Essential Words for
TEPS / ACT / SAT / GRE

Essential Words for
TEPS ACT SAT GRE

초판 1쇄 인쇄일 | 2017년 2월 13일
초판 1쇄 발행일 | 2017년 2월 17일

저　자　| 권오인(Eric Kwon)
펴낸곳　| 북마크
펴낸이　| 정기국
책임편집 | 이헌건
디자인　| 서용석
관　리　| 안영미

주　소　| 서울특별시 동대문구 왕산로23길 17(제기동) 중앙빌딩 305호
전　화　| (02) 325-3691
팩　스　| (02) 335-3691
홈페이지 | www.bmark.co.kr
등　록　| 제 303-2005-34호(2005.8.30)

ISBN　　| 979-11-85846-58-3　13740
값　　　| 20,000원

이 책은 저작권법에 따라 보호를 받는 저작물이므로 무단전재와 무단복제를 금하며,
이 책 내용의 전부 또는 일부를 이용하려면 반드시 저작권자와 북마크의
서면동의를 받아야 합니다.

Essential Words

for

TEPS
ACT
SAT
GRE

권오인(Eric Kwon)

북마크

Preface

TEPS, ACT, SAT, GRE를 준비하는 학생들이나 TIME지, FINANCIAL TIMES,
WASHINGTON POST 등 수준 높은 영어자료를 읽고 싶은 사람들에게
고급 어휘는 꼭 필요합니다.

이런 어려운 단어들을 동의어와 함께 하나씩 하나씩 외우고 훈련하면
짧은 시간 내에 많은 어휘를 습득할 수 있습니다.

이 책에 나오는 2,500개의 표제어 12,000개의 동의어는 TEPS, ACT, SAT,
GRE시험을 치르는 데 꼭 필요한 단어이며 영자신문이나 영어소설에도
자주 등장하는 고급 어휘들입니다.

필자인 저 자신도 이런 방법으로 비교적 단기간에 여기 단어들을 습득하였으며
표제어 2,500개에 대한 모든 예문은 하나하나씩 저자인 제가 100%
직접 영작한 문장들입니다.

동의어 12,000개도 엄선된 것이며 사용자의 편의를 위해서
단어마다 발음기호를 달았습니다.

이 책으로 시험에서 좋은 결과가 있기를 바라며 영어실력 자체가
더욱 향상될 수 있기를 바랍니다. 감사합니다.

권오인(Eric Kwon)

abase[əbéis] v 낮추다, 떨어뜨리다 = debase[dibéis] = degrade[digréid]
= demean[dimíːn] = disgrace[disgréis] = dishonor[disánər]
He abased himself by being involved in the bribery scandal.
그는 뇌물사건에 연루되면서 그의 품격을 떨어뜨렸다.

abash[əbǽʃ] v 당황하게 하다 = baffle[bǽfl] = confuse[kənfjúːz]
= disconcert[dìskənsə́ːrt] = embarrass[imbǽrəs]
The mayor looked abashed at the sight of the flood damage.
시장은 수해 피해를 보고 당황한 듯이 보였다.

abate[əbéit] v 감소시키다, 완화하다, 줄이다 = decrease = diminish[dimíniʃ]
= dwindle[dwíndl] = subside[səbsáid] = wane[wein]
The epidemic started to abate as the winter started.
전염병은 겨울이 시작되면서 완화되기 시작했다.

abbreviate[əbríːvièit] v 단축하다, 줄이다 = abridge[əbrídʒ] = shorten
LAPD is the abbreviated form of Los Angeles Police Department.
LAPD는 Los Angeles Police Department의 약자이다.

abdicate[ǽbdəkèit] v 포기하다, 버리다 = abandon[əbǽndən] = abjure[æbdʒúər]
= relinquish[rilíŋkwiʃ] = waive[weiv]
The king had to abdicate the throne because of his old age.
왕은 노령으로 인해 왕위를 이양해 주었다.

aberration[æbəréiʃən] n 일탈, 일탈적인 행동, 이상 = abnormality[æbnɔːrmǽləti]
= anomaly[ənáməli] = deviation[dìːviéiʃən] = eccentricity[èksəntrísəti]
We sometimes think of aberrations from our daily routine.
우리는 때때로 일상에서 벗어나는 일탈을 생각한다.

abet[əbét] v 부추기다, 선동하다 = goad[goud] = incite[insáit] = instigate[ínstəgèit]
= prod[prad] = provoke[prəvóuk]
A loan shark abetted him in leaking the personal information of all workers in the company.
사채업자는 그에게 회사 직원들의 개인정보를 유출하라고 사주했다.

abeyance[əbéiəns] n 중지, 정지 = intermission = quiescence[kwiésns]
= suspension[səspénʃən]
The vote on free nurture is being held in abeyance in congress.
무상보육에 관한 표결이 국회에 계류되어 있다.

abhor[æbhɔ́ːr] v 혐오하다, 증오하다 = abominate[əbɑ́mənèit] = detest[ditést]
= execrate[éksəkrèit] = loathe[louð]
We abhor any kinds of violence. 우리는 어떤 종류의 폭력도 혐오합니다.

abject[ǽbdʒekt] a 비참한, 절망적인 = dejected[didʒéktid] = deplorable[diplɔ́ːrəbl] = hopeless
= miserable[mízərəbl] = wretched[rétʃid]
He suffered an abject failure in his 40s. 그는 40대 때에 비참한 실패를 겪었다.

abjure[æbdʒúər] v 버리다, 포기하다 = forswear[fɔːrswéər] = give up = recant[rikǽnt]
= renounce[rináuns] = retract[ritrǽkt]
He abjured his belief in the Big Bang theory.
그는 우주의 대폭발 이론에 대한 믿음을 공식적으로 포기했다.

abnegate[ǽbnigèit] v 버리다, 포기하다, 끊다 = abstain from = refrain from = renounce[rináuns]
He has abnegated his right to the ownership of the company.
그는 회사에 대한 소유권을 포기했다.

abominate[əbɑ́mənèit] v 혐오하다, 증오하다 = abhor[æbhɔ́ːr] = despise[dispáiz]
= detest[ditést] = dislike = hate = loathe[louð]
She abominated a man of bluff. 그녀는 허세 부리는 남자를 혐오했다.

aboriginal[æbərídʒənl] a 원주민의 = native = original
The explorer could speak the aboriginal language. 탐험가는 토착어를 할 수 있었다.

abortive[əbɔ́ːrtiv] a 유산의, 실패로 돌아간 = stillborn = unsuccessful
The military coup by the general became abortive.
그 장군이 주도한 군사쿠데타는 실패했다.

abound[əbáund] v 아주 많다, 풍부하다 = flourish[fləˊːriʃ] = infest[infést] = teem[tiːm] = thrive[θraiv]
Spanish- styled houses once abounded in this town.
이 마을에는 한때 스페인 양식의 집들이 많았다.

aboveboard[əbʌ́vbɔ́ːrd] a 공명정대한 = candid[kǽndid] = trustworthy
His personnel policy is open and aboveboard. 그의 인사정책은 아주 공명정대하다.

abrade[əbréid] v 마모시키다 = erode[iróud] = scrape[skreip]
All the rocks in the valley are being abraded by the running water.
계곡의 모든 바위들은 흐르는 물에 의해서 마모된다.

abridge[əbrídʒ] v 요약하다, 단축하다 = abbreviate[əbríːvièit] = abstract[æbstrǽkt] = condense[kəndéns] = shorten
The teacher told his students to abridge the long novel.
선생님은 학생들에게 장편소설을 요약하라고 말했다.

abrogate[ǽbrəgèit] v 폐지하다, 철폐하다, 철회하다 = abolish[əbáliʃ] = annul[ənʌ́l] = invalidate[invǽlədèit] = negate[nigéit] = nullify[nʌ́ləfài] = quash[kwaʃ] = repeal[ripíːl] = retract[ritrǽkt] = revoke[rivóuk] = void[vɔid]
We should have abrogated the racial discrimination law earlier.
우리는 인종차별법을 진작에 폐지했어야 했다.

QUIZ 1

Match each word in the first column with its definition in the second column.
Check your answers in the back of the book.

1.	abbreviate	a.	erode = scrape
2.	abrogate	b.	abolish = annul
3.	aboveboard	c.	baffle = confuse
4.	abase	d.	abandon = abjure
5.	abdicate	e.	debase = degrade
6.	abject	f.	abominate = detest
7.	abrade	g.	abnormality = anomaly
8.	abeyance	h.	forswear = give up
9.	abhor	i.	native = original
10.	aberration	j.	candid = trustworthy
11.	abet	k.	abstain from = refrain from
12.	abnegate	l.	decrease = diminish
13.	abjure	m.	flourish = infest
14.	aboriginal	n.	abbreviate = abstract
15.	abortive	o.	goad = incite
16.	abound	p.	intermission = quiescence
17.	abate	q.	dejected = deplorable
18.	abominate	r.	abridge = shorten
19.	abridge	s.	abhor = despise
20.	abash	t.	stillborn = unsuccessful

abscond[æbskánd] v 종적을 감추다, 도주하다 = decamp[dikǽmp] = depart secretly = disappear = run away = vanish[vǽniʃ]
The CFO of the company absconded with the confidential documents.
회사 재무책임자는 기밀문서를 가지고 종적을 감추었다.

absolve[æbzálv] v 무죄를 선언하다 = acquit[əkwít] = exculpate[ékskʌlpèit]
= exonerate[igzánərèit] = vindicate
Judges absolved the pilot of his sin for the emergency landing on the island.
판사들은 섬에 비상착륙한 조종사에 대해서 무죄를 선언했다.

abstemious[æbstíːmiəs] a 자제하는, 금욕적인 = abstinent[ǽbstənənt]
= ascetic[əsétik] = austere[ɔːstíər] = moderate[mádərət] = restrained
He lives quite an abstemious life. 그는 금욕적인 삶을 산다.

abstinent[ǽbstənənt] a 절제하는, 금욕적인 = abstemious[æbstíːmiəs]
= ascetic[əsétik] = austere[ɔːstíər]
All the monks in the abbey live abstinent lives.
수도원의 모든 수도승들은 금욕적인 삶을 산다.

abstruse[æbstrúːs] a 난해한, 심오한 = esoteric[èsətérik] = recondite[rékəndàit]
His theory is too abstruse to understand. 그의 이론은 너무 난해해서 이해하기 어렵다.

abysmal[əbízməl] a 최악의, 구원할 길 없는 = hopeless = wretched[rétʃid]
The sales performance was abysmal at this quarter. 이번 분기 영업실적은 최악이었다.

abyss[əbís] n 심연, 깊은 구렁 = chasm[kǽzm] = crevasse[krəvǽs]
A group of oceanographers sent a submarine to the deepest abyss in the Pacific Ocean to study the creatures down there.
해양학자들은 태평양의 가장 깊은 심연에 사는 생물들을 연구하기 위해 잠수함을 보냈다.

accede[æksíːd] v 찬성하다, 동의하다 = acquiesce[ækwiés] = agree = assent = comply
= concede[kənsíːd] = consent
He decided to accede to their offer. 그는 그들의 제안에 동의했다.

accentuate[æknséntʃuèit] v 강조하다, 역설하다, 두드러지게 하다
= emphasize[émfəsàiz] = highlight = underline = underscore
She accentuates her eye lines when she puts on her makeup.
그녀는 화장할 때 눈매를 강조한다.

acclaim[əkléim] v 환호하다, 격찬하다 = applaud[əplɔ́ːd] = clap = eulogize[júːlədʒàiz]
= exalt[igzɔ́ːlt] = extol[ikstóul] = hail[heil] = laud[lɔ́ːd] = rave[reiv]
The newly-released movie directed by Renny Harlin has been acclaimed all over the world.
최근 개봉된 레니 할린 감독의 영화가 전 세계적으로 격찬을 받고 있다.

accolade[ǽkəlèid] n 포상, 영예, 칭찬 = award = honor
The brave citizen received an accolade from the mayor.
용감한 시민은 시장으로부터 포상을 받았다.

accord[əkɔ́ːrd] v 일치하다, 조화하다 = agree = conform = correspond = jibe[dʒaib]
His personality almost accord with his appearance. 그의 성격은 외모와 거의 일치한다.

accost[əkɔ́ːst] v 말을 붙이다 = approach for conversation
A scalper accosted me in front of a theater. 암표상이 극장 앞에서 내게 말을 걸었다.
scalper[skǽlpər] n 암표상

accouterments[əkúːtərmənt] n 의복, 장신구, 장비 = outfit = trappings[trǽpiŋz]
The palace guards are checking their accouterments. 근위병들이 그들의 의복을 점검하고 있다.

accrete[əkríːt] v 증대시키다, 부착시키다 = enlarge[inláːrdʒ] = increase
The planet has grown by accreting the satellites around it.
행성은 주변 위성들을 흡수하면서 크기가 커졌다.

accrue[əkrúː] v 누적되다, 축적되다 = accumulate[əkjúːmjulèit] = amass[əmǽs]
Interest accrues from the deposited money in the bank. 은행에 예금한 돈에는 이자가 붙는다.

acerbic[əsə́ːrbik] a 신랄한, 가혹한 = acidulous[əsídʒuləs] = acrid[ǽkrid]
= acrimonious[ækrəmóuniəs] = caustic[kɔ́ːstik]
His speech was full of acerbic wit against the government's tax policy.
그의 연설은 정부 세금정책에 반대하는 신랄한 위트로 가득했다.

achromatic[ækrəmǽtik] a 무색의 = colorless
He prefers achromatic-colored shirts. 그는 무채색 계통의 셔츠를 선호한다.

acidulous[əsídʒuləs] a 신랄한, 통렬한, 신맛이 나는 = acerbic[əsə́ːrbik]
= acrimonious[ækrəmóuniəs] = caustic[kɔ́ːstik]
His acidulous speech against some corrupt politicians made him gain the popularity among the citizens.
일부 타락한 정치인에 대한 신랄한 연설 덕분에 그는 시민들 사이에서 인기를 얻었다.

acme[ǽkmi] n 절정, 정점 = culmination[kʌlmənéiʃən] = pinnacle[pínəkl] = summit
= vertex[və́ːrteks] = zenith[zíːniθ]
She reached the acme of the traditional dance at the age of 60.
그녀는 60세에 전통춤의 절정에 도달했다.

QUIZ 2

Match each word in the first column with its definition in the second column.
Check your answers in the back of the book.

1.	accouterments	a.	acquit = exculpate
2.	absolve	b.	outfit = trappings
3.	accrete	c.	applaud = clap
4.	abstinent	d.	emphasize = highlight
5.	acidulous	e.	abstinent = ascetic
6.	accolade	f.	approach for conversation
7.	acme	g.	award = honor
8.	acerbic	h.	acerbic = acrimonious
9.	accentuate	i.	acquiesce = agree
10.	acclaim	j.	abstemious = ascetic
11.	abysmal	k.	chasm = crevasse
12.	accord	l.	colorless
13.	accost	m.	culmination = pinnacle
14.	abstemious	n.	accumulate = amass
15.	accrue	o.	acidulous = acrid
16.	abscond	p.	esoteric = recondite
17.	accede	q.	hopeless = wretched
18.	achromatic	r.	agree = conform
19.	abstruse	s.	enlarge = increase
20.	abyss	t.	decamp = depart secretly

acquiesce[ækwiés] v 묵인하다, 순종하다 = accede[æksíːd] = assent[əsént]
= conform[kənfǝ́ːrm]
All workers acquiesced in the decision of the company management.
모든 직원들이 회사 경영진의 결정을 묵인했다.

acquisitive[əkwízətiv] a 물욕이 많은, 획득하려고 하는, 탐욕스러운 = avaricious[ævəríʃəs]
= avid[ǽvid] = covetous[kʌ́vitəs] = grasping[grǽspiŋ] = greedy[gríːdi] = rapacious[rəpéiʃəs]
The speculator has been very acquisitive of money. 투기꾼은 돈에 대한 욕심이 매우 크다.

acquit[əkwít] v 무죄를 선고하다, 방면하다 = absolve[æbzálv] = exculpate[ékskʌlpèit]
= exonerate[igzánərèit] = let go = liberate[líbərèit] = vindicate[víndəkèit]
The jury acquitted her of the fraud charge. 배심원은 그녀의 사기혐의에 대해 무죄를 선고했다.

acrid[ǽkrid] a 톡 쏘는 듯한, 신랄한 = acid[ǽsid] = acerbic[əsə́ːrbik] = bitter = caustic[kɔ́ːstik] = pungent[pʌ́ndʒənt]
The room was filled with acrid smell. 그 방은 톡 쏘는 악취로 가득 찼다.

acrimonious[ækrəmóuniəs] a 신랄한, 독살스런, 폭언이 오가는 = acerbic[əsə́ːrbik] = bitter = pungent[pʌ́ndʒənt]
The labor and management exchanged an acrimonious dispute.
노사 간에 독살스러운 언쟁이 오고 갔다.

acronym[ǽkrənim] n 두문자어(頭文字語) 예 NATO(North Atlantic Treaty Organization)
UN is a short acronym for United Nations.
UN은 United Nations의 머리글자만 딴 두문자어다.

acumen[əkjúːmən] n 통찰력, 총명 = discernment = insight = sagacity[səgǽsəti]
He was born with the business acumen 그는 사업 감각을 타고났다.

acute[əkjúːt] a 예리한, 격심한, 민감한 = astute[əstjúːt] = canny[kǽni] = discerning[disə́ːrniŋ] = incisive[insáisiv] = insightful = shrewd[ʃruːd]
Sharks are said to have an acute sense of smell.
상어는 예리한 후각을 가졌다고들 말한다.

adage[ǽdidʒ] n 격언, 속담 = aphorism[ǽfərìzm] = apothegm[ǽpəθèm] = axiom[ǽksiəm] = dictum = maxim = motto
There are many similar adages in Asian countries.
아시아 국가들에는 비슷한 속담들이 많다.

adamant[ǽdəmənt] a 단호한 = inexorable[inéksərəbl] = intransigent[intrǽnsədʒənt] = obdurate[άbdjurit] = obstinate[άbstənət] = pertinacious[pə̀ːrtənéiʃəs]
The police chief was adamant about crushing the illegal protests.
경찰 총수는 불법시위 진압에 대해 단호했다.

adduce[ədjúːs] v 증거로 제시하다, 예증하다 = illustrate[íləstrèit]
A variety of documents and charts were adduced to predict economic growth rate.
경제성장률을 예측하기 위해 다양한 서류와 도표가 제시되었다.

adherent[ædhíːərənt] n 지지자, 추종자 = advocate[ǽdvəkèit] = supporter
Many adherents are supporting the tax policy of the politician.
많은 추종자들이 그 정치인의 조세정책을 지지하고 있다.

adjourn[ədʒə́ːrn] v 연기하다, 휴회시키다 = defer[difə́ːr] = delay
= discontinue[dìskəntínjuː] = postpone[poustpóun] = prorogue[proróug] = put off = recess[risés]
= shelve[ʃelv] = suspend[səspénd]
The chairman adjourned the shareholders' general meeting for two days.
회장님은 주주총회를 이틀 연기시켰다.

adjunct[ǽdʒʌŋkt] n 부속물, 부가물 = addition = appendage[əpéndidʒ]
Road signs and street lights are adjuncts roads.
도로표지판이나 가로등 등은 도로 부속물이다.

adjure[ədʒúər] v 간청하다, 탄원하다, 명령하다 = beseech[bisíːʧ] = entreat[intríːt]
= implore[implɔ́ːr] = supplicate[sʌ́pləkèit]
The priest adjured TV viewers to donate some of their money to save the dying children in Africa.
신부는 TV 시청자들에게 아프리카에서 죽어가는 아이들을 구할 수 있도록 기부해줄 것을 간청했다.

adjust[ədʒʌ́st] v 조정(조절)하다, 적응하다 = fine-tune = modify[mádəfài]
He adjusted angles of the rearview mirrors. 그는 자동차 백미러의 각도를 조정했다

ad-lib[æd líb] v 즉흥적으로 말하다(연주하다) = extemporize[ikstémpəràiz]
= improvise[ímprəvàiz]
Asked to give his views on the FTA with China, the president ad-libbed a speech.
대통령은 중국과의 자유무역협정에 대한 의견을 말해달라고 요청받고 즉석에서 연설을 했다.

admirable[ǽdmərəbl] a 칭찬할 만한, 감탄할 만한 = commendable = laudable[lɔ́ːdəbl]
= praiseworthy
He has made admirable efforts to building the huge tower alone.
그는 거대한 탑을 혼자 쌓는 감탄할 만한 노력을 기울였다.

admonish[ædmɑ́niʃ] v 꾸짖다, 책망하다 = berate[biréit] = censure[sénʃər]
= chide[ʧaid] = denounce[dináuns] = rebuke[ribjúːk] = reprehend[rèprihénd]
= reprimand[réprəmænd] = scold[skould]
The teacher admonished a student for dozing off during class.
선생님은 수업 중에 조는 학생을 꾸짖었다.

adroit[ədrɔ́it] a 능숙한, 노련한 = adept[ədépt] = dexterous[dékstərəs] = talented
James has been adroit at wage bargaining.
James는 임금협상에 능하다.

QUIZ 3

Match each word in the first column with its definition in the second column.
Check your answers in the back of the book.

1.	admonish	a.	ex)NATO
2.	acquisitive	b.	accede = assent
3.	adage	c.	absolve = exculpate
4.	adherent	d.	advocate = supporter
5.	adjure	e.	defer = delay
6.	adamant	f.	commendable = laudable
7.	acumen	g.	extemporize = improvise
8.	acute	h.	avaricious = avid
9.	acquit	i.	aphorism = apothegm
10.	adjust	j.	beseech = entreat
11.	adduce	k.	adept = dexterous
12.	acrid	l.	acerbic = bitter
13.	adjourn	m.	astute = canny
14.	adjunct	n.	addition = appendage
15.	acrimonious	o.	fine-tune = modify
16.	acronym	p.	inexorable = intransigent
17.	ad-lib	q.	discernment = insight
18.	adroit	r.	Illustrate
19.	acquiesce	s.	acid = acerbic
20.	admirable	t.	berate = censure

adulation[ædʒuléiʃən] n 아첨 = blandishment[blændiʃmənt] = bootlicking
= fawning[fɔ́ːniŋ] = flattery = sycophancy[síkəfənsi]
When a monarch gets to like adulation, his country is likely to go wrong.
군주가 아첨을 좋아하는 국가는 그릇될 수 있다.

adulterate[ədʌ́ltərèit] v 품질을 떨어뜨리다, 불순물 섞다 = besmirch[bismə́ːrtʃ]
= contaminate[kəntǽmənèit] = debase[dibéis] = degrade[digréid] = sully[sʌ́li] = taint[teint]
= tarnish[táːrniʃ] = vitiate[víʃièit]
The honey was adulterated with sugar. 꿀에 설탕을 넣어서 품질이 떨어졌다.

advent[ǽdvent] n 출현, 도래 = appearance = arrival
The Best Air has had no fatalities since its advent in the air travel service.
The Best Air 항공은 항공계에 진출한 이후 한 사람의 사망자도 내지 않았다.

adventitious[ædvəntíʃəs] a 우연한, 우발적인 = accidental[æksədéntl] = casual = fortuitous[fɔːrtjúːətəs]
Some foods are the outcomes of adventitious discoveries.
어떤 음식물들은 우연한 발견의 결과물들이다.

adverse[ædvə́ːrs] a 반대의, 역행의, 불리한 = contrary = inauspicious[ìnɔːspíʃəs] = unfavorable = untoward
Too much exercise can have adverse effect on our body.
너무 심한 운동은 우리 몸에 역효과를 줄 수 있다.

advertent[ædvə́ːrtənt] a 주의하는, 조심하는 = alert[ələ́ːrt] = attentive = mindful = regardful = vigilant[vídʒələnt] = watchful
Advertent observations are required in the study of astronomy.
천문학 공부는 주의 깊은 관찰을 요구한다.

advocate[ǽdvəkèit] n 옹호하다, 지지하다, 주장하다 = countenance[káuntənəns] = support = uphold
Some citizens don't advocate sending their troops to overseas war zone.
일부 시민들은 군대를 해외 교전지역에 파견하는 것을 지지하지 않는다.

aerate[ɛ́ərèit] v 공기가 통하게 하다 = give air = oxygenate[áksidʒənèit]
All the fish will die if you don't aerate the water in the tank all the time.
수조 속의 물에 항상 공기가 통하도록 하지 않으면 모든 물고기가 죽어버릴 것이다.

aesthetic[esθétik] a 심미적인, 미학적인 = artistic[aːrtístik]
When we develop the city, we need to consider the aesthetic point of view.
우리가 도시를 개발할 때는 미학적인 관점도 고려할 필요가 있다.

affable[ǽfəbl] a 상냥한, 사근사근한 = amiable[éimiəbl] = amicable[ǽmikəbl] = approachable = genial[dʒíːnjəl] = gracious[gréiʃəs] = suave[swaːv]
All waitresses at the restaurant are very affable. 그 식당의 모든 웨이트리스들은 매우 상냥했다.

affectation[æfektéiʃən] n 가장, 꾸밈 = affectedness = dissemblance[disémbləns] = pretence
He told nothing but the truth without affectation. 그는 꾸밈없이 진실만을 얘‖기했다.

affidavit[æfidéivit] n 선서진술서 = official statement
He submitted an affidavit in relation to the robbery case.
그는 강도사건과 관련된 선서진술서를 제출했다.

affinity[əfínəti] n 좋아함, 친밀감 = attraction = kinship
I have an affinity for sea creatures. 나는 바다생물에 친밀감을 가지고 있다.

affliction[əflíkʃən] n 고통 = distress = hardship = misery = scourge[skə:rdʒ]
= torment[tɔ:rmént] = tribulation[tribjuléiʃən] = woe[wou]
He felt considerable affliction when he got divorced with his wife.
그는 아내와 이혼할 때 상당한 고통을 느꼈다.

affluent[ǽfluənt] a 부유한, 풍족한 = opulent[ápjulənt] = prosperous[práspərəs]
= well-off
He was raised in a very affluent area in the city. 그는 도시의 매우 부유한 지역에서 자랐다.

affront[əfrʌnt] n 모욕, 마음의 상처 = indignity[indígnəti] = insult[insʌlt] =
slight[slait]
His speech sounded like an affront to female voters.
그의 연설은 여성 유권자들에게 모욕으로 들렸다.

aftermath[ǽftərmæθ] n 여파, 후유증 = consequences[kánsəkwèns] = outcome
Stricter rules were set up in the aftermath of the passenger train derailment accident.
열차 탈선사고의 여파로 더 엄격한 규칙들이 제정되었다.

aggrandize[əgrǽndaiz] v 증대(확대, 강화)하다 = augment[ɔ:gmént] = boost
= enlarge = magnify[mǽgnəfài]
The monarch tried to aggrandize himself by building a new massive castle.
군주는 거대한 성을 새로 건설함으로써 자신을 강화하려 했다.

aggravate[ǽgrəvèit] v 악화시키다 = exacerbate[igzǽsərbèit] = worsen[wə́:rsn]
A popular remedy aggravated the illness of the patient.
민간요법이 환자의 병을 악화시켰다.

agrarian[əgrɛ́əriən] a 농업의, 농지의 = agricultural = farming
The agrarian economy of the USA has become the base of the IT economy.
미국의 농업경제는 IT경제의 기반이 되었다.

QUIZ 4

Match each word in the first column with its definition in the second column.
Check your answers in the back of the book.

1.	affidavit		a.	artistic
2.	aggravate		b.	opulent = prosperous
3.	affliction		c.	alert = attentive
4.	adventitious		d.	indignity = insult
5.	adverse		e.	consequences = outcome
6.	affront		f.	distress = hardship
7.	advocate		g.	besmirch = contaminate
8.	adulation		h.	amiable = amicable
9.	aesthetic		i.	augment = boost
10.	agrarian		j.	affectedness = dissemblance
11.	affectation		k.	accidental = casual
12.	aerate		l.	official statement
13.	affinity		m.	blandishment = bootlicking
14.	advent		n.	give air = oxygenate
15.	affable		o.	exacerbate = worsen
16.	advertent		p.	attraction = kinship
17.	aftermath		q.	appearance = arrival
18.	aggrandize		r.	agricultural = farming
19.	affluent		s.	countenance = support
20.	adulterate		t.	contrary = inauspicious

aggregate[ǽgrigət] a 총계의, 종합한 = total
The aggregate operating profit is expected to be 20% higher than the forecast.
총 영업이익은 예상보다 20% 이상 높을 것으로 예상된다.

aggrieve[əgríːv] v 괴롭히다, 고통을 주다 = abuse = afflict[əflíkt] = oppress[əprés]
He has been aggrieved with the death of his wife in car accident.
자동차 사고로 죽은 아내 때문에 그는 고통을 받고 있다.

aghast[əgǽst] a 대경실색한, 경악한 = appalled[əpɔ́ːld] = horrified = surprised
All tourists looked aghast at the sight of the scale of the fall.
모든 관광객들은 폭포의 규모를 보고 경악한 듯 보였다.

agitate[ǽdʒitèit] v 동요시키다, 선동하다 = incite[insáit] = perturb[pərtə́ːrb] = stir[stəːr]
The union leader has agitated his members to go on a strike for a raise.
노조 지도자는 노조원들에게 임금인상을 위한 파업을 하라고 선동했다.

agnostic[ægnóustik] n 불가지론자 = person unsure that God exists.
He is an agnostic, not believing in God. 그는 신의 존재를 믿지 않는 불가지론자이다.

agonize[ǽgənàiz] v 고민하다, 고뇌하다 = excruciate[ikskrúːʃièit] = writhe[raið]
He is agonizing over quitting the sales job. 그는 영업직을 그만둘까 고민하고 있다.

alacrity[əlǽkrəti] n 민첩, 민활 = briskness = promptness
Detectives arrested the criminal with alacrity. 형사들은 민첩하게 범인을 체포했다.

alchemy[ǽlkəmi] n 연금술 = change metals into gold
Alchemy was once popular in Europe. 연금술은 한때 유럽에서 인기가 있었다.

alienable[éiljənəbl] a 양도할 수 있는, 매도 가능한 = transferable
Air travel mileage is not an alienable rights. 항공여행 마일리지는 양도가 가능한 권리가 아니다.

alienate[éiljənèit] v 소원하게 만들다, 소외감을 느끼게 하다 = disaffect[dìsəfékt]
= estrange[istréindʒ]
His arrogance alienated his close friends.
그의 거만함이 가까운 주변 친구들을 떨어져 나가게 했다.

align[əláin] v 일직선으로 맞추다, 조정(조절)하다 = adjust = line up
Sales target is aligned with economic condition. 판매 목표액은 시장상황에 맞추어 조정된다.

allay[əléi] v 가라앉히다, 완화시키다 = alleviate[əlíːvièit] = assuage[əswéidʒ]
= calm[kaːm] = ease = mitigate[mítəgèit] = mollify[máləfài] = pacify[pǽsəfài]
The police tried to allay the fears of the citizens after the bomb explosion.
경찰은 폭탄이 터진 후 시민들의 공포를 진정시키기 위해 노력했다.

allege[əlédʒ] v 단언하다, (증거없이) 주장하다 = affirm = assert = aver[əvə́ːr] = declare
= maintain
The politician is alleged to have manipulated public opinion in the election.
그 정치인은 지난 선거에서 여론을 조작했다는 혐의를 받고 있다.

allegiance[əlíːdʒəns] n 충성 = adherence[ædhíːərəns] = fidelity[fidéləti] = loyalty
Most soldiers swore allegiance to their leader before the military coup.
쿠데타를 일으키기 전에 대부분의 군인들은 그들의 지도자에게 충성을 맹세했다.

allegory[ǽligɔ̀ːri] n 우화 = parable[pǽrəbl]
Many children are touched by the allegory. 많은 아이들은 우화에 감동받는다.

alleviate[əlíːvièit] v 완화시키다 = allay[əléi] = assuage[əswéidʒ] = calm = ease
= mitigate[mítəgèit] = mollify[máləfài] = pacify[pǽsəfài]
This ointment will alleviate the pain from burn wounds.
이 연고가 화상으로 인한 고통을 완화시켜 줄 거야.

allot[əlát] v 할당하다, 배당하다 = allocate[ǽləkèit] = apportion[əpɔ́ːrʃən] = assign[əsáin]
= divvy up = earmark = set aside
The financial executive officer allotted each department U$50,000 for their annual expenses.
재무 담당 임원은 각 부서별로 일년에 50,000달러씩을 비용 처리 금액으로 할당했다.

allocate[ǽləkèit] v 할당하다, 배당하다 = allot[əlát] = apportion[əpɔ́ːrʃən] =
assign[əsáin] = divvy up = earmark
Government allocated some of its budget to the construction of a new expressway.
정부는 예산의 일부를 새로운 고속도로 건설에 배당했다.

alloy[ǽlɔi] n 합금 = mixed metal
Most metals we see around are actually alloys.
우리 주변에 있는 금속은 사실 대부분 합금이다.

allusion[əlúːʒən] n 암시 = implication = insinuation[insìnjuéiʃən] = suggestion
He made an allusion to moving out to Beijing.
그는 북경으로 이사 가는 것을 암시했다.

QUIZ 5

Match each word in the first column with its definition in the second column.
Check your answers in the back of the book.

1.	allusion	a.	briskness = promptness
2.	alloy	b.	appalled = horrified
3.	allegiance	c.	person unsure that God exists
4.	alienable	d.	alleviate = assuage
5.	alleviate	e.	adherence = fidelity
6.	agonize	f.	transferable
7.	alacrity	g.	adjust = line up
8.	alchemy	h.	implication=insinuation
9.	agitate	i.	total
10.	alienate	j.	mixed metal
11.	aggregate	k.	abuse = afflict
12.	allay	l.	parable
13.	allege	m.	disaffect = estrange
14.	aghast	n.	affirm = assert
15.	align	o.	allocate = apportion
16.	agnostic	p.	incite = perturb
17.	allot	q.	change metals into gold
18.	allocate	r.	allot = apportion
19.	aggrieve	s.	excruciate = writhe
20.	allegory	t.	allay = assuage

aloft[əlɔ́:ft] ad 하늘 높이, 높이 = above = high up
The drone was flying aloft in the sky. 드론이 하늘 높이 날고 있었다.

aloof[əlú:f] a 떨어져, 초연한 = detached[ditǽtʃt]
The writer stood aloof from becoming famous. 작가는 유명세를 타는 것에 초연했다.

altercation[ɔ̀:ltərkéiʃən] n 논쟁, 언쟁 = argument = bickering = brawl[brɔ:l]
= fracas[fréikəs] = quarrel[kwɔ́:rəl] = wrangle[rǽŋgl]
Villagers had an altercation over the construction of crematorium in their village.
주민들은 마을에 화장터를 건립하는 것에 대해 논쟁을 벌였다.
crematorium[krì:mətɔ́:riəm] n 화장터

altruist[ǽltruist] n 이타주의자, 박애주의자
= benefactor[bénəfæktər] = philanthropist[filǽnθrəpist]
The ultimate goal of teaching ethics in school is to produce as many altruists as possible.
학교에서 윤리를 가르치는 궁극적 목표는 최대한 많은 박애주의자를 배출하는 것이다.

amalgamate[əmǽlgəmèit] v 합병시키다, 통합시키다 = blend[blend]
= consolidate[kənsɑ́lədèit] = integrate[íntəgrèit] = merge[məːrdʒ]
The business group decided to amalgamate its two companies to create synergy effect.
그룹은 시너지 효과를 내기 위해 그룹 내 두 개의 회사를 합병했다.

amass[əmǽs] v 모으다, 축적하다 = accumulate[əkjúːmjulèit] = garner[gɑ́ːrnər]
= gather[gɑ́ːrnər] = hoard[hɔːrd] = stockpile
He amassed a fortune by investing in the undervalued stocks.
그는 저평가된 주식에 투자해서 큰 돈을 모았다.

ambience[ǽmbiəns] n 분위기 = atmosphere = circumstances = environment = surroundings
The ambience of the restaurant was very cozy. 그 식당의 분위기는 매우 아늑했다.

ambiguous[æmbígjuəs] a 모호한, 분명치 않은 = equivocal[ikwívəkəl]
= obscure[əbskjúər] = vague[veig]
There are some ambiguous clauses in the insurance policy.
보험증서에 몇 개의 애매모호한 조항들이 있다.

ambivalent[æmbívələnt] a 상반하는 감정을 가진, 양면적인 = undecided
People in the town have an ambivalent feeling about the casino in their town
주민들은 마을에 있는 카지노에 양면적인 감정을 가지고 있다.

amble[ǽmbl] v 느긋하게 걷다 = loiter[lɔ́itər] = mosey[móuzi] = ramble[rǽmbl]
= saunter[sɔ́ːntər] = stroll
They ambled along the road. 그들은 느긋하게 길을 따라 걸었다.

ameliorate[əmíːljərèit] v 개선하다 = improve
City government is making an effort to ameliorate the quality of water in the rivers.
시 당국은 강의 수질 개선을 위해 노력하고 있다.

amenable[əmíːnəbl] a 순종하는, 따르는 = agreeable = docile[dɑ́səl]
= obedient[oubíːdiənt] = pliable[pláiəbl] = tractable[trǽktəbl]
The couple had two very amenable girls. 그 부부에게는 아주 말을 잘 듣는 두 딸이 있었다.

amenity[əménəti] n 편의, 편의시설 = comfort = convenience
The silver town has many excellent amenities.
그 실버타운은 훌륭한 편의시설들을 갖추고 있다.

amiable[éimiəbl] a 상냥한, 붙임성 있는 = affable[ǽfəbl] = amicable[ǽmikəbl]
= agreeable = friendly = genial[dʒíːnjəl]
The lawyer has a very amiable secretary. 그 변호사에게는 매우 상냥한 비서가 있다.

amicable[ǽmikəbl] a 우호적인, 원만한 = amiable[éimiəbl] = cordial[kɔ́ːrdʒəl]
= friendly = polite
The two countries has had an amicable relationship since the summit meeting.
두 나라는 정상회담 이후로 우호적인 관계를 유지하고 있다.

amnesty[ǽmnəsti] n 사면, 대사 = absolution[æbsəlúːʃən] = forgiveness
= pardon[páːrdn]
Minister of justice granted an amnesty to many criminals on the independence day.
법무부장관은 광복절에 많은 죄수들을 사면했다.

amok[əmʌ́k] n 정신착란 = in an uncontrolled way
Some elephants escaped from the zoo and ran amok downtown in the city.
일부 코끼리가 동물원을 탈출하여 도심에서 날뛰었다.

amoral[eimɔ́(ː)rəl] a 도덕관념이 없는 = immoral[imɔ́ːrəl] = unethical[ʌnéθikəl]
= unscrupulous
During the war, some people are likely to become amoral.
전쟁 중에 일부 사람들은 도덕관념이 없게 된다.

amorous[ǽmərəs] a 호색적인 = erotic
The young entrepreneur gave an amorous glance to the woman.
그 젊은 사업가는 그녀에게 호색적인 눈길을 보냈다.

amorphous[əmɔ́ːrfəs] a 무정형의, 불규칙 모양의 = nondescript[nɑ̀ndiskrípt]
At night we can see an amorphous mass of stars in the sky.
밤하늘에서 우리는 불규칙한 별의 덩어리를 본다.

QUIZ 6

Match each word in the first column with its definition in the second column.
Check your answers in the back of the book.

amenable	a.	argument = bickering
aloof	b.	undecided
amorphous	c.	improve
amnesty	d.	above = high up
amalgamate	e.	amiable = cordial
amass	f.	accumulate = garner
amoral	g.	equivocal = obscure
ambiguous	h.	affable = amicable
amorous	i.	erotic
amble	j.	detached
ameliorate	k.	blend = consolidate
ambivalent	l.	absolution = forgiveness
amenity	m.	in an uncontrolled way
amiable	n.	benefactor = philanthropist
altercation	o.	immoral = unethical
altruist	p.	loiter = mosey
amok	q.	agreeable = docile
ambience	r.	nondescript
aloft	s.	comfort = convenience
amicable	t.	atmosphere = circumstances

amphibian[æmfíbiən] n 양서류 = cold-blooded vertebrate[və́ːrtəbrət]
Salamanders are amphibians. 도롱뇽은 양서 동물이다.

anachronism[ənǽkrənìzm] n 시대착오적인 것(관습/생각) = error in time placement His 2G phone looks like an anachronism. 그의 2G전화기는 시대착오적인 것으로 보인다.

analgesia[ænəldʒíːziə] n 무통증, 통각상실증 = anesthesia[ænəsθíːʒə]
Analgesia sometimes derives from severe stress.
통각상실증은 때때로 극심한 스트레스에서 온다.

analogy[ənǽlədʒi] n 유사점, 비유 = semblance[sémbləns] = similarity[sìməlǽrəti]
There is an analogy between birds and planes. 새와 비행기 사이에는 유사점이 있다.

anarchy[ǽnərki] n 무정부 상태, 무법 상태 = without rules or laws
We have suffered a few years of anarchy after independence from the nation.
우리는 광복 후에 몇 년간의 무정부 상태를 겪었다.

anathema[ənǽθəmə] n 저주, 몹시 싫어하는 사람(물건) = something hated
Gambling is an anathema to his wife. 그의 부인은 도박에 질색을 한다.

ancillary[ǽnsəlèri] a 보조의, 부가적인 = additional = supplementary[sʌpləméntəri]
If you purchase this tent, some ancillary equipment is provided.
이 텐트를 구입하면 몇 개의 보조장비가 제공된다.

anecdote[ǽnikdòut] n 일화 = episode[épəsòud]
There are some funny anecdotes about the prince. 왕자에 관한 재미있는 일화가 많다.

anesthetic[ænəsθétik] n 마취제, 진통제 = analgesic[ænəldʒíːzik] = anodyne[ǽnədàin] = opiate[óupiət]
The nurse gave an anesthetic to the patient. 간호사가 환자에게 마취제를 투여했다.

angst[aːŋkst] n 불안, 걱정 = agony[ǽgəni] = apprehension[æprihénʃən] = misgiving[misgíviŋ] = uneasiness
The fugitive has lived a life full of angst. 도망자는 불안으로 가득 찬 삶을 살고 있다.

anguish[ǽŋgwiʃ] n 괴로움, 고통, 고뇌 = affliction[əflíkʃən] = agony[ǽgəni] = distress = rue[ruː] = torment[tɔːrmént] = torture[tɔːrtʃər] = woe[wou]
He is in deep anguish over the bribery scandal. 그는 뇌물 스캔들로 깊은 고통 속에 있다.

animate[ǽnəmèit] v 생기를 주다, 기운차게 하다 = bring to life = enliven[inláivən] = energize[énərdʒàiz]
The march of the female soldiers animated the entire military parade.
여군들의 행진이 군사 퍼레이드 전체에 활기를 불어 넣었다.

animosity[ænəmɑ́səti] n 반감, 증오, 악의 = antagonism[æntǽgənìzm] = antipathy[æntípəθi] = enmity[énməti] = hostility[hastíləti] = malevolence[məlévələns] = malice[mǽlis] = rancor[rǽŋkər] = resentment
There is still a religious animosity among the nations in the continent.
대륙에 있는 나라들 간에는 아직도 종교적인 반감이 존재한다.

annex[ənéks] v 병합하다, 통합하다 = add = attach = join = unite
The nation tried to annex its neighboring country. 그 국가는 이웃 나라를 병합하려 했다.

annuity[ənjúːəti] n 연금 = pension = revenue[révənjùː]
We need to make some changes to the annuity system.
우리는 연금제도에 몇 가지 변화를 줘야 한다.

anodyne[ǽnədàin] n 진통제 = painkiller
His passion for painting was an anodyne to the terminally ill patient.
미술에 대한 열정이 말기 암환자에게 진통제가 되었다.

anomalous[ənɑ́mələs] a 변칙의, 이례적인 = aberrant[əbérənt] = bizarre[bizɑ́ːr]
= abnormal = atypical[eitípikəl] = eccentric[ikséntrik] = incongruous[inkɑ́ŋgruəs]
We have recently seen anomalous climate patterns.
최근 우리는 변칙적인 날씨 유형을 보아왔다.

anomaly[ənɑ́məli] n 예외, 변칙, 이례 = aberration[æbəréiʃən] = deviation[dìːviéiʃən]
An earthquake of magnitude 6 in the nation was an anomaly
그 나라에서 진도 6의 지진은 이례적인 것이다.

antagonize[æntǽgənàiz] v 적대감을 불러일으키다, 적의를 품게 하다
= alienate[éiljənèit] = oppose[əpóuz]
Some tourists antagonize the local people by rude manners.
어떤 관광객들은 무례한 매너로 현지인들에게 적대감을 불러일으키게 한다.

antecedent[æntəsíːdnt] n 선례, 선행사건, 선행자 = something existed before
The bombing of Pearl Harbor is an antecedent to the World War II.
진주만 폭격은 제2차 세계대전의 선행 사건이다.

QUIZ 7

Match each word in the first column with its definition in the second column.
Check your answers in the back of the book.

1.	antagonize		a.	semblance = similarity
2.	anachronism		b.	something hated
3.	analgesia		c.	affliction = agony
4.	anodyne		d.	add=attach
5.	anarchy		e.	additional = supplementary
6.	anathema		f.	painkiller
7.	ancillary		g.	something existed before
8.	animosity		h.	antagonism = antipathy
9.	anesthetic		i.	without rules or laws
10.	amphibian		j.	aberration = deviation
11.	annuity		k.	cold-blooded vertebrate
12.	animate		l.	alienate = oppose
13.	anecdote		m.	error in time placement
14.	annex		n.	pension = revenue
15.	anguish		o.	aberrant = bizarre
16.	anomaly		p.	anesthesia
17.	anomalous		q.	analgesic
18.	analogy		r.	bring to life = enliven
19.	antecedent		s.	agony = apprehension
20.	angst		t.	episode

antedate[ǽntidèit] v 먼저 일어나다, 앞서다 = antecede[æntisíːd] = precede[prisíːd] = predate
Chinese civilization antedates any other one from the Europe.
중국 문명은 유럽의 어떤 문명보다도 앞선다.

anterior[æntíəriər] a 앞선, 이전의 = antecedent[æntəsíːdnt] = precedent[présədənt] = prior to
Tonight we will enjoy massive fireworks anterior to the World Cup opening ceremony tomorrow.
오늘 밤 우리는 내일 있을 월드컵 개막식에 앞서 거대한 불꽃놀이를 즐길 예정이다.

anthology[ænθάlədʒi] n 시선집, 문집 = literary collection
Yesterday an anthology of the greatest poets in 20th was published.
어제 20세기 최고 시인들의 시선집이 출판되었다.

anthropomorphic[ænθrəpəmɔ́:rfik] a 의인화된 = humanlike
The movie is about the struggle and success of an anthropomorphic lion and its animal friends.
그 영화는 의인화된 사자와 그의 동물 친구의 고투와 사랑에 관한 것이다.

antic[ǽntik] a 색다른, 괴상한, 이상야릇한 = grotesque[groutésk]
We can sometimes hear antic laughter in the old castle.
우리는 때때로 오래된 성에서 괴상한 웃음소리를 들을 수 있다.

antidote[ǽntidòut] n 해독제, 해소수단, 해법 = antitoxin
The stricter law can be an antidote to the drunk driving.
더 엄격한 법이 음주운전에 대한 해법이 될 수 있다.

antipathy[æntípəθi] n 반감, 혐오 = abhorrence[æbhɔ́:rəns]= animosity[ænəmásəti]
= antagonism[æntǽgənìzm] = aversion[əvə́:rʒən] = enmity[énməti] = hostility[hastílətí]
= loathing[lóuðiŋ] = rancor[rǽŋkər] = repugnance[ripʌ́gnəns]
The gangsters had a deep antipathy to the rich in our society.
범죄단원들은 우리 사회의 부자들에게 반감을 가지고 있었다.

antipodal[æntípədl] a 대척지의, 정반대의 = contrary = opposite
He has an antipodal idea to your proposal.
그는 당신의 제안과는 정반대의 생각을 하고 있습니다.

antiquity[æntíkwəti] n 고대, 아주 오래됨 = ancientness
There are many historic sites of antiquity in Beijing. 북경에는 오래된 유적지가 많다.

antithesis[æntíθəsis] n 대조, 반대 = exact opposite.
Passion is the antithesis of despair 열정은 절망과는 정반대이다.

apartheid[əpá:rtheit] n 인종차별정책 = racial segregation
He struggled against apartheid in the country. 그는 나라 안의 인종차별에 홀로 저항했다.

apathy[ǽpəθi] n 무관심, 냉담 = aloofness[əlú:fnis] = detachment[ditǽtʃmənt] = indifference
Young people feel apathy toward elections. 젊은이들은 선거에 무관심하다.

aperture[ǽpərtʃər] n 구멍, 틈 = chasm[kǽzm] = cleft[kleft] = crack
= crevice[krévis] = fissure[fíʃər] = hole
There were many apertures in the building. 건물에는 작은 구멍들이 많이 있었다.

apex[éipeks] n 꼭대기, 정점 = acme[ǽkmi] = culmination[kʌ̀lmənéiʃən]
= pinnacle[pínəkl] = vertex[və́ːrteks] = zenith[zíːniθ]
He reached the apex of his organization at the age of 55. 그는 55세에 그의 조직의 정점에 올랐다.

aphorism[ǽfərìzm] n 격언, 경구 = adage[ǽdidʒ] = apothegm[ǽpəθèm]
= axiom[ǽksiəm] = dictum = maxim = proverb = saying
The West and the East have something in common in aphorism.
동양과 서양의 격언에는 몇 가지 공통점이 있다.

apocalypse[əpɑ́kəlips] n 파멸, 대재앙, 세계의 종말 = doomsday
Reckless use of the natural resources on our planet can lead to apocalypse.
무분별한 자원의 사용은 인류의 파멸을 가져 올 수 있다.

apocryphal[əpɑ́krəfəl] a 출처가 의심되는, 가짜의 = doubtful[dáutfəl] =
dubious[djúːbiəs] = questionable = spurious[spjúəriəs]
Some figures in his newly released book are apocryphal.
최근 출시된 그의 책 속의 일부 수치들은 출처가 의심스럽다.

apogee[ǽpədʒìː] n 정점, 절정, 원지점(遠地點) : 달이나 인공위성이 궤도상에서 지구로부터 가장
멀어지는 위치 = farthest distance
The moon reached apogee on Apr. 25 this year. 금년 4월 25일에 달이 지구에서 가장 먼 지점에 이르렀다.

apoplectic[æ̀pəpléktik] a 중풍의, 뇌졸중의 = paralyzed
He was in the hospital because of apoplectic stroke. 뇌졸중 때문에 그는 병원에 있었다.

apoplexy[ǽpəplèksi] n 뇌졸중, 중풍 = seizure[síːʒər] = stroke
The ex-president died of apoplexy. 전직 대통령은 중풍으로 사망했다.

QUIZ 8

Match each word in the first column with its definition in the second column.
Check your answers in the back of the book.

1. anthology
2. apoplexy
3. aphorism
4. anthropomorphic
5. antic
6. apogee
7. antipathy
8. apoplectic
9. antiquity
10. apartheid
11. apex
12. apathy
13. aperture
14. antithesis
15. antedate
16. apocalypse
17. antidote
18. antipodal
19. apocryphal
20. anterior

a. abhorrence = animosity
b. contrary = opposite
c. breach = chasm
d. acme = culmination
e. literary collection
f. seizure = stroke
g. paralyzed
h. doomsday
i. antecedent = precede
j. adage = apothegm
k. doubtful = dubious
l. antecede = precede
m. grotesque
n. aloofness = detachment
o. racial segregation
p. antitoxin
q. farthest distance
r. exact opposite
s. humanlike
t. ancientness

apostate[əpǽsteit] n 변절자, 배반자, 배교자 = backslider = renegade[rénigèid]
= traitor[tréitər] = turncoat
During the war many people become apostates. 전쟁 동안에 많은 사람들은 변절자가 된다.

apotheosis[əpɑ̀θióusis] n 신격화, 절정, 극치 = deification[dìːəfəkéiʃən]
= glorification[glɔ̀ːrəfikéiʃən] = idolization
The apotheosis of a leader was common in ancient dynasty.
지도자의 신격화는 고대왕조에서 흔한 일이었다.

appall[əpɔ́ːl] v 오싹하게 하다, 질겁하게 하다 = astound[əstáund] = awe[ɔː] = daunt[dɔːnt]
= horrify[hɔ́ːrəfài] = petrify[pétrəfài]
A slump in the stock market appalled all the investors.
주식시장 폭락이 모든 투자자들을 오싹하게 만들었다.

apparition[æpəríʃən] n 유령 = ghost[goust] = specter[spéktər] = spook[spuːk]
The campers were scared at the sight of the apparition.
캠핑을 간 사람들은 유령을 보고 무서워했다.

appease[əpíːz] v 달래다, 완화하다 = allay[əléi] = alleviate[əlíːvièit] = assuage[əswéidʒ] = mitigate[mítəgèit] = mollify[máləfài] = placate[pléikeit] = soothe[suːð]
The government tried to appease the anger of the farmers.
정부는 농부들의 분노를 달래려고 노력했다.

appellation[æpəléiʃən] n 명칭, 이름 = moniker[mánəkər] = name
There were a number of appellations to refer to the king in the ancient dynasty.
고대왕조에는 왕을 가리키는 많은 명칭이 있었다.

appendage[əpéndidʒ] n 부속물, 첨가물, 부가물 = adjunct[ǽdʒʌŋkt] = appendix[əpéndiks]
A calendar is provided as an appendage to the book. 책의 부록으로 달력이 제공된다.

apportion[əpɔ́ːrʃən] v 배분하다, 할당하다 = allocate[ǽləkèit] = allot[əlát] = divvy up = prorate[prouréit]
The dividend was apportioned to the shareholders according to their shares.
주식 수에 따라 주주들에게 배당금이 배분되었다.

apposite[ǽpəzit] a 적절한, 적합한 = appropriate[əpróupriət] = apropos[æprəpóu] = felicitous[filísətəs] = germane[dʒərméin] = opportune[àpərtjúːn] = pertinent[pə́ːrtənənt] = relevant[réləvənt] = suitable[súːtəbl]
They took apposite measures to the natural disaster. 그들은 자연재해에 적절한 대책을 취했다.

apprehensive[æprihénsiv] a 염려하는, 우려하는 = anxious[ǽŋkʃəs] = disquieted[diskwáiət] = fearful = have cold feet = restless[réstlis] = worried
The parents were apprehensive about their sons engaged in warfare.
부모들은 전쟁에 참가하고 있는 아들들을 염려했다.

apprise[əpráiz] v 알리다, 통지하다 = inform = notify[nóutəfài]
We have to apprise the climbers of the weather condition in the mountain.
우리는 등산객들에게 산의 기상상태를 알려야 한다.

approbation[æprəbéiʃən] n 승인, 찬성, 허가 = approval = consent[kənsént]
The mayor won the approbation of the city council in the construction of the new city hall.
시장은 새로운 시청사 건설에 대한 시의회의 승인을 얻었다.

appropriate[əpróupriət] v 도용하다, 전용하다, 착복하다 = embezzle[imbézl] = steal
He was prosecuted on a charge of appropriating company money.
그는 회사공금을 도용한 혐의로 고발되었다.

appurtenance[əpə́ːrtənəns] n 부속물, 부속품 = accessory = appendage[əpéndidʒ]
= appendix[əpéndiks]
There were two cars and other appurtenances of bikes in the garage.
차고에는 차 두 대와 자전거 부속품들이 있었다.

apropos[æprəpóu] a 적절한, 알맞은 = apposite[ǽpəzit] = appropriate[əpróupriət]
= felicitous[filísətəs] = germane[dʒərméin] = opportune[àpərtjúːn] = pertinent[pə́ːrtənənt]
= relevant[réləvənt] = suitable
His suggestion was not apropos in the meeting. 그의 제안은 그 회의에 적절하지 않았다.

aqueduct[ǽkwədʌkt] n 송수로, 수로, 도관 = conduit[kándwit] = pipeline
There are a number of aqueducts running underneath the city.
도시 바로 아래에 많은 송수로가 흐른다.

arable[ǽrəbl] a 경작에 알맞은, 농작 가능한 = cultivable[kʌ́ltəvəbl] = tillable[tíləbl]
There was no arable in the desert. 사막에는 경작 가능한 땅이 없었다.

arbitrary[áːrbətrèri] a 임의적인, 자유재량에 의한, 제멋대로의, 독단적인 =
capricious[kəpríʃəs] = erratic[irǽtik] = random = wayward = whimsical[hwímzikəl]
The commander had to make an arbitrary decision in a state of emergency.
사령관은 비상사태에서 임의적인 결정을 내렸다.

arcane[aːrkéin] a 불가사의한, 신비로운, 난해한 = cryptic[kríptik]
= enigmatic[ènigmǽtik] = esoteric[èsətérik] = mysterious = mystic
His success story is too arcane to believe. 그의 성공신화는 믿기에 너무 불가사의하다.

archaic[aːrkéiik] a 구식인, 고풍의, 오래된 = ancient[éinʃənt]
= antediluvian[æntidilúːviən] = behind the times = outdated = out of date = vintage[víntidʒ]
The master craftsman still sticks to the archaic way of making furniture.
그 장인은 아직도 가구를 만드는 데 구식 방법을 고수하고 있다.

QUIZ 9

Match each word in the first column with its definition in the second column.
Check your answers in the back of the book.

1.	arcane	a.	deification = glorification
2.	apotheosis	b.	ghost = specter
3.	appall	c.	adjunct = appendix
4.	archaic	d.	anxious = disquieted
5.	appease	e.	embezzle = steal
6.	apropos	f.	accessory = appendage
7.	apostate	g.	allocate = allot
8.	apprehensive	h.	capricious = erratic
9.	apposite	i.	backslider = renegade
10.	appropriate	j.	cryptic = enigmatic
11.	apprise	k.	astound = daunt
12.	approbation	l.	approval = consent
13.	apportion	m.	apposite = appropriate
14.	appurtenance	n.	cultivable = tillable
15.	appellation	o.	ancient = antediluvian
16.	aqueduct	p.	allay = alleviate
17.	apparition	q.	conduit = pipeline
18.	arbitrary	r.	inform = notify
19.	appendage	s.	appropriate = apropos
20.	arable	t.	moniker = name

archetype[ɑ́ːrkitàip] n 원형, 모범, 전형 = paradigm[pǽrədàim] = prototype
He is considered the archetype of the successful IT businessman.
그는 성공한 IT 기업인의 전형으로 간주된다.

archives[ɑ́ːrkaiv] n 기록보관서 = place where records are stored
A variety of documents are stored in the archives.
다양한 문서들이 기록보관소에 저장되어 있다.

ardent[ɑ́ːrdnt] a 열렬한, 열정적인 = avid[ǽvid] = fervent[fə́ːrvənt] = fervid[fə́ːrvid] = impassioned = passionate = vehement[víːəmənt] = zealous[zéləs]
The soccer players were cheered by ardent fans.
축구선수들은 팬들의 열렬한 환호를 받았다.

arduous[ɑ́ːrdʒuəs] a 몹시 힘든, 고된 = backbreaking = grueling[grúːəliŋ] = laborious[ləbɔ́ːriəs] = no picnic = toilsome[tɔ́ilsəm]
The troops continued an arduous march in the snow. 군대는 눈 속에서 고된 행군을 계속했다.

argot[ɑ́ːrgou] n 은어, 속어 = jargon[dʒɑ́ːrgən] = lingo[líŋgou]
The elderly have difficulty understanding the argot of teenagers.
노인들은 십대들의 은어를 이해하기 어렵다.

arid[ǽrid] a 건조한, 불모의 = barren[bǽrən] = dry = parched[pɑːrtʃt]
Some species of foxes are used to living in an arid desert.
몇몇 종의 여우들은 건조한 사막에서 사는 데 익숙해져 있다.

aristocratic[ərìstəkrǽtik] a 귀족의, 귀족정치의 = noble = patrician[pətríʃən]
The rich young man still enjoys aristocratic lifestyle.
그 부유한 젊은이는 아직도 귀족적인 생활방식을 즐긴다.

armament[ɑ́ːrməmənt] n 군비, 병기, 무기 = ammunition[æmjəníʃən] = arms = ordnance[ɔ́ːrdnəns] = weaponry[wépənri]
No nation is allowed to use biological and chemical armaments.
어떤 나라도 생물학무기와 화학무기를 사용해서는 안 된다.

armistice[ɑ́ːrməstis] n 휴전 = ceasefire = truce[truːs]
The two nations signed an armistice agreement. 두 나라는 휴전협정에 서명했다.

arouse[əráuz] v 깨우다, 자극하다 = awaken = excite = instigate[ínstəgèit]
His trip to the island aroused his curiosity in the wild animals.
섬으로의 여행이 야생동물에 대한 그의 호기심을 자극했다.

arraign[əréin] v 죄의 인정 여부를 묻다 = indict[indáit] = summon[sʌ́mən]
The president was arraigned on a charge of embezzlement. 그 사장은 횡령혐의로 소환되었다.

arrant[ǽrənt] a (나쁜 뜻으로) 완전한, 순전한 = flagrant[fléigrənt] = notorious[noutɔ́ːriəs]
His business plan turned out to be arrant fraudulence. 그의 사업계획은 완전한 사기로 드러났다.

arrears[əríər] n 지체, 밀림 = debt[det] = liability[làiəbíləti]
The bankrupt couple was in arrears with utility bills for several months.
그 파산한 부부는 몇 달간 전기 가스 수도 요금을 연체하고 있다.

arrhythmic[əríðmik] a 주기적이 아닌, 불규칙한 = irregular[irégjulər] = without rhythm
An arrhythmic heartbeat is a red flag about your health.
불규칙한 심장박동은 당신 건강의 적신호이다.

arrogate[ǽrəgèit] v 사칭하다, (권리 등을) 가로채다 = appropriate[əpróupriət]
The executive arrogated to himself the management rights of the company when the chairman had been in the hospital.
회장이 입원해 있을 때 회사 임원 한 명이 회사 경영권을 가로챘다.

arsenal[ά:rsənl] n 집합적 무기, 무기고 = storage of weapons
The armed group is holding massive arsenal.
그 무장단체는 큰 규모의 무기들을 보유하고 있다.

artful[ά:rtfəl] a 교활한, 기교 있는, 교묘한 = crafty = cunning = sly[slai] = wily[wáili] = dodgy[dάdʒi]
Guerrillas in the jungle used artful tactics. 정글의 게릴라들은 교묘한 전술을 사용했다.

artless[ά:rtlis] a 꾸밈없는, 소박한 = guileless[gáillis] = ingenuous[indʒénjuəs] = simple
The explorers will not forget the artless smiles of the people on the island.
탐험가들은 섬사람들의 소박한 미소를 잊지 않을 것이다.

articulate[a:rtíkjulət] v 분명히 표현하다, 또렷이 발음하다 = enunciate[inʌnsièit]
He articulated his views on the government's economic policy.
그는 정부의 경제정책에 대한 의견을 분명하게 표현했다.

artifact[ά:rtəfækt] n 인공물, 유물 = antique[æntí:k]= relic[rélik]
A sunken vessel full of artifacts from Song dynasty was salved.
송나라 유물을 가득 실은 침몰선이 인양되었다.

QUIZ 10

Match each word in the first column with its definition in the second column.
Check your answers in the back of the book.

1.	articulate	a.	avid = fervent
2.	arouse	b.	flagrant = notorious
3.	ardent	c.	noble = patrician
4.	archetype	d.	crafty = cunning
5.	arduous	e.	enunciate
6.	arrogate	f.	debt = liability
7.	aristocratic	g.	backbreaking = grueling
8.	armament	h.	paradigm = prototype
9.	arrears	i.	guileless = ingenuous
10.	archives	j.	place where records are stored
11.	arraign	k.	antique = relic
12.	arsenal	l.	barren = dry
13.	armistice	m.	storage of weapons
14.	arrhythmic	n.	appropriate
15.	arid	o.	ceasefire = truce
16.	arrant	p.	indict = summon
17.	artful	q.	jargon = lingo
18.	artless	r.	ammunition = arms
19.	artifact	s.	irregular = without rhythm
20.	argot	t.	awaken = excite

artifice[ɑ́ːrtəfis] n 책략, 계략 = contrivance[kəntráivəns] = dodge[dadʒ] = hoax[houks] = ruse[ruːz] = stratagem[strǽtədʒəm] = subterfuge[sʌ́btərfjùːdʒ]
The general defended the castle against the enemy by using a clever artifice.
그 장군은 적을 상대로 현명한 책략을 사용하여 성을 지켰다.

artisan[ɑ́ːrtizən] n 장인, 기능공 = craftsman
He is an artisan of a traditional bow and arrows. 그는 전통 활과 화살의 장인이다.

ascend[əsénd] v 오르다, 올라가다 = escalate[éskəlèit] = go up = move up
This time of year we see a number of salmon ascend against the river.
해마다 이때쯤 우리는 수많은 연어들이 강을 거슬러 올라가는 것을 볼 수 있다.

ascendancy[əséndənsi] n 우세, 우위, 지배력 = dominance[dámənəns]
= superiority[səpìərió:rəti] = supremacy[səpréməsi]
We gained ascendancy over the enemy by capturing the advantageous position.
우리는 유리한 위치를 점령함으로써 적에 대한 우위를 차지했다.

ascertain[æsərtéin] v 확인하다, 파악하다 = confirm = make sure = verify[vérəfài]
We ascertained that the passenger plane made an emergency landing on the island.
우리는 그 여객기가 섬에 비상착륙한 것을 확인했다.

ascetic[əsétik] a 금욕적인, 금욕주의의 = abstemious[əbstí:miəs] = abstinent[ǽbstənənt]
= austere[ɔ:stíər]
They have led ascetic lives since they came to the abbey.
그들은 수도원에 온 이후로 금욕적인 삶을 살고 있다.

aseptic[əséptik] a 무균의 = sterile[stéril]
The capsule has been kept aseptic for the chemical experiments.
그 캡슐은 화학실험을 위해서 무균상태로 유지되고 있다.

askance[əskǽns] ad 의심(불신)의 눈으로, 비스듬히, 곁눈으로 = dubiously[djú:biəs]
= skeptically = suspiciously[səspíʃəs]
The public looked askance at the mayor involved in the scandal.
대중들은 추문에 관련된 시장을 의심의 눈으로 보았다.

askew[əskjú:] a, ad 비스듬히, 삐딱하게 = awry[ərái] = crooked[krúkid]
The traffic sign was put up on the corner.
코너에 교통표지판이 비스듬히 서 있었다.

ascribe[əskráib] v 다른 탓으로 돌리다 = attribute[ətríbju:t] = impute[impjú:t]
He ascribed his defeat in the power struggle to a whistle blower.
그는 권력투쟁에서의 패배를 내부고발자의 탓으로 돌렸다.

asperity[əspérəti] n 거침, 퉁명스러움, 가혹함 = acerbity[əsə́:rbəti] = acrimony[ǽkrəmòuni] =
bitterness = harshness
She acts with asperity when asked to do troublesome work.
그녀는 귀찮은 일을 해 달라고 부탁받으면 퉁명스럽게 행동한다.

aspersion[əspə́ːrʃən] n 중상, 비난, 비방 = abuse = animadversion[ænəmǽdvə́ːrʒən]
= calumny[kǽləmni] = defamation[dèfəméiʃən] = detraction[ditrǽkʃən] = invective[invéktiv]
= libel[láibəl] = obloquy[ábləkwi] = slander[slǽndər] = smear[smiər] =
vituperation[vaitjùːpəréiʃən]
We should not cast aspersion on his achievements in environmental protection.
우리는 자연보호에 관한 그의 업적을 비방해서는 안 된다.

aspirant[ǽspərrənt] n 성공 지위를 갈망하는 사람, 큰 뜻을 품은 사람 = wannabe[wánəbìː]
He has been an aspirant to become a congressman.
그는 국회의원이 되기를 갈망해 오고 있는 사람이다.

assail[əséil] v 공격하다 = assault[əsɔ́ːlt] = attack
She assailed her competitor with unfounded allegations on the TV debate.
그녀는 TV토론회에서 그녀의 경쟁자를 근거 없는 주장으로 공격했다.

assess[əsés] v 평가하다 = appraise[əpréiz] = estimate[éstəmèit] = evaluate[ivǽljuèit] = gauge[geidʒ]
City officials are busy assessing the damage after the strong earthquake.
시청 관리들은 강력한 지진 후에 발생한 손해를 평가하느라 바쁘다.

assiduity[æsidjúːəti] n 부지런함, 근면 = diligence = sedulousness[sédʒuləsnis]
The farmer has cultivated the farm land with assiduity.
그 농부는 부지런히 농지를 개간하고 있다.

assiduous[əsídʒuəs] a 근면 성실한, 끈기 있는 = diligent[dílədʒənt] = hard-working
= industrious[indʌ́striəs] = sedulous[sédʒuləs]
The engineer has been very assiduous in his job.
그 엔지니어는 그의 업무에 매우 근면 성실했다.

assuage[əswéidʒ] v 누그러뜨리다, 완화시키다, 달래다 = ally[əlái] = alleviate[əlíːvièit]
= appease[əpíːz] = mitigate[mítəgèit] = mollify[máləfài] = pacify[pǽsəfài] = placate[pléikeit]
= relieve[rilíːv] = soothe[suːð]
The airline company officials assuaged the grief of the families of the victims.
항공회사 임원들은 희생자 가족들의 슬픔을 달랬다.

astringent[əstríndʒənt] a 엄한, 엄격한, 신랄한 = rigid[rídʒid] = rigorous[rígərəs]
= strict = stringent[stríndʒənt]
Some lawmakers are considering more astringent immigration law.
일부 의원들은 더 엄격한 이민법을 고려하고 있다.

astronomy[əstrάnəmi] n 천문학 = study of the stars and planets
Astronomy was necessary in the ancient ocean voyage.
천문학은 고대 바다 항해에서 꼭 필요했다.

QUIZ 11

*Match each word in the first column with its definition in the second column.
Check your answers in the back of the book.*

1.	astringent	a.	contrivance = dodge
2.	artisan	b.	attribute = impute
3.	ascend	c.	escalate = go up
4.	artifice	d.	wannabe
5.	ascertain	e.	abstemious = abstinent
6.	ascetic	f.	acerbity = acrimony
7.	assuage	g.	assault = attack
8.	askance	h.	sterile
9.	assiduous	i.	dominance = superiority
10.	ascendancy	j.	confirm = make sure
11.	asperity	k.	ally = alleviate
12.	aspersion	l.	rigid = rigorous
13.	aspirant	m.	dubiously = skeptically
14.	ascribe	n.	study of the stars and planets
15.	assess	o.	diligent = hard-working
16.	assiduity	p.	craftsman
17.	askew	q.	awry = crooked
18.	aseptic	r.	diligence = sedulousness
19.	assail	s.	appraise = estimate
20.	astronomy	t.	abuse = animadversion

astute[əstjúːt] a 통찰력이 있는, 기민한, 약삭빠른 = acute[əkjúːt]
= perspicacious[pə̀ːrspəkéiʃəs] = sharp = shrewd[ʃruːd]
He was a financially astute M&A expert. 그는 재무적으로 약삭빠른 인수합병 전문가이다.

asylum[əsáiləm] n 보호시설, 피난처, 망명 = harbor = haven[héivn] = refuge
= sanctuary[sǽŋktʃuèri] = shelter
He ended up with his life at an asylum for the homeless.
그는 노숙자 보호시설에서 삶을 마감했다.

atone[ətóun] v 속죄하다, 보상하다 = compensate[kámpənsèit] = expiate[ékspièit]
He atoned for his wrongdoings he had committed.
그는 자신이 저지른 잘못에 대해 속죄했다.

atrocious[ətróuʃəs] a 극악무도한, 끔찍한 = flagrant[fléigrənt] = heinous[héinəs]
= nefarious[nifɛ́əriəs]
The rebels will be never forgiven for their atrocious massacre of innocent people.
반군들은 무고한 사람들을 극악무도하게 대량 학살한 것에 대해 결코 용서받지 못할 것이다.

atrophy[ǽtrəfi] n 위축, 쇠퇴 = degeneration = deterioration[ditìəriəréiʃən]
I feel the atrophy of the muscle in my body due to the lack of exercise.
나는 운동부족으로 몸의 근육이 위축되는 걸 느낀다.

attenuate[əténjuèit] v 약화시키다, 가늘게 하다 = debilitate[dibílətèit] = enfeeble[infíːbl]
= sap[sæp] = vitiate[víʃièit] = weaken
Too much stress attenuates the level of immunity.
과도한 스트레스는 면역력을 떨어뜨린다.

attest[ətést] v 증명하다, 입증하다, 증언하다 = authenticate[ɔːθéntəkèit]
= corroborate[kərábərèit] = substantiate[səbstǽnʃièit] = verify[vérəfài]
The certificate of origin attests that the product was made in China.
원산지 증명서는 그 제품이 중국에서 생산됨을 증명한다.

attrition[ətríʃən] n 마찰, 소모, 감소 = abrasion[əbréiʒən] = erosion[iróuʒən]
The surprise attack turned into a long-lasting war of attrition.
기습공격이 장기 소모전으로 바뀌었다.

audacity[ɔːdǽsəti] n 대담함, 뻔뻔함 = boldness = daring[déəriŋ]
= dauntlessness[dɔ́ːntlis] = gallantry[gǽləntri] = guts = intrepidity[intrepídəti] = valor[vǽlər]
The special forces showed the audacity in the battle.
특공대원들은 전투에서 대담함을 보여주었다.

augment[ɔːgmént] v 증대시키다, 늘리다 = aggrandize[əgrǽndaiz] = beef up
The military high command decided to augment the troops in the battle to seize the chance to victory.
군 고위 지휘부는 승기를 잡기 위해 병력을 증원하기로 결정했다

augur[ɔ́:gər] v 전조가 되다, 점치다, 예측하다 = forecast = foreshadow = foretell = harbinger[háːrbindʒər] = herald = portend[pɔːrténd] = predict = presage[présidʒ] = prognosticate[pragnástikèit] = prophesy[práfəsài]
Strong sunlight and much rain in spring augur well for good harvest in fall.
봄철의 강한 햇빛과 많은 비는 가을에 수확이 좋을 것이라는 조짐이다.

august[ɔ́:gəst] a 위엄 있는 = dignified[dígnəfàid] = exalted[igzɔ́:ltid] = lofty[lɔ́:fti] = noble
Our society demands for august leaders
우리 사회는 위엄 있는 지도자를 요구한다.

auspices[ɔ́:spis] n 원조, 후원 = advocacy[ǽdvəkəsi] = aegis[íːdʒis] = patronage[péitrənidʒ] = support
The charity concert was held under the auspices of the city.
자선음악회는 시의 후원 아래 열렸다.

auspicious[ɔ:spíʃəs] a 길조의, 상서로운 = favorable = propitious[prəpíʃəs]
Cumuliform clouds in winter are said to be a auspicious sign.
겨울의 뭉게구름은 상서로운 조짐이라고 한다.

austere[ɔ:stíər] a 꾸밈없는, 소박한, 금욕적인 = abstemious[æbstíːmiəs] = abstinent[ǽbstənənt] = ascetic[əsétik]
The priest has lived an austere life.
신부님은 금욕적인 삶을 살았다.

autocratic[ɔ̀:təkrǽtik] a 독재의, 독재적인 = authoritarian[əθɔ̀:rətéəriən] = despotic[dispátik] = dictatorial[dìktətɔ́:riəl] = tyrannical[tirǽnikəl]
The fighter for democracy was sent to jail during the autocratic government.
민주투사는 독재정부가 통치하던 기간에 투옥되었다.

auxiliary[ɔ:gzíljəri] a 보조의, 예비의 = accessory = ancillary[ǽnsəlèri] = complementary[kàmpləméntəri] = supplementary[sʌpləméntəri]
The new tractor has a lot of auxiliary functions.
새로 나온 트랙터는 많은 보조기능이 있다.

avant-garde[əvὰːntgάːrd] a 전위적인 = liberal = progressive
Many avant-garde paintings are being displayed in the art gallery.
많은 전위적인 그림들이 화랑에 전시되고 있다.

avarice[ǽvəris] n 탐욕, 욕심 = greed = rapacity[rəpǽsəti]
The old man was blind with avarice. 그 노인은 탐욕에 눈이 멀었다.

aversion[ǽvəris] n 혐오, 반감 = abhorrence[æbhɔ́ːrəns] = abomination[əbɑ̀mənéiʃən]
= animosity[ænəmɑ́səti] = antagonism[æntǽgənìzm] = antipathy[æntípəθi]
= detestation[dìːtestéiʃən] = disgust[disgʌ́st] = dislike = distaste = hatred[héitrid]
= odium[óudiəm]= repugnance[ripʌ́gnəns] = hostility[hastíləti] = loathing[lóuðiŋ]
= revulsion[rivʌ́lʃən]
His wife has an aversion to investment in stocks. 그의 부인은 주식투자에 혐오를 갖고 있다.

QUIZ 12

Match each word in the first column with its definition in the second column.
Check your answers in the back of the book.

1.	auspices	a.	advocacy = aegis
2.	asylum	b.	degeneration = deterioration
3.	austere	c.	favorable = propitious
4.	avarice	d.	acute = perspicacious
5.	atrophy	e.	authoritarian = despotic
6.	attenuate	f.	aggrandize = beef up
7.	atone	g.	greed = rapacity
8.	auxiliary	h.	debilitate = enfeeble
9.	aversion	i.	harbor = haven
10.	augment	j.	compensate = expiate
11.	augur	k.	abhorrence = abomination
12.	august	l.	flagrant = heinous
13.	astute	m.	boldness = daring
14.	auspicious	n.	abstemious = abstinent
15.	attest	o.	forecast = foreshadow
16.	autocratic	p.	authenticate = corroborate
17.	attrition	q.	abrasion = erosion
18.	avant-garde	r.	liberal = progressive
19.	atrocious	s.	accessory = ancillary
20.	audacity	t.	dignified = exalted

avert[əvə́ːrt] v 방지하다, 피하다 = avoid = deter[ditə́ːr] = fend off = foil[fɔil]
= forestall = preclude[priklúːd] = prevent[privént] = thwart[θwɔːrt] = ward off
The management of the company tried to avert a strike. 회사 경영진은 파업을 피하려 했다.

avid[ǽvid] a 열렬한, 열광적인 = ardent[άːrdnt] = devoted = eager
= enthusiastic[inθùːziǽstik] = fanatical[fənǽtikəl] = fervent[fə́ːrvənt] = passionate
= vehement[víːəmənt] = zealous[zéləs]
The star baseball player has a number of avid fans.
그 스타플레이어 야구선수는 열렬한 팬들을 많이 가지고 있다.

avow[əváu] v 인정하다, 공언하다, 맹세하다 = admit = affirm = assert[əsə́ːrt]
= aver[əvə́ːr] = proclaim[prouklέim]
He avowed that he would quit gambling on the horses. 그는 경마도박을 끊겠다고 공언했다.

avuncular[əvʌ́ŋkjulər] a 삼촌 같은, (삼촌처럼) 자애로운 = like an uncle
The manager educated the newcomers in his kind and avuncular manner.
매니저는 신입사원들을 친절하고 자애로운 방법으로 교육했다.

awry[ərái] a, ad 엉망이 된, 구부러져, 비뚤어져 = askew[əskjúː] = crooked[krúkid]
Our plan to visit the Jeju Island went awry because of the heavy rain.
제주도를 방문하려던 우리의 계획이 폭우로 엉망이 되었다.

axiom[ǽksiəm] n 자명한 이론, 공리, 격언 = adage[ǽdidʒ] = aphorism[ǽfərìzm]
= apothegm[ǽpəθèm] = dictum[díktəm] = maxim = proverb[právəːrb] = saying
It is an axiom that honesty and diligence leads to success in life.
정직과 근면이 성공으로 연결된다는 것은 자명한 이치이다.

QUIZ 13

Match each word in the first column with its definition in the second column.
Check your answers in the back of the book.

1.	axiom		a.	adage = aphorism
2.	avid		b.	avoid = deter
3.	avow		c.	admit = affirm
4.	avert		d.	ardent = devoted
5.	awry		e.	askew = crooked
6.	avuncular		f.	like an uncle

babble[bǽbl] v 지껄이다, 중얼중얼 말하다, 잡담하다 = drivel[drívəl] = gabble[gǽbl]
A group of high school girls were babbling on something funny.
한 무리의 여고생들이 무슨 재미난 얘기인지 재잘재잘 지껄이고 있다.

bacchanal[bàːkənάːl] n 술 마시며 흥청대는 사람 = debauch[dibɔ́ːʧ] = reveler[révəl]
Some bacchanals was still seen walking around in the streets 2 hours after the festival in the town.
마을에서 있었던 축제가 끝난 지 두 시간이 지났지만 여전히 술을 마시며 흥청대는 사람들 몇 명이 거리에 보인다.

badger[bǽdʒər] v 졸라대다, 계속 묻다 = importune[ìmpɔːrtjúːn] = nag = pester[péstər]
The realtor called and badgered the entrepreneur into investing on an undeveloped area.
그 부동산업자는 기업가에게 전화를 걸어 미개발 지역에 투자하라고 졸라댔다.

bait[beit] v 꾀다, 유인하다 = entice[intáis] = lure[luər] = seduce[sidjúːs]
The animal rescue team was baiting the abandoned dog with a plate of ham and sausages.
동물구조팀은 햄과 소시지 한 접시로 유기견을 유인하고 있었다.

bale[beil] n 재앙, 불행, 고뇌 = calamity[kəlǽməti] = disaster = mishap[míshæp]
= tragedy= tribulation[trìbjuléiʃən]
It the glacier melts at a faster pace, our planet will be faced with a series of bale.
만약 빙하가 더 빠른 속도로 녹는다면 우리 지구는 연속적인 재앙에 직면할 것이다.

baleful[béilfəl] a 해로운, 악의적인 = baneful[béinfəl] = deadly = evil = harmful
= hurtful = injurious[indʒúəriəs] = malevolent[məlévələnt] = malignant[məlígnənt]
= noxious[nάkʃəs] = ominous[άmənəs] = pernicious[pərníʃəs] = ruinous[rúːinəs] = sinister
= threatening[θrétniŋ]
Most of the introduced species of fish exerted baleful consequences on the ecosystem of the river and lakes. 대부분의 외래 어종들은 강이나 호수의 생태계에 해로운 결과를 가져왔다.

balk[bɔːk] v 주저하다, 망설이다 = flinch[flinʧ] =hesitate= recoil[rikɔ́il] = stop short
The champion has balked at the demand for a return match by the challenger.
챔피언은 도전자의 재시합 요청에 망설여 왔다.

ballast[bǽləst] n 안정시키는 것, 가라앉히는 것 = something giving balance
A half an hour of meditation in the morning gives me ballast.
30분간의 아침 명상은 내게 마음의 안정을 준다.

ballyhoo[bǽlihùː] n 떠들썩한 선전, 야단법석, 과대광고 = hype[haip] = propaganda[pràpəgǽndə]
The company raised much ballyhoo in the media, while releasing a new smartphone.
그 회사는 새로운 스마트폰을 출시하면서 방송에 떠들썩하게 광고를 했다.

balm[baːm] n 위안, 완화 = anodyne[ǽnədàin]= consolation[kànsəléiʃən]
= palliative[pǽlièitiv] = solace[sɑ́ləs]
After the death of her husband, the pet dog has been a balm to her.
남편이 죽은 뒤 그 애완견은 그녀에게 위안이 되고 있다.

banal[bənǽl] a 평범한, 흔한, 시시한 = commonplace = clichéd[kliːʃéid]
= hackneyed[hǽknid] = humdrum[hʌmdrʌm] = pedestrian[pədéstriən] = trite[trait]
His commencement speech was full of banal and boring remarks.
그의 졸업연설은 너무 평범하고 따분한 말로 가득 찼다.

bane[bein] n 파멸의 원인, 해로운 것, 골칫거리 = affliction[əflíkʃən] = curse[kəːrs]
= poison = torment[tɔːrmént] = venom[vénəm]
Internet gambling has been the bane for the young businessman.
인터넷 도박은 그 젊은 사업가의 파멸의 원인이 되었다.

baneful[béinfəl] a 사악한, 해로운, 파멸시키는, 치명적인 = baleful[béilfəl] = deadly
= evil = harmful = hurtful = injurious[indʒúəriəs] = malevolent[məlévələnt]
= malignant[məlígnənt] = noxious[nɑ́kʃəs] = ominous[ɑ́mənəs] = pernicious[pərníʃəs]
= ruinous[rúːinəs] = sinister[sínəstər]
The intake of mercury can exercise a baneful effect on the reproductive function.
수은 섭취는 생식능력에 치명적인 영향을 줄 수 있다.

bandy[bǽndi] v 주고받다, 교환하다 = barter[bɑ́ːrtər] = exchange = trade
I didn't want to bandy words with the person who didn't keep his promise.
나는 약속을 지키지 않는 사람과는 말을 주고받고 싶지 않다.

banish[bǽniʃ] v 추방하다, 내쫓다, 배척하다 = deport[dipɔ́ːrt] = dispel[dispél] = exile[égzail]
= expatriate[ekspéitrièit] = expel from place = ostracize[ɑ́strəsàiz]
He was banished for from the casino for playing tricks on the gambling games.
그는 도박 게임에서 속임수를 쓰다가 카지노에서 쫓겨났다.

banter[bǽntər] n 농담, 희롱, 잡담 = chitchat
They started light banter when they met again 30 years after they graduated from the high school.
고등학교를 졸업하고 30년 만에 다시 만난 그들은 가벼운 농담을 시작했다.

barb[bɑːrb] n 비평, 가시 돋친 말, 신랄한 말 = criticism = sarcasm[sάːrkæzm]
The novelist deserves severe barb for his plagiarism.
소설가는 표절행위로 말미암아 신랄한 비난을 들을 만하다.

barbarize[bάːrbəràiz] v 야만스럽게 하다, 잔인하게 만들다 = brutalize[brúːtəlàiz]
He has become barbarized after he joined the criminal world.
그는 범죄세계에 발을 들인 이후 잔인스럽게 되었다.

bare[bɛər] a 발가벗은, 노출된, 드러난 = exposed[ikspóuzd] = uncovered
The hostages escaped in bare feet from the dungeon in the old castle.
인질들은 그 오래된 성의 지하감옥에서 맨발로 탈출했다.

barefaced[bɛrfeɪst] a 뻔뻔스러운, 부끄러운 기색이 없는 = blatant[bléitənt] = brazen[bréizn] = impudent[ímpjudnt] = unabashed
The captain of the ship showed a barefaced attitude to the victims of the tragic accident at sea.
선장은 끔직한 해상사고의 희생자들에게 뻔뻔스러운 태도를 보였다.

QUIZ 14

Match each word in the first column with its definition in the second column.
Check your answers in the back of the book.

1. barbarize
2. barefaced
3. banal
4. bait
5. bale
6. babble
7. balk
8. banter
9. ballyhoo
10. balm
11. badger
12. bane
13. barb
14. bandy
15. banish
16. baleful
17. baneful
18. bare
19. ballast
20. bacchanal

a. calamity = disaster
b. Chitchat
c. drivel = gabble
d. blatant = brazen
e. baneful = deadly
f. hype = propaganda
g. baleful = deadly
h. barter = exchange
i. entice = lure
j. Brutalize
k. debauch = reveler
l. commonplace = clichéd
m. affliction = curse
n. importune = nag
o. criticism = sarcasm
p. something giving balance
q. exposed = uncovered
r. deport = dispel
s. anodyne = consolation
t. flinch = hesitate

baroque[bəróuk] a 현란한, 화려하게 장식한 = decorative[dékərətiv] = flamboyant[flæmbɔ́iənt] = florid[flɔ́:rid] = ornate[ɔ:rnéit]

The walls of the church were filled with a lot of baroque paintings.
그 교회의 벽면들은 화려한 바로크 양식의 그림들로 가득 차 있었다.

barrage[bərɑ́:ʒ] n 포격, 사격, (질문)세례 = bombardment[bamba:rdmənt] = fusillade[fjú:səlèid]= gunfire = salvo[sǽlvou]= volley[váli]

The company president has been faced with a barrage of questions over his company advancing into the Chinese market.
회사의 사장은 중국시장 진출과 관련하여 수많은 질문세례를 받았다.

bastion[bǽstʃən] n 요새, 보루, 수호자 = bulwark[búlwərk] = citadel[sítədl] = fortification[fɔ̀:rtəfikéiʃən] = fortress[fɔ́:rtris] = stronghold
Monthly payments to a state pension can be the last bastion of a happy life in your old age.
매달 납부하는 국민연금은 노후의 행복한 삶을 위한 최후의 보루가 될 수 있다.

bathetic[bəθétik] a 평범한, 진부한, 점강법의 = banal[bənǽl] = cliché[kli:ʃéi] = commonplace = hackneyed[hǽknid] = stereotyped[stériətàipt]
A poem or a novel written in bathetic expressions can't draw attentions any more from readers.
진부한 표현으로 쓰여진 시나 소설은 독자들의 관심을 더 이상 끌지 못한다.

bauble[bɔ́:bl] n 싸구려 물건(보석), 시시한 것, 하찮은 것 = trinket[tríŋkit]
The entrance to the bar was decorated with a variety of baubles.
술집 입구는 다양한 싸구려 보석으로 장식되어 있었다.

beacon[bí:kən] n 신호, 등불, 봉화 = flare[flɛər] = sign
The Texas team professional player has been a beacon of hope to a lot of MLB fans in Asia.
텍사스 팀 소속의 그 프로선수는 아시아의 메이저리그 야구 팬들에게 희망의 빛이다.

bedlam[bédləm] n 대소동, 혼란, 아수라장, 법석 = chaos[kéias] = commotion[kəmóuʃən] = maelstrom[méilstrəm] = pandemonium[pændəmóuniəm] = tumult[tjú:məlt] = turmoil[tə́:rmɔil] = uproar[ʌpró:r]
The airport in Beijing turned into complete bedlam as the global movie star showed up at the arrival section of the airport.
북경의 공항은 세계적인 영화배우가 입국장에 모습을 나타내자 완전한 아수라장으로 변했다.

beget[bigét] v 초래하다, 일으키다, 결과를 낳다 = bring about = bring forth = engender[indʒéndər] = give rise to = generate[dʒénərèit]
Severe confrontation between the police and demonstrators begot gunfire at each other.
경찰과 시위대 간의 심한 대립은 결국 서로의 총격을 초래했다.

begrudg[bigrʌdʒ] v 시기하다, 못마땅해 하다, 주기를 아까워하다 = envy[énvi] = grudge[grʌdʒ]
I don't begrudge him earning a tremendous annual salary.
나는 그가 엄청난 연봉을 받는 것을 시기하지 않는다.

behest[bihést] n 명령, 지령, 요청, 간청 = decree[dikrí:] = injunction[indʒʌ́ŋkʃən] = order
At the behest of the local governor, no one was allowed to catch salmons until December in the rivers.
지방정부 관리자의 명령에 의해 12월까지 그 누구도 강에서 연어를 잡을 수 없도록 금지되었다.

belabor[biléibər] v [논쟁 · 일 등을] 오래도록 계속하다, 길게 늘어놓다 = rehash[rì:hǽʃ]
The mayor belabored the advantage of constructing nuclear power plant in his city.
시장은 원자력발전소를 그 시에 건설할 경우 발생할 이점에 대해 장황하게 이야기했다.

beleaguer[bilí:gər] v 포위하다, 둘러싸다, 괴롭히다 = beset[bisét] = besiege[bisí:dʒ]
= encompass[inkʌ́mpəs] = surround[səráund]
The beleaguered escaped prisoners conspired to commit another crime.
궁지에 몰린 탈옥수들이 또 다른 범죄를 모의하였다.

belie[bilái] v 모순되다, 위반하다, 거짓임을 보여주다 = contradict[kàntrədíkt]
= contravene[kàntrəví:n] = disprove[disprú:v]
His extravagant way of living belies his assertion that he donated all his wealth to a charity.
그의 사치스러운 생활방식은 모든 재산을 자선단체에 기부했다는 그의 주장이 거짓임을 보여준다.
extravagant[ikstrǽvəgənt] a 낭비하는, 사치하는

belittle[bilítl] v 얕보다, 업신여기다, 과소평가하다 = derogate[dérəgèit] = denigrate[dénigrèit]
= deprecate[déprikèit] = disparage[dispǽridʒ]
We should not belittle his love and dedication to the homeless.
우리는 노숙자들에 대한 그의 사랑과 헌신을 과소평가해서는 안 된다.

belligerent[bəlídʒərənt] a 호전적인, 싸우기 좋아하는, 공격적인 = bellicose[bélikòus]
= cantankerous[kæntǽŋkərəs] = contentious[kənténʃəs] = pugnacious[pʌgnéiʃəs]
= truculent[trʌ́kjulənt] = warlike
His belligerent attitude has always kept people away from him.
그의 호전적인 태도는 항상 사람들을 그로부터 멀어지게 했다.

beloved[bilʌ́vd] a 소중한, 친애하는, 사랑하는 = admired[ædmáiərd] = adored[ədɔ́:rd] = dear
The musician lost his beloved wife in a tragic car accident two years ago.
그 음악가는 2년 전에 비극적인 교통사고로 사랑하는 아내를 잃었다.

bemoan[bimóun] v 슬퍼하다, 비탄하다 = bewail[biwéil] = deplore[diplɔ́:r] = lament[ləmént]
= mourn[mɔ:rn]
The citizens bemoaned the deaths of the soldiers in the naval battle.
시민들은 해전에서 병사들이 목숨을 잃은 것을 슬퍼했다.

bemused[bimjúːzd] **a** 넋을 잃은, 당황한, 어리벙벙한 = baffled[bǽfld] = befuddled[bifʌ́dld] = bewildered[biwíldərd] = confused[kənfjúːzd] = discomfited[diskʌ́mfitid] = disconcerted[dìskənsə́ːrtid] = muddled[mʌ́dld] = perplexed[pərplékst] = puzzled[pʌ́zld] = stupefied[stjúːpəfài]

The actor looked a little bemused by fans in large scale rushing to him.
배우는 그에게 달려드는 수많은 팬들 때문에 다소 어리벙벙해 보였다.

QUIZ 15

Match each word in the first column with its definition in the second column.
Check your answers in the back of the book.

1.	benevolent	a.	calamity = disaster
2.	beacon	b.	Chitchat
3.	benediction	c.	drivel = gabble
4.	bathetic	d.	blatant = brazen
5.	bemoan	e.	baneful = deadly
6.	barrage	f.	hype = propaganda
7.	bedlam	g.	baleful = deadly
8.	beget	h.	barter = exchange
9.	begrudge	i.	entice = lure
10.	belabor	j.	Brutalize
11.	bauble	k.	debauch = reveler
12.	beleaguer	l.	commonplace = clichéd
13.	beloved	m.	affliction = curse
14.	belittle	n.	importune = nag
15.	belligerent	o.	criticism = sarcasm
16.	belie	p.	something giving balance
17.	bastion	q.	exposed = uncovered
18.	bemused	r.	deport = dispel
19.	baroque	s.	anodyne = consolation
20.	behest	t.	flinch = hesitate

benediction[bènədíkʃən] **n** 축복, 축복의기도 = prayer = invocation[ìnvəkéiʃən]
The priest gave the benediction for the disabled and elderly.
신부님은 장애인들과 노인들을 위해서 축복기도를 드렸다.

benevolent[bənévələnt] **a** 자비로운, 자애로운, 관대한 = charitable[tʃǽritəbl] = beneficent[bənéfəsənt] = bountiful[báuntifəl] = considerate[kənsídərət] = generous[dʒénərəs] = magnanimous[mægnǽnəməs] = philanthropic[filənθrɑ́pik]

He had been a benevolent ruler before his wife died.
그의 아내가 죽기 전까지는 그는 자비로운 군주였다.

benign[bináin] a 인자한, 상냥한, 온화한 = amiable[éimiəbl] = complaisant[kəmpléisnt] = friendly = genial[dʒíːnjəl]
The benign smiles of the employees in the department made the customers happy all day long.
부서 직원들의 인자한 미소는 손님들을 하루 종일 행복하게 만들었다.

benighted[bináitid] a 무지몽매한, 미개한 = ignorant[ígnərənt] = unenlightened = unlearned
The leader was sure that only education would change the benighted people into intelligent citizens.
지도자는 단지 교육만이 무지몽매한 사람들을 지적인 시민으로 변화시킬 수 있다고 확신했다.

bequest[bikwést] n 유산, 유증 = heritage[héritidʒ] = legacy[légəsi]
The chairman left a huge bequest to his young wife.
회장은 거액의 유산을 그의 젊은 아내에게 남겼다.

berate[biréit] v 질책하다, 비난하다, 책망하다 = castigate[kǽstəgèit] = censure[sénʃər] =chastise[tʃæstáiz] = criticize[krítəsàiz] severely = excoriate[ikskɔ́ːrièit] = lambaste[læmbéist] = lash out at = rebuke[ribjúːk] = reprimand[réprəmænd] = reproach[riróutʃ] = reprove[riprúːv] = revile[riváil] = scold[skould] = tell off = upbraid = vilify[víləfài] = vituperate[vaitjúːpərèit]
He berated his son for spending too much time on the computer games.
그는 아들이 컴퓨터 게임에 너무 많은 시간을 보내는 것을 구짖었다.

bereaved[biríːvd] a 사별한, 유족이 된
She was bereaved of her only son in a plane crash.
그녀는 비행기 추락으로 외아들을 잃었다.

beset[bisét] v 포위하다, 둘러싸다, 괴롭히다 = beleaguer[bilíːgər] = besiege[bisíːdʒ] = encompass[inkʌ́mpəs] = hem in = surround
The citizens are being beset with the severe yellow dust.
시민들은 심한 황사 때문에 괴롭힘을 당하고 있다.

besmirch[bismə́ːrtʃ] v 더럽히다, 모독하다, 먹칠을 하다 = defile[difáil] = dishonor[disǽnər] = smear[smiər] = sully[sʌ́li] = taint[teint]
The unfounded rumor besmirched the presidential candidate.
근거 없는 소문은 대통령 후보자의 얼굴에 먹칠을 했다.

bestow[bistóu] v 수여하다, 주다 = confer[kənfə́ːr] = donate[dóuneit] = entrust[intrʌ́st]
The king bestowed a knighthood on the brave general.
왕은 용감한 장군에게 기사 작위를 내렸다.

bigot[bígət] n 편견이 심한 사람, 고집쟁이 = intolerant and prejudiced person
The police presumed the shooter to be a racial bigot.
경찰은 그 총격자가 인종편견을 가진 사람이라고 추측했다.

bilious[bíljəs] a 심술궂은, 까다로운, 성질이 고약한 = cantankerous[kæntǽŋkərəs]
= choleric[kálərik] = cranky[krǽŋki] = grouchy[ɡráutʃi] = grumpy[ɡrʌ́mpi] = irascible[irǽsəbl]
= irritable[írətəbl] = ornery[ɔ́ːrnəri]
Few customers go to the store where a bilious woman is always sitting.
심술궂은 여자가 앉아 있는 가게에 가는 손님은 거의 없다.

bivouac[bívuæk] n 야영, 야영지 = encampment[inkǽmpmənt]
They set up a bivouac next to a big rock.
그들은 큰 바위 옆에 야영지를 잡았다.

blanch[blæntʃ] v 창백해지다 = pale[peil]
The children blanched at the sight of the wild bear.
아이들은 야생 곰을 보고 창백해졌다.

bland[blænd] a 무미건조한, 지루한, 재미없는, 평범한 = banal[bənǽl] = dull[dʌl] = insipid[insípid]
= tasteless = vapid[vǽpid]
The concert of the rock band was rather boring and bland.
록밴드의 공연은 오히려 지루하고 무미건조했다.

blandishment[blǽndiʃmənt] n 아첨, 아양, 감언 = adulation[ædʒuléiʃən]
= blarney[blɑ́ːrni] = cajolery[kədʒóuləri] = coaxing[kóuksiŋ] = fawning[fɔ́ːniŋ] = sweet talk
= sycophancy[síkəfənsi] = wheedling[hwíːdling]
She couldn't resist his blandishments that he could make her an actress.
그녀는 자기를 영화배우로 만들어 주겠다는 그의 감언이설을 거절하기 어려웠다.

blasphemy[blǽsfəmi] n 신성모독, 불경 = desecration[dèsikréiʃən]
= irreverence[irévərəns] = profanity[prəfǽnəti] = sacrilege[sǽkrəlidʒ]
Blasphemy is considered a serious crime in some countries.
신성모독은 어떤 국가에서는 매우 중한 범죄이다.

blatant[bléitənt] a 뻔뻔스러운, 부끄러운 기색이 없는, 뻔한 = barefaced
= brazen[bréizn] = flagrant[fléiɡrənt] = impudent[ímpjudnt] = unabashed
The nation made a blatant attempt to occupy the island that belongs to another nation.
그 나라는 다른 나라 영토에 속해 있는 섬을 차지하려는 뻔뻔스러운 시도를 했다.

blazon[bléizn] v 꾸미다, 장식하다 = adorn[ədɔ́ːrn] = embellish[imbéliʃ]
The car of the newlywed couple was blazoned with flowers.
신혼부부의 차는 꽃으로 꾸며져 있었다.

blemish[blémiʃ] v 손상시키다, 더럽히다, 흠집을 내다 = flaw[flɔː] = mar[maːr]
= stain[stein] = sully[sʌ́li] = taint[teint] = tarnish[táːrniʃ] = vitiate[víʃièit]
His reputation was blemished by the scandal.
그의 명예는 스캔들로 더럽혀졌다.

blight[blait] v 망치다, 더럽히다, 시들게 하다 = mar = taint[teint] = wither[wíðər]
His life was blighted by gambling.
그의 삶은 도박으로 망쳐졌다.

bliss[blis] n 행복, 환희, 기쁨 = ecstasy[ékstəsi] = euphoria[juːfɔ́ːriə] = felicity[filísəti]
= rapture[rǽptʃər]
The couple was in a state of bliss when their son won the gold medal in wrestling.
부부는 그들의 아들이 레슬링에서 금메달을 땄을때 환희상태 였다.

blithe[blaið] a 쾌활한, 명랑한, 즐거운 = animated = buoyant[bɔ́iənt] = carefree = cheerful
= jaunty[dʒɔ́ːnti] = jocund[dʒákənd] = jolly[dʒáli] = jovial[dʒóuviəl] = lighthearted = merry
= mirthful[məːrθfəl] = spritely[spraitli] = vivaciously[vivéiʃəs]
She is the blithest girl I've ever met.
그녀는 내가 만난 소녀 중 가장 쾌활한 소녀이다.

QUIZ 16

Match each word in the first column with its definition in the second column.
Check your answers in the back of the book.

1.	blithe	a.	defile = dishonor
2.	blanch	b.	heritage = legacy
3.	blemish	c.	confer = donate
4.	berate	d.	pale
5.	beset	e.	cantankerous = choleric
6.	besmirch	f.	flaw = mar
7.	bequest	g.	adulation = blarney
8.	bigot	h.	mar = taint
9.	bilious	i.	ecstasy = euphoria
10.	blandishment	j.	castigate = censure
11.	bestow	k.	banal = dull
12.	bland	l.	encampment
13.	bivouac	m.	adorn = embellish
14.	blasphemy	n.	animated = buoyant
15.	blight	o.	barefaced = brazen
16.	blazon	p.	amiable = complaisant
17.	benighted	q.	beleaguer = besiege
18.	blatant	r.	intolerant and prejudiced person
19.	bliss	s.	desecration = irreverence
20.	benign	t.	ignorant = unenlightened

blunt[blʌnt] a 퉁명스러운, 무뚝뚝한 = brusque[brʌsk] = curt
They heard a blunt answer from him. 그들은 그로부터 퉁명스러운 대답을 들었다.

blurb[blə:rb] n 광고문, 선전문 = advertisement[ædvə́:rtismənt]
There is a blurb on the cover of the book. 책 표지에 광고문이 있다.

blurt[blə:rt] v 불쑥 말하다, 무심코 말하다, 엉겁결에 말하다 = utter suddenly
He blurted out a secret while drinking with his friends.
그는 친구들과 술을 마시다가 엉겁결에 비밀을 말했다.

blush[blʌʃ] v 얼굴이 붉어지다, 빨개지다 = flush[flʌʃ] = turn red
She blushed at his arrival at the party.
그녀는 그 남자가 파티에 도착하자 얼굴이 붉어졌다.

bluster[blʌstər] v 고함치다, 외치다 = holler[hálər] = roar[rɔːr] = rumble[rʌmbl] = yell
" Put your gun down" the police officer blustered. "총을 내려놔" 하고 경찰이 고함쳤다.

bode[boud] v 징조가 되다, 예언하다, 예상하다 = augur[ɔ́ːgər] = forebode = forecast
= foretell = portend[pɔːrténd] = predict[pridíkt] = presage[présidʒ]
The flight of a swarm of locusts bodes ill for farmers.
대규모 메뚜기 떼의 비행은 농부들에게 불길한 징조이다.

bolster[bóulstər] v 지지하다, 보강하다, 강화하다 = boost = buttress[bʌtris] = reinforce
= shore up = support
The government decided to bolster the air power.
정부는 공군력을 강화하기로 결정했다.

bombast[bʌ́mbæst] n 호언장담, 허풍, 허세 = braggadocio[brægədóuʃiòu]
= bravado[brəvάːdou] = grandiloquence[grændíləkwəns]
His bombast made many voters turn their backs on him.
그의 호언장담은 많은 유권자들이 그에게 등을 돌리게 만들었다.

bon vivant[F. bõ vivõ] n 인생을 즐기며 사는 사람, 향락주의자, 미식가 = epicure[épikjùər]
= gourmet[gúərmei]
The artist was a famous bon vivant in his city.
그 예술가는 그 도시에서 유명한 향락주의자였다.

bona fide[bóunə fàid] a 진정한, 진실된, 성실한 = authentic[ɔːθéntik] = genuine[dʒénjuin]
The bona fide purpose of his visit is to ask for money.
그의 방문의 진정한 목적은 돈을 빌리기 위함이다.

bonhomie[bùnəmíː] n 온화함, 상냥함, 친절 = affability[æfəbíləti]
= amiability[èimiəbíləti] = geniality[dʒìːniǽləti]
All the diners felt the bonhomie of the owner at the restaurant.
모든 식사 손님들은 식당 주인의 상냥함을 느꼈다.

boon[buːn] n 혜택, 이익, 요긴한 것 = advantage[ædvǽntidʒ] = benefit[bénəfit] = blessing
The construction of the overpass will be a great boon to the citizens.
고가도로의 건설은 시민들에게 크나큰 혜택이 될 것이다.

boor[buər] n 천박한 사람, 시골뜨기, 촌스러운 사람 = churl[tʃəːrl] = lout[laut]
They considered him a boor. 그들은 그를 촌스러운 사람이라 생각했다.

bootless[bú:tlis] a 무익한, 쓸모없는, 헛된 = futile[fjú:tl] = useless
It will be a bootless effort if he tries to build a city under the water.
그가 만일 수중도시를 건설하려 한다면 그것은 쓸데없는 노력이 될 것이다.

booty[bú:ti] n 전리품, 약탈물 = loot[lu:t] = plunder[plʌndər]
The soldiers came back with a lot of booty. 병사들은 많은 전리품을 가지고 돌아왔다.

botch[batʃ] v 서투른 솜씨로 망쳐놓다, 실수하다, 그르치다 = blunder[blʌndər]
= bungle[bʌŋgl] = fumble[fʌmbl]
The novice cook botched his spaghetti.
초보 요리사가 서투른 솜씨로 그의 스파게티를 망쳐놓았다.

bovine[bóuvain] a 소 같은, 우둔한, 미련한
Doctors are checking if the bovine diseases may infect human beings.
의사들은 소로부터 전염되는 질병이 사람에게 감염되었는지 확인하고 있다.

bracing[bréisiŋ] a 기운을 돋우는, 상쾌한, 활발한 = brisk[brisk] =
exhilarating[igzíləreìtiŋ] = invigorating[invígəreìtiŋ] = refreshing[rifréʃiŋ]
The patient loved to take a deep breath of bracing air.
환자는 상쾌한 상쾌한 공기를 가슴 깊이 들이마시는 것을 좋아했다.

braggart[brǽgərt] n 허풍쟁이 = braggadocio[brægədóuʃiòu]
The salesman is a braggart himself. 그 영업사원은 허풍쟁이다.

brandish[brǽndiʃ] v 무기를 휘두르다 = wield[wi:ld]
The thief brandishied his knife at the policeman. 도둑은 경찰에게 칼을 휘둘렀다.

brash[brǽʃ] a 성급한, 경솔한, 무모한 = impulsive[impʌlsiv] = impetuous[impétʃuəs]
= reckless[réklis]
The brash decision of the general claimed as many as 200 lives.
장군의 성급한 결정 때문에 200명이 목숨을 잃었다.

QUIZ 17

Match each word in the first column with its definition in the second column.
Check your answers in the back of the book.

1.	blurt	a.	holler = roar
2.	boor	b.	augur = forebode
3.	brash	c.	boost = buttress
4.	blush	d.	brisk = exhilarating
5.	braggart	e.	utter suddenly
6.	brandish	f.	braggadocio = bravado
7.	bolster	g.	advantage = benefit
8.	bode	h.	loot = plunder
9.	bon vivant	i.	epicure = gourmet
10.	bona fide	j.	braggadocio
11.	bootless	k.	wield
12.	boon	l.	authentic = genuine
13.	bombast	m.	impulsive = impetuous
14.	bonhomie	n.	advertisement
15.	booty	o.	blunder = bungle
16.	blunt	p.	futile = useless
17.	bracing	q.	churl = lout
18.	blurb	r.	affability = amiability
19.	botch	s.	brusque = curt
20.	bluster	t.	flush = turn red

brat[bræt] n 버릇없는 녀석, 귀찮은 꼬마 = spoiled child
The only son grew up to be a spoiled brat. 외동아들은 버릇없는 아이로 자랐다.

bravado[brəvá:dou] n 허세, 허장성세 = bombast[bάmbæst] = braggadocio[brægədóuʃìou]
He was always full of bravado. 그는 항상 허세로 가득 차 있었다.

brawn[brɔ:n] n 근육, 근력, 체력 = muscle[mʌsl]
You need at least either brawn or brain to survive our society.
우리 사회에서 생존하기 위해서는 체력이나 머리 둘 중 하나는 필요하다.

brazen[bréizn] a 뻔뻔스러운, 부끄러운 기색이 없는 = blatant[bléitənt] =cheeky[tʃí:ki]
= impudent[ímpjudnt] = unabashed
Everyone was mad at his brazen attitude. 모든 사람이 그의 뻔뻔스러운 태도에 화가 났다.

breach[briːtʃ] n 위반, 침해 = contravention[kàntrəvénʃən] = infraction[infrǽkʃən] = infringement[infríndʒmənt] = transgression[trænsgréʃən] = violence[váiələns]
Absence without notice is a breach of contract. 무단결근은 계약 위반이다.

brevity[brévəti] n 짧음, 간결함, 덧없음 = briefness[bríːfnis] = terseness
Consistency and brevity are required in any proposals.
어떤 제안이든 일관성과 간결함이 요구된다.

brink[briŋk] n 직전, 가장자리, 경계 = fringe[frindʒ] = verge[vəːrdʒ]
The company is on the brink of bankruptcy. 그 회사는 부도 직전에 있다.

bristle[brísl] v 성나서 곤두서다, 발끈하다 = fume = seethe[siːð]
All the passengers bristled at the cancellation of the flight.
모든 승객들이 운항 취소에 발끈했다.

broach[broutʃ] v 화제를 끄집어내다, 말을 꺼내다 = bring up a topic
It was hard for me to broach a topic with my mother-in-law.
장모님과 어떤 화제로 이야기를 나눠야 할지 난감했다.

bromide[bróumaid] n 진부한 표현 = cliché[kliːʃéi] = platitude[plǽtitjùːd]
You had better not use bromide while making presentations.
프레젠테이션을 할 때는 진부한 표현을 쓰지 않는 것이 좋겠다.

brouhaha[bruːhάːhaː] n 소동, 소란, 난리법석 = fracas[fréikəs] = uproar[ʌpróːr]
There was a brouhaha over the suicide of the actress. 여배우의 자살 때문에 난리가 났다.

browbeat[braʊbiːt] v 위협하다, 겁주다, 억압하다 = bully = coerce[kouə́ːrs] = intimidate[intímədèit]
The bullies browbeat a boy into buying each of them a fair of shoes.
건달들은 한 소년을 겁주어 그들에게 신발 한 켤레씩을 사주도록 했다.

brusque[brʌsk] a 퉁명스러운, 무뚝뚝한 = blunt[blʌnt] = curt[kəːrt] = gruff[grʌf] = surly[sə́ːrli]
His brusque answer made us stop asking more questions.
그의 퉁명스런 대답은 우리로 하여금 더 이상의 질문을 하지 못하게 만들었다.

bucolic[bjuːkάlik] a 전원적인, 시골의, 소박한 = Arcadian[aːrkéidiən] = idyllic[aidílik] = pastoral[pǽstərəl] = rural = rustic[rʌ́stik]
He lives in a bucolic house. 그는 전원주택에서 살고 있다.

buffoon[bəfúːn] n 어릿광대 = clown
He acted like a buffoon. 그는 어릿광대처럼 행동했다.

bulwark[búlwərk] n 보루, 방어물, 보호막 = bastion[bǽstʃən] = citadel[sítədl] = fortress = rampart[rǽmpaːrt] = redoubt[ridáut] = stronghold
The fair election is a bulwark of democracy.
공정선거는 민주주의의 보루이다.

bumptious[bʌ́mpʃəs] a 거만한, 오만한, 잘난 체하는 = arrogant[ǽrəgənt] = haughty[hɔ́ːti] = imperious[impíəriəs] = pompous[pámpəs] = presumptuous[prizʌ́mptʃuəs] = pretentious[priténʃəs]
The factory chief was a bumptious engineer.
공장 책임자는 거만한 엔지니어였다.

buoyant[bɔ́iənt] a 부력 있는, 기운찬, 활황인 = bouncy[báunsi] = peppy[pépi]
We forecast a buoyant demand for electric cars.
우리는 전기차에 대한 수요가 활발해지리라 예상한다.

burgeon[bə́ːrdʒən] v 싹트다, 급성장하다, 급증하다 = flourish[fləˊːriʃ] = germinate[dʒə́ːrmənèit] = sprout[spraut]
Drone industry started to burgeon from 2000s.
드론 산업은 2000년대부터 급성장했다.

burlesque[bəːrlésk] n 풍자극, 풍자문, 풍자시 = farce[faːrs]
The musical 'Animals' is a burlesque portraying our greedy life.
뮤지컬 'Animals'는 인간의 탐욕스런 삶을 묘사하는 풍자극이다.

QUIZ 18

Match each word in the first column with its definition in the second column.
Check your answers in the back of the book.

1.	burgeon	a.	muscle
2.	bravado	b.	Arcadian = idyllic
3.	broach	c.	cliche = platitude
4.	burlesque	d.	blatant = cheeky
5.	breach	e.	bombast = braggadocio
6.	bromide	f.	spoiled child
7.	brazen	g.	fume = seethe
8.	bristle	h.	bastion = citadel
9.	bulwark	i.	blunt = curt
10.	brink	j.	arrogant = haughty
11.	brouhaha	k.	flourish = germinate
12.	browbeat	l.	contravention = infraction
13.	brusque	m.	clown
14.	bucolic	n.	bouncy = peppy
15.	brevity	o.	fracas = uproar
16.	brat	p.	briefness = terseness
17.	bumptious	q.	bully = coerce
18.	buoyant	r.	farce
19.	brawn	s.	bring up a topic
20.	buffoon	t.	fringe = verge

burnish[bə́ːrniʃ] **v** 닦다, 광을 내다 = furnish[fə́ːrniʃ] = polish[páliʃ]
He likes to burnish his car. 그는 그의 차에 광내기를 좋아한다.

busybody[bɪziba:di] **n** 참견하기 좋아하는 사람 = nosy
The old man was a busybody. 그 나이든 남자는 참견하기 좋아하는 사람이었다.

buttress[bʌtris] **v** 강화하다, 지지하다, 힘을 실어주다 = bolster[bóulstər] = brace = support = uphold
The environmental group buttressed the mayor's plan to regulate the discharge of wastewater.
환경단체는 폐수방류를 규제하려는 시장의 계획을 지지했다.

byzantine[bízəntìːn] **a** 복잡 미묘한, 미로 같은 = complex = daedal[díːdl]
No military general prefers a byzantine chain of command.
어떤 군 장성도 복잡미묘한 명령체계를 좋아하지 않는다.

QUIZ 19

*Match each word in the first column with its definition in the second column.
Check your answers in the back of the book.*

1. byzantine
2. busybody
3. burnish
4. buttress

a. nosy
b. bolster = brace
c. furnish = polish
d. complex = daedal

cabal[kəbǽl] n 음모, 계략 = conspiracy[kənspírəsi] = intrigue[intríːg] = plot = scheme[skiːm]
Their cabal to overthrow the government was foiled.
정부를 전복시키려는 그들의 음모는 실패했다.

cache[kæʃ] n 은닉처, 저장소 = hideout = repository[ripázətɔ̀ːri]
FBI's search using the GPS system detected the arms cache of the terrorists.
FBI는 위치추적 시스템을 이용하여 테러분자들의 무기 은닉처를 찾아냈다.

cacophony[kəkáfəni] n 불협화음, 불일치 = discord[dískɔːrd] = dissonance[dísənəns]
Conference participants from difficult backgrounds and cultures made cacophony at first.
서로 다른 배경과 문화적 배경을 가진 회의 참석자들은 처음에 불협화음을 냈다.

cadence[kéidns] n 리듬, 운율 = rhythm[ríðm]
All the villagers in the town danced in slow cadence.
마을 사람들은 느린 리듬으로 춤을 추었다.

cajole[kədʒóul] v 아첨하다, 구슬리다, 감언으로 꾀다 = blarney[bláːrni] = coax[kouks]
= sweet-talk = inveigle[invéigl] = wheedle[hwíːdl]
The realtor cajoled the newly-wed couple into a house.
그 부동산 중개인은 집을 사도록 신혼부부를 꾀었다.

calamity[kəlǽməti] n 재난, 재앙, 불행 = adversity[ædvə́ːrsəti]
= catastrophe[kətǽstrəfi] = disaster = mishap[míshæp] = tragedy = woe[wou]
The crash of the helicopter, killing 7 marines and 3 soldiers, was a huge calamity to the Army.
해병대원 7명과 군인 3명이 사망한 헬리콥터 추락사고는 군에게 커다란 재앙이었다.

calibrate[kǽləbrèit] v 조정하다 = adjust = fine-tune
Astronomers calibrated their telescopes to observe the stars.
천문학자들은 별을 관측하기 위해 망원경을 조정했다.

callous[kǽləs] a 냉담한, 무감각한, 무정한 = apathetic[æpəθétik] = indifferent
= insensitive[insénsətiv] = uncaring = unsympathetic
They showed a callous indifference to the tragic story of the boat people.
그들은 보트피플에 대한 비극적인 이야기에 냉담한 무관심을 보였다.

callow[kǽlou] a 미숙한, 경험이 없는, 풋내기인 = immature[ìmətʃúər] = inexperienced = unskilled
He was just a callow young man when he started his own e-commerce business.
전자상거래 사업을 시작했을 때 그는 그저 풋내기 청년이었다.

calumny[kǽləmni] n 중상, 비방, 명예훼손 = aspersion[əspə́ːrʃən]
= defamation[dèfəméiʃən] = denigration[dènigréiʃən] = disparagement[dispǽridʒmənt]
= libel[láibəl] = obloquy[ábləkwi] = slander = smear[smiər] = vituperation[vaitjùːpəréiʃən]
The loyal admiral has been the victim of calumny for a long time.
그 충성스러운 제독은 오랫동안 중상모략의 희생자가 되었다.

candor[kǽndər] n 공평무사, 솔직, 정직, 성실 = honesty[ánisti] = sincerity[sinsérəti]
= veracity[vərǽsəti]
Most companies emphasize the candor and communication ability from their new employees.
대부분의 회사는 신입사원들에게 정직과 의사소통 능력을 강조한다.

canon[kǽnən] n 법령, 규범, 명령 = edict[íːdikt] = precept[príːsept] = rule = tenet[ténit]
Western settlers established the canons of behavior.
서부 정착민들은 행동규범을 제정했다.

cant[kænt] n 위선적인 말, 겉치레, 빈말 = hypocrisy[hipákrəsi] = pretense[priténspríːtens]
= sanctimony[sǽŋktəmòuni]
The politician's speech was full of cant and self-conceit.
그 정치인의 연설은 위선과 자만으로 가득 차 있다.

cantankerous[kæntǽŋkərəs] a 툭하면 싸우는, 심술궂은, 성질이 고약한
= choleric[kálərik] = crabby[krǽbi] = cranky[krǽŋki] = grouchy[gráutʃi] = grumpy[grʌmpi]
= irascible[irǽsəbl] = morose[məróus] = ornery[ɔ́ːrnəri] = peevish[píːviʃ] = petulant[pétʃulənt]
= quarrelsome[kwɔ́ːrəlsəm] = testy[tésti]
The owner of the store is such a cantankerous old man that we rarely go there.
가게 주인은 성질이 고약한 노인이라 우리는 거의 그곳에 가지 않는다.

canvass[kǽnvəs] v 여론조사를 하다 = poll = solicit[səlísit]
Before he officially announced his candidacy for the election, he decided to canvass the opinions of the electorate.
공식적으로 출마를 선언하기 전에 그는 유권자들의 여론을 조사하기로 결심했다.

capacious[kəpéiʃəs] a 넓은, 널찍한, 큼직한 = ample = commodious[kəmóudiəs]
= comprehensive[kàmprihénsiv] = expansive[ikspǽnsiv] = extensive[iksténsiv]
= spacious[spéiʃəs] = voluminous[vəlúːmənəs]
His new house has a capacious back yard.
그의 새 집에는 널찍한 뒷마당이 있다.

capitulate[kəpítʃulèit] v 항복하다, 굴복하다, 포기하다 = give in = succumb[səkʌm]
= surrender[səréndər] = yield[ji:ld]
The hostage-takers didn't capitulate to the police to the last ditch.
인질범들은 끝까지 경찰에 항복하지 않았다.

captivate[kǽptəvèit] v 매혹하다, 사로잡다 = allure[əlúər] = attract
= enchant[intʃǽnt] = enthrall[inθrɔ́:l] = fascinate[fǽsənèit] = hypnotize[hípnətàiz]
= mesmerize[mézməràiz]
The beauty and elegance of the actress at the awards ceremony captivated a lot of movie fans.
시상식에서 여배우의 미모와 우아함은 많은 영화 팬들을 매료시켰다.

capricious[kəpríʃəs] a 변덕스러운, 변화무쌍한, 예측할 수 없는 = erratic[irǽtik]
= fanciful[fǽnsifəl] = fickle = mercurial[mərkjúəriəl] = wayward[wéiwərd]
= whimsical[hwímzikəl]
A caravan of merchants suffered from a capricious climate when crossing the desert.
대상들은 사막을 건널 때 변덕스러운 날씨 때문에 고생했다.

carcinogenic[kɑ̀:rsənədʒénik] a 발암성의, 암을 유발하는 = lethal[lí:θəl]
= mortal[mɔ́:rtl] = virulent[vírjulənt]
Some of the chemical emissions are said to contain carcinogenic properties.
몇몇 화학 배출물들은 암을 유발하는 성분을 포함하고 있다고 한다.

QUIZ 18

Match each word in the first column with its definition in the second column.
Check your answers in the back of the book.

1.	cant		a.	immature = inexperienced
2.	canvass		b.	blarney = coax
3.	capricious		c.	hypocrisy = pretense
4.	cadence		d.	choleric = crabby
5.	cajole		e.	aspersion = defamation
6.	carcinogenic		f.	adjust = fine-tune
7.	calibrate		g.	hideout = repository
8.	capacious		h.	give in = succumb
9.	callow		i.	allure = attract
10.	calumny		j.	honesty = sincerity
11.	cacophony		k.	adversity = catastrophe
12.	canon		l.	discord = dissonance
13.	cabal		m.	erratic = fanciful
14.	cantankerous		n.	lethal = mortal
15.	candor		o.	ample = commodious
16.	capitulate		p.	rhythm
17.	cache		q.	apathetic = indifferent
18.	captivate		r.	poll = solicit
19.	callous		s.	conspiracy = intrigue

cardinal[kά:rdənl] a 주요한, 중요한 = important = overriding = prime[praim]
The cardinal virtue in mountain climbing is to follow the safety rules.
등산에서 가장 중요한 덕목은 안전수칙을 따르는 것이다.

careen[kərí:n] v 기울다, 경사지다 = tilt[tilt]
The overladen ship caught in a storm and careened to one side.
짐을 너무 많이 실은 배가 폭풍을 만나 한쪽으로 기울어졌다.

carouse[kəráuz] v 술 마시며 흥청대다, 흥겹게 마시며 놀다 = booze[bu:z]
= revel[révəl] = roister[rɔ́istər]
After the soccer club winning the championship, the fans of the team caroused until late at night.
축구팀이 우승하자 팬들은 밤 늦게까지 술을 마시고 흥청댔다.

carp[kaːrp] v 트집잡다, 불평하다, 잔소리하다 = cavil[kǽvəl] = complain = gripe[graip] = grumble[grʌmbl] = nag[næg] = quibble[kwíbl]
Nancy sometimes carps at her husband about the way he is dressed.
Nancy는 남편의 옷 입는 방식에 대해 때때로 트집을 잡는다.

cartography[kaːrtágrəfi] n 지도제작법 = geography[dʒiágrəfi] = topography[təpágrəfi]
It took him 5 years and a lot of field trips to master the cartography.
그가 지도제작법을 터득하기까지는 5년의 시간과 많은 현장답사가 필요했다.

cascade[kæskéid] n 작은폭포 = waterfall
A group of climbers went past a cascade and were headed for the peak of the mountain.
한 무리의 등산객들은 작은 폭포를 지나 산 정상으로 향했다.

castigate[kǽstəgèit] v 혹평하다, 징계하다, 질책하다, 비난하다 = criticize severely
= berate[biréit] = censure[sénʃər] = chastise[tʃæstáiz] = condemn[kəndém]
= excoriate[ikskɔ́ːrièit] = lambaste[læmbéist] = lash out at = rebuke[ribjúːk]
= reprimand[réprəmænd] = reproach[ripróutʃ] = reprove[riprúːv] = revile[riváil] = scold = tell off
= upbraid = vilify[víləfài] = vituperate[vaitjúːpərèit]
The president of the company castigated the sales manager for the steep sales drop.
회사의 사장님 가파른 매출 감소에 대해 영업부장을 질책했다.

cataclysm[kǽtəklìzm] n 대재앙, 대변동, 대재난 = calamity[kəlǽməti]
= catastrophe[kətǽstrəfi] = convulsion[kənvʌlʃən] = debacle[deibáːkl] = deluge[déljuːdʒ]
= disaster = upheaval[ʌphiːvl]
The country has been going through a political and social cataclysm after the war of independence.
그 나라는 독립전쟁 후에 정치적, 사회적 대변동을 겪고 있다.

catalyst[kǽtəlist] n 촉매, 자극, 기폭제 = impetus[ímpətəs] = incentive[inséntiv]
= motivation[mòutəvéiʃən]
The death of a young college student became the catalyst for the nationwide protests.
젊은 대학생의 죽음은 전국적인 시위의 기폭제가 되었다.

categorical[kætəgɔ́ːrikəl] a 절대적인, 무조건의, 단정적인, 명확한
= absolute[ǽbsəlùːt] = definite[défənit] = definitive[difínətiv] = unconditional[ʌnkəndíʃənl]
The singer called for a news conference to make a categorical statement that he did not violated the foreign exchange control law.
그 가수는 외환관리법을 위반하지 않았다는 단정적인 진술을 하기 위해 기자회견을 요청했다.

catholic[kǽθəlik] a 보편적인, 치우치지 않는, 도량이 넓은, 폭이 넓은 = all-bracing
= comprehensive[kàmprihénsiv] = ecumenical[èkjuménikəl] = universal[jù:nəvə́:rsəl]
All the democratic countries guarantee a catholic truth of freedom of speech.
모든 민주국가들은 보편적 가치인 언론의 자유를 보장한다.

caucus[kɔ́:kəs] n 전당대회, 회의, 집회 = convention[kənvénʃən]
The democratic party held the caucus to select a presidential candidate.
민주당은 대통령 후보 선출을 위한 전당대회를 개최했다.

caustic[kɔ́:stik] a 부식성의, 톡 쏘는, 신랄한 = acerbic[əsə́:rbik] = acrid[ǽkrid]
= corrosive[kəróusiv] = pungent[pʌ́ndʒənt]
The movie which received caustic remarks from some of the domestic film critics won the grand award at a foreign film festival.
국내 영화 평론가들로부터 신랄한 비평을 받은 영화가 해외 영화제에서 대상을 탔다.

cavalier[kævəlíər] a 거만한, 건방진, 무신경한 = arrogant[ǽrəgənt] = assuming[əsú:miŋ]
= condescending[kàndəséndiŋ] = haughty[hɔ́:ti] = imperious[impíəriəs]
= insolent[ínsələnt] = overbearing = overweening[òuvərwí:niŋ] = supercilious[sù:pərsíliəs]
His cavalier attitude led to most of his friends to turn their backs on him.
그의 거만한 태도 때문에 대부분의 친구들이 그에게 등을 돌렸다.

caveat[kéiviæt] n 경고, 절차정지통고 = admonition[ædməníʃən] = warning[wɔ́:rniŋ]
The actress entered a caveat against using her portraits on the cosmetic products by a company.
그 여배우는 어떤 회사의 화장품에 자기 초상화를 쓰지 못하도록 사용정지가처분을 신청했다.

cavern[kǽvərn] n 동굴 = cave[keiv]
Every year a lot of visitors come to this mountainous area to explore the famous cavern.
매년 많은 방문객들이 유명한 거대 동굴을 탐사하기 위해서 이 산동네로 온다.

cavil[kǽvəl] v 잔소리하다, 트집잡다 = carp[ka:rp] = gripe[graip] = grumble[grʌ́mbl]
= quibble[kwíbl]
Some passengers sometimes cavil at the meals on the plane.
가끔 일부 승객이 기내식에 트집을 잡는다.

cavort[kəvɔ́:rt] v 신이 나서 뛰어다니다, 깡총거리다 = frolic[frálik] = gambol[gǽmbl]
When our family arrived at the camping site, my two sisters started cavorting on the grass.
우리 가족이 캠핑장에 도착하자 두 여동생은 잔디 위를 신이 나서 뛰어다니기 시작했다.

celibacy[séləbəsi] n 금욕, 순결, 절제 = abstinence from sex = abstention[əbsténʃən]
= chastity[tʃæstəti] = continence[kántənəns]
Some bachelors try to keep a vow of celibacy before their marriages.
일부 미혼 남성들은 결혼 전까지 순결 서약을 지키기 위해 노력한다.

censure[sénʃər] v 질책하다, 혹평하다, 비난하다 = castigate[kǽstəgèit] = criticize
= severely = berate[biréit] = chastise[tʃæstáiz] = excoriate[ikskɔ́ːrièit] = lambaste[læmbéist]
= lash out at = rebuke[ribjúːk] = reprimand[réprəmænd] = reproach[ripróutʃ] = reprove[riprúːv]
= revile[riváil] = scold = tell off = upbraid = vilify[víləfài] = vituperate[vaitjúːpərèit]
The president of the company censured the factory manager for violating the environmental
protection law. 사장님은 환경보호법을 위반한 공장 관리자를 질책했다.

QUIZ 21

Match each word in the first column with its definition in the second column.
Check your answers in the back of the book.

1.	censure	a.	important = overriding
2.	cavort	b.	booze = revel
3.	caucus	c.	geography
4.	caveat	d.	all-bracing = comprehensive
5.	cataclysm	e.	convention
6.	cascade	f.	acerbic = acrid
7.	castigate	g.	cavil = complain
8.	cardinal	h.	arrogant = assuming
9.	catalyst	i.	waterfall
10.	categorical	j.	admonition = warning
11.	cavern	k.	cave
12.	cartography	l.	carp = gripe
13.	caustic	m.	calamity = catastrophe
14.	cavalier	n.	frolic = gambol
15.	careen	o.	impetus = incentive
16.	carouse	p.	tilt
17.	cavil	q.	abstinence from sex = abstention
18.	carp	r.	criticize severely = berate
19.	celibacy	s.	castigate = criticize
20.	catholic	t.	absolute = definite

cerebral[sərí:brəl] a 뇌의, 지적인, 이지적인 = brainy[bréini]
= intellectual[intəléktʃuəl] = intelligent[intélədʒənt] = smart
The inventor is creative and cerebral. 그 발명가는 창의적이고 이지적이다.

cessation[seséiʃən] n 중지, 정지 = abeyance[əbéiəns] = hiatus[haiéitəs] = respite[réspit]
The workers were running the factory without cessation to meet the demand for the new phone.
직원들은 새로 나온 전화기 수요를 맞추기 위해 쉴 새 없이 공장을 가동했다.

chaff[tʃæf] n 쓰레기, 찌꺼기, 잡동사니 = waste[weist]
While producing the chemical products, the factory is generating chaff and dust at the same time.
그 공장은 화학제품을 생산하는 동시에 쓸모없는 찌꺼기도 생산한다.

chagrin[ʃəgrín] v 굴욕을 느끼게 하다, 분하게 여기게 하다 = abase[əbéis]
= humiliate[hju:mílièit] = mortify[mɔ́:rtəfài]
The judoka felt chagrined at the defeat by his biggest rival at the final.
그 유도선수는 결승전에서 그의 최대 라이벌에게 패한 것에 굴욕감을 느끼고 있다.

chameleon[kəmí:liən] n 지조 없는 사람, 변덕스러운 사람 = inconstant person
The loan shark is a chameleon, who changes his mind all the time.
그 사채업자는 변덕스런 사람이야, 항상 마음을 바꾸거든.

champion[tʃǽmpiən] v 위해 싸우다, 옹호하다, 지지하다 = advocate[ǽdvəkèit]
= espouse[ispáuz] = support = uphold[ʌphóuld]
A majority still champions the presidential system of government in the country.
그 나라의 대다수는 아직도 대통령제를 지지한다.

channel[tʃǽnl] v 나르다, 전달하다, 옮기다 = convey[kənvéi] = direct[dirékt]
= funnel[fʌnl] = siphon[sáifən]
A large amount of the liquefied natural gas is channeled through the gas pipeline to the capital of the country. 많은 액화천연가스가 가스 라인을 따라 그 나라 수도로 전달된다.

chaotic[keiátik] a 무질서한, 혼란의 = confused = tumultuous[tju:mʌltʃuəs] = turbulent[tɔ́:rbjulənt]
The war declaration sent the entire nation into a chaotic state.
전쟁 선포로 그 나라 전체가 무질서와 혼란의 상태로 빠졌다.

charade[ʃəréid] n 위장, 가식, 속임수 = disguise[disgáiz] = pretense[priténs, prí:tens]
His loyalty to the company has been a charade because he has leaked important information to the rival firm. 중요한 정보를 경쟁회사에 누설한 걸로 보아 그의 회사 충성도는 위장이었다.

chary[tʃéəri] a 조심성 있는, 신중, 주의 깊은 = careful[kéərfəl] = cautious[kɔ́:ʃəs]
= circumspect[sə́:rkəmspèkt]
She is chary of eating fatty foods. 그녀는 기름기 많은 음식은 피한다.

charlatan[ʃɑ́:rlətn] n 허풍쟁이, 사기꾼, 돌팔이 = con man = mountebank[máuntəbæŋk]
= quack[kwæk] = sham[ʃæm] = swindler[swíndlər]
It seems that he is a charlatan doctor, frequently prescribing wrong medicine.
돌팔이 의사로 보이는 그는 자주 엉뚱한 약을 처방한다.

chasm[kǽzm] n 간격, 틈 = cleft[kleft] = crevice[krévis] = fissure[fíʃər] = gap
The income chasm between haves and have-nots is getting deeper.
부유층과 빈곤층 간의 소득격차가 점점 커지고 있다.

chaste[tʃeist] a 순결한, 정숙한, 단정한 = decorous[dékərəs] = immaculate[imǽkjulət]
= incorrupt[ìnkərʌ́pt] = pure
After her husband death at war, Clara has lived as a chaste and beautiful widow for the rest of her life.
전쟁에서 남편이 죽은 뒤 Clara는 평생 지조 있고 아름다운 미망인으로 살았다.

chastise[tʃæstáiz] v 호되게 책망하다, 질책하다, 비난하다 = censure[sénʃər] = castigate[kǽstəgèit]
= criticize severely = berate[biréit] = excoriate[ikskɔ́:rièit] = lambaste[læmbéist] = lash out at
= rebuke[ribjú:k] = reprimand[réprəmænd] = reproach[ripróutʃ] = reprove[riprú:v] = revile[riváil]
= scold = tell off = upbraid = vilify[víləfài] = vituperate[vaitjú:pərèit]
The director of the tax office chastised its officials for being treated to food and drink.
국세청장은 직원들이 향응받은 것을 호되게 책망했다.

cherub[vaitjú:pərèit] n 천사, 천사 같은 아이 = angel
When he paints on the ceiling of a church, some cherubs often show up in the painting.
그가 교회 지붕에 그리는 그림에는 천사들이 자주 등장한다.

chicanery[ʃikéinəri] n 속임수, 핑계, 구실 = artifice[ɑ́:rtəfis] = cheating = deception[disépʃən]
= dodge[dadʒ] = ruse[ru:z] = stratagem[strǽtədʒəm] = subterfuge[sʌ́btərfjù:dʒ] = trickery[tríkəri]
The formation of a political party was his chicanery to become the candidate of the presidency in
the party. 창당은 그가 그 정당의 대통령 후보가 되기 위한 속임수였다.

chimera[kimíərə] n 망상, 환상, 허구 = fantasy[fǽntəsi] = hallucination[həlù:sənéiʃən]
= illusion[ilú:ʒən]
The belief that all terrors will disappear on the earth by the power of the religions is a chimera.
종교의 힘으로 지구상에서 모든 테러행위가 없어질 것이라는 믿음은 환상이다.

choleric[kάlərik] a 화를 잘 내는, 걸핏하면 화를 내는, 불 같은 = fractious[frǽkʃəs]
= grumpy[grʌmpi] = irascible[irǽsəbl] = irritable[írətəbl] = peevish[píːviʃ] = petulant[pétʃulənt]
= short-tempered = testy[tésti]
He is such a choleric person that people rarely talk to him.
그는 너무 화를 잘 내는 성격이라 사람들은 그에게 이야기를 잘 하지 않는다.

chord[kɔːrd] n 심금, 감정, 화음 = musical accordance
The tragic life story touched a chord with TV viewers.
그녀의 슬픈 인생사는 시청자들의 심금을 울렸다.

choreography[kɔ̀(ː)riάgrəfi] n 안무, 무용술 = dance
Helen is in charge of choreography in a ballet company.
Helen은 발레단에서 안무를 책임지고 있다.

QUIZ 22

Match each word in the first column with its definition in the second column.
Check your answers in the back of the book.

1.	choleric	a.	waste
2.	cessation	b.	abeyance = hiatus
3.	choreography	c.	abase = humiliate
4.	chagrin	d.	advocate = espouse
5.	chameleon	e.	careful = cautious
6.	champion	f.	cleft = crevice
7.	charlatan	g.	fantasy = hallucination
8.	cherub	h.	confused = tumultuous
9.	cerebral	i.	disguise = pretense
10.	chaff	j.	con man = mountebank
11.	chastise	k.	artifice = cheating
12.	chasm	l.	angel
13.	chaste	m.	decorous = immaculate
14.	chimera	n.	musical accordance
15.	charade	o.	dance
16.	chord	p.	inconstant person
17.	chary	q.	brainy = intellectual
18.	channel	r.	convey = direct
19.	chicanery	s.	fractious = grumpy
20.	chaotic	t.	censure = castigate

chortle[tʃɔ́ːrtl] v 기쁜 듯이 웃다, 깔깔거리다 = chuckle[tʃʌkl] = giggle[gígl]
Some girls chortled at the sight of frogs. 소녀들은 개구리를 보고 깔깔 웃었다.

chronic[kránik] a 만성적인, 습관적인, 상습적인 = constant[kánstənt]
= entrenched[intréntʃ] = habitual[həbítʃuəl] = ingrained[ingréind] = inveterate[invétərət]
The war veteran has been suffering from chronic bronchitis.
그 퇴역 군인은 만성적인 기관지염으로 고생하고 있다.

chronicle[kránikl] n 연대기, 연보 = annals[ǽnlz]
His autobiography contains a chronicle of historical events from 1905 to 1990.
그의 자서전은 1905년부터 1990년까지의 역사적 연대기를 포함하고 있다.

churl[tʃəːrl] n 무례한 사람, 시골뜨기, 막된 사람 = boor[buər] = yokel[jóukəl]
He is a churl, doing all kinds of misdeeds. 그는 온갖 비행을 다 저지르는 막된 사람이다.

churlish[tʃə́ːrliʃ] a 무례한, 천한 = boorish[búəriʃ] = crude
It is churlish of him to talk and laugh loudly at the funeral.
그가 장례식장에서 크게 말하고 웃는 것은 무례한 것이다.

chutzpah[hútspə] n 당돌함, 대담함, 뻔뻔함 = effrontery[ifrʌntəri] = impudence[ímpjudns]
He had the chutzpah to walk into the enemy's camp alone and have the negotiation with his counterpart.
그는 적진으로 홀로 걸어가서 상대와 협상을 하는 대담함이 있었다.

cipher[sáifər] n 암호 = code
During the world war II headquarters of the allied forces sent all the messages in cipher to their corps.
제2차 세계대전 중 연합군사령부는 예하부대에 암호로 된 메시지를 보냈다.

circuitous[sərkjúːətəs] a 우회적인, 빙 돌아가는 = roundabout
He made a circuitous criticism about the development of the nuclear bomb.
그는 핵무기 개발에 대해 우회적으로 비판을 했다.

circumlocution[səːrkəmloukjúːʃən] n 에두른(완곡한) 표현, 우회적 표현
= beating around the bush = euphemism[júːfəmìzm]
Without circumlocution, your presentation fell short of our expectations.
단도직입적으로 말해서 당신의 프레젠테이션은 우리들의 기대에 못미쳤다.

circumnavigate[sə̀ːrkəmnǽvəgèit] v 일주하다 = travel around
His dream is to circumnavigate the world in his yacht.
그의 꿈은 그의 요트를 타고 전 세계를 일주하는것이다.

circumscribe[s3ːrkəmskraıb] v 제한하다, 억제하다 = confine[kənfáin] = curb
= hamper[hǽmpər] = hinder[híndər] = restrict[ristríkt]
The power and privileges of the lawmakers will be circumscribed by the revision of the parliamentary law. 국회의원들의 힘과 특권은 국회법 개정으로 제한될 것이다.

circumspect[sə́ːrkəmspèkt] a 신중한, 조심성 있는 = attentive[əténtiv] = canny
= cautious[kɔ́ːʃəs] = discreet[diskríːt] = gingerly[dʒíndʒərli] = prudent[prúːdnt]
= vigilant[vídʒələnt] = wary
The fund manager was very circumspect in buying and selling stocks.
자금 운용자는 주식을 사고파는 데 매우 신중했다.

circumvent[sə̀ːrkəmvént] v 우회하다, 피하다, 회피하다 = avoid[əvɔ́id] = bypass
= evade[ivéid] = skirt
The businessman tried to circumvent the corporation tax by setting up a paper company in overseas tax havens.
그 사업가는 해외 조세피난처에 가짜 회사를 세워서 법인세 납부를 회피하려 했다.

cistern[sístərn] n 물탱크, 물통, 수조 = reservoir[rézərvwɑ̀ːr] = tank
All the tenants in the building used the water from the cistern on the rooftop.
모든 세입자들은 옥상에 있는 물탱크의 물을 사용했다.

citadel[rézərvwɑ̀ːr] n 성채, 요새, 최후의 거점 = bastion[bǽstʃən] = fortress[fɔ́ːrtris] = stronghold
All the citizens gathered in the citadel to be ready to for their last ditch fight with their enemy.
모든 시민들은 적과의 최후의 결전을 준비하기 위해 성채에 모였다.

clandestine[klændéstin] a 은밀한, 비밀의 = covert[kóuvərt] = furtive[fɔ́ːrtiv]
= secret = sneaky = stealthy[stélθi] = sub rosa = surreptitious[sə̀ːrəptíʃəs]
The clandestine relationship between the drug dealers and the police was revealed by the witness of a whistleblower.
마약 공급상과 경찰관의 은밀한 관계는 내부고발자의 증언에 의해 폭로되었다.

cleave[kliːv] v 쪼개다, 나누다 = divide = hew[hjuː] = split = sunder[sʌ́ndər]
An entomologist was cleaving some trees open to find the rare insects inside.
한 곤충학자가 나무 속에서 진귀한 곤충들을 찾기 위해 나무를 쪼개고 있었다.
entomologist[èntəmɑ́lədʒist] n 곤충학자

cleft[kleft] n 쪼개진 틈, 갈라진 틈 = chasm[kǽzm] = crevice[krévis] = fissure[fíʃər]
The snow-covered mountain contains a variety of clefts on the rocks and grounds.
눈 덮인 그 산은 바위와 지면에 다양한 모양의 갈라진 틈이 있다.

clement[klémənt] a 관대한, 온화한, 너그러운 = benevolent[bənévələnt]
= benign[bináin] = charitable[tʃǽritəbl] = forgiving = lenient[líːniənt] = merciful[məˊːrsifəl]
The chief justice gave a clement judgment to the defendant who was a young first offender.
재판장은 초범인 어린 피고인에게 관대한 판결을 내렸다.

cliché[kliːʃéi] n 진부한 표현, 상투적 표현 = commonplace = platitude[plǽtitjùːd] = stereotype
Most interviewers were disappointed at the presentation of the applicant because he used too much cliché.
면접관들은 너무 많은 진부한 표현을 사용하는 지원자의 프레젠테이션에 실망했다.

QUIZ 23

Match each word in the first column with its definition in the second column.
Check your answers in the back of the book.

1. circumlocution   a. annals
2. clement   b. roundabout
3. chortle   c. travel around
4. cistern   d. code
5. churlish   e. boor = yokel
6. chronicle   f. confine = curb
7. cipher   g. boorish = crude
8. circuitous   h. reservoir = tank
9. chutzpah   i. bastion = fortress
10. circumnavigate   j. covert = furtive
11. circumscribe   k. beating around the bush = euphemism
12. chronic   l. attentive = canny
13. circumvent   m. avoid = bypass
14. churl   n. divide = hew
15. circumspect   o. chasm = crevice
16. clandestine   p. chuckle = giggle
17. cleave   q. constant = entrenched
18. cliche   r. benevolent = benign
19. citadel   s. commonplace = platitude
20. cleft   t. effrontery = impudence

clique[kli:k] n 파벌, 패거리 = cabal[kəbǽl] = faction
There was a clique in the company, all members of which graduated from the same school.
그 회사 내에 파벌이 있었는데 회원들은 모두 같은 학교 출신들이었다.

clog[klag] v 막다, 방해하다 = block = choke = hamper = hinder = impede[impí:d] = plug
The accumulation of the bad cholesterol clogs the blood flow in the blood vessel.
나쁜 콜레스테롤 축적은 혈관 내의 피의 흐름을 막는다.

cloister[klɔ́istər] n 수도원, 수녀원, 회랑, 은둔장소 = abbey[ǽbi] = convent[kάnvent]
= nunnery[nΛnəri]
There used to be a cloister by the river. 강 옆에 수도원이 있었다.

clone[kloun] v 복제하다, 모사하다 = duplicate[djú:plikət] = replicate[répləkèit]
A research team of veterinarians and physicians succeeded in cloning the wild mammoth.
수의사들과 의사들로 이루어진 연구팀이 야생 매머드를 복제하는 데 성공했다.

clout[klaut] n 영향력 = influence
The law professor carries enormous political clout among young voters.
그 법대 교수는 젊은 유권자들에게 엄청난 정치적인 영향을 미친다.

cloy[klɔi] v 물리다, 질리다, 싫증나게 하다 = satiate[séiʃièit] = surfeit[sɔ́:rfit]
Rice rarely cloys us even though we eat it every day. 쌀은 매일 먹어도 거의 물리지 않는다.

coagulate[kouǽgjulèit] v 응고시키다, 응고하다, 굳어지다 = clot = congeal[kəndʒí:l]
= solidify[səlídəfài]
It took a few hours for the paint to coagulate on the floor.
바닥 페인트가 응고되는 데 몇 시간이 걸렸다.

coalesce[kòuəlés] v 합동하다, 통합하다, 연합하다 = amalgamate[əmǽlgəmèit] = blend
= integrate = merge[mə:rdʒ] = mingle[míŋgl]
A lot of planets and stars coalesce to become a galaxy.
많은 행성과 별들이 모여서 은하계가 된다.

coarse[kɔ:rs] a 상스러운, 거친, 천한 = crude = rough[rΛf] = uncouth[Λnkú:θ] = unrefined
The precious Song porcelain was covered in the coarse cloth when discovered first.
그 귀중한 송나라 자기는 처음 발견되었을 때 거친 천에 싸여 있었다.
porcelain[pɔ́:rsəlin] n 도자기

coax[kouks] v 구슬르다, 달래다, 꾀다 = cajole[kədʒóul] = entice[intáis] = induce = inveigle[invéigl] = wheedle[hwíːdl]
His mother coaxed her son out of exploring the deep sea.
그의 어머니는 그의 아들을 구슬려 심해 탐사를 그만두게 했다.

coda[kóudə] n 종결부, 결말 = epilogue[épəlɔːg]
The actress keeps singing in a high pitched voice at the coda of the musical.
여배우는 뮤지컬의 마지막 부분에서 계속 고음으로 노래한다.

coddle[kάdl] v 애지중지하다, 응석받이로 기르다 = cosset[kάsit] = indulge[indʌ́ldʒ] = pamper[pǽmpər]
A boy born of an old couple can be coddled by his parents.
늦둥이 아들은 응석받이로 길러질 수 있다.

coerce[kouə́ːrs] v 강압하다, 강요하다 = force = pressure
The coach of the baseball team coerced his players returning to their training camp by pm 6 on Saturdays. 야구팀 코치는 선수들이 일요일 오후 6시까지 합숙소로 돌아오도록 강요했다.

cogent[kóudʒənt] a 설득력 있는, 납득시키는 = convincing = persuasive[pərswéisiv]
The prosecution office presented some cogent evidences to indict him on charges of homicide.
검찰은 그를 살인죄로 기소할 수 있는 몇 가지 설득력 있는 증거를 제시했다.

cogitate[kάdʒətèit] v 숙고하다, 생각하다, 명상하다 = contemplate[kάntəmplèit] = deliberate[dilíbərət] = meditate = mull over = muse = ponder = ruminate[rúːmənèit]
The business group chairman cogitated on the selection of his heir among the three sons.
회장님은 그의 세 아들 가운데 후계자를 고르기 위해 숙고했다.

cognitive[kάgnitiv] a 인식의, 인지의, 경험적 지식에 입각한 = cerebral[səríːbrəl] = intellectual
Traveling is said to build up the cognitive ability of children.
여행은 아이들의 인지능력을 길러준다고 말한다.

cognizant[kάgnəzənt] a 인식한, 깨달은 = acquainted[əkwéintid] = aware = conscious
All the astronauts were cognizant of the risk facing them before they reached the space station.
모든 우주인들은 우주정거장에 도착하기 전에 겪을 위험을 잘 알고 있었다.

coherent[kouhíərənt] a 일관성 있는, 논리정연한 = consistent
The minister gave a coherent explanation about the measures the ministry took.
장관은 자신의 부처에서 취한 조치에 대해 일관성 있는 설명을 했다.

cohort[kóuhɔːrt] n 무리, 집단 = companion = comrade[kǽmræd]
The labor union leader and his cohorts are demanding wage hike and shorter working hours.
노조위원장과 노조원들은 임금인상과 근무시간 단축을 요구하고 있다.

colander[kʌ́ləndər] n 여과기, 체, 소쿠리 = strainer[stréinər]
My mother placed the noodle in colander before preparing for sauce.
어머니는 양념을 준비하기 전에 국수를 소쿠리에 놓았다.

QUIZ 24

Match each word in the first column with its definition in the second column.
Check your answers in the back of the book.

1.	coax	a.	amalgamate = blend
2.	cognitive	b.	crude = rough
3.	cloister	c.	convincing = persuasive
4.	clique	d.	influence
5.	clout	e.	strainer
6.	cloy	f.	contemplate = deliberate
7.	cogent	g.	cabal = faction
8.	coalesce	h.	block = choke
9.	coagulate	i.	force = pressure
10.	clog	j.	cerebral = intellectual
11.	coda	k.	epilogue
12.	coarse	l.	cosset = indulge
13.	coerce	m.	abbey = convent
14.	clone	n.	acquainted = aware
15.	coddle	o.	consistent
16.	colander	p.	duplicate = replicate
17.	cognizant	q.	clot = congeal
18.	cogitate	r.	cajole = entice
19.	cohort	s.	companion = comrade
20.	coherent	t.	satiate = surfeit

colloquial[kəlóukwiəl] a 구어체의, 회화체의, 격식을 차리지 않는 = conversational
[kànvərséiʃənl]
You need to learn colloquial English to understand the American dramas.
미국 드라마를 이해하기 위해서는 구어체 영어를 배워야 한다.

collusion[kəlúːʒən] n 공모, 음모, 결탁 = complicity[kəmplísəti] = conspiracy[kənspírəsi]
The poachers were in collusion with some rangers to hunt the wild animals in the wildlife sanctuary.
밀렵꾼들은 야생동물보호구역에서 사냥하기 위해 순찰대원들과 공모를 했다.

colonnade[kɑ̀lənéid] n 기둥 = columns
The huge Pantheon is supported by numerous colonnades.
거대한 신전은 여러 개의 기둥에 의해 지탱되고 있다.

combust[kəmbʌst] v 연소하다, 타다 = burn
Hybrid car is moving in the combination of combusting fuel in the engine and using electricity motor.
하이브리드 차는 엔진에서 연료를 연소해서 얻는 힘과 전기모터에서 얻는 두 가지 힘에 의해 움직인다.

comity[kɑ́məti] n 상호예의, 예절 = civility[sivíləti] = courtesy[kɜːrtəsi]
= deference[défərəns] = reverence[révərəns]
The comity of nations is more emphasized in time of more frequent territorial disputes.
영토분쟁이 더 흔해질 때는 나라 간의 친교가 더 강조된다.

commend[kəménd] v 칭찬하다, 추천하다, 권하다 = compliment[kɑ́mpləmənt]
= extol[ikstóul] = laud[lɔːd]
The judges all commended the chef for his excellent dishes using lamb and mushrooms.
심사위원들 모두 양고기와 버섯을 사용한 그 요리사의 음식을 칭찬했다.

commemorate[kəmémərèit] v 기념하다, 축하하다 = celebrate = honor
= memorialize[məmɔ́ːriəlàiz] = observe
The government is preparing for a massive military parade to commemorate the victory in the war.
정부는 전쟁에서의 승리를 기념하는 대규모 군사 퍼레이드를 준비하고 있다.

commensurate[kəménsərət] a 적당한, 동등한, 비례하는 = appropriate
= corresponding[kɔ̀ːrəspɑ́ndiŋ] = equal = proportionate[prəpɔ́ːrʃənit]
The workers will be rewarded commensurate with the dedication and achievements they make.
작업자들에게는 그들의 헌신과 업적에 비례해서 보상이 주어질 것이다.

commiserate[kəmízərèit] v 동정하다, 가엾게 여기다 = sympathize
He commiserated with her on her son's failure to join the national soccer team.
그는 그녀의 아들이 축구 국가대표 팀에 합류하지 못한 것에 대해 그녀를 가엾게 여겼다.

commodious[kəmóudiəs] a 넓은, 넉넉한 = ample = capacious[kəpéiʃəs]
= expansive = spacious[spéiʃəs]
The hotel on the beach has some commodious rooms and conference halls.
해변가 호텔은 널찍한 방과 회의실을 갖추고 있다.

commonsensical[kámənsénsəkl] a 상식적인, 합리적인 = judicious[dʒu:díʃəs] = sensible
It is commonsensical to yield up our seats to the old and the weak and pregnant women.
노약자나 임신부에게 자리를 양보하는 것은 상식적인 일이다.

commotion[kəmóuʃən] n 소란, 소동, 동요 = agitation[ædʒitéiʃən] = ferment[fə́:rment]
= turbulence[tə́:rbjuləns]
Some audience caused a commotion after hearing the abrupt announcement that the music concert would be cancelled.
음악회가 취소될 것이라는 갑작스러운 방송을 듣고 일부 관객들은 소란을 일으켰다.

compatible[kəmpǽtəbl] a 양립할 수 있는, 화합할 수 있는 = adaptable[ədǽptəbl]
= consistent = congenial[kəndʒí:njəl] = congruous[káŋgruəs] = consonant[kánsənənt]
= harmonious = in sync with
I don't think a lifetime employment can be compatible with job creations among young graduates.
나는 평생고용과 젊은 졸업생들의 일자리 창출은 양립할 수 없다고 생각한다.

compelling[kəmpéliŋ] a 강제적인, 설득력 있는, 주목하지 않을 수 없는 = forceful
A compelling evidence is supporting his theory that land animals came to the island during the ice age.
육지 동물들이 빙하기에 그 섬에 왔다는 그의 주장을 받쳐주는 설득력 있는 증거가 있다.

compendious[kəmpéndiəs] a 간결한, 모든 필요한 내용을 담은
= abridged[əbrídʒd] = concise[kənsáis] = curt[kə:rt] = laconic[ləkánik] = succinct[səksíŋkt]
The professor has published a compendious history book.
교수는 모든 필요한 내용을 담은 역사책 한 권을 출판했다.

compendium[kəmpéndiəm] n 요약, 개요 = abridgment[əbrídʒmənt] = abstract
= digest = epitome[ipítəmi] = summary = synopsis[sinápsis]
He wrote a one-page compendium of the code of conducts in the library.
그는 한 페이지로 요약된 도서관 행동수칙을 썼다.

complacent[kəmpléisnt] a 자기만족의, 현실에 안주하는 = contented = self-satisfied = smug[smʌg]
You shouldn't get complacent about the number of home runs you hit before you set a new record.
너는 신기록을 수립할 때까지 네가 친 홈런 개수에 스스로 만족하지 말아라.

complaisance[kəmpléisns] **n** 정중, 공손, 상냥함 = deference[défərəns]
= politeness[pəláitnis]
She has never lost her complaisance although she has been working in harsh environment.
그녀는 어려운 환경에서 일하고 있지만 결코 상냥함을 잃지 않는다.

complement[kάmpləmənt] **v** 보완하다, 완벽하게 하다 = complete[kəmplí:t]
The unexpected president's visit complemented the political convention of the party.
예정에 없던 대통령의 방문이 그 정당의 전당대회를 완벽하게 했다.

complicity[kəmplísəti] **n** 공모, 공범 = collusion[kəlú:ʒən] = conspiracy[kənspírəsi]
He was sentenced to 5 years in prison on charges of complicity in drug trafficking.
그는 마약밀매 공모혐의로 징역 5년형을 선고받았다.

QUIZ 25

Match each word in the first column with its definition in the second column.
Check your answers in the back of the book.

1.	commotion	a.	sympathize
2.	commodious	b.	ample = capacious
3.	colloquial	c.	civility = courtesy
4.	combust	d.	compliment = extol
5.	colonnade	e.	forceful
6.	commend	f.	contented = self-satisfied
7.	commemorate	g.	adaptable = consistent
8.	comity	h.	abridged = concise
9.	commiserate	i.	deference = politeness
10.	complicity	j.	celebrate = honor
11.	commensurate	k.	appropriate = corresponding
12.	collusion	l.	judicious = sensible
13.	compatible	m.	conversational
14.	complacent	n.	complete
15.	compendious	o.	complicity = conspiracy
16.	commonsensical	p.	columns
17.	compelling	q.	collusion = conspiracy
18.	complaisance	r.	burn
19.	complement	s.	agitation = ferment
20.	compendium	t.	abridgment = abstract

compliment[kámpləmənt] n 칭찬, 찬사 = commendation[kàməndéiʃən]
= praise = tribute[tríbju:t]
Compliment can be the best motivation for workers to achieve their goals in the workplace.
칭찬은 작업장에서 근로자들이 목표를 달성하는 데 가장 좋은 동기부여가 된다.

composed[kəmpóuzd] a 침착한, 차분한 = calm = collected = poised[pɔizd]
= serene[sərí:n] = tranquil[trǽŋkwil] = unflappable
She has remained composed even when she was held hostage.
그녀는 인질로 잡혀 있을 때도 침착함을 유지했다.

comprise[kəmpráiz] v 구성되다, 이루어지다, 포함하다 = be composed of = be made up of
= consist of
The 10-member committee comprises 3 lawyers, 3 doctors, 2 government officials and 2 Volunteers.
10명의 위원회는 3명의 변호사, 3명의 의사, 2명의 공무원과 2명의 자원봉사자로 구성되어 있다.

compromise[kámprəmàiz] n 양보, 타협, 절충안, 조정 = adjustment
= concession[kənséʃən] = settlement
School authorities and protesting students reached a compromise on the tuition hike.
학교 당국과 시위 학생들은 등록금 인상에 대해 타협에 이르렀다.

compunction[kəmpʌ́ŋkʃən] n 양심의 가책, 뉘우침, 죄책감, 참회 = contrition[kəntríʃən]
= penitence[pénitəns] = regret = remorse[rimɔ́:rs] = repentance[ripéntəns] = rue[ru:]
The president of the company showed no compunction about selling the outdated foods.
그 회사 사장은 유통기한이 지난 음식을 판 것에 대해 뉘우치는 기색이 없었다.

concave[kankéiv] a 오목한 = curved[kə:rvd] = dented[dentid]
Leaves on some trees in the desert turn concave due to the lack of water.
사막에 사는 일부 나무의 잎은 물 부족으로 인해 오목한 형태로 변한다.

concede[kənsí:d] v 동의하다, 인정하다 = accede[æksí:d] = accept[æksépt] =
acknowledge[æknálidʒ] = acquiesce[ækwiés] = assent[æksí:d] = endorse[indɔ́:rs]
He has been cautiously conceded to be the best pitcher as an Asian player in the Major League Baseball.
그는 조심스럽게 메이저리그 야구에서 아시아 선수 가운데 최고로 인정받는다.

concentric[kənséntrik] a 중심이 같은, 동심의 = having a common center
The planets on the solar system have the concentric orbits.
태양계 행성들은 중심이 같은 궤도를 돌고 있다.

concert[kánsəːrt] n 일치, 조화, 협동, 협력 = agreement = consonance[kánsənəns] = harmony
The city officials in concert with the residents are trying to hold the winter sports games.
시청 공무원들은 시민들과 협력하여 동계스포츠 경기를 개최하려고 애쓰고 있다.

conciliate[kənsílièit] v 달래다, 회유하다 = appease[əpíːz] = pacify[pǽsəfài]
= placate[pléikeit]
The mother of the deserter was trying to conciliate the runaway soldier.
탈영병의 어머니가 아들을 설득하고 있었다.

conciliatory[kənsíliətɔ̀ːri] a 달래는, 회유하는 = compromising[kámprəmàiziŋ]
= flexible[fléksəbl]
The local government offered conciliatory measures to angry farmers.
지방정부는 화난 농민들을 회유하기 위한 조치를 제안했다.

concise[kənsáis] a 간결한, 명료한 = brief[briːf] = compendious[kəmpéndiəs]
= curt[kəːrt] = in a nutshell = laconic[ləkánik] = pithy[píθi] = succinct[səksíŋkt] = terse[təːrs]
= to the point
The politician made a concise statement before going to the prosecution office to be questioned.
그 정치인은 검찰에 조사를 받으러 들어가기 전에 간결한 진술을 했다.

concoct[kankákt] v 고안하다, 만들어내다, 꾸며내다 = contrive[kəntráiv]
= devise[diváiz] = fabricate[fǽbrikèit]
He concocted a fraud to distribute fake designer brands across the nation.
그는 '짝퉁' 유명 디자이너 제품을 전국적으로 유통하려는 사기극을 꾸며냈다.

concord[kánkɔːrd] n 일치, 조화 = accord = agreement = harmony = unity[júːnəti]
You need to learn how to live in concord with even mosquito in the country life.
시골 생활에서는 심지어 모기와도 화목하게 사는 법을 배워야 한다.

concomitant[kankámətənt] a 수반하는, 공존하는, 부수하는 = accompanying
The government announcement to import rice and the concomitant violent responses from the farmers sent the nation in turmoil.
정부의 쌀 수입 발표와 그에 따른 농민들의 격렬한 반응은 전국을 혼란 속으로 빠뜨렸다.

concur[kənkə́ːr] v 일치하다, 동의하다 = acquiesce[ækwiés] = accord = agree = jibe[dʒaib]
The labor union concurred with the management in some sticky issues.
노사는 몇몇 까다로운 문제에 대해 의견 일치를 보았다.

condemn[kəndém] v 비난하다, 혹평하다, 질책하다 = castigate[kǽstəgèit] = criticize severely = berate[biréit] = censure[sénʃər] = chastise[ʧæstáiz] =excoriate[ikskɔ́:rièit] = lambaste[læmbéist] = lash out at = rebuke[ribjú:k] = reprimand[réprəmænd] = reproach[ripróuʧ] = reprove[riprú:v] = revile[riváil] = scold[skould] = tell off = upbraid = vilify[víləfài] = vituperate[vaitjú:pərèit]

Most western countries condemned the dictator in South America for his violent suppression of the protest.
대부분의 서방 국가들은 남미의 한 독재자가 폭력적으로 시위를 진압한 것을 비난했다.

condense[kəndéns] v 응축시키다, 압축하다, 요약하다, 단축하다 = compress
The manager submitted a 2-page new business report to the president, which condensed a lot of business analysis and forecast   매니저는 2페이지짜리 사업보고서를 사장에게 제출했는데, 이 보고서는 많은 사업 분석과 예측을 압축 요약한 것이다.

condescend[kùndəsénd] v 자신을 낮추는 척하다, 겸손하게 하려 하다 = humble oneself = patronize[péitrənàiz] = stoop[stu:p]
The candidate condescended to talk and shake hands with some voters during the campaign.
후보자는 유세기간 중에 일부 유권자들에게 몸을 낮추어 이야기하고 악수를 하려고 했다.

QUIZ 26

Match each word in the first column with its definition in the second column.
Check your answers in the back of the book.

1. burgeon
2. bravado
3. broach
4. burlesque
5. breach
6. bromide
7. brazen
8. bristle
9. bulwark
10. brink
11. brouhaha
12. browbeat
13. brusque
14. bucolic
15. brevity
16. brat
17. bumptious
18. buoyant
19. brawn
20. buffoon

a. calm = collected
b. commendation = praise
c. contrive = devise
d. accompanying
e. acquiesce = accord
f. curved = dented
g. coincident = concomitant
h. accede = accept
i. accord = agreement
j. castigate = criticize
k. having a common center
l. be composed of = be made up of
m. compress
n. appease = pacify
o. humble oneself = patronize
p. agreement = consonance
q. brief = compendious
r. adjustment = concession
s. compromising = flexible
t. contrition = penitence

condone[kəndóun] v (죄, 위법을) 용서하다, 눈감아주다 = absolve[æbzálv] = excuse = forgive = look the other way
We should not condone any crimes involving children.
우리는 어린이들을 끌어들이는 어떤 범죄도 용서해 줘서는 안 된다.

conducive[kəndjúːsiv] a 공헌하는, 기여하는, 도움이 되는 = contributive[kəntríbjutiv]
Walking or jogging an hour a day will be conducive to lowering blood pressure.
하루에 한 시간 걷기나 조깅은 혈압을 떨어뜨리는 데 기여한다.

confederate[kənfédərət] n 동맹자, 공모(공범)자 = accomplice[əkámplis] = ally[əlái] = collaborator[kəlǽbərèitər]
The principal and his confederate surrendered to the police after the robbery.
강도 행각을 벌인 후 주범과 공범은 경찰에 자수했다.

confer[kənfə́ːr] v 상의하다, 의논하다 = consult[kənsʌ́lt] = deliberate[dilíbərət] = discuss[diskʌ́s]
The student wanted to have some time to confer with his teacher about deciding on his major in college.
그 학생은 대학에서의 전공 결정과 관련, 선생님과 이야기할 시간이 필요했다.

confidant[kánfədænt] n 절친한 친구, 믿을 만한 사람 = close friend
= companion[kəmpǽnjən] = crony[króuni]
He has no close confidant to talk about his secret with.
그는 자신의 비밀에 대해 상의할 절친한 친구가 없다.

configuration[kənfìgjuréiʃən] n 배열, 배치, 구성 = arrangement[əréindʒmənt]
= composition[kàmpəzíʃən]
The efficient configuration of the components in the boiler system is very important.
보일러 시스템에서 효율적인 부품 배치는 매우 중요하다.

conflagration[kànfləgréiʃən] n 대화재, 큰불 = inferno[infə́ːrnou] = large fire
The conflagration last night in the city started from a furniture factory.
그 도시에서 일어난 대형 화재는 가구공장에서 시작되었다.

confluence[kánfluəns] n 합류, 집합, 모임 = convergence[kənvə́ːrdʒəns] = junction[dʒʌ́ŋkʃən]
We can find a variety of fish at a confluence of the two rivers.
우리는 두 강이 합류하는 지점에서 여러 가지 다양한 물고기를 볼 수 있다.

confound[kənfáund] v 당황하게 하다, 어리둥절하게 하다, 혼동하다 = abash[əbǽʃ]
= baffle[bǽfl] = bewilder[biwíldər] = confuse = discombobulate[dìskəmbɑ́bjulèit]
= discomfit[diskʌ́mfit] = dumbfound[dʌ́mfáund] = embarrass = faze = flabbergast[flǽbərgæst]
= mystify[místifài] = nonplus[nanplʌ́s] = perplex = puzzle
Some difficult questions at the interview confounded most applicants.
면접 시 몇몇 어려운 질문들은 대부분의 지원자들을 당황하게 만들었다.

congeal[kəndʒíːl] v 응고시키다, 굳히다 = coagulate[kouǽgjulèit] = concrete
= curdle[kə́ːrdl] = solidify[səlídəfài]
Eating too much fatty foods can congeal the blood, slowing the flow of it.
기름기 있는 음식을 과다하게 섭취하면 피를 응고시키고, 피의 흐름을 느리게 한다.

congenial[kəndʒíːnjəl] a 같은 성질인, 마음이 맞는, 잘 통하는 = agreeable[əgríːəbl]
= compatible[kəmpǽtəbl]
He usually enjoys tofu because the food is congenial to his physiology.
그는 보통 두부를 즐기는데, 두부가 그의 생리에 잘 맞는다.

congenital[kəndʒénətl] a 타고난, 선천적인 = inborn = indigenous[indídʒənəs]
= ingrained[ingréind] = inherent[inhíərənt] = innate = intrinsic[intrinsik]
Her congenital hearing problem couldn't stop her from becoming an excellent composer.
선천적인 청각장애도 그녀가 뛰어난 작곡가가 되는 것을 막지는 못했다.

congruent[káŋgruənt] a 합동의, 적합한, 부합하는 = concurring[kənkə́:riŋ] = harmonious
His behaviors and words were not congruent with his position at the party.
파티에서 그의 행동과 말은 그의 지위에 부합하지 않았다.

conjugal[kándʒugəl] a 결혼의, 부부간의 = connubial[kənjú:biəl] = marital[mǽrətl]
= nuptial[nʌpʃəl]
Their conjugal relations began to crack after they suffered from a financial hard time.
그들의 결혼관계는 경제적인 어려움을 겪고 나서 금이 가기 시작했다.

conjecture[kəndʒéktʃər] v 추측하다, 짐작하다, 가정하다 = guess = hypothesize[haipáθisàiz]
= speculate[spékjulèit] = surmise[sərmáiz] = suppose = theorize[θí:əràiz]
The realtor conjectured that the housing prices would jump for the years to come.
그 부동산업자는 앞으로 집값이 매우 오르리라고 예측했다.

connive[kənáiv] v 공모하다, 도모하다, 음모를 꾸미다 = cabal[kəbǽl]
= collude[kəlú:d] = conspire[kənspáiər] = machinate[mǽkənèit] = plot[plat] = scheme[ski:m]
The vice president connived with some of the directors to depose the president of the
Company. 회사의 부사장은 일부 임원들과 공모하여 사장을 물러나게 하려고 했다.

connoisseur[kànəsə́:r] n 감식가(감정가), 전문가, 권위자 = authority[əθɔ́:rəti]
= expert = guru[gúəru:] = pundit[pʌ́ndit]
A panel of food connoisseurs selected the dish cooked by the Chinese chef as the winner in the
cooking contest. 음식 전문가들은 요리대회에서 중국 요리사가 만든 요리를 우승자로 선택했다.

consecrate[kánsəkrèit] v 신성하게 하다 = hallow[hǽlou] = sanctify[sǽŋktəfài]
The birthplace of the saint has been consecrated for over 2000 years.
그 성인이 태어난 장소는 2000년 넘게 신성한 상태로 내려오고 있다.

consensus[kənsénsəs] n 의견 일치, 합의 = general agreement = unanimity[jù:nəníməti]
The representatives from 5 cities reached a consensus on building a dam.
5개 도시 대표들은 댐 건설에 관해 의견일치를 보았다.

conservatory[kənsə́:rvətɔ̀:ri] n 음악(미술, 연극)학교
= conservatoire[kənsə́:rvətwὰ:r]
The pianist is from the Eastman Conservatory of Music.
그 피아니스트는 이스트만 음악학교 출신이다.

QUIZ 27

Match each word in the first column with its definition in the second column.
Check your answers in the back of the book.

1.	congenital	a.	consult = deliberate
2.	connive	b.	coagulate = concrete
3.	congeal	c.	concurring = harmonious
4.	confer	d.	abash = baffle
5.	conducive	e.	agreeable = compatible
6.	congruent	f.	connubial = marital
7.	conflagration	g.	hallow = sanctify
8.	confidant	h.	arrangement = composition
9.	confound	i.	general agreement = unanimity
10.	confederate	j.	close friend = companion
11.	confluence	k.	accomplice = ally
12.	condone	l.	guess = hypothesize
13.	configuration	m.	cabal = collude
14.	congenial	n.	contributive
15.	conjecture	o.	authority = expert
16.	conservatory	p.	absolve = excuse
17.	conjugal	q.	inferno = large fire
18.	consecrate	r.	convergence = junction
19.	consensus	s.	inborn = indigenous
20.	connoisseur	t.	conservatoire

consign[kənsáin] v 맡기다, 위임하다, 위탁하다 = assign = commission = entrust
Before he died, the business man consigned all his wealth to his lawyer.
죽기 전에 그 사업가는 전 재산을 변호사에게 위임했다.

consolidate[kənsάlədèit] v 합병하다, 결합하다 = amalgamate[əmǽlgəmèit]
= combine = conjoin[kəndʒɔ́in] = incorporate[inkɔ́:rpərèit] = unify[jú:nəfài]
The board of directors decided to consolidate its two electronics companies to maximize the synergy effect.
이사회는 시너지 효과를 최대화하기 위해서 두 개의 전자회사를 합병하기로 결정했다.

consonant[kánsənənt] a 일치하는, 조화하는 = congruous[káŋgruəs]
= corresponding[kɔ̀:rəspándiŋ] = harmonious[ha:rmóuniəs]
The life of the religious leader is consonant with what he has been teaching to his followers.
그 종교 지도자의 삶은 그의 추종자들에게 가르쳐 온 것과 일치한다.

conspicuous[kənspíkjuəs] a 눈에 잘 띄는, 이목을 끄는, 두드러진
= distinct[distíŋkt] = noticeable[nóutisəbl]
His goal and dribble in the debut game made him conspicuous among the players.
데뷔 경기에서의 득점과 드리블은 선수들 사이에서 그를 돋보이도록 만들었다.

conspire[kənspáiər] v 공모하다, 음모를 꾸미다 = cabal[kəbǽl] = collude[kəlú:d]
= connive[kənáiv] = machinate[mǽkənèit] = plot = scheme with others
The students conspired to steal the test paper a day before the test.
학생들은 시험 하루 전에 시험지를 훔치기로 공모했다.

constellation[kànstəléiʃən] n 별자리 = arrangement of stars
Most constellations were named after animals and figures in the myth.
대부분의 별자리들은 동물이나 신화 속 인물들의 이름을 따서 명명되었다.

consternation[kànstərnéiʃən] n 깜짝 놀람, 대경실색, 경악 = awe[ɔ:]
= dismay[disméi] = trepidation[trèpədéiʃən]
To his consternation, he realized that he had left his bag on the train.
그는 가방을 기차에 두고 내린 걸 알고 깜짝 놀랐다.

constituency[kənstítʃuənsi] n 유권자, 투표자, 선거구 = electorate[iléktərət] = voters
The constituency in the rural area welcomed the government announcement to build another expressway in their area.
그 지방의 유권자들은 또 다른 고속도로를 짓겠다는 정부의 발표를 환영했다.

constrict[kənstríkt] v 억제하다, 억누르다, 수축시키다 = cramp[kræmp]
Some scholars insist that grinding constricts the creativity of the students.
어떤 학자들은 주입식 교육이 학생들의 창의력을 억제한다고 주장한다.
grinding[gráindiŋ] n 주입식 교육

construe[kənstrú:] v ~으로 해석하다, 이해하다 = decipher[disáifər] = figure out = understand
His tears were construed as his acknowledgement to committing a blunder.
그의 눈물은 그가 큰 실수를 했다는 것을 인정하는 것으로 받아들여졌다.
blunder[blʌ́ndər] n 큰 실수

consummate[kənsʌmət] a 완전한, 완벽한, 순전한 = arrant[ǽrənt] = flawless
= impeccable[impékəbl] = perfect = supreme[səprí:m]
Ronald is a consummate soccer player. 호날두는 완벽한 축구선수다.

contagious[kəntéidʒəs] a 전염성의, 전염병의 = communicable[kəmjú:nəkəbl]
= infectious[infékʃəs]
We were relieved to hear the news that the virus was not contagious.
우리는 그 바이러스가 전염성이 아니라는 뉴스를 듣고 안도했다.

contempt[kəntémpt] n 경멸, 모욕, 조롱 = derision[dirízən] = disdain[disdéin] = disregard
= jeer[dʒiər] = mockery[mɑ́kəri] = ridicule[rídikjù:l] = scoff = scorn = slight = sneer = taunt[tɔ:nt]
He has been held in contempt since he started to brag about his money.
그는 돈 자랑을 시작한 이후 경멸을 받고 있다.

contentious[kənténʃəs] a (사람이) 논쟁을 좋아하는, 논쟁을 불러일으키는
= argumentative[ὰ:rgjuméntətiv] = quarrelsome[kwɔ́:rəlsəm]
Tax increase has been a contentious issue in this country.
이 나라에서 세금 인상은 논쟁을 불러일으키는 주제이다.

contiguous[kəntígjuəs] a 인접한, 인근의 = abutting[əbʌtiŋ] = adjacent[ədʒéisnt]
= adjoining = conterminous[kantə́:rmənəs] = neighboring[néibəriŋ]
We stayed at a hotel contiguous to a lake in the countryside.
우리는 시골 호숫가에 인접한 호텔에 묵었다.

contingent[kəntíndʒənt] a 조건으로 하는, 의존하는 = conditional[kəndíʃənl] = dependent
He was released from the police station contingent on his promise that he would not violate the law again. 그는 법을 다시는 위반하지 않겠다는 약속을 하고 경찰서에서 풀려났다.

continuum[kəntínjuəm] n 연속, 연속체 = continuation = sequence[sí:kwəns]
The houses and buildings along the road formed a continuum.
도로를 따라 집과 건물들이 연속체를 이루었다.

contraband[kɑ́ntrəbænd] n 밀수품 = smuggled products
The customs officials uncovered much contraband in the container.
세관 관리들은 컨테이너에서 대량의 밀수품을 적발했다.

contraction[kəntrǽkʃən] n 수축, 축소 = shrinkage[ʃríŋkidʒ]
We can feel the contraction of the muscle in our body in winter.
우리는 겨울에 우리 몸의 근육이 축소되는 걸 느낄 수 있다.

contravene[kɑ̀ntrəvíːn] v 위반하다, 어기다 = breach[briːʧ] = infringe[infrínʤ] = violate
Some protester contravened law on assembly and demonstration.
일부 시위자들이 집회와 시위에 관한 법률을 위반했다.

QUIZ 28

Match each word in the first column with its definition in the second column. Check your answers in the back of the book.

1.	contravene	a.	electorate = voters
2.	contagious	b.	cramp
3.	consign	c.	decipher = figure out
4.	conspicuous	d.	assign = commission
5.	conspire	e.	amalgamate = combine
6.	consonant	f.	shrinkage
7.	consternation	g.	breach = infringe
8.	constituency	h.	smuggled products
9.	contraction	i.	congruous = corresponding
10.	construe	j.	derision = disdain
11.	consummate	k.	arrant = flawless
12.	constrict	l.	distinct = noticeable
13.	contempt	m.	communicable = infectious
14.	consolidate	n.	continuation = sequence
15.	contiguous	o.	conditional = dependent
16.	contingent	p.	arrangement of stars
17.	contentious	q.	argumentative = quarrelsome
18.	contraband	r.	cabal = collude
19.	constellation	s.	abutting = adjacent
20.	continuum	t.	awe = dismay

contretemps[kɑ̀ntrətɑ̀ːŋ] n 안 좋은 일, 사건, 사소한 언쟁 = misadventure
= mishap[míshæp] = predicament[pridíkəmənt]
He was involved in a series of contretemps in 2014.
2014년에 그는 좋지 않은 사건에 연이어 휩싸였다.

contrite[kəntráit] a 후회하는, 회개한, 뉘우치는 = compunctious[kəmpʌ́ŋkʃəs]
= penitent[pénətənt] = regretful[rigrétfəl] = remorseful[rimɔ́ːrsfəl]
He felt contrite after driving under the influence.
음주운전 후에 그는 뉘우쳤다.

contrived[kəntráivd] a 인조적인, 억지로 꾸민 듯한, 인위적인 = artificial
The smiles on the face of the children in the impoverished area seemed contrived.
가난한 지역의 아이들의 미소는 억지로 꾸민 듯 보였다.

contumacious[kòntjuméiʃəs] a 고집 센, 반항적인, 완고한 = headstrong[hédstrɔ̀(ː)ŋ]
= intractable[intrǽktəbl] = intransigent[intrǽnsədʒənt] = obdurate[ábdjurit] = obstinate[ábstənət]
= recalcitrant[rikǽlsitrənt] = refractory[rifrǽktəri]
He was contumacious to the police officers even in the police station.
그는 심지어 경찰서 내에서도 경찰관들에게 반항적이었다.

contumely[kántuməli] n 오만불손, 모욕적 취급 = arrogance[ǽrəgəns]
= contempt[kəntémpt] = disdain[disdéin] = humiliation[hjuːmìliéiʃən] = insolence[ínsələns]
= insult = rudeness[rúːdnis] = scorn[skɔːrn]
Many people were disappointed with the contumely of the rich businessman.
많은 사람들이 부유한 사업가의 오만불손에 실망했다.

conundrum[kənʌ́ndrəm] n 수수께끼, 난제 = enigma[əním gə] = mystery = puzzle = riddle
No one knew the answer to the conundrum posed by a witch.
아무도 그 마녀가 낸 수수께끼에 대한 답을 알지 못했다.

convalesce[kànvəlés] v 회복하다, 차도가 있다, 요양하다 = recover
= recuperate[rikjúːpərèit] = rejuvenate[ridʒúːvənèit]
He is convalescing from the injuries in the car accident.
그는 자동차 사고의 부상에서 점점 회복되고 있다.

convene[kənvíːn] v 소집하다, 모으다 = gather = congregate[káŋgrigèit] = muster[mʌ́stər]
The chairman convened the board of directors to discuss the acquisition of another company.
회장은 또 다른 회사를 인수하는 것을 논의하기 위해 이사회를 소집했다.

conversant[kənvə́ːrsənt] a 지식이 있는, 정통한, 숙련된 = acquainted[əkwéintid]
= experienced = proficient = skilled[skild] = versed[vəːrst]
The doctor is conversant with arthritis. 그 의사는 관절염에 정통하다.

converse[kənvə́ːrs] n 정반대 = antipode[ǽntipòud] = contrary = opposite
John was driving toward the east coast and Joe was driving the converse.
John은 동해안으로 운전해 가고 있었고 Joe는 정반대로 가고 있었다.

convey[kənvéi] v 전달하다, 운반하다 = transfer = transport
The pipeline was conveying the water from the river to the city.
파이프라인은 강에서 시내로 물을 전달하고 있다.

conviction[kənvíkʃən] n 유죄선고 = condemnation[kàndemnéiʃən] = guilty sentence
He got a conviction for his drunk driving last month.
그는 지난 달 음주운전으로 유죄판결을 받았다.

convince[kənvíns] v 납득시키다, 확신시키다, 설득하다 = assure
The developer of the project tried to convince the investors of the high return on their investments.
프로젝트 개발자는 투자가들에게 고수익이 돌아온다고 확신시키려 했다.

convivial[kənvíviəl] a 명랑한, 사교적인, 유쾌한 = cheerful = festive
= jocund[dʒákənd] = jolly[dʒáli] = jovial[dʒóuviəl] = sociable
The reception party was being held in a convivial atmosphere.
연회는 유쾌한 분위기에서 진행되고 있었다.

convoluted[kánvəlùːtid] a 복잡한, 뒤얽힌, 난해한 = complicated
= intricate[íntrikət] = labyrinthine[læbərínθin] = tangled[tæŋgld] = tortuous[tɔ́ːrtʃuəs]
His theory is too convoluted for students to understand.
그의 이론은 너무 복잡하고 난해해서 학생들이 이해하기 어렵다.

convulsion[kənvʌ́lʃən] n 경기, 경련 = contraction[kəntrækʃən] = cramp[kræmp]
The patient in the intensive care unit had severe convulsions.
중환자실의 환자가 심한 경련을 일으켰다.

copious[kóupiəs] a 풍부한, 막대한, 다량의 = abundant[əbʌ́ndənt] = ample
= bountiful[báuntifəl] = plentiful[pléntifəl] = profuse[prəfjúːs] = replete[riplíːt]
The semiconductor company had copious operating profits in the last fourth quarter.
그 반도체회사는 지난 4분기에 막대한 영업이익을 올렸다.

coquette[koukét] n 요부, 바람난 여자 = flirt[fləːrt]
The elegant lady turned out to be a coquette. 그 우아한 여인은 요부로 판명되었다.

cordial[kɔ́ːrdʒəl] a 애정 어린, 진심의 = affectionate = amicable[ǽmikəbl]
= congenial[kəndʒíːnjəl] = friendly = gracious[gréiʃəs] = hearty = warmhearted
He conveyed a cordial condolence on the death of her son.
그녀의 아들의 사망에 대해 그는 진심어린 조의를 표했다.

corollary[kɔ́ːrəlèri] **n** 필연적 결과, 당연한 귀결 = conclusion
= consequence[kánsəkwèns] = ramification[ræməfikéiʃən]
The size of the rainforest in Amazon has reduced significantly as a corollary of the reckless development of the area by the humans.
아마존의 열대우림 숲의 규모는 상당히 줄어들었는데, 무모한 개발에 따른 당연한 귀결이다.

QUIZ 29

*Match each word in the first column with its definition in the second column.
Check your answers in the back of the book.*

1.	contretemps	a.	gather = congregate
2.	convince	b.	condemnation = guilty sentence
3.	contrived	c.	assure
4.	contumacious	d.	affectionate = amicable
5.	corollary	e.	misadventure = mishap
6.	conundrum	f.	cheerful = festive
7.	convalesce	g.	complicated = intricate
8.	copious	h.	compunctious = penitent
9.	conversant	i.	acquainted = experienced
10.	converse	j.	antipode = contrary
11.	convene	k.	flirt
12.	conviction	l.	contraction = cramp
13.	convulsion	m.	artificial
14.	cordial	n.	transfer = transport
15.	convoluted	o.	headstrong = intractable
16.	contrite	p.	recover = recuperate
17.	convivial	q.	enigma = mystery
18.	coquette	r.	conclusion = consequence
19.	convey	s.	arrogance = contempt
20.	contumely	t.	abundant = ample

coronation[kɔ̀ːrənéiʃən] **n** 대관식, 취임식 = crowning = inauguration[inɔ̀ːgjuréiʃən]
The visitors had a chance to see the coronation held in the palace.
관광객들은 궁전에서 열리는 대관식을 볼 기회를 가졌다.

corporeal[kɔːrpɔ́ːriəl] **a** 실체적인, 형태를 가진, 신체의 = bodily = carnal
= fleshly[fléʃli] = physical = tangible[tǽndʒəbl]
We don't believe that most of the gods in Greek mythology had corporeal bodies.
우리는 그리스 신화에 등장하는 대부분의 신들이 실체적인 형태를 가졌다고는 믿지 않는다.

[kɔ̀ːrəléiʃən] n 상호관계, 상관관계 = reciprocity[rèsəprásəti]
A group of psychologists insist that there is a considerable correlation between poverty and crime rates.
일단의 심리학자들은 가난과 범죄율 사이에 상당한 상관관계가 있다고 주장한다.

corroborate[kərábərèit] v 확증하다, 확인하다 = confirm[vérəfài] = verify[vérəfài]
The scientist tried to corroborate his theory by doing a series of experiments.
그 과학자는 연속 시험을 통해 그의 이론을 확증하려고 노력했다.

corrosive[kəróusiv] a 부식성의, 부식을 일으키는 = caustic[kɔ́ːstik] = erosive[iróusiv]
The valley has a number of grotesque rocks due to the long corrosive activities by water.
그 골짜기는 오랫동안 물에 의한 침식 활동 덕분에 기이한 바위가 많다.

corrugated[kɔ́ːrəgèitid] a 물결 모양의, 주름 잡힌, 골진 = crumpled[krʌmpld]
Most houses in the country in 1970s had corrugated slate roofs.
1970년대 시골의 대부분의 집들은 골이 파진 슬레이트 지붕이었다.

cosmopolitan[kɑ̀zməpálətn] a 세계적인, 세계주의적인 = global = worldwide
Shanghai has been a cosmopolitan city since 1900s.
상하이는 1900년대부터 국제적인 도시이다.

cosset[kásit] v 애지중지하다, 귀여워하다 = fondle[fándl] = pamper[pǽmpər]
The only son in the family has been cosseted by his parents.
외동아들은 그의 부모님으로부터 귀여움을 받았다.

coterie[kóutəri] n 소집단, 파벌 = clique[kliːk]
A coterie of hardliners in the army supported the coup.
군대 내의 강경파 파벌들이 그 쿠데타를 지지했다.

countenance[káuntənəns] n 얼굴, 용모, 표정 = appearance = features = visage[vízidʒ]
The couple at the wedding ceremony had jovial countenance.
결혼식장의 신혼 커플은 즐거운 표정을 지었다.

counterfeit[káuntərfit] a 위조의, 모조의, 가짜의 = copied = fake = false
= forged[fɔːrdʒd] = phony[fóuni] = simulated = spurious[spjúəriəs]
Recently it is not easy to discern the counterfeit money from the real one.
요즘은 위조 화폐와 진짜 화폐를 구별하기가 쉽지 않다.

countermand[kàuntərmǽnd] v 철회하다, 취소하다, 무효로 하다 = annul[ənʌ́l]
= repeal = rescind[risínd] = retract[ritrǽkt] = revoke[rivóuk]
The general countermanded his order to bombard the enemy's airfields.
장군은 적의 비행장을 폭격하라는 명령을 철회했다.

court[kɔːrt] v 환심을 사려 하다, 추구하다, 얻으려고 애쓰다 = seek = solicit[səlísit] = woo[wuː]
All candidates in the general elections are courting the voters.
총선에서 후보자들이 유권자들에게 표를 얻으려고 환심을 사고 있다.

coven[kʌ́vən] n 마녀의 모임, 집회 = assembly = gathering
Once a month there is a coven in the backyard of the old castle.
한 달에 한번 고성의 뒤뜰에서 마녀들의 집회가 있다.

covenant[kʌ́vənənt] n 계약, 약속 = agreement = contract
The entrepreneur tried to keep covenant with the director of an orphanage.
그 기업가는 고아원 원장과의 약속을 지키려 노력했다.

covert[kóuvərt] a 은밀한, 비밀의 = camouflaged[kǽməflàːʒ] = clandestine[klændéstin]
= concealed = furtive[fə́ːrtiv] = hidden = secret = stealthy[stélθi] = surreptitious[sə̀ːrəptíʃəs]
He has been carrying out the covert operations in the USA since 1990s.
그는 1990년대 이후 미국에서 비밀공작을 수행해 오고 있다.

covet[kʌ́vit] v 몹시 탐내다, 갈망하다 = crave[kreiv] = desire strongly
He has long been coveting the position of being a congressman.
그는 오랫동안 국회의원이 되기를 갈망해 오고 있다.

cower[káuər] v 움츠리다, 웅크리다, 숙이다 = cringe[krindʒ] = crouch[krautʃ]
= flinch[flintʃ] = quail[kweil] = recoil[rikɔ́il] = shrink[ʃriŋk] = wince[wins]
A few lions cowered when they saw a herd of buffalos coming toward them.
몇몇 사자는 버팔로 무리가 그들에게 다가가자 움츠렸다.

crass[kræs] a 세련되지 못한, 거친, 우둔한, 무신경한 = boorish[búəriʃ] = coarse[kɔːrs] = vulgar[vʌ́lgər]
The minister made comments of crass ignorance on the nuclear power plants.
장관은 원자력발전소에 관한 무신경할 정도의 무지에 대해 언급했다.

craven[kréivn] a 비겁한, 겁많은 = dastardly[dǽstərdli] =
pusillanimous[pjùːsəlǽnəməs] = timid[tímid] = timorous[tímərəs]
The man described his boss craven and mean.
그 남자는 자신의 상사를 비겁하고 비열하다고 표현했다.

QUIZ 30

Match each word in the first column with its definition in the second column.
Check your answers in the back of the book.

1. cosset
2. corporeal
3. correlation
4. craven
5. coterie
6. corroborate
7. cosmopolitan
8. coronation
9. corrugated
10. countenance
11. counterfeit
12. corrosive
13. crass
14. coven
15. covenant
16. countermand
17. covet
18. cower
19. court
20. covert

a. clique
b. fondle = pamper
c. annul = repeal
d. copied = fake
e. appearance = features
f. dastardly = pusillanimous
g. boorish = coarse
h. reciprocity
i. global = worldwide
j. cringe = crouch
k. camouflaged = clandestine
l. assembly = gathering
m. seek = solicit
n. crave = desire strongly
o. confirm = verify
p. caustic = erosive
q. crowning = inauguration
r. bodily = carnal
s. crumpled
t. agreement = contract

credence[krí:dəns] n 신임, 믿음, 신뢰 = credit = trust
At first the swindler gained credence from the investors.
처음엔 그 사기꾼도 투자자들로부터 신뢰를 얻었다.

credulous[krédʒuləs] a 쉽사리 믿는, 잘 속는 = gullible[gʌ́ləbl] = naïve
Innocent people are sometimes likely to be credulous.
순진한 사람들이 때때로 쉽게 속는 경향이 있다.

crescendo[kriʃéndou] n 점점 세어지기, 단계적 확대 = escalation[èskəléiʃən]
The soldiers were singing a war song in a crescendo.
군인들은 군가를 점점 크게 불렀다.

crestfallen[krestfɔ:lən] a 의기소침한, 기가 죽은 = dejected = depressed
 = despondent[dispándənt] = discouraged = dispirited[dispíritid] = down in the dumps
Marcus looked crestfallen when he realized that he could not advance to the final.
Marcus는 자기가 결승전에 오르지 못한다는 것을 알고 의기소침한 듯 보였다.

crevice[krévis] n 갈라진 틈, 균열 = abyss[əbís] = crack = fissure[fíʃər] = gap
There were a lot of crevices on the way to the summit of the mountain.
산 정상으로 가는 길에 많은 갈라진 틈들이 있었다.

cringe[krindʒ] v 움츠리다, 굽실거리다 = cower[káuər] = crouch[krautʃ] = flinch[flintʃ]
 = quail[kweil] = recoil[rikɔ́il] = shrink[ʃriŋk]= wince[wins]
All the dogs cringed at the sight of the wild bears. 모든 개들은 야생 곰들을 보고 움츠렸다.

critique[kritíːk] n 비평, 평론 = analysis = appraisal[əpréizəl] = assessment[əsésmənt]
 = commentary[káməntèri] = review
The newly released novel has received good critiques from most critics.
최근 출시된 그 소설은 대부분의 비평가들로부터 좋은 평가를 받았다.

criterion[kraitíəriən] n 기준, 표준, 척도 = standard = touchstone
The city government has recently raised the criterion of food sanitation.
시 정부는 최근 식품위생에 대한 기준을 상향 조정했다.

croon[kruːn] v (낮은 목소리로 감상적으로) 노래하다 = sing
The stranger crooned walking along the trail.
나그네는 오솔길을 걸어가면서 낮은 소리로 노래했다.

crumble[krʌmbl] v 바스러지다, 가루로 만들다, 무너지다 = break up = fall into pieces
The meteorite crumbled into pieces while hitting the ground.
운석은 지상에 떨어지면서 바스러져 가루가 되었다.

crux[krʌks] n 핵심, 요점 = bottom line = core = essence = gist[dʒist] = nub[nʌb]
The crux of his economic policy is the growth of the economy.
그의 경제정책의 핵심은 경제성장이다.

cryptic[kríptik] a 비밀의, 불가사의한, 은밀한 = arcane[aːrkéin]
 = enigmatic[ènigmǽtik] = esoteric[èsətérik] = mysterious[mistíəriəs] = mystic[místik]
The scholars are trying to decipher the cryptic symbols in the tomb.
학자들은 무덤 속에서 나온 불가사의한 상징을 해독하려 하고 있다.
decipher[disáifər] v 해독하다

cuisine[kwizíːn] n 요리, 요리법 = cooking
Many people like French cuisine.
많은 사람들이 프랑스 요리를 좋아한다.

culinary[kjúːlənèri] a 요리의, 부엌의 = relating to cooking
The executive chef of the restaurant in the hotel has great culinary skills.
호텔 식당의 총 주방장은 대단한 요리실력을 가지고 있다.

cull[kʌl] v 고르다, 추려내다 = glean[gliːn] = select = sift[sift] = winnow[wínou]
The ingredients of the foods for the reception were culled from each food vendor in the region.
환영 연회에 쓰이는 음식 재료는 그 지역 식품 판매상들로부터 공급받은 것이었다.

culminate[kʌ́lmənèit] v 최고조에 달하다, ~으로 끝이 나다 = climax[kláimæks]
The debate between the two candidates culminated in blaming each other.
두 후보자 간의 토론은 결국 서로를 비난하는 것으로 끝이 났다.

culpable[kʌ́lpəbl] a 과실이 있는, 비난할 만한, 유죄의 = blameworthy
= censurable[sénʃərəbl] = guilty[gílti] = reprehensible[rèprihénsəbl]
The jury agreed to hold the captain of the plane culpable for not following the safety rules.
배심원들은 항공기 기장이 안전수칙을 따르지 않은 것에 대해 과실이 있다고 평결했다.

curmudgeon[kəːrmʌ́dʒən] n 심술궂은 구두쇠, 괴팍한 사람 = griper[gráipər]
= growler[gráulər] = grumbler[grʌ́mblər]
The grocery store on the corner was being run by a curmudgeon.
길 모퉁이 식료품 가게는 심술궂은 구두쇠가 운영하고 있다.

cursory[kə́ːrsəri] a 피상적인, 서두르는 = hasty[héisti] = perfunctory[pərfʌ́ŋktəri]
= sketchy = superficial[sùːpərfíʃəl]
The politician made a cursory apology for the bribery scandal.
그 정치인은 뇌물 스캔들에 대해서 피상적인 사과를 했다.

curb[kəːrb] v 억제하다, 제한하다 = constrain[kənstréin] = contain = control
= fetter[fétər] = hamper[hǽmpər] = hinder[híndər] = hold down = impede[impíːd]
= inhibit[inhíbit] = leash[liːʃ] = repress = restrain = restrict = shackle[ʃǽkl] = suppress[səprés]
= withhold[wiðhóuld]
The government tried to curb the prices of daily necessities.
정부는 생필품 가격을 억제했다.

curt[kəːrt] a 퉁명스러운, 무뚝뚝한 = blunt[blʌnt] = brusque[brʌsk]
= compendious[kəmpéndiəs] = laconic[ləkánik] = pithy[píθi] = succinct[səksíŋkt] = terse[təːrs]
The owner of the guesthouse was very curt when they entered the house.
그들이 들어가자 게스트하우스 주인은 매우 퉁명스러웠다.

curtail[kəːrtéil] v 단축하다, 줄이다 = cut back = cut short = truncate[trʌ́ŋkeit]
We have to curtail the use of fossil fuel.
우리는 화석연료의 사용을 줄여야 한다.

QUIZ 31

Match each word in the first column with its definition in the second column.
Check your answers in the back of the book.

1.	curtail	a.	cower = crouch
2.	curb	b.	abyss = crack
3.	credence	c.	credit = trust
4.	criterion	d.	escalation
5.	crevice	e.	break up = fall into pieces
6.	crescendo	f.	constrain = contain
7.	critique	g.	gullible = naïve
8.	crestfallen	h.	griper = growler
9.	cuisine	i.	sing
10.	crumble	j.	hasty = perfunctory
11.	crux	k.	standard = touchstone
12.	culpable	l.	blunt = brusque
13.	croon	m.	dejected = depressed
14.	culinary	n.	arcane = enigmatic
15.	cull	o.	climax
16.	culminate	p.	blameworthy = censurable
17.	cringe	q.	bottom line = core
18.	curmudgeon	r.	cut back = cut short
19.	cryptic	s.	analysis = appraisal
20.	credulous	t.	glean = select

dabble[dǽbl] v 취미 삼아 해보다, 장난 삼아 손대다 = play at
When he was living on the coastal town, he started dabbling in farming the fish.
그는 해안가 마을에 살 때 취미 삼아 물고기 양식을 했다.

daft[dæft] a 어리석은, 미친 듯한, 바보 같은 = insane[inséin] = lunatic[lú:nətik]
She went daft when she heard about the news that her son died.
그녀는 아들이 죽었다는 뉴스를 듣고 미쳤다.

damp[dæmp] a 축축한, 습기 찬 = dank[dæŋk] = humid = moist = soaked = soggy [sági] = wet
The inside of the cave was damp and cold. 동굴 안은 축축하고 추웠다.

dank[dæŋk] a 눅눅한, 축축한 = clammy[klǽmi] = chilly = damp = humid[hjú:mid]
= muggy[mʌgi] = wet
The abandoned basement storage was dark and dank. 버려진 지하창고는 어둡고 축축했다.

dapper[dǽpər] a 깔끔한, 말쑥한 = jaunty[dʒɔ́:nti] = natty = neat = well-groomed
All the male cadets look very dapper in their suits.
모든 남자 사관생도들이 정장을 입으니 참 말쑥해 보인다.

dappled[dǽpld] a 얼룩무늬의, 얼룩진, 얼룩덜룩한 = mottled[mátld]
This strange-looking crab is dappled green on one side and orange on the other.
이상하게 생긴 그 게는 반은 얼룩덜룩한 녹색이고 다른 반쪽은 오렌지색이다.

daredevil[dɛ́ərdèvl] n 앞뒤를 헤아리지 않는 사람, 저돌적인 사람 = thrill-seeker
The traffic signal couldn't stop the daredevils from carrying out the car racing along the street in broad daylight.
교통신호는 대담무쌍한 사람들이 대낮에 거리에서 자동차 경주를 하는 것을 막지 못했다.

daunt[dɔ:nt] v 위협하다, 겁먹게 하다, 무섭게 하다 = frighten[fráitn] = appall[əpɔ́:l]
= browbeat = consternate[kánstərnèit] = intimidate[intímədèit] = scare
The postman was daunted at the sight of a fierce dog 그 집배원은 무서운 개를 보고 겁이 났다.

deadpan[dedpæn] a (특히 농담하는 사람이) 무표정한, 감정을 드러내지 않는
= expressionless[ikspréʃənlis] = impassive[impǽsiv] = poker-faced
His deadpan humor made him popular across the nation.
그는 무표정한 유머로 전국적으로 인기 있는 사람이 되었다.

deafening[défəniŋ] a 떠들썩한, 귀청이 터질 듯한 = blaring[blɛ́əriŋ] = vociferous[vousífərəs]
The noise of the machine at the factory was deafening 공장의 기계소리 때문에 귀가 먹먹했다.

dearth[də:rθ] n 결핍, 부족 = deficiency[difíʃənsi] = meagerness[mí:gər] = paucity[pɔ́:səti] = privation[praivéiʃən] = scarcity[skɛ́ərsəti]
The refugees are suffering from a dearth of food. 난민들은 식량부족으로 고통받고 있다.

debase[dibéis] v 떨어뜨리다, 낮추다, 저하시키다 = degrade = demean[dimí:n] = deteriorate[ditíəriərèit] = vitiate[víʃièit]
Inflation has debased the country's currency. 인플레이션은 그 나라의 통화가치를 떨어뜨렸다.

debacle[deibɑ́:kl] n 대 실패, 파괴, 붕괴 = collapse[kəlǽps] = fiasco[fiǽskou]
His challenge to send the manned spaceship to the Mars by 2016 ended up a debacle.
2016년까지 유인 우주선을 화성에 보내겠다는 그의 도전은 대 실패로 끝났다.

debauchery[dibɔ́:tʃəri] n 방탕, 난봉 = dissoluteness[dísəlù:tnis] = profligacy[prɑ́fligəsi] = sybaritism[síbəràit]
A life of debauchery surely shortens the careers of all athletes.
방탕한 생활은 모든 운동선수들의 수명을 확실히 단축시킨다.

debilitate[dibílətèit] v 약화시키다, 쇠약하게 하다 = attenuate[əténjuèit] = enervate[énərvèit] = enfeeble[infí:bl]
The infection to the virus slowly debilitates the patients.
바이러스에 감염되면 환자는 천천히 쇠약하게 된다.

debrief[di:brí:f] v 보고를 듣다 = listen to briefing
The fighter pilot was debriefed on the military situations along the border.
그 전투기 조종사는 국경지역의 군사상황에 대해 보고했다.

debunk[dibʌ́ŋk] v 정체를 폭로하다, 틀렸음을 밝히다 = demystify[di:místəfài] = unmask
The invention of the Hubble space telescope debunked a lot of theories on the universe.
허블 우주망원경의 발명으로 우주에 대한 많은 이론들이 틀렸음이 밝혀졌다.

decadent[dékədənt] a 타락한, 퇴폐적인, 부패한 = debauched[dibɔ́:tʃt] = depraved = self-indulgent[sèlfindʌ́ldʒənt] = sybaritic[sìbərítik] = voluptuous[vəlʌ́ptʃuəs]
The couple finally got divorced due to the decadent lifestyle of the husband.
그 부부는 남편의 퇴폐적인 생활방식 때문에 결국 이혼을 했다.

decant[dikǽnt] v 가만히 따르다, 병에서 다른 병으로 따르다 = pour out
She always used to decant the boiled water into a jug.
그녀는 늘 끓인 물을 주전자에 옮겨 따랐다.

deceive[disíːv] v 속이다, 기만하다 = dupe[djuːp] = fool = bamboozle[bæmbúːzl] = beguile[bigáil] = cheat = deceive = defraud = delude = hoax[houks] = hoodwink = mislead = swindle[swíndl] = trick

The car dealer deceived him into buying an unnecessary pick-up truck.
그 차의 판매상은 그를 속여서 필요하지도 않은 픽업트럭을 사게 했다.

QUIZ 32

Match each word in the first column with its definition in the second column.
Check your answers in the back of the book.

1.	deceive	a.	frighten = appall
2.	daft	b.	dupe = fool
3.	deadpan	c.	expressionless = impassive
4.	dank	d.	debauched = depraved
5.	debauchery	e.	pour out
6.	damp	f.	deficiency = meagerness
7.	daredevil	g.	jaunty = natty
8.	dappled	h.	Mottled
9.	dabble	i.	collapse = fiasco
10.	deafening	j.	degrade = demean
11.	daunt	k.	dissoluteness = profligacy
12.	debase	l.	attenuate = enervate
13.	debacle	m.	listen to briefing
14.	dearth	n.	blaring = vociferous
15.	debilitate	o.	demystify = unmask
16.	dapper	p.	thrill-seeker
17.	debunk	q.	play at
18.	decadent	r.	insane = lunatic
19.	decant	s.	dank = humid
20.	debrief	t.	clammy = chilly

decelerate[diːsélərèit] v 속도를 줄이다, 감속하다 = slow down
He decelerated his car at the sight of the sobriety checkpoint.
그는 음주운전 단속하는 것을 보고 차의 속도를 줄였다. sobriety[səbráiəti] n 취해 있지 않음, 금주

decimate[désəmèit] v 대량으로 죽이다, 학살하다 = annihilate[ənáiəlèit] = eradicate[irædəkèit] = massacre[mǽsəkər] = wipe out
The persistent drought decimated the sheep and cattle herds.
계속된 가뭄으로 양떼와 소떼가 대량으로 죽었다.

decode[diːkóud] v 해독하다, 번역하다 = decipher[disáifər] = decrypt[diːkrípt]
He spent many years decoding the ancient manuscript.
그는 고대의 필사본을 해독하느라 수년간의 시간을 보냈다.

decorous[dékərəs] a 품위 있는, 예의 바른, 단정한 = courteous[kə́ːrtiəs] = seemly
I, as a principal of this school, asked all of you students to learn decorous attitudes first.
나는 이 학교의 교장으로서 학생들 모두가 우선 예의 바른 태도를 배우길 바랍니다.

decree[dikríː] n 명령, 법령, 포고 = behest[bihést] = edict[íːdikt]
= injunction[indʒʌ́ŋkʃən] = legal order = ordinance[ɔ́ːrdənəns]
An official decree invalidated the vote in the election.
법령 포고로 그 투표는 무효가 되었다.

decrepit[dikrépit] a 노쇠한, 쇠약한 = debilitated[dibílətèitid] = feeble = rickety[ríkiti]
She is so decrepit that she can hardly walk. 그녀는 매우 노쇠하여 걸을 수조차 없다.

decry[dikrái] v 헐뜯다, 비난하다, 매도하다 = asperse[əspə́ːrs] = belittle[bilítl] = blame
= calumniate[kəlʌ́mnièit] = censure = condemn[kəndém] = criticize = defame = degrade
= denigrate[dénigrèit] = deprecate[déprikèit] = deride = disdain = disparage[dispǽridʒ]
= malign[məláin] = reprehend[rèprihénd] = ridicule[rídikjùːl] = scorn = slander = traduce
[trədjúːs] = vilify[víləfài]
The movie critic decried the violence of modern films.
그 영화비평가는 현대 영화의 폭력성을 공공연히 비난했다.

deduce[didjúːs] v 추론하다, 추정하다 = infer
The doctor deduced the time of the death of the victim from the autopsy.
의사는 시체 부검을 통해 피해자의 사망시간을 추정했다. autopsy[ɔ́ːtapsi] n 검시

deem[diːm] v 여기다, 간주하다, 생각하다 = assume[əsúːm] = consider = regard
All the passengers and crew on the crashed plane are deemed dead.
추락한 비행기의 모든 승객과 승무원들은 사망한 것으로 추정된다.

defame[diféim] v 중상하다, 비방하다, 비난하다, 헐뜯다 = calumniate[kəlʌ́mnièit]
= cast aspersions on = denigrate[dénigrèit] = disparage = libel[láibəl] = malign[məláin]
= slander[slǽndər] = vilify[víləfài]
Some lawmakers of the opposition party defamed the welfare policy of the government.
일부 야당 의원들은 정부의 복지정책을 비난했다.

deference[défərəns] n 경의, 존경, 존중 = admiration[ædməréiʃən] = veneration[vènəréiʃən]
All TV stations stopped comedy programs in deference to the deceased soldiers.
모든 TV 방송국은 사망한 병사들에게 경의를 표하는 의미로 코미디 프로그램 방영을 중지했다.

deficit[défəsit] n 부족액, 결손, 적자 = lack = loss = paucity[pɔ́ːsəti] = shortfall
The mayor is very concerned about the budget deficit of the city government.
시장은 시정부의 예산부족에 대해 매우 우려한다.

defile[difáil] v 더럽히다, 모독하다 = adulterate[ədʌ́ltərèit] = befoul[bifául] = besmirch[bismə́ːrtʃ]
= debase = degrade = desecrate[désikrèit] = dishonor[disánər] = maculate[mǽkjulèit] =
profane[prəféin] = smear = stain = sully[sʌ́li] = taint = tarnish[táːrniʃ] = vitiate[víʃièit]
The invaders defiled a holy place by sacrilegious deeds.
침략자들은 불경한 소행으로 영지(靈地)를 더럽혔다. sacrilegious[sækrəlídʒəs] a 신성을 더럽히는

definitive[difínətiv] a 최종적인, 결정적인, 확실한 = conclusive = decisive[disáisiv]
The definitive decision by the mayor can make a huge change in our project.
시장의 최종 결정은 우리의 프로젝트에 큰 변화를 줄 수 있다.

deft[deft] a 솜씨 좋은, 능숙한, 숙달된 = adept = adroit = agile[ǽdʒəl] = dexterous[dékstərəs]
= handy = ingenious[indʒíːnjəs] = nimble = proficient = skillful
The man working at the pizza place was deft at dealing with dough.
피자가게에서 일하는 남자는 밀가루 반죽을 다루는 데 능숙하다.

defunct[difʌ́ŋkt] a 쇠퇴한, 죽은 = extinct = not functioning = obsolete[ɑ̀bsəlíːt]
Mark Dean was the leader of the now defunct Democratic Green Party.
Mark Dean은 지금은 없어진 민주녹색당의 총수였다.

defuse[diːfjúːz] v 신관을 제거하다, 완화시키다; 비활성화하다 = deactivate[diːǽktəvèit]
An explosives disposal unit has defused a bomb found in a downtown building.
폭발물 처리반이 시내의 한 건물에서 발견된 폭탄을 제거했다.

defy[difái] v 무시하다, 반대하다, 거부하다 = disregard = oppose = resist
The civic groups defied the Government's policy on the construction of the nuclear power plant.
시민단체들은 정부의 핵발전소 건설 정책을 정면으로 반대했다.

degenerate[didʒénərèit] v 저하하다, 퇴화하다 = decline = deteriorate[ditíəriərèit]
Your joints naturally degenerate over time.
여러분의 관절은 시간이 지나면서 자연스럽게 퇴화됩니다.

degrade[digréid] v 손상시키다, 떨어뜨리다, 타락시키다 = debase = demean
= deteriorate[ditíəriərèit] = impair = vitiate[víʃièit]
You should not degrade yourself by accepting bribes.
뇌물을 받아서 자기의 품위를 떨어뜨려서는 안 된다.

QUIZ 33

*Match each word in the first column with its definition in the second column.
Check your answers in the back of the book.*

1.	degenerate	a.	admiration = veneration
2.	decimate	b.	courteous = seemly
3.	deficit	c.	calumniate = cast aspersions on
4.	degrade	d.	adept = adroit
5.	decree	e.	infer
6.	decode	f.	lack = loss
7.	decry	g.	debase = demean
8.	deduce	h.	adulterate = befoul
9.	defile	i.	behest = edict
10.	decrepit	j.	extinct = not functioning
11.	deference	k.	deactivate
12.	decelerate	l.	slow down
13.	deem	m.	annihilate = eradicate
14.	defame	n.	assume = consider
15.	deft	o.	disregard = oppose
16.	defunct	p.	decipher = decrypt
17.	definitive	q.	debilitated = feeble
18.	defy	r.	conclusive = decisive
19.	defuse	s.	decline = deteriorate
20.	decorous	t.	asperse = belittle

deign[dein] v 자신을 낮추어[부끄러움을 참고, 자존심을 버리고] ~~ 하다 = condescend
[kàndəsénd] = lower oneself
The Queen deigned to visit my daughter's wedding ceremony in person.
여왕은 황송하게도 내 딸의 결혼식에 몸소 와주셨다.

deity[díːəti] n 신, 신격, 신위 = divinity[divínəti] = god
Bears used to be worshiped as a deity in some ancient countries.
어떤 고대국가는 곰을 신처럼 숭배하였다.

dejected[didʒéktid] a 의기소침한, 풀이 죽은, 낙담한 = crestfallen[krestfɔ:lən]
= depressed = despondent[dispándənt] = discouraged[diskə́:ridʒd] = disheartened[dishá:rtnd]
= dispirited = gloomy = glum = morose[məróus]
Losing the game in the final, they looked extremely dejected.
결승전에서 패한 그들은 극도로 낙담한 얼굴을 하고 있었다.

delectable[diléktəbl] a 맛있는, 기쁜, 유쾌한 = delicious = delightful = enjoyable
= luscious[lʌ́ʃəs] = palatable[pǽlətəbl] = sapid[sǽpid] = savory[séivəri] = scrumptious[skrʌ́mpʃəs]
All the guests in the party enjoyed delectable foods and drinks.
파티의 모든 손님은 맛있는 음식과 음료들을 즐겼다.

deleterious[dèlitíəriəs] a 해로운, 유해한 = baleful[béilfəl] = baneful[béinfəl]
= harmful = detrimental[dètrəméntl] = hurtful = inimical[inímikəl] = injurious
= mischievous[místʃəvəs] = noxious[nákʃəs] = pernicious[pərníʃəs]
Mercury has a deleterious effect on the nervous system.
수은은 신경계에 해로운 영향을 미친다.

deliberate[dilíbərət] a 고의의, 계획적인, 의도적인 = intentional = premeditated[pri:medıteıtıd]
The police are investigating whether it was a deliberate homicide or not.
경찰은 그것이 고의적인 살인인지 아닌지 조사 중이다.

delineate[dilínièit] v 상세히 기술하다, 표현하다, 묘사하다 = describe = depict = limn[lim]
= portray
The old painting delineates the traditional wrestling and its environmental scenes.
그 오래된 그림은 전통 레슬링과 주변 장면을 묘사한 것이다.

delinquent[dilíŋkwənt] a 의무 불이행의, 연체된, 태만한 = defaulting[difɔ́:lting]
= irresponsible[irispánsəbl] = overdue = unpaid
He received a call from a credit card company urging him to pay his delinquent payments.
그는 신용카드 회사로부터 연체된 금액을 결제하라는 전화를 받았다.

delirium[dilíəriəm] n 망상, 정신착란, 헛소리 = hallucination[həlù:sənéiʃən]
= insanity[insǽnəti]
The ex-president suffered from delirium in his later life.
전직 대통령은 인생의 말년에 정신착란으로 고생을 했다.

delude[dilúːd] v 속이다, 착각하게 하다 = beguile[bigáil] = cheat = con = cozen[kʌzn]
= deceive = fool = hoodwink = take in
The con man deluded a lot of innocent investors into putting their money on almost bankrupt company.
그 사기꾼은 많은 순수한 투자자들을 속여서 거의 부도난 회사에 돈을 투자하게 했다.
con man 사기꾼

deluge[déljuːdʒ] n 대홍수, 호우, 쇄도, 범람 = flood = inundation[ìnəndéiʃən]
The rising star was happy with a deluge of request for interview.
인기가 치솟고 있는 그 스타는 쇄도하는 인터뷰 요청에 행복해 했다.

delusion[dilúːʒən] n 망상, 착각, 현혹 = hallucination[həlùːsənéiʃən] = illusion[ilúːʒən] He is under a delusion that he will be a millionaire soon.
그는 곧 백만장자가 될 것이라는 망상에 사로잡혀 있다.

delve[delv] v 철저히 조사하다, 깊이 탐구하다 = probe
The Attorney General ordered the prosecutors to delve into the fraudulent election scandal.
검찰총장은 검사들에게 부정선거에 대해 철저히 조사하라고 명령했다.

demagogue[déməgɑ̀g] n 선동가, 선동 정치가 = agitator[ǽdʒitèitər] = instigator
The demagogue urged more young people to participate in the anti-government protests.
선동가는 더 많은 젊은이들이 반정부 시위에 가담하도록 촉구했다.

demeanor[dimíːnər] n 행실, 처신, 태도 = attitude = behavior
Car dealers should have a kind and gentle demeanor.
자동차 판매상은 친절하고 점잖은 태도를 가져야만 한다.

demise[dimáiz] n 붕어, 종말, 죽음, 사망 = decease
The cardinal's sudden demise was shocking news to the whole nation.
추기경의 갑작스런 서거는 전 국민에게 충격적인 소식이었다.

demography[dimɑ́grəfi] n 인구통계학, 인구학 = study of human population
She has been teaching demography in college for 5 years.
그녀는 대학에서 인구통계학을 5년째 가르치고 있다.

demolish[dimɑ́liʃ] v 파괴하다, 부수다 = destroy = devastate = dilapidate[dilǽpidèit]
= dismantle[dismǽntl] = flatten = pulverize[pʌ́lvəràiz] = wreck
A team of explosion experts is going to demolish that old apartment.
폭파 전문가들로 이루어진 팀이 그 낡은 아파트를 철거할 예정이다.

demur[pʌlvəràiz] v 반대하다, 이의를 제기하다 = disagree
Land owners didn't demur to accepting the offer from the property developer.
집주인들은 부동산개발업자의 제안을 받아들이는 것을 반대하지 않았다.

demure[dimjúər] a 얌전한, 조용한 = prudish[prú:diʃ] = sedate[sidéit] = unassuming
The demure girl from the small town grew up to be a world famous ballerina.
작은 마을 출신의 그 얌전한 소녀는 세계적인 발레리나가 되었다.

QUIZ 34

Match each word in the first column with its definition in the second column.
Check your answers in the back of the book.

1.	demur	a.	intentional = premeditated
2.	deity	b.	destroy = devastate
3.	dejected	c.	describe = depict
4.	delectable	d.	defaulting = irresponsible
5.	delve	e.	decease
6.	deluge	f.	baleful = baneful
7.	delineate	g.	study of human population
8.	delinquent	h.	disagree
9.	demeanor	i.	condescend = lower oneself
10.	delude	j.	prudish = sedate
11.	deign	k.	hallucination = insanity
12.	delusion	l.	beguile = cheat
13.	deleterious	m.	divinity = god
14.	demagogue	n.	agitator = instigator
15.	deliberate	o.	flood = inundation
16.	demure	p.	probe
17.	delirium	q.	crestfallen = depressed
18.	demolish	r.	hallucination = illusion
19.	demography	s.	delicious = delicious
20.	demise	t.	attitude = behavior

denigrate[dénigrèit] v 폄하하다, 헐뜯다, 중상하다 = asperse[əspə́:rs] = belittle[bilítl]
= besmirch[bismə́:rtʃ] = calumniate[kəlʌ́mnièit] = decry= defame = disparage[dispǽridʒ]
= impugn[impjú:n] = libel[láibəl] = malign[məláin] = revile[riváil] = slander[slǽndər] =
traduce[trədjú:s] = vilify[víləfài]
We should not denigrate the passion of the young politician trying to reform the political circles.
우리는 정치계를 개혁하려는 젊은 정치인들의 열정을 폄하해서는 안 된다.

denizen[dénəzən] n 주민 = citizen = dweller = resident = inhabitant
Most denizens of the coastal village depend on the marine products for their income.
해변 마을 주민들의 대부분은 주 수입을 수산물에 의존하고 있다.

denomination[dinὰmənéiʃən] n 명칭, 종류 = appellation[æpəléiʃən] = name
She is taking care of plants of various denominations in her garden.
그녀는 정원에서 여러 가지 종류의 식물을 돌보고 있다.

denote[dinóut] v 나타내다, 지시하다, 뜻하다 = indicate = mean = stand for
The medical checkup chart of a patient shows symptoms that denote cancer.
환자의 건강진단표는 암의 징후를 보여준다.

denounce[dináuns] v 비난하다, 고발하다 = accuse = blame = castigate[kǽstəgèit]
= censure = condemn[kəndém] = criticize = decry = excoriate[ikskɔ́:rièit] = impeach
= impugn[impjú:n] = rebuke = reprehend = reprimand = reproach = reprobate[réprəbèit]
= reprove = revile[riváil] = scold = upbraid = vilify[víləfài] = vituperate[vaitjú:pərèit]
All the countries on the globe denounced the assassination as an act of terrorism.
지구상의 모든 국가는 그 암살을 테러 행위라며 맹렬히 비난했다.

depict[dipíkt] v 그리다, 묘사하다 = delineate[dilínièit] = describe = limn[lim] = portray
This painting depicts the birth of the queen in its true colors and proportions.
이 그림은 여왕의 탄생을 있는 그대로의 색채와 크기로 묘사하고 있다.

deplete[diplí:t] v 고갈시키다, 격감시키다 = empty = use up
That country has depleted its natural resources completely.
그 나라의 천연자원은 완전히 고갈되었다.

deplore[diplɔ́:r] v 깊이 뉘우치다, 개탄하다 = bemoan[bimóun] = bewail[biwéil]
= lament[ləmént] = mourn[mɔ:rn] = regret = repent[ripént] = rue[ru:]
We cannot but deplore the poor educational conditions in the rural areas.
우리는 시골의 열악한 교육환경을 개탄하지 않을수 없다.

deploy[diplɔ́i] v 배치하다, 알맞게 사용하다 = arrange = station troops.
We'll continue to deploy forces to the border. 우리는 국경에 병력 배치를 계속할 것이다.

depose[dipóuz] v 물러나게 하다, 퇴위시키다 = dethrone[di:θróun] = overthrow
= unseat = out from position = subvert[səbvə́:rt]
Many professors hope the people will rise up in anger and depose the dictator.
많은 교수들은 분노한 민중들이 봉기하여 독재자를 끌어내리길 바라고 있다.

depravity[diprǽvəti] n 타락, 부패 = corruption[kərʌpʃən]
= depravation[dèprəvéiʃən] = turpitude[tə́:rpətjù:d]
The stockbroker doesn't want to have a life with depravity anymore.
그 주식중개인은 더 이상 방탕하게 살고 싶지 않아 한다.

deprecate[déprikèit] v 비난하다, 반대하다 = denigrate[dénigrèit] = disparage
= vilipend[víləpènd]
Most employees of the company deprecated the M&A decision by the management.
대부분의 종업원들은 경영진의 인수합병 결정을 비난했다.

depreciate[diprí:ʃièit] v 가치를 떨어뜨리다 = devalue[di:vǽlju:]
Housing and property rarely depreciate in the developing country.
개발도상국에서는 주택과 부동산 가치가 거의 떨어지지 않는다.

depredate[dépridèit] v 강탈하다, 약탈하다 = despoil[dispɔ́il] = loot =
maraud[mərɔ́:d] = pillage[pílidʒ] = plunder[plʌ́ndər] = ravage[rǽvidʒ] = sack = spoliate[spóulièit]
The pirates depredated livestock and even pets in the coastal areas.
해적들은 해안 지역에서 가축은 물론 심지어 애완동물들까지 약탈했다.

deprivation[dèprəvéiʃən] n 박탈, 결핍 = destitution[dèstətjú:ʃən] = privation[praivéiʃən]
Hair loss is one of the earliest signs of protein deprivation.
탈모는 단백질 결핍을 가장 먼저 알려주는 신호 중 하나이다.

deracinate[dirǽsənèit] v 뿌리채 뽑다, 근절하다, 쫓아내다 = abolish = annihilate
[ənáiəlèit] =eliminate[ilímənèit] = exterminate[ikstə́:rmənèit] = stamp out = wipe out
Religious leaders need to try hard to deracinate superstitions and pseudo-religions.
종교 지도자들은 미신과 사이비 종교를 근절하기 위해 노력할 필요가 있다.

derelict[dérəlìkt] a 버려진, 유기된 = abandoned = deserted = discarded = forsaken[fərséikən]
The derelict building had been used as a shelter for the homeless.
버려진 그 건물은 집 없는 사람들을 위한 은신처로 사용되어 왔었다.

deride[diráid] v 조소하다, 비웃다, 조롱하다 = contemn[kəntém]
= despise[dispáiz] = disdain = disparage = flout[flaut] = insult = jeer = make fun of = mock
= ridicule = scoff = scorn = sneer = taunt[tɔ:nt]
We should not deride his efforts to build the wind power plant on the hill.
우리는 언덕에 풍력발전소를 짓겠다는 그의 노력을 무시해서는 안 된다.

derivative[dirívətiv] n 파생품, 파생상품 = transmitted from source
The financial crisis in the US originated from the sub-prime derivatives.
미국의 금융위기는 서브프라임 파생상품에서 시작되었다.

derogatory[dirágətɔ̀:ri] a 손상시키는, 경멸하는, 깔보는 = degrading = disdainful [disdéinfəl] = disparaging[dispǽridʒiŋ] = opprobrious[əpróubriəs] = scurrilous[skə́:rələs]
My boss called me by a derogatory name. 나의 상사는 나에게 모욕적인 말을 했다.

QUIZ 35

Match each word in the first column with its definition in the second column.
Check your answers in the back of the book.

1.	denigrate		a.	dethrone = overthrow
2.	derogatory		b.	arrange = station troops
3.	deride		c.	denigrate = disparage
4.	denote		d.	devalue
5.	derivative		e.	despoil = loot
6.	depict		f.	asperse = belittle
7.	depreciate		g.	citizen = dweller
8.	deplore		h.	appellation = name
9.	deploy		i.	indicate = mean stand for
10.	depose		j.	destitution = privation
11.	denizen		k.	abolish = annihilate
12.	deprecate		l.	delineate = describe
13.	depravity		m.	accuse = blame
14.	depredate		n.	banter = contemn
15.	deprivation		o.	degrading = disdainful
16.	deplete		p.	empty = use up
17.	derelict		q.	transmitted from source
18.	denounce		r.	bemoan = bewail
19.	deracinate		s.	corruption = depravation
20.	denomination		t.	abandoned = deserted

---

desecrate[désikrèit] v 신성 모독하다, 훼손하다 = blaspheme[blæsfí:m] = defile = profane[prəféin]
We shouldn't desecrate a sacred place.
우리는 신성한 장소를 훼손해서는 안 된다.

desiccate[désikèit] v 건조시키다 = dehydrate[di:háidreit] = exsiccate[éksəkèit]
The oriental medical doctor desiccates some herbs to use them as medicine.
그 한의사는 일부 약초를 바짝 건조시켜서 약으로 쓴다.

desist[dizíst] v 그만두다, 단념하다 = abstain[əbstéin] = cease = quit
The police called on the demonstrators to desist from violence.
경찰은 시위대에게 폭력을 중지하라고 요청했다.

despicable[déspikəbl] a 비열한, 야비한 = contemptible[kəntémptəbl] = reprehensible[rèprihénsəbl] = vile[vail]
The rigged election was a despicable and reprehensible crime.
부정선거는 비열하고 비난받을 범죄이다. rig v 부정수단으로 조작하다

despondent[dispándənt] a 낙담한, 풀 죽은 = depressed = dejected = discouraged[diskə́:ridʒd] = dispirited = downcast = down in the mouth = gloomy = in despair
The patient has been despondent about his ill health.
그 환자는 병이 난 것을 비관하고 있다.

despot[déspət] n 폭군 = autocrat[ɔ́:təkræt] = dictator[díkteitər] = tyrant[táiərənt]
The king was so a cruel despot so the citizens always hated him.
그는 잔인한 독재자였기 때문에 시민들은 항상 그를 싫어했다.

destitute[déstətjù:t] a 가난한, 궁핍한 = down and out = deficient = impecunious[ìmpikjú:niəs] = impoverished[impávəriʃt] = indigent[índidʒənt] = penurious[pənjúəriəs]
Most homeless in the cities are in destitute circumstances.
도시의 노숙자들은 대부분 궁핍한 처지에 놓여있다.

desultory[désəltɔ̀:ri] a 무질서한, 산만한 = haphazard[hæphǽzərd] = rambling[rǽmbliŋ]
His speech continued in so a very desultory manner that some audience couldn't focus on it.
그의 연설은 너무 산만해서 일부 청중들은 집중하기 어려웠다.

detach[ditǽtʃ] v 분리하다, 떼어내다 = cut off = disconnect = separate = sever[sévər]
After arriving at the station, the driver was detaching a locomotive from a train.
역에 도착한 후 기관사는 열차에서 기관차를 분리하고 있었다.

detect[ditékt] v 탐지하다, 간파하다, 찾아내다, 발견하다 = discover = identify = reveal
The sensitive medical device can be used to detect viral diseases and cancer early.
그 민감한 의료기구는 바이러스성 질병과 암을 조기에 발견하는 데 사용될 수 있다.

deter[ditə́:r] v 단념시키다, 그만두게 하다, 방해하다 = block = hinder[híndər] = impede[impí:d] = obstruct[əbstrʌ́kt] = preclude[priklú:d] = prevent = prohibit[prouhíbit]
The sudden downpour deterred us from going fishing to the island.
갑작스러운 호우 때문에 우리는 섬으로 낚시 가는 것을 단념했다.

deterrent[ditə́:rənt] n 제지하는 것, 억제력, 방해물 = hindrance[híndrəns] = impediment[impédəmənt] = obstacle[ɑ́bstəkl]
The presence of the army should serve as a major deterrent effect to war.
군대가 주둔하는 것이 주요한 전쟁 억지 효과가 있을 것이다.

detour[dí:tuər] n 우회로, 둘러가는 길 = bypass
We got to make a detour because of a road construction.
도로공사 때문에 우리는 우회해야 합니다.

devastate[dévəstèit] v 황폐화하다, 완전히 파괴하다 = demolish[dimɑ́liʃ] = destroy = ravage[rǽvidʒ] = wreck[rek]
Many countries in Europe were devastated during the World War II.
많은 유럽 국가들이 제2차 세계대전 중에 황폐화되었다.

devout[diváut] a 독실한, 경건한 = faithful[féiθfəl] = pious[páiəs] = religious[rilídʒəs]
She considers herself a devout Catholic. 그녀는 자신을 독실한 가톨릭 신자라고 생각한다.

dexterous[dékstərəs] a 솜씨 좋은, 능란한 = adept[ədépt] = adroit[ədrɔ́it] = ingenious[indʒí:njəs] = nimble[nímbl] = proficient[prəfíʃənt] = skilled
The floor manager is dexterous in displaying clothes.
그 매장 지배인은 옷을 진열하는 솜씨가 좋다.

diaphanous[daiǽfənəs] a 아주 얇은, 속이 내비치는 = see-through
His young son saw the burglar clearly through the diaphanous curtain.
그의 어린 아들은 훤히 비치는 커튼을 통해 강도를 명확하게 보았다.

diatribe[dáiətràib] n 비난, 혹평 = harangue[hərǽŋ] = invective[invéktiv] = tirade[táireid]
The opposition lawmaker launched a diatribe against the unemployment policy of the government.
야당 의원은 정부의 실업정책을 비난했다.

dichotomy[daikɑ́təmi] n 양분, 이분 = division[divíʒən]
Students are not taught to look upon the world as a dichotomy between the haves and the have-nots.
학생들은 가진 자와 못 가진 자라는 이분법으로 세상을 바라보도록 교육받아서는 안 된다.

dictum[díktəm] n 격언, 속담 = axiom[ǽksiəm] = adage[ǽdidʒ] = aphorism[ǽfərìzm]
= apothegm[ǽpəθèm] = maxim = proverb[právə:rb] = saying
This reminds us of the old dictum that look before you leap.
이것은 돌다리도 두드려보고 건너라는 속담을 생각나게 한다.

QUIZ 36

*Match each word in the first column with its definition in the second column.
Check your answers in the back of the book.*

1.	desecrate	a.	cut off = disconnect
2.	dexterous	b.	discover = identify
3.	dichotomy	c.	haphazard = rambling
4.	despicable	d.	autocrat = dictator
5.	dictum	e.	depressed = dejected
6.	despot	f.	block = hinder
7.	detour	g.	down and out = deficient
8.	desultory	h.	see-through
9.	detach	i.	bypass
10.	desiccate	j.	abstain = cease
11.	deter	k.	adept = adroit
12.	deterrent	l.	faithful = pious
13.	detect	m.	axiom = adage
14.	devastate	n.	dehydrate = exsiccate
15.	devout	o.	hindrance = impediment
16.	destitute	p.	division
17.	diaphanous	q.	blaspheme = defile
18.	diatribe	r.	contemptible = reprehensible
19.	despondent	s.	harangue = invective
20.	desist	t.	demolish = destroy

didactic[daidǽktik] a 교훈적인, 설교적인 = enlightening[inláitniŋ] = pedantic[pədǽntik]
The didactic movie produced by the government didn't appeal to many moviegoers.
정부에 의해 제작된 그 교훈적인 영화는 많은 영화 팬들의 호응을 받지 못했다.

diffident[dífidənt] a 자신 없는, 내성적인, 조심스러운 = bashful[bǽʃfəl] = coy
= demure[dimjúər] = timid = timorous[tímərəs]
He was diffident about delivering a speech in public.
그는 대중 앞에서 연설하는 데 자신이 없었다.

diffuse[difjú:z] v 퍼뜨리다, 확산시키다 = disperse[dispə́:rs] = disseminate[disémənèit]
= distribute[distríbju:t] = scatter = strew[stru:]
The core technology to make fake money was diffused immediately through the internet.
위조 화폐를 만드는 핵심기술은 인터넷을 통해 즉시 퍼져나갔다.

dignify[dígnəfài] v 위엄을 주다, 엄숙하게 하다 = exalt[igzɔ́:lt] = glorify[glɔ́:rəfài]
The forum was dignified by the presence of a lot of government dignitaries.
그 토론장은 많은 정부 고위 관리들의 참석 덕분에 무게가 더해졌다.

digress[daigrés] v 주제에서 벗어나다, 빗나가다 = deviate[dí:vièit]
The speaker was talking about his own history, digressing from the point at issue.
연사는 문제의 요점에서 벗어나 본인의 성장과정에 대해 이야기하고 있었다.

dilapidate[dilǽpidèit] v (건물 등을) 헐다, 황폐케 하다, 파손하다 = demolish = destroy
= devastate[dévəstèit]
The old apartment complex was dilapidated to construct to sports stadium.
오래된 아파트 단지는 종합스포츠 운동장을 짓기 위해 해체되었다.

dilate[dailéit] v 팽창시키다, 확장시키다 = amplify[ǽmpləfài] = distend[disténd]
= inflate[infléit] = enlarge = swell
When explorers entered the dark cave, the pupils of their eyes dilated.
어두운 동굴에 들어섰을 때 탐험가들은 눈의 동공이 확장되었다.

dilemma[dilémə] n 딜레마, 궁지, 진퇴양난 = impasse[ímpæs] = plight[plait]
= predicament[pridíkəmənt] = quandary[kwándəri]
She was facing a dilemma of obeying her father or marrying a poor man.
그녀는 아버지에게 순종하느냐 그 가난한 남자와 결혼하느냐의 진퇴양난에 빠져 있었다.

dilettante[dìlitá:nti] n 애호가, 호사가, 아마추어 = dabbler[dǽblər]
He's a professional cyclist, not a dilettante. 그는 아마추어가 아닌 전문적인 사이클리스트다.

dilute[dilú:t] v 묽게 하다, 희석하다 = make thinner = water down
The melting ice dilutes the orange juice. 얼음이 녹으면서 음료를 희석시킨다.

diminish[dimíniʃ] v 줄이다, 감소시키다, 감소하다 = abate[əbéit] = curtail[kə:rtéil] = decline =
decrease = dwindle[dwíndl] = ebb[eb] = lesson = lower = reduce = shrink[ʃriŋk] = wane[wein] = weaken
The police chief tried to diminish the crime rates in his precinct.
경찰서장은 관할지역에서 범죄율을 줄이려고 노력했다.

diminution[dìmənjúːʃən] n 축소, 감소 = abatement[əbéitmənt] = curtailment[kəːrtéilmənt] = reduction = retrenchment[ritréntʃmənt]
We have seen a diminution in population growth in some countries in Europe.
우리는 유럽 일부 국가에서 인구증가의 감소 현상을 보고 있다.

din[din] n 크고 시끄러운 소리, 소음 = loud and continuous noise
We heard a sudden din of explosions. 우리는 갑작스런 큰 폭발소리를 들었다.

dingy[díndʒi] a 우중충한, 칙칙한 = drab[dræb]
His car was parked in a dingy garage. 그의 차는 우중충한 차고에 주차되어 있었다.

diocesan[daiɑ́səsən] n 주교, 감독 = bishop[bíʃəp]
The diocesan kept his church open to the people in need poor 24 hours a day.
주교는 어려운 사람들에게 그의 교회를 하루 24시간 개방하도록 했다.

dire[daiər] a 긴급한, 절박한 = desperate[déspərət] = urgent[ə́ːrdʒənt]
The flood victims are in dire need of relief items.
수재민들은 구호품을 절실히 필요로 하고 있다.

dirge[dəːrdʒ] n 애도가, 만가, 장송곡 = elegy[élədʒi]
A dirge was played at a cemetery. 공동묘지에서 장송곡이 울려 퍼졌다.

disabuse[dìsəbjúːz] v 바로 잡아주다, 오해를 풀어주다 = disenchant[dìsentʃǽnt] = disillusion[dìsilúːʒən] = enlighten[inláitn]
I want to disabuse him of his prejudices that man is better than woman at math.
나는 남자가 여자보다 수학을 더 잘한다는 편견을 가진 그를 깨우쳐주고 싶다.

disaffect[dìsəfékt] v 불만을 품게 하다 = alienate[éiljənèit] = antagonize[æntǽgənàiz]
Farmland tax increase by the local government disaffected most farmers.
지방정부의 농지세 인상은 대다수의 농부들에게 불만을 품게 했다.

disarray[dìsəréi] n 무질서, 혼란 = chaos[kéias] = confusion = disorder = mess = shambles[ʃǽmblz]
The powerful earthquake put the citizens in the ancient city into disarray.
강력한 지진이 고대도시의 시민들을 혼란에 빠뜨렸다.

QUIZ 37

Match each word in the first column with its definition in the second column.
Check your answers in the back of the book.

1.	din		a.	abate = curtail
2.	disarray		b.	drab
3.	disaffect		c.	enlightening = pedantic
4.	dingy		d.	bishop
5.	digress		e.	deviate
6.	dilapidate		f.	demolish
7.	dilate		g.	bashful = coy
8.	diminution		h.	amplify = distend
9.	dignify		i.	impasse = plight
10.	dilute		j.	exalt = glorify
11.	diminish		k.	desperate = urgent
12.	diffident		l.	disperse = disseminate
13.	dilettante		m.	elegy
14.	dilemma		n.	disenchant = disillusion
15.	diocesan		o.	dabbler
16.	dire		p.	alienate = antagonize
17.	dirge		q.	make thinner = water down
18.	disabuse		r.	abatement = curtailment
19.	didactic		s.	loud and continuous noise
20.	diffuse		t.	chaos = confusion

disavow[dìsəváu] v 부인하다, 부정하다 = deny = disown[disóun] = repudiate[ripjú:dièit]
The bank clerk disavowed any knowledge of the embezzlement.
은행 직원은 횡령사건에 대해 아무것도 모른다고 부인했다.

discern[disə́:rn] v 식별(판별, 분간)하다 알아보다 = descry = distinguish[distíŋgwiʃ]
= espy[ispái] = recognize = tell apart
It is not easy for even experts to discern the genuine paintings from the counterfeit ones.
심지어 전문가들도 진품 그림과 위조 작품을 식별하기 어렵다.

disclaim[diskléim] v 부인하다, 거부하다 = disavow[dìsəváu] = disown[disóun]
The stockbroker disclaimed being involved in the affair.
그 주식중개인은 그 사건에 관련되었다는 것을 부인했다.

discomfit[diskʌmfit] v 당황시키다, 혼란스럽게 하다 = disturb[distə́:rb] = embarrass
= fluster[flʌ́stər] = nonplus[nanplʌ́s] = perplex = perturb[pərtə́:rb] = puzzle
The violent protesters were discomfited by the sudden dispatch of the police SWAT team.
폭력적인 시위대들은 갑작스런 경찰특공대의 출동으로 당황했다.

discommode[dìskəmóud] v 불편하게 하다, 폐를 끼치다, 난처하게 하다 = bother = harass
The guest discommoded the host by overstaying at the host house with three sons.
손님은 그의 아들 세 명과 함께 그를 초대해준 집에 너무 오래 머물면서 폐를 끼쳤다.

discompose[dìskəmpóuz] v 뒤숭숭하게 하다, 심란하게 하다, 평정을 잃게 만들다
= confuse[kənfjú:z] = discomfit[diskʌ́mfit]
Having spent so many years on the sea, he was not discomposed by the storm and high waves.
바다 위에서 몇 년을 보냈던 덕분에 그는 폭풍과 높은 파도에도 평정을 잃지 않았다.

disconcert[dìskənsə́:rt] v 당황하게(쩔쩔매게) 하다, 혼란시키다 = abash[əbǽʃ]
= baffle[bǽfl] = bewilder[biwíldər] = confound[kanfáund] = discombobulate[dìskəmbábjuleit]
The software programmers were disconcerted with a sudden failure in the computer system.
소프트웨어 프로그래머들은 갑작스런 컴퓨터 시스템의 고장으로 당황했다.

discord[dískɔ:rd] n 불일치, 부조화, 불화 = disharmony = dissonance[dísənəns]
There was no obvious sign of discord among the members of the party.
당원들 사이에 불화의 명백한 징조는 없었다.

discredit[diskrédit] v 믿을 수 없는 것으로 간주하다, 신용을 손상하다, 신용하지 않다
= distrust = doubt[daut]
Judges discredited the statement of the suspect made under coercion.
판사들은 강압에 의한 피의자 진술을 신뢰하지 않았다.

discrepancy[diskrépənsi] n 차이, 불일치, 모순 = conflict[kənflíkt] = disagreement
= disparity[dispǽrəti] = divergence[divə́:rdʒəns] = inconsistency[ìnkənsístənsi]
= discordance[diskɔ́:rdəns] = dissonance[dísənəns]
The inspectors found a large discrepancy in quality between the two products.
검열관은 두 제품 사이의 품질에 큰 차이가 있는 것을 발견했다.

discreet[diskrí:t] a 신중한, 분별 있는, 조심스러운 = careful = circumspect
[sə́:rkəmspèkt] = gingerly[dʒíndʒərli] = prudent[prú:dnt]
The scientist was very discreet in giving his opinion on the test result.
그 과학자는 테스트 결과에 대한 자기의 의견을 말하는 데 몹시 신중했다.

discrete[diskríːt] a 별개의, 분리된, 불연속의 = disconnected
The England in the middle ages was controlled by discrete feudal lords.
중세시대 영국은 분리된 각각의 봉건영주들에 의해 다스려졌다. feudal[fjúːdl] a 봉건제도의

discriminate[diskrímənèit] v 식별하다, 차별하다, 구별하다 = differentiate[dìfərénʃièit]
= segregate[ségrigèit]
We should not discriminate against any race or religion.
우리는 어떤 인종이나 종교에 대해서도 차별해서는 안 된다.

discursive[diskə́ːrsiv] a 산만한, 두서 없는 = rambling[ræmbliŋ]
The novel by the psychologist is discursive but quite interesting.
그 심리학자가 쓴 소설은 두서는 없지만 꽤 흥미진진해.

disdain[disdéin] n 경멸, 멸시 = contempt[kəntémpt] = derision[diríʒən] = ridicule
= scorn[skɔːrn]
Some of the immigrants were treated with disdain. 일부 이민자들은 모욕적인 대우를 받았다.

disentangle[dìsentǽŋgl] v 해방시키다, 구분하다, 얽힘을 풀어주다 = emancipate
[imǽnsəpèit] = extricate[ékstrəkèit] = unravel = unwind
The new CEO tried to disentangle the complicated disputes between the labor union and the management. 새로 온 대표이사는 노사간에 얽힌 복잡한 논쟁을 풀려고 노력했다.

disgorge[disgɔ́ːrdʒ] v 게워내다, 구토하다 = regurgitate[rigə́ːrdʒətèit] = spew[spjuː]
= upchuck[ʌptʃʌk] = vomit[vámit]
The dog disgorged the bone it had swallowed. 그 개는 삼켰던 뼈를 토해냈다.

disgruntle[disgrʌ́ntl] v 언짢게 하다, 불만을 품게 하다 = discontent = displease
The direction of the warden of a prison that it will reduce the amount of meat in the meals disgruntled all of the inmates.
교도소 수감자들 식사에 고기량을 줄이라는 교도소장의 지시는 모든 수감자들에게 불만을 품게 했다.

disguise[disgáiz] v 위장하다, 변장시키다 = camouflage[kǽməflɑ̀ːʒ]
The prison breaker disguised himself as a lady. 탈옥범은 여성으로 변장했다.

disinformation[disìnfərméiʃən] n 허위 정보, 잘못된 사실
= misrepresentation[mìsreprizentéiʃən]
The spokesman of the government is releasing the disinformation about the recent project.
정부 대변인은 최근 프로젝트에 대해 허위정보를 발표하고 있다.

QUIZ 38

Match each word in the first column with its definition in the second column.
Check your answers in the back of the book.

1.	disinformation	a.	abash = baffle
2.	discommode	b.	disharmony = dissonance
3.	disguise	c.	conflict = disagreement
4.	discomfit	d.	confuse = discomfit
5.	disgorge	e.	deny = disown
6.	discompose	f.	descry = distinguish
7.	disconcert	g.	misrepresentation
8.	disdain	h.	Camouflage
9.	discredit	i.	differentiate = segregate
10.	discrepancy	j.	discontent = displease
11.	disavow	k.	disavow = disown
12.	discrete	l.	careful = circumspect
13.	discriminate	m.	distrust = doubt
14.	discursive	n.	disconnected
15.	discreet	o.	disturb = embarrass
16.	disentangle	p.	Rambling
17.	discord	q.	regurgitate = spew
18.	disgruntle	r.	contempt = derision
19.	discern	s.	bother = harass
20.	disclaim	t.	emancipate = extricate

disingenuous[dìsindʒénjuəs] a 솔직하지 않은, 부정직한, 불성실한 = deceitful[disí:tfəl]
= dishonest[disánist] = insincere[ìnsinsíər]
When the driver was asked by the traffic police to realize whether he violated the traffic sign, he was disingenuous.
교통경찰이 신호위반 사실을 알았느냐고 물어봤을 때 그 운전자는 솔직하지 않았다.

disintegrate[disíntəgrèit] v 붕괴하다, 분해하다, 무너지다 = break up =crumble
[krʌmbl] = decompose[dì:kəmpóuz] = dismantle[dismǽntl] = fall apart
Even after the free trade agreement with China, I think the rice market in our country will not disintegrate. 중국과의 자유무역협정 이후에도 나는 우리 쌀시장이 붕괴되리라고 보지 않는다.

disinterested[disíntərèstid] a 편견이 없는, 청렴한, 공정한 = equitable[ékwətəbl]
= impartial[impá:rʃəl] = unbiased[ʌnbaɪəst]
The panel of judges was disinterested in selecting the winner of the contest.
판정단들은 대회 우승자를 뽑는 데 공평무사했다.

dismal[dízməl] a 음울한, 쓸쓸한, 우울한 = bleak = depressing = desolate[désələt] = dingy[díndʒi] = discouraging[diskə́:ridʒiŋ] = disheartening = gloomy[glú:mi]
The prospects for the economy of next year remain dismal due to various external factors.
다양한 외부 악재로 인해서 내년의 경제전망은 여전히 암울하다.

dismantle[dismǽntl] v 분해하다, 해체하다 = break up = demolish[dimáliʃ] = disassemble[dìsəsémbl] = take apart
The engineers dismantled the security system from the wall after the field test.
엔지니어들은 현장 테스트를 하고 그 보안시스템을 벽으로부터 철거했다.

dismay[disméi] v 당황하게 하다, 움츠리게 하다, 겁먹게 하다 = abash[əbǽʃ] = bewilder = confound = decompose = discomfit[diskʌ́mfit] = disconcert[dìskənsə́:rt] = dumbfound[dʌmfáund] = faze = flummox[flʌ́məks] = fluster[flʌ́stər] = nonplus[nanplʌ́s] = perplex = puzzle
The news of a plane crash dismayed many passengers waiting at the airport.
비행기가 추락했다는 뉴스는 공항에서 대기 중인 많은 승객들을 당황하게 했다.

disparage[dispǽridʒ] v 비난하다, 헐뜯다, 깔보다 = belittle = criticize = decry = defame[diféim] = degrade = denigrate[dénigrèit] = deprecate[déprikèit] = deride[diráid] = disdain[disdéin] = malign[məláin] = ridicule[rídikjù:l] = scorn[skɔ:rn] = slander[slǽndər] = traduce[trədjú:s] = vilify[víləfài]
We should not disparage his efforts to save the rain forest by purchasing the land.
우리는 열대우림의 땅을 구매해서 그곳을 보존하려는 그의 노력을 폄하해서는 안 된다.

disparate[díspərit] a 종류가 다른, 본질적으로 다른, 이질적인 = contrasting = different = discordant[diskɔ́:rdənt] = divergent[divə́:rdʒənt] = diverse[divə́:rs]
The two economists had disparate ideas in solving the economic crisis.
두 경제학자는 경제위기를 해결하는 데 있어서 본질적으로 다른 견해를 가지고 있었다.

dispassionate[dispǽʃənət] a 감정에 좌우되지 않는, 냉정한, 선입견 없는, 공평한 = detached[ditǽtʃt] = disinterested = impartial[impá:rʃəl] = unbiased = unprejudiced[ʌnprédʒədist]
The arbiter dealt with the conflict in prudent and dispassionate manner.
중재자는 그 분쟁을 신중하게, 감정에 좌우되지 않고 처리했다.

disperse[dispə́:rs] v 흩어지게 하다, 퍼뜨리다 = disseminate[disémənèit] = dissipate[dísəpèit] = scatter[skǽtər] = strew[stru:]
The technique required to produce privately manufactured explosions was dispersed through the Internet across the nation.
사제 폭탄을 만드는 데 필요한 기술은 인터넷을 통해 전국으로 퍼졌다.

dispirit[dispírit] v 기를 꺾다, 낙담하게 하다 = dampen[dǽmpən] = deject[didʒékt]
= depress = demoralize[dimɔ́:rəlàiz] = discourage = dishearten[dishá:rtn] = sadden[sǽdn]
The red card given to the leader of the team dispirited the rest of the players.
주장에게 주어진 퇴장 명령은 나머지 선수들의 기를 꺾었다.

disposition[dìspəzíʃən] n 성질, 성향, 경향 = inclination[ìnklənéiʃən]
= predisposition[pri:dɪspəzɪʃn] = propensity[prəpénsəti] = tendency
The job opening in the sales team requires a man of a genial and cheerful disposition.
영업팀에서 구하는 사람은 친절하고 활달한 성질의 사람이어야 한다.

disproportionate[dìsprəpɔ́:rʃənət] a 균형이 안 맞는, 불균형의, 어울리지 않는
= asymmetric[èisəmétrik] = incommensurate[ìnkəménsərət] = out of balance
A disproportionate amount of budget being assigned to building the swimming center, they had to raise more money.
수영장 건설에 어울리지 않을 만큼 지나치게 많은 예산이 배정되어 그들은 더 많은 돈을 모아야 했다.

disprove[disprú:v] v 오류를 입증하다, 반증하다, 논박하다 = prove false = rebut[ribʌ́t]
= refute[rifjú:t]
The new discovery of the cooking utensils used by ancient humans disprove his theory that only modern humans have been using the tools.
고대 인류가 사용했던 주방도구의 발견은 단지 현생인류만 그런 도구를 쓰고 있다는 그의 이론에 오류가 있음을 보여준다.

disregard[dìsrigá:rd] v 무시하다, 경시하다, 외면하다 = despise[dispáiz] = disdain[disdéin]
= disparage[dispǽridʒ] = ignore = make light of = neglect[niglékt] = slight[slait] = snub[snʌb]
= vilipend[víləpènd]
The local government disregarded the recommendations of the environmentalists in the construction of the roads. 지방정부는 도로를 건설하는 데 있어 환경론자들의 권고를 무시하였다.

disrespect[dìsrispékt] n 실례, 무례 = discourtesy[diskə́:rtəsi] = rudeness[rú:dnis]
= impiety[impáiəti]
You should not show disrespect to the interviewers at the job interview.
면접 시에는 면접관에게 무례해서는 안 된다.

disquiet[diskwáiət] v 불안하게 하다, 걱정시키다 = agitate[ǽdʒitèit] = annoy = bother
= fret[fret] = perturb[pərtə́:rb] = pester[péstər] = unsettle = vex[veks]
Investors have become disquieted about the collapse of the stock market.
투자자들은 주식시장 붕괴에 대해 불안해 하고 있다.

dissemble[disémbl] v 속이다, 숨기다, 가장하다 = camouflage[kǽməflà:ʒ]
= disguise[disgáiz] = dissimulate[disímjulèit] = feign[fein] = pretend[priténd]
Lily always tried to wear designer brand clothes to dissemble her poverty.
Lily는 가난을 감추기 위해 항상 명품 의류를 입으려고 노력했다.

disseminate[disémənèit] v 퍼뜨리다, 보급하다 = diffuse[difjú:z] = disperse[dispə́:rs]
= dissipate[dísəpèit] = distribute = propagate[prɑ́pəgèit] = scatter = strew
The new theory about the birth of the universe was disseminated fast among the astrophysicists.
우주 탄생에 대한 새로운 이론이 천체물리학자들 사이에서 빠르게 전파되었다.

dissent[disént] v 의견이 다르다, 이의를 주장하다 = demur[dimə́:r] = disagree = differ = discord
There were a lot of economists who dissented from the free trade deal with the neighboring country.
이웃나라와 자유무역협정을 체결하는 데 반대하는 경제학자가 매우 많았다.

QUIZ 39

*Match each word in the first column with its definition in the second column.
Check your answers in the back of the book.*

1.	disquiet	a.	bleak = depressing
2.	disregard	b.	discourtesy = rudeness
3.	disparage	c.	equitable = impartial
4.	dismal	d.	asymmetric = incommensurate
5.	dismantle	e.	belittle = criticize
6.	dismay	f.	agitate = annoy
7.	disrespect	g.	camouflage = disguise
8.	dissent	h.	deceitful = dishonest
9.	dissemble	i.	contrasting = different
10.	disperse	j.	diffuse = disperse
11.	disintegrate	k.	break up = crumble
12.	disposition	l.	demur = disagree
13.	dispassionate	m.	prove false = rebut
14.	disprove	n.	detached = disinterested
15.	disparate	o.	break up = demolish
16.	disingenuous	p.	despise = disdain
17.	dispirit	q.	abash = bewilder
18.	disproportionate	r.	inclination = predisposition
19.	disseminate	s.	disseminate = dissipate
20.	disinterested	t.	dampen = deject

disservice[dissə́:rvis] n 구박, 학대, 해 = detriment[détrəmənt] = injustice
The coach did a great disservice to the baseball world by fixing games.
그 감독은 승부조작으로 야구계에 큰 해를 끼쳤다.

dissident[dísidnt] n 반체제인사, 반대자 = dissenter[diséntər] = nonconformist
= protester[proutéstər]
In recent years, more than 30 political dissidents have been sent to prison.
최근 몇 년간 30명이 넘는 반정부 인사들이 감옥에 보내졌다.

dissipate[dísəpèit] v 분산시키다, 소실시키다, 흩뜨리다 = disperse[dispə́:rs]
= dissolve = evanesce[èvənés]
The entrepreneur dissipated all his wealth in gambling.
그 사업가는 도박으로 모든 재산을 날렸다.

dissolute[dísəlù:t] a 방종한, 무절제한 = debauched[dibɔ́:tʃt] = depraved[dipréivd]
= libertine[líbərtì:n]
Ryan admitted that he had been leading a dissolute life from his youth.
Ryan은 젊었을 때부터 방탕한 삶을 살았다고 인정했다.

dissolution[dìsəlú:ʃən] n 분해, 해산, 소멸, 해체 = disintegration[disìntəgréiʃən]
After coming into power, the dictator ordered the dissolution of the parliament.
권력을 잡은 그 독재자는 의회 해산 명령을 내렸다.

dissolve[dizálv] v 녹이다(녹다), 용해시키다(용해되다), 해산시키다 = melt
When I have a hangover, I dissolve some honey in warm water and drink it.
난 숙취가 있으면 더운물에 꿀을 조금 타서 마신다.

dissonance[dísənəns] n 불협화음, 불일치, 부조화 = discord = incongruity[ìnkəŋgrú:əti]
The polotical party has lost many seates in the election due to the dissonance among the members of supreme council.
그 정당은 최고위원들과의 불화로 인해 선거에서 많은 의석을 잃었다.

dissuade[diswéid] v 설득하다, 단념시키다 = deter[ditə́:r] = divert[divə́:rt] = prevent
= talk out of = thwart[θwɔ:rt]
Owen tried to dissuade his only and weak son from enlisting in the special forces.
Owen은 몸이 약한 그의 외동아들이 특수부대에 입대하는 것을 단념시키려 했다.

distend[disténd] v 팽창시키다, 부풀리다, 확장시키다 = bloat[blout] = bulge[bʌldʒ]
= dilate[dailéit] = expand = inflate[infléit] = swell
His liver was distended with repeated accumulation of alcohol and stress.
그의 간은 반복되는 알코올의 축적과 스트레스로 인해 부어 있었다.

distillate[dístələt] n 추출물, 증류액 = extract
Malt whiskey is very popular across the nation, which is a distillate of nothing but barley.
보리에서만 추출된 증류액인 몰트 위스키가 전국적으로 인기가 있다.

distinct[distíŋkt] a 별개의, 전혀 다른, 뚜렷한 = different = disparate[díspərit]
= peculiar[pikjú:ljər] = unique
The geographical features of the Mars are distinct from those of the Earth.
화성의 지형특성은 지구와 전혀 다르다. geographical[dʒì:əgrǽfikəl] a 지리학의

distinguish[distíŋgwiʃ] v 구별하다, 식별하다, 분간하다 = demarcate[dimá:rkeit]
= differentiate = discriminate[diskrímənèit]
It is not easy to distinguish between the sound of the violin and the sound of the viola in an orchestra.
오케스트라에서 바이올린과 비올라 소리를 구분하기는 쉽지 않다.

distort[distɔ́:rt] v 왜곡하다, 비틀다 = falsify[fɔ́:lsəfài] = pervert[pərvə́:rt] = warp[wɔ:rp]
No country is allowed to distort its historical truth.
어떤 국가도 그 나라의 역사적 진실을 왜곡해서는 안 된다.

distract[distrǽkt] v 집중이 안 되게 하다, 산만하게 하다 = detract[ditrǽkt] = divert[divə́:rt]
Cell phone use while driving distracts the attention of the drivers.
운전 중 휴대폰 사용은 운전자의 주의를 산만하게 한다.

distraught[distrɔ́:t] a 마음이 산란해진, 당황한, 제정신이 아닌 = distracted = distrait[distréi]
He was distraught with the bankruptcy of his company. 그는 회사의 부도로 제정신이 아니었다.

distress[distrés] n 고뇌, 고통, 고난, 걱정 = affliction = agony[ǽgəni]
= anguish[ǽŋgwiʃ] = pain = suffering
Rising sea level is a source of great distress to the island country.
해수면 상승은 그 섬나라의 심각한 걱정거리이다.

ditty[díti] n 짤막한 노래, 소곡 = song
The widow was taking a walk, singing a sad ditty.
그 미망인은 슬픈 노래를 부르며 산책 중이었다.

diurnal[daiə́:rnl] a 낮 동안의, 주행성의 = during the day
Most bees are diurnal, mostly collecting honey at daytime.
대부분의 벌은 주행성이고, 낮에 꿀을 수집한다.

divergent[divə́:rdʒənt] a 분기하는, 서로 다른, 불일치의 = different = diverse[divə́:rs]
The two economic professors have divergent views on the opening of the nation's rice market.
경제학 교수 두 사람은 국내 쌀시장 개방에 대해 서로 다른 견해를 갖고 있다.

divine[diváin] v 예언하다, 점치다 = conjecture[kəndʒéktʃər] = foresee
= foretell = infer = intuit[intjú:it] = predict = prognosticate[pragnǽstikèit] = prophesy[práfəsài]
= surmise[sərmáiz]
The shaman divined that there would be big floods in the village.
그 주술사는 마을에 큰 홍수가 있을 것이라고 예언했다.

QUIZ 40

Match each word in the first column with its definition in the second column.
Check your answers in the back of the book.

1.	divergent	a.	debauched = depraved
2.	dissident	b.	disintegration
3.	distress	c.	distracted = distrait
4.	dissolute	d.	disperse = dissolve
5.	distort	e.	detract = divert
6.	divine	f.	affliction = agony
7.	dissonance	g.	detriment = injustice
8.	distinct	h.	demarcate = differentiate
9.	distend	i.	dissenter = nonconformist
10.	distillate	j.	during the day
11.	dissolve	k.	falsify = pervert
12.	distinguish	l.	melt
13.	dissuade	m.	discord = incongruity
14.	distract	n.	deter = divert
15.	distraught	o.	bloat = bulge
16.	diurnal	p.	extract
17.	ditty	q.	different = diverse
18.	dissolution	r.	different = disparate
19.	dissipate	s.	song
20.	disservice	t.	conjecture = foresee

divulge[divʌldʒ] v 누설하다, 폭로하다 = disclose[disklóuz] = leak[li:k] = reveal[riví:l]
The sports agent divulged the terms of the contract between the baseball player and the club. 스포츠 에이전트는 야구선수와 구단 간의 계약조건을 누설했다.

docile[dásəl] a 순한, 고분고분한, 다루기 쉬운 = amenable[əmí:nəbl] = compliant[kəmpláiənt] = meek = obedient[oubí:diənt] = pliable[pláiəbl] = submissive[səbmísiv]
The UFC fighter had been a docile boy until he became 19 years old.
그 UFC 파이터는 열아홉 살이 될 때까지 순한 소년이었다.

doctrinaire[dùktrinɛ́ər] a 교조적인, 광신도적인 = dogmatic[dɔ:gmǽtik] = opinionated
He is a doctrinaire seclusionist, being opposed to signing free trade agreements with any nation.
그는 광적인 쇄국주의자로, 어떤 나라와도 자유무역협정을 맺는 것을 반대한다.

document[dákjumənt] v 인용하다 = cite
The economic analyst documented the financial data to forecast the economic situation of next year.
그 경제분석가는 내년 경제상황을 예측하기 위해 금융자료를 인용했다.

dodder[dádər] v 비틀거리다, 몸을 떨다 = quiver[kwívər] = shiver[ʃívər] = shudder[ʃʌ́dər] = shake = stagger[stǽgər] = sway = teeter[tí:tər] = totter[tátər] = tremble = wobble[wábl]
The old man dodder along the street leaning on his stick.
노인은 지팡이에 의지한 채 비틀거리며 길을 걸어갔다.

dogged[dɔ́:gid] a 고집 센, 쉽사리 굽히지 않는, 끈덕진 = resolute[rézəlù:t] = stubborn[stʌ́bərn] = tenacious[tənéiʃəs]
The dogged passion of the doctor led to the discovery of the new vaccine.
집요한 의사의 열정이 마침내 새로운 백신의 발견을 가져왔다.

doggerel[dɔ́:gərəl] n 엉터리 시, 우스꽝스러운 시 = poetry[póuitri] = verse[və:rs]
The general wrote a doggerel, which made soldiers relaxed.
장군이 쓴 한 편의 엉터리 시가 병사들의 긴장을 풀어주었다.

dogmatic[dɔ:gmǽtik] a 독단적인, 독선적인 = arbitrary[á:rbətrèri] = arrogant[ǽrəgənt] = assertive[əsə́:rtiv] = bigoted[bígətid] = bullheaded
The newly appointed coach was dogmatic about selecting players.
새로 임명된 코치는 선수 선발에 독단적이었다.

doldrums[dóuldrəmz]n 침체, 침울, 우울 = depression = gloom[glu:m]
= malaise[mæléiz] = stagnation[stægnéiʃən] = stupor[stjú:pər]
The growth of the smartphone sales has remained in the doldrums due to market saturation.
스마트폰 시장은 포화 상태로 침체되어 있다.

doleful[dóulfəl] a 슬픔(비탄, 수심)에 잠긴, 우울한, 침울한 = dejected = dismal[dízməl]
= dolorous[dóulərəs] = lugubrious[lugjú:briəs] = sorrowful[sárəfəl]
All the family members and visitors were standing at the funeral with doleful faces.
장례식장의 모든 가족과 손님들은 슬픈 표정으로 서 있었다.

dolt[doult] n 얼간이, 멍청이, 바보 = idiot[ídiət]
I think Ryan a dolt because he has dumped a good girl like Cathy.
난 Cathy처럼 좋은 여자를 걷어찬 Ryan은 멍청이라고 생각해.

dormant[dɔ́:rmənt] a 잠복 중인, 비활성의, 휴면기의, 수면 중의 = inactive[inæktiv]
= inert[inə́:rt] = latent[léitnt] = lethargic[ləθá:rdʒik] = quiescent[kwaiésnt] = sleeping
= sluggish[slʌ́giʃ] = torpid[tɔ́:rpid]
I think we humans can go farther in the space if we can develop the technique to keep us dormant in a capsule.
사람을 캡슐 안에서 휴면상태로 머물게 하는 기술을 개발하면 우리 인류는 더 먼 우주로 갈 수 있다고 생각한다.

dour[duər] a 시무룩한, 음울한, 음침한, 재미없는 = glum[glʌm] = morose[məróus]
= saturnine[sǽtərnàin] = sulky[sʌ́lki] = sullen[sʌ́lən] = surly[sə́:rli]
After a massive pyramid scam swept through the town, the towners have remained depressed and dour.
대규모의 다단계 신용사기가 마을을 쓸고 간 후 마을 사람들은 낙담하고 시무룩해 하고 있다.

downcast[dáunkæst] a 풀이 죽은, 고개를 숙인 = bummed out = crestfallen[krestfɔ:lən]
= dejected = depressed = despondent[dispándənt] = disappointed = disconsolate[diskánsələt]
= discouraged = disheartened = dispirited = doleful[dóulfəl] =droopy[drú:pi]
= forlorn[fərlɔ́:rn] = gloomy = glum[glʌm] = morose[məróus]
The coaching staff and the players of the national team looked downcast after eliminated from the tournament.
국가대표 코치진과 선수들은 예선 탈락 후 풀이 죽은 모습이었다.

downplay[daʊnpleɪ] v 경시하다, 얕보다 = devalue[di:vǽlju:]
The health ministry officials downplayed the potential threat of the endemic at the outbreak of it.
보건부 관리들은 전염병 발생 시의 잠재적 위험을 경시했다.

doyen[dɔién] n 권위자, 대가, 원로, 제일인자 = connoisseur[kànəsə́ːr]
He is still in active service as the the doyen of the announcers of the broadcasting station.
방송가의 원로 아나운서인 그는 아직 현역 활동 중이다.

drab[dræb] a 칙칙한, 우중충한, 생기 없는, 단조로운 = bleak = desolate[désəlet]
= dingy[díndʒi] = dreary[dríəri] = somber[sámbər]
After she lost her husband in traffic accident, she has been leading a drab life.
그녀는 교통사고로 남편을 잃은 후로 단조로운 삶을 살고 있다.

draconian[dreikóuniən] a 엄격한, 가혹한 = brutal[brúːtl] = cruel = harsh
= oppressive[əprésiv]
I think draconian sentences can cause the crime rates to drop.
나는 가혹한 형벌이 범죄율을 떨어뜨릴 수 있다고 생각한다.

drawl[drɔːl] v 점잔을 빼며 천천히 이야기하다, 길게 늘려 이야기하다 = draw out
The man from Alabama drawled " How are you doing you guys?" when he met us for the first time.
앨라배마 출신의 그 남자는 처음 우리를 만났을 때 "안녕 여러분"이라고 점잔을 빼며 느릿느릿 말했다.

dread[dred] n 근심, 불안, 공포 = horror = panic = trepidation[trèpədéiʃən]
Most teenagers have a dread of spiders.
십대들은 대부분 거미를 무서워한다.

QUIZ 41

Match each word in the first column with its definition in the second column.
Check your answers in the back of the book.

1.	dread		a.	dejected = dismal
2.	document		b.	Idiot
3.	draconian		c.	amenable = compliant
4.	downplay		d.	brutal=cruel
5.	doyen		e.	dogmatic = opinionated
6.	dogged		f.	Cite
7.	doggerel		g.	quiver = shiver
8.	divulge		h.	inactive = inert
9.	dour		i.	poetry = verse
10.	doleful		j.	bleak = desolate
11.	dolt		k.	disclose=reveal
12.	dormant		l.	draw out
13.	dogmatic		m.	resolute = stubborn
14.	downcast		n.	Connoisseur
15.	drawl		o.	Devalue
16.	doldrums		p.	horror = panic
17.	drab		q.	arbitrary = arrogant
18.	dodder		r.	depression = gloom
19.	docile		s.	bummed out = crestfallen
20.	doctrinaire		t.	glum = morose

drench[drentʃ] v 흠뻑 적시다, 담그다 = douse[daus] = saturate[sǽtʃərèit] = soak[souk] = steep
She was drenched in cold sweat after watching a horror movie for 2 hours.
그녀는 2시간짜리 공포영화를 보고 나서 식은땀에 흠뻑 젖었다.

drivel[drívəl] v 계속 쓸데없는 말을 늘어놓다 = babble[bǽbl] = gabble[gǽbl]
He driveled on what he had experienced in his 20s.
그는 이십대에 경험한 것에 대해 계속 쓸데없는 말을 늘어놓았다.

droll[droul] a 우스꽝스러운, 익살스런 = farcical[fɑ́ːrʃəl] = jocular[dʒɑ́kjulər]
= humorous[hjúːmərəs] = ludicrous[lúːdəkrəs]
The comedian gained huge popularity across the nation due to his droll costume on a show.
그 코미디언은 어떤 쇼에서의 우스꽝스러운 복장으로 전국적인 큰 인기를 얻었다.

dross[drɔːs] n 싸구려 물건, 찌꺼기, 가치 없는 것 = remains = waste
People are throwing away a variety of dross in the back street of the city at night.
사람들은 밤에 온갖 종류의 가치 없는 물건들을 도시의 뒷골목에 버린다.

drudgery[drʌdʒəri] n 힘든 일, 고역 = hard, tedious work = toil[tɔil]
She has been doing the drudgery of collecting tolls at the toll gate for 10 years.
그녀는 톨게이트에서 통행료를 걷는 단조로운 일을 10년째 하고 있다.

dubious[djúːbiəs] a 의심하는, 분명치 않은, 미심쩍어 하는 = doubtful[dáutfəl]
= equivocal[ikwívəkəl] = fishy = questionable[kwéstʃənəbl] = skeptical[sképtikəl]
= suspicious[səspíʃəs]
The detective was dubious about the alibi of the suspect.
탐정은 피의자의 알리바이를 의심하고 있었다.

dulcet[dʌlsit] a 감미로운, 아름다운 = agreeable[əgríːəbl] = melodious[məlóudiəs]
The princess fell in love with a night who had a dulcet voice.
공주는 감미로운 목소리를 가진 기사와 사랑에 빠졌다.

dune[djuːn] n 모래언덕 = sand hill
A series of huge waves created a various forms of dune on the beach.
연속적인 큰 파도는 해변에 여러 가지 형태의 모래언덕을 만들었다.

dupe[djuːp] v 속이다, 사기를 치다 = fool = bamboozle[bæmbúːzl] = beguile[bigáil]
= cheat = deceive = defraud[difrɔ́ːd] = delude[dilúːd] = hoax[houks] = hoodwink = mislead
= swindle[swíndl] = trick
He was duped by a fraudulent realtor into buying a huge amount of useless vacant land.
그는 부동산 사기꾼에게 속아서 대규모의 쓸모없는 나대지를 샀다.

duplicity[djuːplísəti] n 표리부동, 이중성, 겉 다르고 속 다름 = artifice[ɑ́ːrtəfis]
= chicanery[ʃikéinəri] = deception = falsehood = guile[gail] = hypocrisy[hipákrəsi]
= perfidy[pə́ːrfədi] = treachery[trétʃəri]
The bank manager has showed a behavior of duplicity in dealing with his clients.
은행 지점장은 그의 고객을 대할 때 이중적인 행동을 보이고 있다.

duration[djuréiʃən] n 지속, 계속, 지속 기간 = continuation[kəntìnjuéiʃən] = period[píːəriəd]
= span[spæn]
He explored every corner of the island for the long duration of his staying there.
그는 오랫동안 섬에 머물며 구석구석을 탐험했다.

duress[djuərés] n 협박, 압박, 구속 = coercion[kouə́ːrʃən] = compulsion[kəmpʌ́lʃən]
= threat[θret]
The owner of the building promised to turn over all his businesses to the gangsters under duress.
건물 주인은 협박 때문에 그의 모든 사업체를 갱들에게 넘겨준다고 약속했다.

dwindle[dwíndl] v 점점 작아지다, 감소하다, 줄어들다 = diminish[dimíniʃ] = abate[əbéit]
= curtail[kəːrtéil] = decline = decrease = ebb = lesson = lower = reduce[ridjúːs]
= shrink = wane[wein] = weaken[wíːkən]
The number of self-employed people has been dwindling due to economic downturn.
경기 침체로 자영업자들의 수가 줄어들고 있다.

dyspeptic[dispéptik] a 소화불량의, 우울하고 화를 잘 내는, 성질이 나쁜 = crabby[krǽbi]
= grouchy[gráutʃi] = ornery[ɔ́ːrnəri]
He is too dyspeptic to spend a day without quarreling with his neighbor.
그는 우울하고 화를 잘 내는 성격이라 단 하루도 이웃과 싸우지 않고 지나가는 날이 없다.

QUIZ 42

Match each word in the first column with its definition in the second column.
Check your answers in the back of the book.

1. dyspeptic
2. dubious
3. duress
4. dross
5. duplicity
6. drivel
7. dulcet
8. dune
9. dupe
10. drench
11. duration
12. drudgery
13. dwindle
14. droll

a. continuation = period
b. artifice = chicanery
c. fool – bamboozle
d. crabby = grouchy
e. diminish = abate
f. coercion = compulsion
g. sand hill
h. agreeable = melodious
i. babble = gabble
j. douse = saturate
k. doubtful = equivocal
l. farcical = jocular
m. hard, tedious work
n. remains = waste

earshot[íərʃàt] n 목소리가 닿는 거리, 부르면 들리는 거리 = stone's throw
As he came within earshot of the gladiators, he was ready to die in the fighting.
검투사들의 말소리가 들리는 거리쯤에 다가가자 그는 싸움에서 죽을 각오를 했다.

earsplitting a 귀청이 찢어질 듯한, 천지를 진동하는 = blaring[blɛəriŋ] = deafening[défəniŋ]= loud
As the tourists were approaching the fall, they were soon surrounded by the earsplitting roar.
폭포에 다가간 관광객들은 귀청이 찢어지는 듯한 굉음에 둘러싸였다.

ebb[eb] v 쇠퇴하다, 감퇴하다, 희미해지다 = abate[əbéit] = decline = diminish = dwindle[dwíndl]
= lesson = recede[risíːd] = shrink[ʃriŋk] = slacken[slǽkən] = wane[wein] = weaken[wíːkən]
As time goes by, his grief of losing his son began to ebb away.
시간이 가면서 아들을 잃은 그의 슬픔도 희미해지기 시작했다.

ebullient[ibʌ́ljənt] a 원기 왕성한, 사기 충천한, 열광적인 = enthusiastic[inθùːziǽstik]
= effervescent[èfərvésnt] = vivacious[vivéiʃəs]
The soldiers were ebullient with the upcoming battle. 군인들은 다가올 전투에 대해 사기가 충천해 있다.

eccentric[ikséntrik] a 괴짜인, 별난, 비정상적인, 엉뚱한 = bizarre[bizάːr] = aberrant
[əbérənt] = abnormal[æbnɔ́ːrməl] = anomalous[ənάmələs] = erratic[irǽtik] = freak =
idiosyncratic[ìdiousiŋkrǽtik] = irregular[irégjulər] = outlandish[autlǽndiʃ] = queer[kwiər]
He is called an eccentric man in the neighborhood. 그는 이웃에서 괴짜로 통한다.

ecclesiastical[iklìːziǽstikəl] a 교회에 관한, 성직자에 관한 = churchly[tʃə́ːrtʃli]
Four–hour class is open for those who want to learn about ecclesiastical authority and history.
교회의 권위와 역사를 배우고 싶어 하는 사람들을 위해 네 시간짜리 강의가 개설되어 있다.

eclectic[ikléktik] a 취사선택하는, 절충주의의, 다방면에 걸친 = assorted[əsɔ́ːrtid] = selective
The gallery is exhibiting eclectic works of art. 그 미술관은 다양한 미술작품을 전시하고 있다.

eclipse[iklíps] v 어둡게 하다, 실추시키다, 가리다 = dim[dim] = obscure[əbskjúər]
= overshadow = veil[veil]
Many paintings were eclipsed by the great work of Philip Miller in the exhibition.
전시회에 나온 많은 그림들이 Philip Miller의 대작 때문에 그 존재가 무색해졌다.

ecumenical[èkjuménikəl] a 전 기독교적인, 세계교회주의의, 전반적인, 보편적인
= catholic[kǽθəlik] = general
Some churches don't follow the ecumenical doctrine.
어떤 교회는 세계기독교주의를 따르지 않는다.

edible[édəbl] a 먹을 수 있는, 식용의 = able to be eaten
They were not edible mushrooms. 그것들은 식용버섯이 아니었다.

edict[í:dikt] n 칙령, 포고, 명령 = commandment[kəmǽndmənt] = decree[dikrí:]
= directive[diréktiv] = injunctio[indʒʌ́ŋkʃən] = order = ordinance[ɔ́:rdənəns]
As he became a king, he issued an edict banning gambling.
그는 왕이 되고 나서 도박을 금지하는 칙령을 내렸다.

edifice[édəfis] n 건물, 대 건축물 = monument[mɑ́njumənt] = structure[strʌ́ktʃər]
A new edifice was built in memory of the dead queen.
새로운 대 건축물이 죽은 왕비를 기념하기 위해서 지어졌다.

edify[édəfài] v 덕성을 함양하다, 교화하다, 지식을 높이다 = educate = enlighten[inláitn]
The king tried to edify his subjects. 왕은 그의 백성들을 교화시키려고 노력했다.

efface[iféis] v 지우다, 삭제하다, 없애다 = delete = erase = expunge[ikspʌ́ndʒ] = obliterate[əblítərèit]
His efforts and dedication to the invention of the rain gauge will never be effaced.
측우기를 발명한 그의 노력과 헌신은 결코 지워지지 않을 것이다.

effectual[iféktʃuəl] a 효과적인, 유효한 = effective = efficacious[èfəkéiʃəs]
The labor minister took effectual steps to solve the unemployment problem.
노동부 장관은 실업 문제를 해결하기 위해 효과적인 조치를 취했다.

effervescent[èfərvésnt] a 사람이 쾌활한, 열광하는, 기운이 넘치는
= ebullient[ibʌ́ljənt] = jolly[dʒɑ́li] = vivacious[vivéiʃəs]
The female merchant in the market was very effervescent. 시장 안의 여성 상인은 매우 활달했다.

effete[ifí:t] a 기운이 빠진, 나약한, 쇠약한 = burnt out = exhausted[igzɔ́:stid]
= enervated[énərvèitid] = enfeebled[infí:bld] = worn out
Some young people have become more effete in the modern society.
현대 사회에서 일부 젊은이들은 더 나약해지고 있다.

efficacy[éfikəsi] n 유효성, 효험 = adequacy[ǽdikwəsi] = effectiveness = potency[póutnsi]
They should perform several clinical tests to confirm the efficacy of the new medicine.
그들은 새로운 약의 효험을 확인하기 위해서 몇 번의 임상실험을 해야 한다.

effigy[éfidʒi] n 조상, 모형, 인형 = dummy[dʌ́mi] = puppet[pʌ́pit]
Angry people were burning their ousted dictator in effigy in the street.
화난 사람들이 축출된 독재자의 인형을 거리에서 불태우고 있었다.

effulgent[ifʌ́ldʒənt] a 찬란히 빛나는, 눈부신 = beaming[bíːmiŋ] = glowing[glóuiŋ]
= incandescent[inkəndésnt] = luminous[lúːmənəs] = radian[réidiənt] = resplendent[rispléndənt]
The effulgent UFO disappeared into clouds.
눈부시게 빛나는 UFO는 구름 속으로 사라졌다.

QUIZ 43

*Match each word in the first column with its definition in the second column.
Check your answers in the back of the book.*

1.	effulgent	a.	delete = erase
2.	effigy	b.	bizarre = aberrant
3.	effervescent	c.	educate = enlighten
4.	ebullient	d.	enthusiastic = effervescent
5.	earshot	e.	able to eaten
6.	ecclesiastical	f.	beaming = glowing
7.	eclectic	g.	abate = decline
8.	edifice	h.	adequacy = effectiveness
9.	ecumenical	i.	ebullient = jolly
10.	edible	j.	blaring = deafening
11.	effete	k.	effective = efficacious
12.	efface	l.	stone's throw
13.	edify	m.	commandment = decree
14.	eclipse	n.	monument = structure
15.	effectual	o.	burnt out = exhausted
16.	eccentric	p.	churchly
17.	edict	q.	assorted = selective
18.	efficacy	r.	dim = obscure
19.	ebb	s.	dummy = puppet
20.	earsplitting	t.	catholic = general

---

effusion[ifjúːʒən] n 유출, 분출, 감정토로 = outpouring = emanation[èmənéiʃən] = ooze[uːz]
A huge effusion of crude oil along the coastline of the island was reported.
섬의 해안선을 따라서 엄청난 양의 원유 유출이 있다고 보도되었다.

effusive[ifjúːsiv] a 감정 표현이 야단스러운, 과장된, 심정을 토로하는, 뿜어 나오는
= ebullient[ibʌ́ljənt] = exuberant[igzúːbərənt] = gushing[gʌ́ʃiŋ]
The retired boxer becomes effusive when talking about boxing.
은퇴한 그 복서는 복싱 이야기를 할 때면 감정 표현이 야단스럽게 된다.

egocentric[ìːgouséntrik] a 자기중심적인, 이기적인 = egotistic[ìːgətístik] = self-centered
No one can be the leader of our society with his egocentric behavior.
아무도 자기중심적인 행동으로 우리 사회의 지도자가 될 수 없다.

egregious[igríːdʒəs] a 지독한, 어처구니없는 = arrant[ǽrənt] = flagrant[fléigrənt]
The train derailment accident was a egregious man-made calamity.
기차 탈선 사고는 어처구니없는 인재였다.

elated[iléitid] a 우쭐한, 의기양양한 = delighted[diláitid] = ecstatic[ekstǽtik]
= euphoric[juːfɔ́ːrik] = exhilarated[igzílərèitid] = exultant[igzʌ́ltənt] = jubilant[igzʌ́ltənt]
= overjoyed
He was highly elated at his first victory in the battle.
전투에서의 첫 승리에 대해 그는 매우 우쭐해 했다.

electorate[iléktərət] n 선거민, 유권자 = constituency[kənstítʃuənsi] = voters[vóutər]
Most of the electorate didn't want the charnel house built in their area.
대부분의 유권자들은 그들 지역에 납골당이 건설되는 것을 원하지 않았다.
charnel[tʃɑ́ːrnl] n 납골당

eleemosynary[èlimǽsənèri] a 자선적인, 은혜를 베푸는, 적선하는 = benevolent
[bənévələnt] = charitable[tʃǽritəbl] = generous = philanthropic[filənθrǽpik]
The charity organization is emphasizing an eleemosynary act, asking for some donations from the rich.
그 자선단체는 부자들에게 기부를 부탁하면서 자선행동을 강조하고 있다.

elevate[éləvèit] v 높이다, 들어올리다, 승격(승진)시키다 = heighten[háitn] = lift up = raise = uplift
I think that the police chief should be elevated to the Cabinet ministerial level.
경찰총수는 장관급으로 격상되어야 한다고 나는 생각한다.

elicit[ilísit] v 끌어내다, 유도해내다 = draw out = educe[idjúːs] = extract[ikstrǽkt]
Pollster's job is to elicit their opinions from a wide range of people.
여론조사요원들의 업무는 다양한 사람들로부터 의견을 이끌어내는 것이다.

elliptical[ilíptikəl] a 타원형의, 생략적인, 생략의 = oval-shaped
The airship has an elliptical shape. 그 비행선은 타원형 모양이었다.

elocution[èləkjúːʃən] n 웅변술, 연설조 = eloquence[éləkwəns]
The presidential candidate was excellent at elocution.
그 대통령 후보는 웅변술에 매우 뛰어났다.

elongate[ilɔ́:ŋgeit] v 연장하다, 길게 하다, 길게 되다 = extend = lengthen[léŋkθən]
= prolong = protract[proutrǽkt]
The blacksmith was elongating the iron by heating and pounding it.
대장장이는 쇠에 열을 가하고 내리치면서 길게 늘리고 있었다.

elucidate[ilú:sədèit] v 해명하다, 밝히다, 설명하다 = clarify[klǽrəfài] = explain
= explicate[ékspləkèit] = expound[ikspáund] = illustrate[íləstrèit]
The reporters asked the minister to elucidate the recent measures.
기자들은 장관에게 최근에 취한 조치에 대해 해명해 주기를 요청했다.

elude[ilú:d] v 잘 피하다, 교묘하게 벗어나다, 도망치다 = avoid = dodge[dadʒ] =
escape[iskéip] = evade[ivéid] = shun[ʃʌn]
The forgers eluded the pursuit of the police. 위조범들은 경찰의 추격을 벗어났다.

elusive[ilú:siv] a 파악하기 어려운, 알기 어려운, 눈에 띄지 않는 = evasive[ivéisiv]
His theory is too elusive to understand. 그의 이론은 너무 파악하기 어려워서 이해하기 힘들다.

emaciate[iméiʃièit] v 야위게 하다, 쇠약하게 하다 = attenuate[əténjuèit] = weaken
The famous wrestler was emaciated by drug addiction.
그 유명한 레슬러는 마약중독으로 쇠약해져 있었다.

emanate[émənèit] v 나오다, 발산하다, 퍼지다 = derive[diráiv] = emit[imít]
= exude[igzú:d] = give off = radiate[réidièit]
An aroma of roses emanated from the woods. 수풀에서 장미향이 났다.

emancipate[imǽnsəpèit] v 해방시키다, 석방하다 = affranchise[əfrǽntʃaiz] =
disencumber[dìsenkʌ́mbər] = manumit[mæ̀njmít] = set free = unfetter = unshackle[ʌnʃǽkl]
The edict issued by the king emancipated all slaves.
왕은 칙령에 의해 모든 노예들을 해방시켰다.

embargo[imbá:rgou] n 통상 정지, 수출입 금지 = ban = prohibition[pròuibíʃən]
= restriction[ristríkʃən]
UN has imposed an embargo on weapons sales to the country in Africa.
유엔은 아프리카에 있는 그 나라에 무기 금수 조치를 내렸다.

embed[imbéd] v 박아 넣다, 심다, 깊이 새겨두다, 끼워 넣다 = implant[implǽnt] = insert = install[instɔ́:l]
The company is selling smart phones embedded with high quality operating system.
그 회사는 수준 높은 운영체제가 내장된 스마트폰을 팔고 있다.

QUIZ 44

*Match each word in the first column with its definition in the second column.
Check your answers in the back of the book.*

1. embed
2. eleemosynary
3. emancipate
4. egregious
5. elude
6. elocution
7. effusive
8. effusion
9. elicit
10. elliptical
11. elevate
12. elongate
13. electorate
14. emaciate
15. elusive
16. elated
17. emanate
18. elucidate
19. embargo
20. egocentric

a. egotistic = self-centered
b. arrant = flagrant
c. heighten = lift up
d. benevolent = charitable
e. outpouring = emanation
f. ebullient = exuberant
g. affranchise = disencumber
h. ban = prohibition
i. clarify = explain
j. constituency = voters
k. draw out = educe
l. evasive
m. delighted = ecstatic
n. attenuate = weaken
o. avoid = dodge
p. implant = insert
q. extend = lengthen
r. derive = emit
s. oval-shaped
t. eloquence

embellish[imbéliʃ] v 아름답게 꾸미다, 장식하다 = adorn[ədɔ́ːrn] = bedeck[bidék] = decorate = embroider[imbrɔ́idər] = festoon[festúːn] = garnish[gáːrniʃ]
Before the ceremony, some girls were embellishing the wedding hall with flowers.
식을 시작하기 전에 몇몇 소녀들이 예식장을 꽃으로 장식하고 있었다.

embody[imbádi] v 구현하다, 구체화하다, 실현하다 = materialize[mətíəriəlàiz] = represent = symbolize[símbəlàiz]
The flight to the moon was to embody the dreams of the mankind.
달 여행은 인류의 꿈을 실현하기 위한 것이었다.

embolden[imbóuldən] v 대담하게 만들다, 용기를 돋우어 주다, 격려하다 = encourage = invigorate[invígərèit]
He was emboldened to dive into deep water by her praise.
그녀의 칭찬에 용기를 얻어 그는 깊은 바다로 다이빙했다.

embrace[imbréis] v 포용하다, 기꺼이 받아들이다, 수용하다 = accept[æksépt] = adopt[ədápt]
The player embraced the new annual salary system by the club.
그 선수는 구단이 새롭게 만든 연봉제를 수용했다.

embroil[imbrɔ́il] v 분쟁에 끌어들이다, 휘말리게 하다 = enmesh[inméʃ]
= ensnare[insnɛ́ər] = entangle[intǽŋgl] = implicate[ímplikèit] = involve
We were reluctant to get embroiled in the conflict with the labor union.
우리는 노동조합과의 분쟁에 휘말리는 것을 꺼렸다.

embryonic[èmbriánik] a 초기의, 미발달의 = evolving = germinal[dʒə́:rmənl]
= immature[imətʃúər] = incipient[insípiənt] = rudimentary[rù:deméntəri]
The space shuttle industry in India is still in embryonic stage.
인도에서의 우주왕복선 산업은 아직 초기 단계이다.

emigrate[émigrèit] v 이주하다, 이민가다 = migrate[máigreit] = move to new country
The family didn't want to emigrate to South America.
그 가족은 남미로 이민을 가고 싶지 않았다.

eminent[émənənt] a 저명한, 탁월한, 걸출한 = distinguished[distíŋgwiʃt] =
elevated[éləvèitid] = exalted[igzɔ́:ltid] = lofty[lɔ́:fti] = prestigious[prestídʒəs] =
prominent[prámənənt] = renowned[rináund]
He is eminent in genetic engineering. 그는 유전공학에 있어서 탁월하다.

emissary[éməsèri] n 사절, 특사 = deputy[dépjuti] = envoy[énvɔi]
We sent an emissary to the military parade on the China's 70th Victory Day.
우리는 중국의 승전 70주년 기념일에 열리는 군사 퍼레이드에 특사를 한 명 보냈다.

empathy[émpəθi] n 감정이입, 공감 = sympathy[símpəθi]
All the audience in the auditorium felt empathy with the speaker on the issue.
강당의 모든 청중들은 그 주제에 대해 연사의 이야기에 공감했다.

empirical[impírikəl] a 경험에 의한, 실험에 의한 = based on experience
The scientist only believes in the empirical theory. 그 과학자는 경험에 의한 이론만 믿는다.

empower[impáuər] v 권리(권한)를 주다, 할 수 있게 하다, 허락하다
= authorize[ɔ́:θəràiz]= entitle[intáitl]
The tax bureau officials are empowered to conduct a tax investigation of a company.
국세청 직원들은 회사의 세무조사를 할 수 있는 권한이 부여된다.

emulate[émjulèit] v 지지 않으려고 애쓰다, 맞먹다, 필적하다, 모방하다
= imitate[ímətèit] = mimic[mímik]
Silvia wants to emulate her master in dancing.
Silvia는 무용에서 그녀의 스승과 필적하게 되기를 원한다.

enact[inækt] v 제정하다, 성립시키다 = legislate[lédʒislèit]
The law protecting trans genders should be enacted.
성전환자를 보호하는 법이 제정되어야 된다.

enclose[inklóuz] v 에워싸다, 둘러싸다, 동봉하다 = encase = encircle
= encompass[inkʌmpəs] = put inside = surround
A traditional house was enclosed by tall buildings.
전통가옥 한 채가 높은 빌딩에 둘러싸여 있었다.

encomium[enkóumiəm] n 찬사, 칭찬 = accolade[ǽkəlèid]
= compliment[kámpləmənt] = eulogy[júːlədʒi] = panegyric[pænidʒírik] = praise[preiz]
= tribute[tríbjuːt]
Her acting in the movie brought a lot of encomiums.
영화에서의 그녀의 연기는 많은 찬사를 불러왔다.

encroach[inkróutʃ] v 침범하다, 침략하다, 침해하다 = impinge[impíndʒ]
= infringe[infríndʒ] = intrude[intrúːd] = invade[invéid] = trespass[tréspəs]
The violent nomads were trying to encroach on their territory.
난폭한 유목민들이 그들의 영토를 침범하려 하였다.

encumber[inkʌmbər] v 방해하다, 지장을 주다 = hamper[hǽmpər]
= hinder[híndər] = impede[impíːd] = obstruct[əbstrʌkt]
The construction of the bridge was encumbered by the heavy rain for 5 days.
교량건설공사는 5일간의 폭우로 인해 지장을 받았다

endear[indíər] v 사랑받게 하다, 귀엽게 여기게 하다
= captivate[kǽptəvèit] = cherish[tʃériʃ]
His diligence and ability endeared him to the management.
그는 근면하고 능력이 있어서 경영진의 사랑을 받았다.

endemic[endémik] a 어떤 지방에 고유한, 풍토성의 = indigenous[indídʒənəs]
Doctors found a cure to the disease endemic to the high mountains.
의사들은 고산지대의 풍토병에 대한 치료법을 찾아냈다.

QUIZ 45

Match each word in the first column with its definition in the second column.
Check your answers in the back of the book.

1.	endemic	a.	migrate = move to new country
2.	embody	b.	imitate = mimic
3.	encumber	c.	legislate
4.	encomium	d.	distinguished = elevated
5.	encroach	e.	accept = adopt
6.	embryonic	f.	deputy = envoy
7.	enclose	g.	encase = encircle
8.	endemic	h.	encourage = invigorate
9.	emissary	i.	captivate = cherish
10.	empathy	j.	materialize = represent
11.	enact	k.	hamper = hinder
12.	empower	l.	accolade = compliment
13.	emulate	m.	adorn = bedeck
14.	empower	n.	indigenous
15.	empirical	o.	enmesh = ensnare
16.	encomium	p.	impinge = infringe
17.	emigrate	q.	evolving = germinal
18.	embroil	r.	sympathy
19.	endear	s.	based on experience
20.	embolden	t.	authorize = entitle

endorse[indɔ́ːrs] v 지지하다, 보증하다 = advocate[ǽdvəkèit] = approve[əprúːv]
The civic group didn't endorse the measures by the government.
시민단체는 정부의 조치를 지지하지 않았다.

endure[indjúər] v 견디다, 참다, 지탱하다 = ride out = tolerate[tɑ́lərèit] = weather = withstand[wiðstǽnd]
The house could not endure the strong tornado.
그 집은 강력한 토네이도를 견뎌내지 못했다.

enervate[énərvèit] v 약화시키다, 무기력하게 하다, 기력을 떨어지게 하다 = debilitate[dibílətèit] = enfeeble[infíːbl] = unnerve[ʌnnə́ːrv] = weaken
The sultry weather in Africa continent enervated the workers from China.
아프리카 대륙의 무더운 날씨는 중국에서 온 근로자들을 무기력하게 했다.

enfeeble[infíːbl] v 약화시키다, 쇠약하게 하다 = attenuate[əténjuèit] = debilitate[dibílətèit] = exhaust[igzɔ́ːst] = sap[sæp] = unnerve[ʌnnə́ːrv] = weaken
His long illness enfeebled the eminent writer. 저명한 저자는 오랜 지병으로 쇠약해졌다.

enfranchise[infrǽntʃaiz] v 참정권을 주다, 선거권을 주다
A law will be enacted to enfranchise those over 19 years old.
열아홉 살이 넘은 사람들에게 선거권을 주는 법이 제정될 것이다.

engaging[ingéidʒiŋ] a 매력적인, 매혹하는, 호감이 가는 = alluring[əlúəriŋ] = appealing = captivating[kǽptəvèitiŋ] = fascinating[fǽsənèitiŋ] = charming = intriguing[intríːgiŋ]
Sarah has an engaging dimple on her left cheek.
Sarah는 왼쪽 뺨에 매력적인 보조개가 있다.

engender[indʒéndər] v 발생(야기)시키다, 불러일으키다, 낳다 = beget[bigét] = create = generate[dʒénərèit] = father
The lack of sleeping engenders the concentration problem.
수면부족은 집중력 문제를 야기시킨다.

engrave[ingréiv] v 새기다, 조각하다, 명심하다, 감명시키다 = etch[etʃ] = inscribe[inskráib]
Names of the great players and coaches were engraved on the central wall in the hall of fame.
명예의전당 중앙 벽에는 위대한 선수들과 감독들의 이름이 새겨져 있었다.

engross[ingróus] v 몰두시키다, 마음을 빼앗다 = immerse[imə́ːrs] = preoccupy
All of the students were engrossed in the lecture of the scientist.
모든 학생들은 과학자의 강의에 몰두했다.

enhance[inhǽns] v 높이다, 향상시키다, 강화하다 = boost = improve = upgrade
The new product will enhance the brand image of our company.
새로운 제품은 우리 회사의 브랜드 이미지를 높일 것이다.

enigma[ənígmə] n 수수께끼 = conundrum[kənʌ́ndrəm] = mystery = puzzle = riddle[rídl]
The birth of the moon still remains an enigma to many scientists.
달의 탄생은 여전히 많은 과학자들에게 수수께끼로 남아 있다.

enlarge[inlɑ́ːrdʒ] v 크게 하다, 확대하다, 확장하다 = magnify[mǽgnəfài] = swell[swel]
Traveling and learning the 2nd language can enlarge your point of view.
여행과 제2외국어 공부는 사람들의 식견을 넓혀 줄 수 있다.

enlighten[inláitn] v 계몽하다, 교화하다, 가르치다 = civilize[sìvəlàiz] = edify[édəfài] = educate
The invention and distribution of the easy writing system helped enlighten people.
쉬운 문자의 발명과 보급이 민중들을 계몽하는 데 일조했다.

enmity[énməti] n 원한, 증오, 적대감 = animosity[ӕnəmásəti] = antipathy[ӕntípəθi] = dislike = hatred[héitrid] = hostility[hastíləti] = loathing[lóuðiŋ] = rancor[rӕŋkər]
We should not be at enmity with the immigrants. 우리는 이민자들에게 적의를 품어선 안 된다.

ennui[a:nwí:] n 권태감, 지루함, 울적함 = boredom[bɔ́:rdəm] = languor[lӕŋgər] = tedium[tí:diəm]
Thirty years of married life can cause ennui for the couple.
결혼생활 30년이면 부부에게 권태가 올 수 있다.

enormity[inɔ́:rməti] n 심각함, 엄청남, 잔인한 범죄행위(pl) = horribleness[hɔ́:rəblnis] = atrocity[ətrásəti] = depravity[diprӕvəti] = heinousness[héinəsnis] = nefariousness [niféəriəs] = turpitude[tə́:rpətjù:d] = wickedness[wíkidnis]
The conqueror committed numerous enormities in the colony.
정복자들은 식민지에서 잔인한 범죄행위를 수없이 저질렀다.

ensconce[inskάns] v 안락하게 자리를 잡다, 안치하다 = situate
Mark ensconced himself in the sofa to watch the soccer game on TV.
Mark는 TV로 축구경기를 보기 위해 소파에 편안하게 자리를 잡았다.
.

enslave[insléiv] v 포로로 하다, 노예로 만들다, 예속시키다 = make someone a slave = shackle[ʃӕkl] = subjugate[sΛbdʒugèit]
Some middle aged women are enslaved to speculation in real estates.
일부 중년 부인들은 부동산 투기에 사로잡혀 있다.

ensue[insú:] v 일어나다, 뒤따르다, 잇따라 일어나다 = arise[əráiz] = befall[bifɔ́:l]
The two countries exchanged bombardments each other and a war ensued.
두 나라가 포격을 주고받고 나서 전쟁이 일어났다.

entail[intéil] v 수반하다, 필요로 하다, 일으키다 = bring out = encompass[inkΛmpəs] = lead to = necessitate[nəsésətèit] = require = result in
The presidency entails leadership and responsibility. 대통령직은 지도력과 책임감이 필요하다.

entice[intáis] v 꾀다, 유혹하다, 시키다 = allure[əlúər] = beguile[bigáil] = cajole[kədʒóul] = coax[kouks] = inveigle[invéigl] = seduce[sidjú:s] = tempt = wheedle[hwí:dl]
She enticed him away from studying abroad. 그녀는 그를 부추겨 유학 가는 걸 그만두게 했다.

QUIZ 46

Match each word in the first column with its definition in the second column.
Check your answers in the back of the book.

1.	entice	a.	advocate = approve
2.	entail	b.	bring out = encompass
3.	enervate	c.	alluring = appealing
4.	ensconce	d.	arise = befall
5.	enigma	e.	make someone a slave = shackle
6.	engender	f.	conundrum = mystery
7.	ennui	g.	ride out = tolerate
8.	engross	h.	beget = create
9.	enmity	i.	etch = inscribe
10.	endorse	j.	Situate
11.	enlarge	k.	attenuate = debilitate
12.	enlighten	l.	magnify = swell
13.	enmity	m.	civilize = edify
14.	engaging	n.	immerse = preoccupy
15.	ensue	o.	boost = improve
16.	engrave	p.	animosity = antipathy
17.	enslave	q.	debilitate = enfeeble
18.	ensue	r.	boredom = languor
19.	enfeeble	s.	allure = beguile
20.	engrave	t.	horribleness = atrocity

entity[éntəti] n 독립체, 존재, 본질 = existence[igzístəns] = presence
The tribe in the pacific ocean became a political entity. 태평양의 한 부족이 독립국가가 되었다.

entrap[intrǽp] v 덫으로 잡다, 함정에 빠뜨리다, 위험에 빠뜨리다 = ensnare[insnɛ́ər]
The con man entrapped a young innocent man into buying drugs.
사기꾼은 계략을 써서 젊고 순진한 남자에게 마약을 사게 했다.

entreat[intríːt] v 간청하다, 애원하다, 탄원하다 = beg = beseech[bisíːtʃ] = crave
= implore[implɔ́ːr] = petition[pətíʃən] = supplicate[sʌ́pləkèit]
The homeless entreated some money from the passers-by.
노숙자는 지나가는 행인들에게 얼마간의 돈을 간청했다.

entrepreneur[àːntrəprənəːr] n 기업가, 사업가 = industrialist[indʌ́striəlist]
He's an ambitious entrepreneur. 그는 야심 있는 사업가다.

enumerate[injú:mərèit] v 하나하나 열거하다, 차례로 들다 = list = specify[spésəfài]
The detective enumerated all the evidence to the suspect.
형사는 피의자에게 하나하나씩 증거를 열거했다.

enunciate[inʌnsièit] v 분명하게 발음하다, 선언하다 = articulate[a:rtíkjulət]
The young girl enunciated each word on the letter.
어린 소녀는 편지의 모든 단어를 분명하게 발음했다.

envision[invíʒən] v 장래를 상상하다, 계획하다 = anticipate = foresee = predict[pridíkt]
We sometimes envision the world where there is no war.
우리는 때때로 전쟁 없는 세상을 상상하곤 한다.

ephemeral[ifémərəl] a 덧없는, 단명한, 잠깐의 = brief[bri:f] = evanescent[èvənésnt]
= fleeting[flí:tiŋ] = short-lived = transient[trǽnʃənt]
Our life is too ephemeral to seek something foolish.
우리 인생은 어리석은 것을 좇기에는 너무 덧없다.

epicure[épikjùər] n 미식가, 식도락가 = foodie[fú:di] = gourmet[gúərmei]
She is an epicure of French food. 그녀는 프랑스 요리를 즐기는 미식가다.

epigram[épəgræm] n 경구, 짧은 시 = aphorism[ǽfərìzm]
We can see a lot of epigrams in traditional Chinese novels.
고대 중국 소설에서 우리는 많은 경구를 볼 수 있다.

epilogue[épəlɔ̀:g] n 끝맺는 말, 종결 부분, 에필로그 = coda[kóudə]
The director sends a significant message at the epilogue of the play.
연출가는 연극의 종결 부분에서 의미심장한 메시지를 보낸다.

epitome[ipítəmi] n 요약, 줄거리 = compendium[kəmpéndiəm]
= abridgment[əbrídʒmənt] = abstract[ǽbstrǽkt]= digest[daidʒést] = summary = synopsis[sinápsis]
His epic novel in epitome was also the best seller.
요약된 형태의 대하소설도 그의 베스트셀러 작품이었다.

epoch[épək] n 시대, 세기, 신기원 = era[íərə] = period
We will move into the new epoch by sending the astronauts to Mars.
우리는 우주인들을 화성에 보내면서 새로운 시대로 돌입할 것이다.

equable[ékwəbl] a 한결같은, 온화한, 침착한 = consistent
= imperturbable[ìmpərtə́:rbəbl] = placid[plǽsid] = steady[stédi]
Equable temperature is required to grow flowers in the green house.
꽃을 키우기 위해서는 늘 한결같은 온도가 필요하다.

equanimity[ì:kwəníməti] n 침착, 평정, 냉정 = calm = composure[kəmpóuʒər]
= equilibrium[ì:kwəlíbriəm] = imperturbability[ìmpərtə̀:rbəbíləti] = poise[pɔiz]
The homemaker dealt with the threat of the robbers with equanimity.
그 주부는 강도들의 위협에 침착하게 대응했다.

equestrian[ikwéstriən] n 승마자, 기수 = horse rider
The equestrian did some wonderful performances on the horse back.
기수는 말의 등에서 몇 가지 묘기를 선보였다.

equipoise[í:kwəpɔ̀iz] n 균형, 평형 = balance = equilibrium[ì:kwəlíbriəm]
The sense of equipoise is required to run the company.
회사를 운영하는 데는 균형감각이 필요하다.

equitable[ékwətəbl] a 공정한, 공평한, 합리적인 = disinterested
= dispassionate[dispǽʃənət] = objective = square[skwɛər] = unbiased
The flood victims are asking for an equitable distribution of the relief supplies.
홍수 피해자들은 구호물자의 공평한 분배를 원한다.

equivocal[ikwívəkəl] a 분명치 않은, 애매한, 모호한 = ambiguous[æmbígjuəs]
= obscure[əbskjúər] = vague[veig]
His statement was so equivocal that we couldn't catch his real intention.
그의 말이 너무 애매모호해서 진짜 의도를 파악하지 못했다.

equivocate[ikwívəkèit] v (속이려고) 얼버무리다, 모호하게 말하다 = avoid
= dodge[dadʒ] = elude[ilú:d] = escape = eschew[istʃú:] = evade[ivéid] = palter[pɔ́:ltər]
= parry[pǽri] = prevaricate[privǽrəkèit] = quibble[kwíbl] = sidestep =
tergiversate[tə́:rdʒivərsèit]
When the suspect was grilled about the crime, he often equivocated.
범죄에 대해서 심문을 받을 때 그 용의자는 자주 말을 얼버무렸다.

QUIZ 47

Match each word in the first column with its definition in the second column.
Check your answers in the back of the book.

1.	equivocate	a.	list = specify
2.	equitable	b.	articulate
3.	entreat	c.	horse rider
4.	equivocal	d.	existence = presence
5.	enumerate	e.	calm = composure
6.	equanimity	f.	beg = beseech
7.	equable	g.	balance = equilibrium
8.	ephemeral	h.	ensnare
9.	epitome	i.	era = period
10.	epigram	j.	consistent = imperturbable
11.	epilogue	k.	industrialist
12.	entity	l.	gourmet
13.	epoch	m.	aphorism
14.	epicure	n.	disinterested = dispassionate
15.	equestrian	o.	ambiguous = obscure
16.	envision	p.	coda
17.	equipoise	q.	compendium = abridgment
18.	entrepreneur	r.	anticipate = foresee
19.	enunciate	s.	bricf = cvancsccnt
20.	entrap	t.	avoid = dodge

errant[érənt] a 잘못된, 정도를 벗어난, 바람을 피우는 = aberrant[əbérənt]
= deviant[díːviənt] = erratic[irǽtik]
No journalists were allowed to write an errant article. 어떤 기자도 정도를 벗어난 기사를 써서는 안 된다.

erode[iróud] v 서서히 파괴하다, 침식(풍화)시키다, 약화시키다 = abrade[əbréid]
= corrode[kəróud] = wear away
The hills and grasslands has been eroded by the meandering river.
굽이굽이 흐르는 강에 의해 언덕과 목초지가 침식되었다.

erratic[irǽtik] a 별난, 괴상한, 변덕스러운, 일정치 못한 = abnormal
= arbitrary[άːrbətrèri] = capricious[kəpríʃəs] = eccentric[ikséntrik] = mercurial[mərkjúəriəl]
= wayward = whimsical[hwímzikəl]   velocity[vəlάsəti] n 속도
It is not recommendable to build a wind power plant here because the velocity of the wind is erratic.
풍속이 일정하지 않기 때문에 여기에 풍력발전소를 세우는 것은 바람직하지 않다.

erudite[érjudàit] a 학구적인, 유식한, 박식한 = learned = savvy[sǽvi] = versed[vəːrst] = well-educated
The venerable high school released many erudite scholars.
그 유서 깊은 고등학교는 박식한 학자들을 많이 배출했다. venerable[vénərəbl] a 유서 깊은

eschew[istʃúː] v 피하다, 삼가다, 회피하다 = avoid = forgo[fɔːrgóu] = forswear[fɔːrswέər] = shun[ʃʌn]
She eschews fatty foods to achieve her goal in the diet.
그녀는 다이어트를 위해 기름진 음식을 피한다.

esoteric[èsətérik] a 소수만 이해하는, 난해한, 심원한, 은밀한 = arcane[aːrkéin]
= cryptic[kríptik] = enigmatic[ènigmǽtik] = mysterious[mistíəriəs] = mystic[místik]
The professor enjoys quoting the esoteric philosophy during the class.
교수는 수업시간에 난해한 철학을 인용하는 것을 즐긴다.

espouse[ispáuz] v 신봉하다, 지지하다, 옹호하다 = advocate[ǽdvəkèit] = champion
= stand behind = stand up for = support = uphold
Most citizens espouse the policies of the female candidate in education.
대부분의 시민들은 교육에 관해서 여성후보자의 정책을 지지한다.

estimable[éstəməbl] a 존경(존중)할 만한, 평가할 수 있는 = esteemed = honorable
= laudable[lɔ́ːdəbl] = meritorious[mèritɔ́ːriəs] = praiseworthy = venerable[vénərəbl]
The environmental group is being led by an estimable leader.
그 환경단체는 존경할 만한 지도자에 의해서 이끌어지고 있다.

estrange[istréindʒ] v 이간시키다, 소원하게 하다, 사이를 틀어지게 하다
= alienate[éiljənèit] = disaffect[dìsəfékt]
Money estranged him from his friends. 돈 때문에 그는 친구들과 소원하게 되었다.

ethereal[iθíəriəl] a 공기 같은, 아주 우아한, 천상의 = celestial[səléstʃəl] = heavenly
The diva has an ethereal voice. 그 유명 여가수는 천상의 목소리를 가지고 있다.

euphemism[júːfəmìzm] n 완곡어법(어구) = circumlocution[sə̀ːrkəmloukjúːʃən]
"Let me think about it" is a euphemism for "No".
"생각해볼게요"는 "No"의 완곡한 표현이다.

eulogize[júːlədʒàiz] v 칭송하다, 찬사를 보내다 = commend = extol[ikstóul]
= glorify[glɔ́ːrəfài] = idolize[áidəlàiz] = laud[lɔːd] = praise
Many film critics have eulogized his new movie 'Avatar'.
영화 평론가들은 그의 새 영화 'Avatar'에 찬사를 보냈다.

eulogy[júːlədʒi] n 찬양하는 글, 찬사, 추도연설 = acclamation[ækləméiʃən]
= encomium[enkóumiəm] = exaltation[ègzɔːltéiʃən] = paean[píːən] = panegyric[pænidʒírik]
= praise = tribute
The movie director won the eulogy of the best movie of the year.
그 영화감독은 올해의 작품의 찬사를 받았다.

euphonious[juːfóuniəs] a 음조가 좋은, 듣기 좋은 = dulcet[dʌlsit]
= mellifluous[melífluəs] = melodious
She composed a lot of songs full of euphonious melodies.
그녀는 듣기 좋은 선율이 가득한 많은 곡을 작곡했다.

evade[ivéid] v 회피하다, 피하다, 빠져나가다 = avoid = bypass = circumvent[sə̀ːrkəmvént]
= dodge[dadʒ] = elude[ilúːd] = escape = fend off = sidestep
Some hocky players tried to evade military service.
일부 하키 선수들이 병역의무를 회피하려고 했다.

evanescent[èvənésnt] a 덧없는, 사라져 가는 = ephemeral[ifémərəl] = fleeting
= passing = short-lived = transient[trǽnʃənt] = vanishing[vǽniʃiŋ]
A poet says that our life is as evanescent as one night's dream in the summer.
어떤 시인은 우리 인생은 한여름 밤의 꿈만큼 덧없다고 말한다.

evict[ivíkt] v 퇴거시키다, 쫓아버리다 = dislodge[dislɑ́dʒ] = eject[idʒékt] = expel = force out
The musician was evicted from his apartment because he had made noises at night.
음악가는 밤에 소음을 내서 아파트에서 쫓겨났다.

evince[ivíns] v 분명히 밝히다, 증명하다, 명시하다 = attest = demonstrate
= manifest[mǽnəfèst] = prove = reveal
He evinced his views on the issue 그는 쟁점에 대한 자신의 견해를 분명히 밝혔다.

evoke[ivóuk] v 불러일으키다, 환기시키다 = arouse = conjure[kɑ́ndʒər] = elicit[ilísit]
= invoke
This picture evokes the memories of my elementary school days in the countryside.
이 사진은 내가 지방에서 초등학교를 다닐 때의 기억을 불러일으킨다.

exacerbate[igzǽsərbèit] v 악화시키다 = aggravate[ǽgrəvèit] = worsen
Global warming will exacerbate food shortage in Africa.
지구온난화는 아프리카의 식량부족을 악화시킬 것이다.

QUIZ 48

Match each word in the first column with its definition in the second column.
Check your answers in the back of the book.

1.	exacerbate		a.	arcane = cryptic
2.	erode		b.	advocate = champion
3.	erudite		c.	aggravate = worsen
4.	evoke		d.	avoid = forgo
5.	eschew		e.	celestial = heavenly
6.	evict		f.	esteemed = honorable
7.	espouse		g.	dulcet = mellifluous
8.	evade		h.	dislodge = eject
9.	estrange		i.	alienate = disaffect
10.	ethereal		j.	abnormal = arbitrary
11.	eulogy		k.	learned = savvy
12.	eulogize		l.	acclamation = encomium
13.	evanescent		m.	attest = demonstrate
14.	euphonious		n.	abrade = corrode
15.	euphemism		o.	arouse = conjure
16.	errant		p.	aberrant = deviant
17.	estimable		q.	circumlocution
18.	evince		r.	ephemeral = fleeting
19.	esoteric		s.	avoid = bypass
20.	erratic		t.	commend = extol

exacting[igzǽktiŋ] a 사람이 엄격한, 일이 혹독한, 까다로운 = demanding = fastidious[fæstídiəs]
He has gone through exacting courses to be the best chef.
그는 최고의 셰프가 되기 위해 혹독한 과정을 거쳤다.

exaggerate[igzǽdʒərèit] a 과장하다, 과장해서 말하다 = overstate
Some people exaggerate their annual incomes.
어떤 사람들은 자신의 연봉을 과장해서 말한다.

exalt[igzɔ́ːlt] v 칭찬하다, 찬양하다, 지위 명예를 높이다 = acclaim = applaud = commend
= extol[ikstóul] = glorify[glɔ́ːrəfài] = laud[lɔːd] = praise
The public exalted the young archers participating in Olympic Games.
국민들은 올림픽에 참가하고 있는 젊은 궁사들을 칭찬했다.

exasperate[ikstóul] v 분개시키다, 성나게 하다 = incense[ínsens] = infuriate[infjúərièit]
Cancellations of the flights exasperated many airline passengers.
비행기 운항 취소는 많은 승객들을 성나게 했다.

excerpt[éksə:rpt] n 발췌, 초록, 인용 = citation[saitéiʃən] = extract = quotation[kwoutéiʃən]
His report is an excerpt from a recently released statement by government.
그의 보고서는 정부에서 최근 발표한 성명서에서 발췌한 것이다.

excise[éksaiz] v 삭제하다, 잘라내다 = amputate[ǽmpjutèit] = cut out = delete
= expunge[ikspʌndʒ] = remove
Some lewd expressions and illustrations were excised from the novel.
그 소설에서 일부 외설스러운 표현 및 삽화들이 삭제되었다.

excoriate[ikskɔ́:rièit] v 혹평하다, 심하게 비난하다 = denounce[dináuns] = accuse
= blame = castigate[kǽstəgèit] = censure = condemn[kəndém] = criticize[krítəsàiz] = decry
= impeach[impí:tʃ] = impugn[impjú:n] = lambaste = rebuke = reprehend = reprimand
[réprəmænd] = reproach[ripróutʃ] = reprobate[réprəbèit] = reprove = revile[riváil] = scold
= upbraid = vilify[víləfài] = vituperate[vaitjú:pərèit]
The book written by the wannabe politician was excoriated by many political critics.
신인 정치 지망생이 쓴 책은 정치비평가들에게 혹평을 받았다.

exculpate[ékskʌlpèit] v 무죄를 입증하다, 면하게 하다 = absolve = acquit[əkwít]
= amnesty[ǽmnəsti] = condone[kəndóun] = exonerate[igzánərèit] = pardon = vindicate[víndəkèit]
His alibi exculpated him from arson charge. 그는 알리바이 덕분에 방화 혐의를 벗었다.

excursive[ikskə́:rsiv] a 본론에서 벗어난, 탈선하는, 산만한 = desultory[désəltɔ̀:ri]
= digressive[diskə́:rsiv] = discursive[diskə́:rsiv] = rambling[rǽmbliŋ]
The lecturer was excursive from the beginning, so no students could catch his points.
강사가 처음부터 주제를 벗어나는 바람에 어떤 학생도 요점을 이해하지 못했다.

execrate[éksəkrèit] v 혐오하다, 질색하다, 헐뜯다 = abhor[æbhɔ́:r]
= abominate[əbámənèit] = detest[ditést] = loathe[louð]
The neighbors execrated the professor indicted on charges of child molester.
이웃 사람들은 아동 성추행으로 기소된 교수를 혐오했다.

exemplify[igzémpləfài] v 예증하다, 예가 되다, 실증하다 = demonstrate[démənstrèit]
= illustrat[íləstrèit]
Black suits exemplify the respect to the dead at funerals.
검정 양복은 장례식장에서 망자에 대한 존경을 나타낸다.

exempt[igzémpt] v 면제하다, 면해주다 = absolve[æbzálv] = excuse
= exonerate[igzánərèit] = free = spare
His skin disease exempted him from military service. 그는 피부병으로 병역을 면제받았다.

exhaust[igzɔ́:st] v 고갈시키다, 다 써버리다, 기진맥진하다 = deplete = run out = use up
Her lavish lifestyle has exhausted all the wealth of the couple.
그녀의 사치생활이 부부의 모든 재산을 고갈시켰다.

exhaustive[igzɔ́:stiv] a 철저한, 완전한, 포괄적인 = comprehensive = extensive
= in-depth = intensive = thorough[θə́:rou]
The police made an exhaustive investigation into the kidnapping case.
경찰은 유괴사건에 대해 철저히 조사했다.

exhort[igzɔ́:rt] v 간곡히 타이르다, 권고하다, 훈계하다 = admonish[ædmániʃ]
The doctor exhorted the patient to start walking right away.
의사는 그 환자에게 즉시 걷기를 시작하라고 권고했다.

exhume[igzjú:m] v 파내다, 발굴하다 = dig up = unbury[ʌnbéri] = unearth
The team of archeologists has exhumed the remains of the now-defunct mammoth.
고고학자 팀은 멸종된 매머드의 유골을 발굴해냈다.

exigency[éksədʒənsi] n 긴급사태, 급한 볼일 = emergency = pinch
Some countries in Europe are struggling with economic and political exigencies.
유럽의 일부 국가는 경제적, 정치적 긴급사태로 어려움을 겪고 있다.

exodus[éksədəs] n 탈출, 이동, 출국, 나가기 = evacuation[ivækjuéiʃən] = migration[maigréiʃən]
We can see the huge exodus to foreign countries at the airport during the long holiday.
우리는 공항에서 연휴기간에 해외로 나가려는 엄청난 수의 출국자들의 모습을 볼 수 있다.

exonerate[igzánərèit] v 해방하다, 면제하다 = absolve[æbzálv] = acquit[əkwít] = assoil[əsɔ́il]
= exculpate[ékskʌlpèit] = exempt[igzémpt] = vindicate[víndəkèit]
The soldier was exonerated from the duty of vigilant sentry.
그 병사는 불침번의 의무에서 면제되었다.   sentry[séntri] n 보초

exorbitant[igzɔ́:rbətənt] a 터무니없는, 과도한 = excessive[iksésiv]
= extravagant[ikstrǽvəgənt] = inordinate[inɔ́:rdənət] = unreasonable
Some merchants demand an exorbitant price in tourist attractions.
관광지에서 어떤 상인들은 터무니없는 가격을 요구한다.

QUIZ 49

Match each word in the first column with its definition in the second column.
Check your answers in the back of the book.

1.	exorbitant	a.	absolve = excuse
2.	exaggerate	b.	demonstrate = illustrate
3.	exodus	c.	abhor = abominate
4.	exasperate	d.	evacuation = migration
5.	exhume	e.	demanding = fastidious
6.	excise	f.	deplete = run out
7.	excoriate	g.	desultory = digressive
8.	exculpate	h.	absolve = acquit
9.	exhaustive	i.	acclaim = applaud
10.	execrate	j.	admonish
11.	exemplify	k.	overstate
12.	exacting	l.	comprehensive = extensive
13.	exhaust	m.	denounce = accuse
14.	exempt	n.	dig up = unbury
15.	exhort	o.	citation = extract
16.	exalt	p.	excessive = extravagant
17.	exigency	q.	absolve = acquit
18.	excerpt	r.	incense = infuriate
19.	exonerate	s.	emergency – pinch
20.	excursive	t.	amputate = cut out

expatriate[ekspéitrièit] v 추방하다, 고국을 떠나다, 국적을 버리다
The politician expatriated himself in search for a country that supports his ideology.
정치인은 그의 이념을 지지해주는 나라를 찾아 망명을 떠났다.

expedient[ikspí:diənt] a 편리한, 적당한 = beneficial[bènəfíʃəl] = convenient = practical
I think it will be expedient for post offices to provide banking service.
나는 우체국이 금융서비스를 제공해주면 매우 편리하리라 생각한다.

expedite[ékspədàit] v 촉진시키다, 신속히 처리하다 = facilitate[fəsílətèit] = hasten[héisn]
Automatic packing can expedite the deliveries to the customers.
자동포장 방식은 고객들에게 신속하게 배달할 수 있게 해줄 것이다.

expenditure[ikspénditʃər] n 지출, 소비 = expense = payment = spending
City government plans to slash expenditure on the universal welfare.
시 정부는 무상복지(보편적 복지)에 쓰이는 지출을 삭감할 계획이다.

expiate[ékspièit] v 보상하다, 속죄하다 = atone[ətóun] = compensate[kámpənsèit]
He wanted to expiate his sin by donating some of his wealth to the society.
그는 재산 일부를 사회에 기부함으로써 자신의 죄를 속죄하고 싶어 했다.

explicate[ékspləkèit] v 해명하다, 해석하다, 설명하다 = clarify[klǽrəfài] = elucidate[ilú:sədèit] = expatiate[ikspéiʃièit] = explain = expound[ikspáund] v = illustrate
The world-famous scientist explicated the big bang theory to the students.
세계적인 과학자는 학생들에게 빅뱅이론을 설명해주었다.

explicit[iksplísit] a 명백한, 숨김없는, 솔직한 = outspoken = trenchant[trénʧənt]
He was explicit about the difficulties facing him.
그는 당면하고 있는 어려움을 솔직하게 털어놓았다.

exponent[ikspóunənt] n 주창자, 옹호자, 지지자 = proponent[prəpóunənt] = supporter
The doctor is an exponent of euthanasia. 그 의사는 안락사 옹호자이다.

exposition[èkspəzíʃən] n 해설, 설명 = elucidation[ilù:sədéiʃən] = explanation = explication[èksplikéiʃən]
Reporters are listening to the exposition of the FTA between the two nations.
기자들은 두 나라 사이의 자유무역협정에 대한 설명을 듣고 있다.

expostulate[ikspástʃulèit] v 훈계하다, 반대하다, 타이르다 = remonstrate[rimánstreit]
He expostulated his son against gambling on the horses.
그는 아들에게 경마도박을 하지 말라고 타일렀다.

expunge[ikspʌndʒ] v 지우다, 삭제하다 = abolish[əbáliʃ] = annihilate[ənáiəlèit]
= destroy = delete[dilí:t] = efface[iféis] = eradicate[irǽdəkèit] = erase
= exterminate[ikstə́:rmənèit] = extirpate[ékstərpèit] = obliterate[əblítərèit] = wipe out
His flight record has been expunged from the computer database.
그의 비행기록이 컴퓨터 데이터베이스에서 삭제되었다.

expurgate[ékspə:rgèit] v [책·영화 등] (외설·부적당한 부분을) 삭제하다, 수정하다
= bowdlerize[bóudləràiz] = censor = cut
The obscene scene was expurgated by the inspector from the movie.
검열관에 의해서 영화의 외설적인 장면이 삭제되었다.

exquisite[ékskwizit] a 아름다운, 정교한, 완벽한 = elegant = excellent = polished
Dumped furniture became an exquisite work of art. 버려진 가구가 정교한 예술작품이 되었다.

extant[ékstənt] a 현존하는, 잔존하는, 현역의 = existing = surviving
Historians attempt to preserve extant remains of the temple.
역사학자들은 잔존하는 사찰의 유물을 보존하고자 한다.

extenuate[iksténjuèit] v 경감하다, 가볍게 하다, 정상참작하다 = excuse = lessen
= mitigate[mítəgèit] = palliate[pǽlièit]
The mental illness of the suspect extenuated the sentence in final trial.
피고인은 정신병 때문에 최종판결에서 형량이 경감되었다.

extinguish[ikstíŋgwiʃ] v 불을 끄다, 진화하다 = put out a fire = quench[kwentʃ]
It took 50 fire engines to extinguish the flames. 그 불길을 잡기 위해 소방차 50대가 출동했다.

extol[ikstóul] v 칭찬하다, 격찬하다, 찬양하다 = exalt[igzɔ́ːlt] = acclaim[əkléim]
= applaud[əplɔ́ːd] = commend = glorify = laud = praise
The unmanned car was extolled as the future of the car. 그 무인자동차는 자동차의 미래로 격찬 받았다.

extort[ikstɔ́ːrt] v 강탈하다, 빼앗다 = blackmail = coerce[kouə́ːrs]
The pirates extorted all the money and valuables from the sailors.
해적들은 선원들에게서 모든 돈과 귀중품을 강탈했다.

extract[ikstrǽkt] v 뽑다, 빼내다, 추출하다 = cull[kʌl] = derive[diráiv] = elicit[ilísit]
The workers were working hard to extract sap from trees.
일꾼들은 나무에서 수액을 추출하기 위해 열심히 일하는 중이었다.

extraneous[ikstréiniəs] a 관계없는, 이질적인, 본질에서 벗어난 = extra
= irrelevant[iréləvənt] = unneeded = unnecessary
The guest speaker mentioned his personal stories extraneous to the subject.
초청 연사는 주제와 무관한 개인 사생활을 이야기했다.

extrapolate[ikstrǽpəlèit] v 기존의 자료에 기초하여 추론하다, 추정하다
= deduce[didjúːs] = infer = predict
Astrophysicists extrapolated the distance between the two stars on the basis of their brightness.
천체물리학자들은 별의 밝기를 근거로 두 별 사이의 거리를 추정했다.

QUIZ 50

Match each word in the first column with its definition in the second column.
Check your answers in the back of the book.

1. expunge
2. expedite
3. extraneous
4. expiate
5. explicate
6. extrapolate
7. extenuate
8. exposition
9. expostulate
10. extant
11. expedient
12. exquisite
13. extant
14. exponent
15. extinguish
16. expurgate
17. extol
18. extract
19. explicit
20. extort

a. atone = compensate
b. clarify = elucidate
c. excuse = lessen
d. expense = payment
e. extra = irrelevant
f. existing = surviving
g. facilitate = hasten
h. elegant = excellent
i. bowdlerize = censor
j. beneficial = convenient
k. deduce = infer
l. put out a fire = quench
m. outspoken = trenchant
n. exalt = acclaim
o. abolish = annihilate
p. blackmail = coerce
q. proponent = supporter
r. elucidation = explanation
s. remonstrate
t. cull = derive

extravagant[ikstrǽvəgənt] a 낭비하는, 낭비벽이 있는, 사치스러운 = lavish[lǽviʃ] = wasteful
You should not select an extravagant girl as your bride.
낭비벽이 있는 소녀를 너의 신부로 선택하지 말아라.

extremity[ikstréməti] n 맨 끝, 말단, 극도 = terminus[tə́ːrmənəs]
Hanam is located at the southern extremity of the Korean peninsula.
해남은 한반도 최남단에 위치한다.

extricate[ékstrəkèit] v 구출하다, 해방하다 = disentangle[dìsentǽŋgl]
= emancipate[imǽnsəpèit] = get off the hook = manumit[mǽnjmít] = untangle
It took a few hours to extricate the children trapped in the elevator.
엘리베이터에 갇힌 아이들을 구하는 데 몇 시간이 걸렸다.

extrinsic[ikstrínsik] a 비본질적인, 외부의, 외적인 = foreign
He talked about some conditions extrinsic to the trade agreement.
그는 거래 계약과는 상관없는 조건들을 이야기했다.

extrovert[ékstrəvə̀:rt] n 외향적인 사람, 사교적인 사람 = sociable person
While she is an introvert, her husband is an extrovert.
그녀는 내성적인 반면에 그녀의 남편은 외향적인 사람이다.

exuberant[igzú:bərənt] a 활기 넘치는, 원기 왕성한, 열광적인 = animated = ardent[ά:rdnt]
= ebullient[ibʌ́ljənt] = effervescent[èfərvésnt] = energetic = enthusiastic[inθù:ziǽstik] = passionate
= sprightly[spráitli] = vigorous[vígərəs] = vivacious[vivéiʃəs]
We will visit the exuberant ball park as the final destination.
우리는 마지막 목적지로 활기 넘치는 야구장을 방문합니다.

exult[igzʌ́lt] v 기뻐 날뛰다, 환호하다 = be delighted = be elated = be in high spirits
= be jubilant[dʒú:bələnt] = rejoice[ridʒɔ́is]
She exulted at the news that her son had been accepted to the Harvard Univ..
그녀는 아들이 Harvard대에 합격했다는 소식에 기뻐 날뛰었다.

exultant[igzʌ́ltənt] a 기뻐서 어쩔 줄 모르는, 의기양양한 = delighted = elated
= jubilant[dʒú:bələnt] = overjoyed = rejoicing[ridʒɔ́isiŋ]
He was exultant to hear that his son passed the bar exam.
그는 아들이 사법고시에 합격했다는 소식에 기뻐서 어쩔 줄을 몰랐다.

QUIZ 51

*Match each word in the first column with its definition in the second column.
Check your answers in the back of the book.*

1. exultant
2. exult
3. exuberant
4. extrinsic
5. extrovert
6. extravagant
7. extremity
8. extricate

a. disentangle = emancipate
b. foreign
c. delighted = elated
d. sociable person
e. terminus
f. animated = ardent
g. be delighted = be elated
h. lavish = wasteful

fabricate[fǽbrikèit] v 제작하다, 꾸며내다, 조작하다 = concoct[kankákt]
= contrive[kəntráiv] = counterfeit[káuntərfit] = falsify[fɔ́:lsəfài]
The scientists fabricated the research data to get the fund from the government.
과학자들은 정부 기금을 얻기 위해서 연구자료를 조작했다.

facade[fəsá:d] n 정면, 외관, 겉치레 = appearance = exterior[ikstíəriər] = front
The facade of the department store was decorated with colorful neon lights.
백화점 정면은 외관이 화려한 네온 등불로 장식되었다.

facet[fǽsit] n 측면, 양상, 국면 = aspect[ǽspekt] = surface[sə́:rfis]
The war took on a new facet after the intervention of the UN.
UN의 개입 후에 전쟁은 새로운 양상을 띠었다.

facetious[fəsí:ʃəs] a 익살맞은, 경박한, 까부는 = droll[droul] = farcical[fá:rsikəl]
= humorous[hjú:mərəs] = jocular[dʒákjulər] = ludicrous[lú:dəkrəs]
I think the businessman was facetious in his way of talking at the reception.
사업가는 환영식에서 익살맞게 이야기한 것 같다.

facile[fǽsil] a 수월하게 일하는, 술술 하는, 능란한 = deft = dexterous[dékstərəs] = fluent = skillful
His facile packing skills mean that he spent a lot of time in the delivery job.
그의 능란한 포장기술은 그가 배달 일에 오랫동안 종사했다는 것을 보여준다.

facilitate[fəsílətèit] v 수월하게 하다, 용이하게 하다 = aid[eid] = assist = expedite[ékspədàit]
Robots facilitate the assembly job in the car manufacturing factory.
자동차 생산 공장에서의 로봇들은 조립작업을 수월하게 해준다.

faction[fǽkʃən] n 당파, 파벌 = cabal[kəbǽl] = clique[kli:k]
Two factions in the party are fighting each other for the nominations before the general elections.
당내 두 파벌이 총선 후보자 공천 문제로 싸우고 있다.

fade[feid] v 바래다, 희미해지다, 서서히 사라지다 = disappear = evaporate[ivǽpərèit] = vanish[vǽniʃ]
Their hopes to find the survivors has faded away.
생존자를 찾겠다는 그들의 희망이 서서히 사라졌다.

fallacious[fəléiʃəs] a 허위의, 거짓의, 잘못된 = beguiling[bigáiliŋ] = deceptive[diséptiv]
= delusive[dilú:siv] = fraudulent[frɔ́:dʒulənt] = misleading = spurious[spjúəriəs]
The forced fallacious confession shouldn't be accepted in the court.
강압에 의한 허위 자백이 법정에서 받아들여져선 안 된다.

fallacy[fǽləsi] n 잘못된 생각, 착오, 오류 = falsehood = illusion = untruth = misconception[mɪskənsepʃn]
It is a widespread fallacy that fasting is the best diet.
단식이 최고의 다이어트라는 것은 널리 알려진 잘못된 상식이다.

falter[fɔ́:ltər] v 비틀거리다, 흔들리다, 머뭇거리다 = flounder[fláundər] = lurch[lə:rtʃ] = reel[ri:l] = stagger[stǽgər] = totter[tátər] = wobble[wábl]
His determination to quit smoking has never faltered so far.
금연을 하리라는 그의 결심은 지금까지 전혀 흔들리지 않고 있다.

fanatic[fənǽtik] n 광적인 사람, 광신자, 애호가 = enthusiast[inθú:ziæst] = zealot[zélət]
She is an organic food fanatic. 그녀는 유기농산물 애호가이다.

farce[fa:rs] n 소극, 익살극, 웃음거리 = burlesque[bə:rlésk]
A series of farces were playing in the local theater.
그 지역 극장에서 일련의 소극(笑劇)이 상연되었다.

farcical[fá:rsikəl] a 웃음거리가 된, 소극의, 익살스런 = facetious[fəsí:ʃəs] = droll = humorous[hjú:mərəs] = jocular[dʒákjulər] = ludicrous[lú:dəkrəs]
Their failure in the first round became a farcical event. 그들의 1회전 탈락은 웃음거리가 되었다.

fast[fæst] v 단식하다, 절식하다 = go without food
All Muslims fast during Ramadan. 모든 이슬람교도들은 라마단 기간 중에 단식을 한다.

fastidious[fæstídiəs] a 성미가 까다로운, 꼼꼼한 = demanding = exacting = finicky = meticulous[mətíkjuləs] = picky = punctilious[pʌŋktíliəs]
The designer is very fastidious about the quality of the fabric.
디자이너는 직물의 품질에 대해 매우 까다롭다.

fathom[fǽðəm] v 헤아리다, 가늠하다, 추측하다 = comprehend[kàmprihénd] = discern[disə́:rn] = figure out = plumb = understand
It is hard to fathom what will happen to the mankind in 100 years.
100년 후 인류에게 어떤 일이 일어날지 가늠하기는 어렵다.

fatuous[fǽtʃuəs] a 어리석은, 바보 같은, 어수룩한 = asinine[ǽsənàin] = daft = inane[inéin] = vacuous[vǽkjuəs]
The fatuous measures taken by the city government made the flood disaster worse.
시 정부에서 취한 어리석은 조치들이 홍수로 인한 재난을 악화시켰다.

faux[fou] a 모조의, 가짜의 = artificial[à:rtəfíʃəl] = counterfeit[káuntərfit] = ersatz[έərza:ts] = fabricated = factitious[fæktíʃəs] = fake = false = imitation = spurious[spjúəriəs]
She was wearing a faux diamond ring. 그녀는 모조 다이아몬드 반지를 끼고 있었다.

fawn[fɔːn] v 비위 맞추다, 알랑거리다, 아양떨다 = apple-polish = be servile = bootlick[búːtlìk] = flatter = genuflect[dʒénjuflèkt] = grovel[grʌvəl] = ingratiate[ingréiʃièit] = kowtow[káutáu] = toady[tóudi]
Most subjects fawned over the strong monarch.
대부분의 신하들은 그 강력한 군주의 비위를 맞추었다.

QUIZ 52

*Match each word in the first column with its definition in the second column.
Check your answers in the back of the book.*

1.	faux	a.	disappear = evaporate
2.	façade	b.	apple-polish = be servile
3.	fawn	c.	artificial = counterfeit
4.	farcical	d.	beguiling = deceptive
5.	fastidious	e.	demanding = exacting
6.	facilitate	f.	concoct = contrive
7.	farce	g.	enthusiast = zealot
8.	fade	h.	facetious = droll
9.	fallacious	i.	flounder = lurch
10.	fallacy	j.	asinine = daft
11.	falter	k.	aspect = surface
12.	fanatic	l.	burlesque
13.	fabricate	m.	falsehood = illusion
14.	facetious	n.	go without food
15.	fast	o.	cabal = clique
16.	faction	p.	comprehend = discern
17.	facile	q.	droll = farcical
18.	fatuous	r.	appearance = exterior
19.	facet	s.	aid = assist
20.		t.	

faze[feiz] v 당황시키다, 곤란하게 하다 = embarrass = confound = dismay = dumbfound[dʌmfáund] = nonplus
He was fazed by the news that his son had been injured in the car accident.
그의 아들이 교통사고로 다쳤다는 뉴스에 그는 당황했다.

feckless[féklis] a 무기력한, 무능한, 무책임한 = feeble = incompetent[inkámpətənt]
He is considered too feckless to take responsibility for the entire project.t
그는 전체 프로젝트를 책임지기에는 능력이 모자란다고 생각된다.

fecund[fíkənd] a 비옥한, 다산성의, 창조력이 풍부한 = fertile[fə́:rtl] = productive = prolific[prəlífik]
Three tribes waged fierce wars each other to take the fecund land along the river.
세 부족은 강 유역의 비옥한 토지를 차지하기 위해 치열하게 싸웠다.

feign[fein] v 가장하다, 인척하다 = camouflage[kǽməflà:ʒ] = dissemble[disémbl]
= dissimulate[disímjulèit] = pretend
He could dodge the forcible conscription by feigning sickness during the colonial days.
그는 식민지 치하에서 아픈 사람인 척 가장하여 강제징집을 피했다.

felicity[filísəti] n 더할 나위 없는 행복, 적절함 = bliss = euphoria[ju:fɔ́:riə]
= exhilaration[igzìləréiʃən] = happiness = joviality[dʒòuviǽləti] = jubilation[dʒù:bəléiʃən]
= mirth[mə:r] = rapture[rǽptʃər]
The winning in the World Cup brought much felicity to the soccer fans.
월드컵 우승은 축구 팬들에게 더할 나위 없는 행복을 안겨주었다.

fervid[fə́:rvid] a 열렬한, 열정적인 = ardent[ɑ́:rdnt] = passionate[pǽʃənət]
Peter is a fervid fan of LA Dodgers. Peter는 LA 다저스의 열렬한 팬이다.

fervor[fə́:rvər] n 열렬, 진지, 열정 = ardor[ɑ́:rdər] = enthusiasm[inθú:ziæzm] = passion
= vehemence[ví:əməns] = zeal
He drew the paintings with fervor to prepare for his first exhibition.
그는 첫 번째 전시회를 준비하기 위해 열정적으로 그림을 그렸다.

fester[féstər] v 곪다, 곪아 터지다, 심해지다 = become inflamed = decay[dikéi] = rot
We should not let the factional conflict in our party fester.
우리는 당내에서 계파간 갈등이 곪아터지게 해서는 안 된다.

fetid[fétid] a 악취가 나는, 냄새가 고약한 = putrid[pjú:trid] = rancid[rǽnsid] = smelly = stinking
We can't tolerate the fetid odor from the contaminated river any longer.
우리는 오염된 강에서 나는 악취를 더 이상 참지 못한다.

fetish[fétiʃ] n 집착, 고집 = obsession[əbséʃən]
My weak grandmother has a fetish about health supplement food.
몸이 허약한 나의 할머니는 건강보조제에 집착한다.

fetter[fétər] v 속박하다, 구속하다 = bind[baind] = confine = curb = encumber[inkʌ́mbər] = hamper = hinder = leash[li:ʃ] = shackle[ʃǽkl]
They were fettered by the get-rich-quick schemes.
그들은 벼락부자가 될 것이라는 계획에 사로잡혀 있다.

fiasco[fiǽskou] n 대 실패, 완패 = blunder[blʌ́ndər] = debacle[deibá:kl] = failure[féiljər]
Their plan to build a city on the Mars ended in fiasco.
화성에 도시를 건설하겠다는 그들의 계획은 대 실패로 끝났다.

fiat[fí:a:t] n 명령, 포고, 지시 = decree[dikrí:] = edict[í:dikt] = order = ordinance[ɔ́:rdənəns]
He was sent to a prison by the fiat. 그는 명령에 의해 감옥에 보내졌다.

fickle[fíkl] a 변덕스러운, 마음이 잘 변하는 = capricious[kəpríʃəs] = erratic[irǽtik] = flighty = mercurial[mərkjúəriəl] = mutable[mjú:təbl] = temperamental[tèmpərəméntl] = whimsical[hwímzikəl]
The fickle weather will continue until May in this area.
이 지역의 변덕스러운 날씨는 5월까지 계속될 것이다.

fidget[fídʒit] v 안절부절못하다, 조바심 내다, 초조해하다 = fret[fret] = jitter[dʒítər]
He started to fidget when his son was carried to the operating room.
그는 아들이 수술실로 실려갔을 때 초조해하기 시작했다.

figment[fígmənt] n 허구, 꾸며낸 것, 공상 = fabrication[fæbrikéiʃən] = falsehood = fiction
Dragon is an imaginary animal, a figment of our imagination.
용은 상상 속의 동물, 우리의 상상으로 꾸며낸 동물이다.

fidelity[fidéləti] n 충실함, 충성, 절개, 신의 = allegiance[əlí:dʒəns] = constancy[kánstənsi] = devotion[divóuʃən] = loyalty
The seven knights swore their fidelity to their king before going to the battle.
칠인의 기사는 전투에 나가기 전에 왕에게 충성을 맹세했다.

figurative[fígjurətiv] a 비유적인, 은유적인 = metaphorical[mètəfɔ́:rikəl]
He used a lot of figurative expressions in his poetry.
그는 자신의 시에 많은 비유적 표현을 사용했다.

filibuster[fíləbʌstər] n 의사진행 방해 = hindrance[híndrəns] = obstruction[əbstrʌ́kʃən] of progress
A few democrats used filibusters to stop the law from passing.
몇몇 민주당원들은 그 법이 통과되지 못하도록 의사진행을 방해했다.

finesse[finés] n 책략, 수완, 재간 = artifice =gimmick[gímik] = guile[gail] = ruse[ru:z]
= tact[tækt]

The new manager showed exceptional finesse in the wage negotiation with the union leaders.
신임 매니저는 노조 지도자와의 임금협상에서 놀라운 수완을 보여주었다.

QUIZ 53

Match each word in the first column with its definition in the second column.
Check your answers in the back of the book.

1.	filibuster	a.	Obsession
2.	fetid	b.	camouflage = dissemble
3.	fidelity	c.	bliss = euphoria
4.	feign	d.	feeble = incompetent
5.	felicity	e.	bind = confine
6.	finesse	f.	hindrance = obstruction
7.	fervor	g.	ardent = passionate
8.	fickle	h.	blunder = debacle
9.	feckless	i.	embarrass = confound
10.	faze	j.	Metaphorical
11.	fetter	k.	ardor = enthusiasm
12.	fiasco	l.	fertile = productive
13.	fiat	m.	capricious = erratic
14.	fetish	n.	decree = edict
15.	fidget	o.	allegiance = constancy
16.	figment	p.	artifice = gimmick
17.	fester	q.	become inflamed = decay
18.	figurative	r.	putrid = rancid
19.	fecund	s.	fabrication = falsehood
20.	fervid	t.	fret = jitter

---

flaccid[flǽksid] a 늘어진, 무른, 무기력한 = drooping[drú:piŋ] = slack[slæk]

The old man we met on the island had flaccid skins on his face.
우리가 섬에서 만난 노인은 얼굴 피부가 축 늘어져 있었다.

flagrant[fléigrənt] a 악명 높은, 파렴치한, 노골적인 = atrocious[ətróuʃəs] = brazen[bréizn]
= egregious[igrí:dʒəs] = heinous[héinəs] = nefarious[nifɛ́əriəs] = notorious[noutɔ́:riəs]

The bombardment on the civilian targets is a flagrant breach of the truce agreement.
민간인을 목표로 포격하는 것은 파렴치한 휴전협정 위반이다.

flatter[flǽtər] v 아첨하다, 알랑거리다, 빌붙다 = adulate[ǽdʒəlèit] = apple-polish = be servile[sə́ːrvil] = blandish[blǽndiʃ] = bootlick[búːtlìk] = fawn = genuflect[dʒénjuflèkt] = grovel[grʌ́vəl] = ingratiate[ingréiʃièit] = kowtow[káutáu] = toady[tóudi]
Some managers flattered their president about the speech he made during the shareholder's meeting.
일부 매니저들은 주주총회 기간에 사장이 한 연설에 대해서 잘했다고 아첨을 했다.

flaunt[flɔːnt] v 과시하다, 뽐내다 = boast = brag = gasconade[gæskənéid] = show off = vaunt[vɔːnt]
He was flaunting his wealth at the car dealership.
그는 자동차 판매 대리점에서 자기의 부를 과시했다.

flavor[fléivər] n 맛, 풍미, 향미 = relish[réliʃ] = savor[séivər]
This seaweed powder will add a fresh flavor to the soup.
이 김가루는 수프에 신선한 풍미를 더해줄 것이다.

flaw[flɔː] n 결점, 결함, 흠 = blemish[blémiʃ] = defect[díːfekt] = fault[fɔːlt] = foible[fɔ́ibl] = glitch[glitʃ] = imperfection[impərfékʃən]
My boss pointed out some flaws in my presentation.
사장님은 나의 프레젠테이션에서 몇 가지 결점을 지적했다.

fledgling[flédʒliŋ] a 경험이 없는, 미숙한 = budding[bʌ́diŋ] = burgeoning[bə́ːrdʒəniŋ] = developing = embryonic[èmbriánik] = germinating[dʒə́ːrmənèitiŋ] = incipient[insípiənt] = nascent[nǽsnt] = sprouting[sprautiŋ]
He was giving business advice to the fledgling venture companies.
그는 경험이 없는 벤처회사에 조언을 해주고 있었다.

fleet[fliːt] a 빠른, 급속히 움직이는 = rapid = speedy
The tourists transferred from the train to the fleet plane.
관광객들은 기차에서 빠르게 움직이는 비행기로 옮겨 탔다.

flinch[flintʃ] v 주춤하다, 움찔하다, 물러서다 = cower[káuər] = cringe[krindʒ] = recoil = wince[wins]
The playful puppies flinched away from a snake.
장난스런 강아지는 뱀으로부터 움찔하고 물러섰다.

flippant[flípənt] a 경박한, 건방진 = frivolous[frívələs] = harebrained[héərbrèind] = irreverent[irévərənt]
He failed the interview because of his flippant attitude and tone.
그는 경박한 태도와 억양 때문에 면접에서 떨어졌다.

165

flirt[flə:rt] v 장난 삼아 해보다, 집적거리다 = banter[bǽntər] = coquet[koukét]
He flirted with the thought of crossing the Pacific ocean in a yacht.
그는 요트를 타고 태평양을 건너볼까 하는 생각을 장난 삼아 해보았다.

flit[flit] v 휙 움직이다, 경쾌하게 돌아다니다 = fleet[fli:t]
In the future there will be many spaceships flitting from planet to planet.
미래에서는 우주선들이 행성과 행성 사이를 훨훨 날아다닐 것이다.

florid[flɔ́:rid] a 화려한, 현란한 = decorative = elaborate = embellished[imbéliʃd]
= flamboyant[flæmbɔ́iənt] = garnished[gá:rniʃd] = ornate[ɔ:rnéit]
The creditors denounced his presentation as a set of florid language.
채권자들은 그의 발표를 한 세트의 화려한 말잔치라고 비난했다.

flounder[fláundər] v 버둥거리다, 허둥대다 = struggle[strʌgl] = stumble[stʌmbl] = wallow[wálou]
The lost explorers were floundering in the deep snow in the mountain.
길 잃은 탐험가들은 그 산의 깊은 눈 속에서 허둥대고 있었다.

flout[flaut] v 어기다, 멸시하다, 무시하다 = affront = deride[diráid] = disregard
= gibe[dʒaib] = insult = jeer = laughat = mock = ridicule = scoff[skɔ:f] = scorn[skɔ:rn]
= sneer[sniər] = spurn[spə:rn] = taunt[tɔ:nt]
The newcomer was accused of flouting the rules in the dorm.
신입생은 기숙사 규정을 어겨서 비난받았다.

foible[fɔ́ibl] n 사소한 약점, 결점 = frailty[fréilti] = shortcoming = weakness
He is trying to make up for his own foibles. 그는 사소한 약점을 보완하려 노력한다.

fodder[fádər] n 꼴, 사료 = animal feed
He was feeding fodder to his cattle. 그는 가축들에게 사료를 먹이고 있었다.

foment[foumént] v 유발하다, 선동하다, 조장하다 = abet[əbét] = agitate[ǽdʒitèit]
=goad = incite = instigate[ínstəgèit] = spur = stimulate = stir[stə:r] up
The demagogue was arrested on charge of fomenting a rebellion.
선동 정치가는 반란을 선동한다는 혐의로 체포되었다.

foot-dragging[fútdrægiŋ] n 지체, 주저, 더딤 = deterrent[ditə́:rənt]
= impediment[impédəmənt] = obstacle[ábstəkl] = stumbling block
The city government's foot-dragging in dealing with the disaster made the situation worse.
시 정부가 그 재해를 제때 처리하지 못하는 바람에 상황이 더 어렵게 되었다.

footloose[fʊtluːs] **a** 어디든지 갈 수 있는, 마음대로의, 자유분방한 = free = unattached
He was still footloose and fancy-free, staying single.
그는 어디든지 갈 수 있는 자유분방한 독신이다.

forbear[fɔːrbɛ́ər] **v** 삼가다, 억제하다, 참다 = abstain = avoid = curb = desist[dizíst]
= eschew[istʃúː] = evade[ivéid] = refrain = restrain = withhold
She forbore from making complaints about the poor service in the restaurant.
그녀는 수준 낮은 식당의 서비스에 대해 불평하는 것을 삼갔다.

QUIZ 54

Match each word in the first column with its definition in the second column.
Check your answers in the back of the book.

1.	footloose	a.	frailty = shortcoming
2.	flagrant	b.	drooping = slack
3.	foment	c.	free = unattached
4.	flaunt	d.	atrocious = brazen
5.	foible	e.	adulate = apple-polish
6.	fledgling	f.	struggle = stumble
7.	flaccid	g.	animal feed
8.	forbear	h.	boast = brag
9.	flippant	i.	blemish = defect
10.	fleet	j.	affront = deride
11.	flit	k.	decorative = elaborate
12.	florid	l.	deterrent = impediment
13.	fodder	m.	budding = burgeoning
14.	flout	n.	rapid = speedy
15.	flinch	o.	cower = cringe
16.	flirt	p.	abet = agitate
17.	flaw	q.	frivolous = harebrained
18.	foot-dragging	r.	rapid = speedy
19.	flatter	s.	banter = coquet
20.	flounder	t.	abstain = avoid

---

forgo[fɔːrgóu] **v** 그만두다, 포기하다 = abandon = abdicate[ǽbdəkèit] = abstain[æbstéin]
= eschew[istʃúː]= forsake[fərséik] = relinquish[rilíŋkwiʃ] = renounce[rináuns] = waive[weiv]
= do without
He forwent the pleasure of going to sauna every day. 그는 매일 사우나 가는 재미를 포기했다.

forsake[fərséik] v 저버리다, 그만두다 = abandon = abdicate[ǽbdəkèit] = desert[dézərt] = relinquish[rilíŋkwiʃ] = renounce[rináuns]
He forsook the hectic days in the city and went to the countryside to go back to farming.
그는 도시의 바쁜 생활을 접고 시골로 가서 다시 농업에 종사했다.

forthright[fɔ́:rθrait] a 솔직한, 똑바른 = candid = outspoken = straightforward
The manager was forthright in the assessment of the employee's performance.
매니저는 종업원 업무평가를 올바르게 했다.

fortuitous[fɔ:rtjú:ətəs] a 우발성의, 우연한, 행운의 = accidental[æksədéntl] = fluky[flú:ki] = inadvertent[ìnədvə́:rtnt] = incidental = serendipitous[sèrəndípətəs] = unexpected = unintentional
Their fortuitous encounter led to the marriage. 그들의 우연한 만남은 결혼으로 이어졌다.

foster[fɔ́:stər] v 촉진하다, 조장하다, 육성하다 = foment[foumént] = promote
Many voters expect the new party leader to foster political reforms.
많은 유권자들은 새로운 정당 지도자가 정치 개혁을 촉진하리라 기대한다.

founder[fáundər] v 실패하다, 무너지다, 가라앉다 = break down = collapse[kəlǽps] = fall through = stumble[stʌmbl]
The luxurious cruise ship foundered in the ocean on her maiden voyage.
호화 유람선은 처녀 항해에서 바다에 가라앉았다.

fragmentary[frǽgməntèri] a 단편적인, 부분적인, 조각조각의 = broken = incomplete = scattered = sketchy
You can't solve this problem with fragmentary knowledge on the computer.
우리는 컴퓨터에 대한 단편적인 지식만 가지고는 이 문제를 풀 수 없다.

fraternal[frətə́:rnl] a 우애의, 형제의, 공제의 = brotherly[brʌ́ðərli]
We could feel their fraternal love while we stayed in their house.
우리는 그들의 집에 머무는 동안 그들의 형제애를 느꼈다.

frenetic[frənétik] a 정신 없이 바쁘게 돌아가는, 제정신이 아닌, 열광적인 = delirious[dilíəriəs] = distraught[distrɔ́:t] = frantic = frenzied[frénzid]
She was working in the market of frenetic activity.
그녀는 정신 없이 바쁘게 돌아가는 시장에서 일하고 있었다.

frenzy[frénzi] n 열광, 광란, 격분 = craze = furor[fjúərɔːr] = passion
His incendiary speech drove the large crowd into frenzy.
그의 선동적인 연설은 수많은 군중들을 열광시켰다.

friable[fráiəbl] a 무른, 깨지기 쉬운 = breakable[bréikəbl] = brittle[brítl]
= crumbly[krʌmbli] = fragile[frǽdʒəl]
You should not set up a tent on a friable rock.
깨지기 쉬운 무른 바위 위에 텐트를 설치해선 안 된다.

frigid[frídʒid] a 몹시 찬, 냉담한, 쌀쌀맞은 = extremely cold = freezing
The immigrants had to get used to a frigid climate.
이민자들은 몹시 추운 날씨에 적응해야만 했다.

frivolity[frivάləti] n 경박, 경솔, 천박함 = flippancy[flípənsi] = levity[lévəti]
His frivolity during the business meeting asked for trouble.
사업회의 중 보여준 그의 경박함이 문제를 자초했다.

frugal[frúːgəl] a 검소한, 절약하는, 인색한 = economical[èkənάmikəl]
= provident[prάvədənt] = prudent[prúːdnt] = thrifty[θrífti]
He has lived a frugal life. 그는 검소한 삶을 살았다.

frustrate[frʌstreit] v 좌절시키다, 훼방 놓다, 망치다 = baffle = depress
= discourage[diskə́ːridʒ] – disappoint = dishearten = thwart[θwɔːrt]
The loss of eyesight in the accident frustrated his dream of being a designer.
사고로 시력을 잃음으로써 디자이너가 되겠다는 그의 꿈은 좌절되었다.

fulminate[fʌlmənèit] v 격렬하게 비난하다, 맹렬히 비판하다 = berate[biréit]
= castigate[kǽstəgèit] = censure[sénʃər] = chastise[tʃæstáiz] = condemn[kəndém]
= criticize harshly = decry = denounce[dináuns] = excoriate[ikskɔ́ːrièit] = execrate[éksəkrèit]
= lambaste[læmbéist] = lash = rebuke[ribjúːk] = reprimand[réprəmænd] = reproach[ripróutʃ]
= reprove = revile[riváil] = scold = upbraid = vilify[víləfài] = vituperate[vaitjúːpərèit]
All nations fulminated against the massacre of innocent people by suicide bombing.
모든 국가들은 자살폭탄에 의한 대량의 민간인 학살에 대해 맹렬히 비판했다.

fulsome[fúlsəm] a (칭찬, 사과 등이) 지나친, 진실성이 안 느껴지는
= adulatory[ǽdʒulətɔːri] = fawning[fɔ́ːniŋ] = flattering = ingratiating[ingréiʃièitiŋ]
Unfounded praise or fulsome compliments should be avoided in communication with others.
타인과 소통을 할 때는 근거 없는 칭찬이나 지나친 찬사를 피해야 한다.

furtive[fə́:rtiv] a 은밀한, 엉큼한, 수상쩍은 = clandestine[klændéstin] = covert[kóuvərt]
= insidious[insídiəs] = secretive[sí:kritiv] = sly[slai] = sneaky = stealthy[stélθi]
= surreptitious[sə̀:rəptíʃəs]
The master succumbed to the furtive temptation of the maid.
주인은 하녀의 은밀한 유혹에 빠졌다. succumb[səkʌ́m] v 굴복하다

fuss[fʌs] n 호들갑, 야단법석, 소란 = commotion[kəmóuʃən] = disturbance[distə́:rbəns]
= ruckus[rʌ́kəs]
My neighbors made a fuss about the appearance of the wild raccoon in our area.
내 이웃들은 마을에 나타난 야생 너구리 때문에 야단법석을 떨었다.

QUIZ 55

Match each word in the first column with its definition in the second column.
Check your answers in the back of the book.

1.	forgo	a.	broken = incomplete
2.	fuss	b.	brotherly
3.	forthright	c.	foment = promote
4.	foster	d.	baffle = depress
5.	fulminate	e.	break down = collapse
6.	founder	f.	berate = castigate
7.	fragmentary	g.	delirious = distraught
8.	friable	h.	flippancy = levity
9.	frenetic	i.	accidental = fluky
10.	frigid	j.	clandestine = covert
11.	frivolity	k.	candid = outspoken
12.	fraternal	l.	extremely cold = freezing
13.	frenzy	m.	adulatory = fawning
14.	frustrate	n.	commotion = disturbance
15.	forsake	o.	abandon = abdicate
16.	fulsome	p.	abandon = abdicate
17.	furtive	q.	breakable = brittle
18.	fortuitous	r.	craze = furor

gaffe[gæf] n 실수, 결례 = blooper[blú:pər] = blunder[blʌ́ndər] = goof[gu:f]
= indiscretion[ìndiskréʃən] = mistake
She made a gaffe in the party. 그녀는 파티에서 결례를 했다.

gainsay[géinsèi] v 부정하다, 반대하다 = deny[dinái] = negate[nigéit] = repudiate[ripjú:dièit]
The actor didn't gainsay the rumor that he had smoked marihuana in his 20s.
그 배우는 이십대 때 마리화나를 피웠다는 소문을 부정하지 않았다.

gait[geit] n 걸음걸이, 보조 = walk
Soldiers in the parade walked with a majestic gait.
퍼레이드에 참가한 군인들은 위엄 있는 걸음걸이로 걸었다.

gall[gɔ:l] v (피부) 쓸리게 하다, 화나게 하다 = exasperate[igzǽspərèit] = irritate[írətèit]
= peeve[pi:v] = rile[rail] = upset
His rude manners galled everyone in the wedding reception.
그의 무례한 태도가 결혼피로연에 참가한 모든 사람들을 화나게 했다.

galvanize[gǽlvənàiz] v 자극하다, 격려하다, 북돋우다 = arouse[əráuz]
= inspire[inspáiər] = invigorate[invígərèit] = motivate[móutəvèit] = spur[spə:r]
= stimulate[stímjulèit] = stir[stə:r]
The slim models on TV galvanized her into diet.
그녀는 TV 속의 날씬한 모델들에게 자극을 받아 다이어트를 시작했다.

gambit[gǽmbit] n 수, 계략 = artifice[á:rtəfis] = gimmick[gímik]
= maneuver[mənú:vər] = plot = ploy[plɔi] = ruse[ru:z]
The coach played a bold gambit in the match. 코치는 경기에서 대담한 수를 사용했다.

gamut[gǽmət] n 전체, 전반, 전 영역 = range[reindʒ] = spectrum[spéktrəm]
The class will run the entire gamut of Chinese history. 이 수업은 중국역사 전체를 다룰 것이다.

garble[gá:rbl] v 왜곡하다, 혼동하다 = distort[distɔ́:rt] = pervert[pərvə́:rt] = warp[wɔ:rp]
No country is supposed to garble history. 어떠한 국가도 역사를 왜곡해서는 안 된다.

gargantuan[ga:rgǽntʃuən] a 거대한, 엄청난 = colossal[kəlásəl]
= enormous[inɔ́:rməs] = gigantic[dʒaigǽntik] = huge = humongous[hju:mʌ́ŋgəs]
= immense[iméns] = massive = prodigious[prədídʒəs] = tremendous[triméndəs] = vast[væst]
The tourists were amazed at the sight of the gargantuan waterfall.
관광객들은 거대한 폭포의 모습을 보고 놀랐다.

garish[gέəriʃ] a 화려한, 지나치게 꾸민 = flashy[flǽʃi] = gaudy[gɔ́:di]
= glittering[glítəriŋ] = ornate[ɔ:rnéit] = ostentatious[àstəntéiʃəs] = showy[ʃóui] = tawdry[tɔ́:dri]
Some singers enjoy wearing garish clothes on the stage.
어떤 가수들은 지나치게 화려한 옷을 입는 것을 즐긴다.

garner[gá:rnər] v 저장하다, 축적하다, 모으다 = accumulate[əkjú:mjulèit]
= amass[əmǽs] = collect = hoard[hɔ:rd] = stockpile
The farmer garners his crops in the storage. 농부는 곡식을 창고에 저장한다.

garrulous[gǽrələs] a 수다스러운, 잘 지껄이는 = loquacious[loukwéiʃəs]
= talkative[tɔ́:kətiv] = verbose[və:rbóus] = wordy[wə́:rdi]
The three ladies were very garrulous during the fashion show.
패션쇼 동안 세 명의 여인들은 매우 수다스러웠다.

gash[gæʃ] n 큰 상처, 깊은 상처 = slash[slæʃ]
The fight with buffalo made a deep gash on the left leg of the female lion.
물소와의 싸움에서 암사자는 왼쪽 다리에 큰 상처를 입었다.

gastronomy[gæstránəmi] n 미식법, 미식학, 요리법 = cuisine[kwizí:n]
The Korean chef has learned Chinese gastronomy in Beijing.
그 한국인 요리사는 북경에서 중국식 요리법을 배웠다.

generic[dʒənérik] a 일반 명칭의, 포괄적인 = common = universal[jù:nəvə́:rsəl]
Most convenience stores sell generic medicine.
대부분의 편의점에서 상표명이 없는 일반약을 판매한다.

genesis[dʒénəsis] n 기원, 발생, 유래 = inception[insépʃən] = origin = provenance[právənəns]
No scientists have explained for sure the genesis of the solar system yet.
아직까지 어떤 과학자도 태양계의 기원에 대해 확실하게 설명하지 못하고 있다.

genial[dʒí:njəl] a 친절한, 다정한, 온난한 = affable[ǽfəbl] = amiable[éimiəbl]
= gracious[gréiʃəs] = jolly[dʒáli] = jovial[dʒóuviəl] = upbeat[Λpbì:t]
The female owner of the restaurant has a genial smile.
식당 여주인은 상냥한 미소를 띠고 있다.

genocide[dʒénəsàid] n 대량 학살, 집단 학살 = carnage[ká:rnidʒ]
= holocaust[háləkɔ̀:st] = mass murder = massacre[mǽsəkər] = slaughter[slɔ́:tər]
The occupying forces committed genocide of innocent citizens.
점령군들은 무고한 시민들을 대량 학살했다.

genteel[dʒentíːl] a 과장되게 고상한, 상류층의 = civilized[sívəlàizd]
= cultivated[kʌltəvèitid] = polished[páliʃt] = refined[rifáind]
Her genteel smile and gestures mean that she might be from rich family.
고상한 웃음과 제스처는 그녀가 부유한 집안 출신일 수도 있다는 것을 의미한다.

germane[dʒərméin] a 밀접한 관련이 있는, 적절한 = applicable[ǽplikəbl]
= apropos[æprəpóu] = apposite[ǽpəzit] = appropriate[əpróupriət] = felicitous[filísətəs]
= opportune[àpərtjúːn] = pertinent[pə́ːrtənənt] = relevant[réləvənt] = suitable[súːtəbl]
The detectives found decisive evidence germane to the crimes of the suspect.
형사들은 피의자의 범죄와 밀접한 관련이 있는 결정적 증거를 찾았다.

QUIZ 56

Match each word in the first column with its definition in the second column.
Check your answers in the back of the book.

1.	genteel		a.	distort = pervert
2.	genial		b.	accumulate = amass
3.	gait		c.	cuisine
4.	generic		d.	range = spectrum
5.	galvanize		e.	common = universal
6.	gambit		f.	flashy = gaudy
7.	garrulous		g.	colossal = enormous
8.	garble		h.	affable = amicable
9.	gaffe		i.	artifice = gimmick
10.	garish		j.	civilized = cultivated
11.	garner		k.	arouse = inspire
12.	germane		l.	inception = origin
13.	gash gall		m.	exasperate = irritate
14.	gastronomy		n.	carnage = holocaust
15.	gainsay		o.	slash
16.	genesis		p.	deny = negate
17.	gash		q.	walk
18.	genocide		r.	blooper = blunder
19.	gamut		s.	applicable = apropos
20.	gargantuan		t.	loquacious = talkative

gesticulate[dʒestíkjulèit] v 몸짓(손짓)으로 가리키다, 몸짓으로 이야기하다
= gesture[dʒéstʃər] = signal[sígnəl]
The castaway gesticulated wildly towards the rescue workers.
조난자는 구조대원들에게 미친 듯이 손짓을 했다.

ghastly[gǽstli] a 무시무시한, 지독한, 섬뜩한 = appalling[əpɔ́:liŋ] = dreadful[drédfəl]
= frightening[fráitniŋ] = grisly[grízli] = gruesome[grú:səm] = hideous[hídiəs]
= horrendous[hɔ:réndəs] = horrible = horrid[hɔ́:rid] = horrifying[hɔ́:rəfàiiŋ] = lurid[lúərid]
= macabre[məkɑ́:brə] = terrifying[térəfàiŋ]
We have recently heard ghastly crimes on the news.
우리는 최근 들어 뉴스에서 무시무시한 범죄 소식을 듣는다.

gibberish[dʒíbəriʃ] n 횡설수설, 지껄여대는 뜻 모를 말 = babble[bǽbl] = drivel[drívəl]
= jabber[dʒǽbər] = prattle[prǽtl]
Some drunken men were talking gibberish on the street.
술 취한 사람 몇 명이 길에서 횡설수설하고 있었다.

gibe[dʒaib] v 조롱하다, 우롱하다 = deride[diráid] = dis = disrespect = flout[flaut]
= jeer[dʒiər] = mock[mak] = ridicule[rídikjù:l] = scoff[skɔ:f] = scorn[skɔ:rn] = sneer[sniər]
= taunt[tɔ:nt]
You should not gibe at those who failed the test.
테스트에 떨어진 사람들을 조롱해서는 안 된다.

glaze[gleiz] v 광택제를 바르다, 윤을 내다 = burnish[bə́:rniʃ] = furbish[fə́:rbiʃ]
= lacquer[lǽkər] = varnish[vɑ́:rniʃ]
After cutting the details of the furniture, the craftsman glaze it.
세부적으로 손질을 하고 나서 장인은 가구에 광택제를 발랐다.

glib[glib] a 입심 좋은, 말 잘하는 = garrulous[gǽrələs] = loquacious[loukwéiʃəs] = slick[slik]
The glib salesperson talked the homemaker into buying the unnecessary camera.
입심 좋은 영업사원은 가정주부를 설득해 불필요한 카메라를 사게 했다.

gloat[glout] v 고소해하다, 흡족해하다, 만족스럽게 바라보다
The president gloated over the well-organized parade of the soldiers.
대통령은 군사들이 펼치는 잘 조직된 퍼레이드를 만족스럽게 바라봤다.

glossy[glɑ́si] a 윤이 나는, 반들반들한 = gleaming[gli:miŋ] = glistening[glísniŋ]
= lustrous[lʌ́strəs] = shiny
All the girls in the mountain village had innocent eyes and glossy hair.
산속 마을의 모든 소녀들이 순진한 눈동자와 윤이 나는 머릿결을 가지고 있었다.

glut[glʌt] n 공급 과잉, 포식 = overabundance = surfeit[sə́:rfit] = surplus
A glut of tomatoes has lowered its price. 토마토 과다 공급이 토마토 가격을 떨어뜨렸다.

gobble[gábl] v 급하게 먹다, 게걸스럽게 먹어치우다 = devour[diváuər] = gorge[gɔːrdʒ] = gulp[gʌlp] = guzzle[gʌzl] = ingurgitate[ingəˊːrdʒitèit]
The two escapees gobbled all the foods in the kitchen of a farmhouse.
두 명의 도망자들은 농가의 부엌에서 모든 음식을 게걸스럽게 먹어치웠다.

gorge[gɔːrdʒ] v 게걸스럽게 먹다, 삼키다 = devour[diváuər] = gobble[gábl] = gulp[gʌlp] = guzzle[gʌzl] = ingurgitate[ingəˊːrdʒitèit]
The amateur wrestlers gorged themselves on the grilled pork after a hard training.
아마추어 레슬러들은 힘든 훈련을 마친 뒤에 구운 돼지고기를 게걸스럽게 먹었다.

gouge[gaudʒ] n 둥근 끌 = scoop
The carpenter used a gouge to make a few holes on the door.
목수는 둥근 끌을 써서 문 위에 몇 개의 구멍을 뚫었다.

gourmet[gúərmei] n 미식가, 식도락가 = epicure[épikjùər]
The gourmet contributes an article on local foods to the food magazine.
그 미식가는 지역 음식에 관한 기사를 음식 관련 잡지에 기고하고 있다.

gossamer[gásəmər] a 얇고 가벼운, 섬세한 = gauzy[gɔˊːzi] = thin
The bride was wearing a wedding veil of gossamer silk.
그 신부는 얇고 가벼운 비단으로 만든 신부 베일을 쓰고 있었다.

grandeur[grǽndʒər] n 위엄, 위풍, 장관 = dignity[dígnəti] = grandiosity[græ̀ndiásəti] = magnificence[mægnífəsns] = majesty[mǽdʒəsti]
The general had the grandeur that all of the soldiers followed him.
그 장군은 모든 군사들이 따를 만한 위엄을 가졌다.

grandiloquent[mægnífəsns] a 허풍 떠는, 과장된 = bombastic[bambǽstik] = pompous[pámpəs]
He failed to get a job because of his grandiloquent way of speaking during the job interview.
그는 구직 면접에서의 과장된 말투 때문에 직장을 얻는 데 실패했다.

grandiose[grǽndiòus] a 웅장한, 장엄한 = imposing[impóuziŋ] = magnificent[mægnífəsnt]
The emperor stuck to his grandiose plan of building the Great Wall.
황제는 만리장성을 짓겠다는 웅장한 계획에 매달렸다.

gratify[grǽtəfài] v 만족시키다, 기쁘게 하다 = delight[diláit] = please = satisfy[sǽtisfài]
Her son's admission to Harvard Uni. gratified her pride.
아들의 하버드대 입학은 그녀의 자존심을 만족시켜줬다.

gratis[grǽtis] a 무료로, 거저의 = complimentary[kàmpləméntəri] = free = for nothing
= gratuitous[grətjúːətəs]
Some musically gifted children were being educated gratis in the music school.
몇몇 음악 영재들은 음악학교에서 무료로 교육받고 있다.

QUIZ 57

*Match each word in the first column with its definition in the second column.
Check your answers in the back of the book.*

1.	gesticulate	a.	garrulous = loquacious
2.	gouge	b.	immature = inexperienced
3.	green	c.	complimentary = costless
4.	gratuitous	d.	babble = drivel
5.	gossamer	e.	gauzy = thin
6.	ghastly	f.	dignity = grandiosity
7.	glossy	g.	gleaming = glistening
8.	gibberish	h.	imposing = magnificent
9.	gobble	i.	appalling = dreadful
10.	gorge	j.	bombastic = pompous
11.	gratify	k.	overabundance = surfeit
12.	gourmet	l.	delight = please
13.	glib	m.	gesture = signal
14.	grandeur	n.	epicure
15.	grandiloquent	o.	deride = dis
16.	grandiose	p.	burnish = furbish
17.	glut	q.	complimentary = free
18.	gratis	r.	devour = gorge
19.	gibe	s.	devour = gobble
20.	glaze	t.	scoop

gratuitous[grətjúːətəs] a 무료의, 무보수의 = complimentary[kàmpləméntəri]
= costless = gratis[grǽtis]
The quiz winner will be given a gratuitous Hawaii sightseeing.
퀴즈 우승자에게는 무료 하와이 관광 혜택이 주어질 것이다.

green[griːn] a 미숙한, 경험 없는 = immature[ìmətʃúər] = inexperienced[ìnikspíəriəns]
The new employee is still green at his job. 신입사원은 여전히 업무에 미숙하다.

gregarious[grigɛ́əriəs] a 사교적인 = convivial[kənvíviəl] = sociable[sóuʃəbl]
The dancer was known as a gregarious person. 그 댄서는 사교적인 사람으로 알려졌다.

grieve[griːv] v 비통해 하다, 슬퍼하다, 비탄하다 = bemoan[bimóun] = deplore[diplɔ́ːr]
= lament[ləmént] = mourn[mɔːrn] = wail[weil] = weep[wiːp]
He deeply grieved over the death of his son. 그는 아들의 사망에 매우 비통해 했다.

grievous[gríːvəs] a 통탄할, 극심한, 비통한, 슬픈 = afflicting[əflíktiŋ]
= agonizing[ǽgənàiziŋ] = calamitous[kəlǽmətəs] = deplorable[diplɔ́ːrəbl]
= lamentable[lǽməntəbl] = painful = tragic[trǽdʒik]
Most citizens were frustrated with the grievous natural disaster.
대부분의 시민들은 극심한 자연재해에 좌절했다.

grimace[gríməs] v (얼굴)찡그리다 = contort[kəntɔ́ːrt] = frown[fraun] = scowl[skaul]
The actress grimaced at the strong sunlight. 여배우는 강한 햇빛에 얼굴을 찡그렸다.

grind[graind] v 으깨다, 잘게 갈다, 가루로 만들다 = grate[greit] = pulverize[pʌ́lvəràiz]
The chef ground beans to make tofu. 셰프는 두부를 만들기 위해 콩을 으깼다.

groove[gruːv] n 관행, 상투적인 방식 = daily routine[ruːtíːn]
Most wedding ceremony these days seems to fall into a groove.
요즘 대부분의 결혼식은 상투적인 방식에 빠진 것 같다.

grotesque[groutésk] a 기괴한, 터무니없는 = bizarre[bizɑ́ːr] = eerie[íəri] = ugly
= misshapen[misʃéipən]
We can see a lot of grotesque creatures in the deep sea.
우리는 심해 바다에서 많은 기괴한 생명체를 볼 수 있다.

grouch[grautʃ] v 토라지다, 불평하다, 시무룩해지다 = carp[kaːrp] = gripe[graip]
= grouse[graus] = grumble[grʌ́mbl] = whine[hwain]
He grouched about the failure of his promotion to the manager.
그는 매니저 승진에 실패해서 토라졌다.

grove[grouv] n 작은 숲, 과수원 = orchard[ɔ́ːrtʃərd]
The old couple was managing a few groves. 노부부는 몇 개의 과수원을 경영 중이었다.

grudge[grʌdʒ] v 내 주기를 꺼리다, 주기 싫어하다 = begrudge[bigrʌdʒ] = give unwillingly
The rich man grudged donating even a small amount of money.
부유한 그 사람은 작은 금액의 돈도 기부하기를 꺼렸다.

guile[gail] n 간사한 꾀, 책략, 속임수 = artifice[ɑ́:rtəfis] = chicanery[ʃikéinəri] = cunning[kʌ́niŋ]
= deceit[disí:t] = deception[disépʃən] = duplicity[dju:plísəti] = ruse[ru:z] = treachery[trétʃəri]
We should not fall into the guile of voice phishing swindlers.
우리는 보이스피싱 사기범들의 속임수에 넘어가서는 안 된다.

guise[gaiz] n 겉치레, 가장, 변장 = disguise[disgáiz] = pretense[priténsprí:tens]
He exploited many homeless boys under the guise of charity.
그는 자선을 가장하여 많은 집 없는 소년들을 이용했다.

gull[gʌl] v 속이다, 부추겨 시키다, 속여 빼앗다 = bamboozle[bæmbú:zl] = cheat
= defraud[difrɔ́:d] = dupe[dju:p] = hoodwink
They gulled some old people into buying fake ginseng at extravagant price.
그들은 노인들을 속여서 가짜 인삼을 터무니없는 가격에 사게 했다.

gush[gʌʃ] v 분출하다, 흘러나오다, 쏟아지다 = flush[flʌʃ] = pour out = spout[spaut]
The magma was gushing from the volcanic region. 화산 지역에서 마그마가 분출되고 있었다.

QUIZ 58

Match each word in the first column with its definition in the second column.
Check your answers in the back of the book.

1.	gregarious	a.	bemoan = deplore
2.	gush	b.	grate = pulverize
3.	grievous	c.	daily routine
4.	gull	d.	contort = frown
5.	grind	e.	carp = gripe
6.	guile	f.	afflicting = agonizing
7.	grotesque	g.	convivial = sociable
8.	grudge	h.	bizarre = eerie
9.	grove	i.	begrudge = give unwillingly
10.	grieve	j.	flush = pour out
11.	grouch	k.	orchard
12.	groove	l.	bamboozle = cheat
13.	guise	m.	disguise = pretense
14.	grimace	n.	artifice = chicanery

habituate[həbítʃuèit] v 길들이다, 습관 들게 하다 = acclimate[ǽkləmèit]
= accustom[əkʌ́stəm] = familiarize[fəmíljəràiz] = inure[injúər]
They habituated themselves to the cold climate during the journey.
그들은 여행을 하는 동안 추운 기후에 익숙해졌다.

hackneyed[hǽknid] a 진부한, 평범한 = banal[bənǽl] = cliché[kliːʃéi]
= commonplace = pedestrian[pədéstriən] = quotidian[kwoutídiən] = stale[steil] = stock[stak]
= trite[trait]
Too many hackneyed scenes in the movie made moviegoers bored.
그 영화에 나오는 너무나 많은 진부한 장면들 때문에 영화 팬들은 따분해졌다.

halcyon[hǽlsiən] a 평온한, 평화로운 = calm[kaːm] = peacefu[píːsfəl]l
A variety of laws and rules were set during the halcyon rein of the king.
그 왕의 평화로운 통치 기간에 다양한 법과 규칙이 정해졌다.

hale[heil] a 정정한, 강건한 = stout[staut] = strapping[strǽpiŋ]
My grandfather is still hale, jogging 5km everyday.
아직 정정하신 우리 할아버지는 매일 5km를 조깅하신다.

hamper[hǽmpər] v 방해하다, 저지하다 = block = curb[kəːrb] = deter[ditə́ːr]
= hinder[híndər] = impede[impíːd] = interfere[ìntərfíər] = obstruct[əbstrʌ́kt] = stymie[stáimi]
= thwart[θwɔːrt]
The heavy continuous rain hampered the construction of the bridge over the river.
계속되는 폭우 때문에 강 위에 교량을 건설하는 데 방해를 받았다.

hangdog[hǽŋdɔ̀(ː)g] a 처량한, 쭈뼛거리는, 처량한 = cowering[káuəriŋ]
= downcast[dáunkæst]
The loser exited from the press conference with a hangdog look on his face.
패배자는 처량한 표정으로 기자회견장을 떠났다.

hankering[hǽŋkəriŋ] n 동경, 갈망 = craving[kréiviŋ] = yearning[jə́ːrniŋ]
The old couple has a hankering for a pastoral life. 그 노부부는 전원생활을 동경하고 있다.

haphazard[hæphǽzərd] a 계획성 없는, 되는 대로의 = desultory[désəltɔ̀ːri]
= indiscriminate[ìndiskrímənət]
The sports events were being held in a haphazard manner.
그 스포츠 행사는 계획성 없이 되는 대로 진행되고 있었다.

hapless[hǽplis] a 불행한, 불운한 = miserable[mízərəbl] = unlucky = wretched[rétʃid]
The movie is about a hapless prince who was killed by his uncle.
그 영화는 삼촌에게 살해당하는 어떤 불행한 왕자에 관한 것이다.

harbinger[hɑ́ːrbindʒər] n 선구자, 조짐 = augury[ɔ́ːgjuri] = herald[hérəld]
= omen[óumən] = portent[pɔ́ːrtent] = precursor[prikə́ːrsər]
The sound of ice-cracking is a harbinger of spring. 얼음 깨지는 소리는 봄이 오는 조짐이다.

harebrained[héərbrèind] a 경솔한, 무모한 = careless[kéərlis] = reckless[réklis]
The chairman's harebrained business plan put his company in the danger of bankruptcy.
회장의 경솔한 사업계획은 회사를 부도 위험으로 내몰았다.

harp[hɑːrp] v 같은 소리를 되풀이하다, 중언부언하다 = reiterate[riːtəreit] = repeat[ripíːt]
The sales director has been harping on the importance of the sales increase.
영업 담당 임원은 매출 증가의 중요성에 대해서 같은 소리를 되풀이하고 있었다.

harry[hǽri] v 괴롭히다, 못살게 굴다 = annoy = badger[bǽdʒər] = bedevil[bidévəl]
= beleaguer[bilíːgər] = gnaw[nɔː] = harass[hərǽs] = hassle[hǽsl] = pester[péstər] = plague[pleig]
The ex-minister has been harried by reporters waiting outside his home.
전직 장관은 그의 집 밖에서 대기하는 기자들로부터 괴롭힘을 받았다.

hash[hæʃ] v 저미다, 다지다 = mince[mins]
You need to hash the beef completely to make a beef patty for hamburgers.
햄버거용 패티를 만들기 위해서는 쇠고기를 완전히 저밀 필요가 있다.

haunt[hɔːnt] v 자주 가다, 출몰하다 = obsess[əbsés]
Some seniors believe that many ghosts haunt the cemetery in the town on rainy days.
일부 노인들은 비 오는 날 마을의 공동묘지에 많은 귀신들이 출몰한다고 믿고 있다.

havoc[hǽvək] n 파괴, 대혼란 = calamity[kəlǽməti] = cataclysm[kǽtəklìzm]
= catastrophe[kətǽstrəfi] = chaos[kéias] = devastation[dèvəstéiʃən]
Grape-sized hailstones wreaked havoc on the crops in the area.
포도알만 한 우박이 그 지역 농작물에 심각한 피해를 주었다.

headlong[hedlɔːŋ] a 저돌적인, 무모한, 몹시 서두르는 = brash[bræʃ] = foolhardy
= impetuous[impétʃuəs] = rash[ræʃ] = reckless[réklis]
His headlong decision ended up incurring a great loss in his business.
그의 저돌적인 결정은 결국 사업에서 큰 손실을 초래했다.

hearten[háːrtn] v 용기를 북돋우다, 격려하다 = cheer = embolden[imbóuldən] = encourage[inkə́ːridʒ]
The workers were heartened by the announcement of pay raise.
근로자들은 급여 인상 발표로 기운이 났다.

hedge[hedʒ] v 예방책을 세우다, 피하다 = avoid[əvɔ́id] = dodge[dadʒ] = sidestep
We can hedge a variety of dangers by taking out insurances.
우리는 보험을 들어서 여러 가지 위험에 대비할 수 있다.

hedonist[híːdənist] n 쾌락주의자 = epicure[épikjùər] = sybarite[síbəràit]
The millionaire was a hedonist. 그 백만장자는 쾌락주의자다.

QUIZ 59

*Match each word in the first column with its definition in the second column.
Check your answers in the back of the book.*

1.	hedonist		a.	craving = yearning
2.	hackneyed		b.	desultory = indiscriminate
3.	headlong		c.	acclimate = accustom
4.	haunt		d.	miserable = unlucky
5.	hedge		e.	annoy = badger
6.	hangdog		f.	reiterate = repeat
7.	harebrained		g.	mince
8.	haphazard		h.	cowering = downcast
9.	hapless		i.	cheer = embolden
10.	harbinger		j.	banal = cliché
11.	hash		k.	obsess
12.	harp		l.	avoid = dodge
13.	harry		m.	augury = herald
14.	habituate		n.	careless = reckless
15.	hankering		o.	calm = peaceful
16.	havoc		p.	calamity = cataclysm
17.	hale		q.	brash = foolhardy
18.	hearten		r.	epicure = sybarite
19.	hamper		s.	stout = strapping
20.	halcyon		t.	block = curb

---

hegemony[hidʒémən i] n 주도권, 지배권 = dominion[dəmínjən] = leadership
The two religious factions severely fought for hegemony.
두 개의 종교 파벌은 주도권을 잡기 위해 심하게 싸웠다.

heinous[héinəs] a 극악무도한, 가증스러운, 악랄한 = atrocious[ətróuʃəs]
= flagitious[fləd͡ʒíʃəs] = flagrant[fléigrənt] = hideous[hídiəs] = horrendous[hɔːréndəs]
= horrifying[hɔ́ːrəfàiiŋ] = iniquitous[iníkwətəs] = monstrous[mánstrəs]
= nefarious[niféəriəs] = vicious[víʃəs]
No one thought that the professor committed such a heinous crime.
아무도 그 교수가 그런 극악무도한 범죄를 저질렀으리라 생각하지 않았다.

herald[hérəld] n 전령사, 선구자 = harbinger[háːrbindʒər] = messenger[mésəndʒər]
The increased water in the valley is a herald of spring.
계곡에 불어난 물은 봄이 오는 것을 알리는 전령사이다.

heresy[hérəsi] n 이단, 이교 = pagan[péigən]
The religious law in the country prevents any religious leader from preaching heresy.
그 나라의 종교법에 따르면 어떤 종교 지도자도 이단적인 내용을 설교하지 못한다.

heretic[hérətik] n 이단자, 이교도 = pagan[péigən]
The famous religious leader turned out to be a heretic.
유명한 종교 지도자가 이단자로 판명이 되었다.

hermetic[həːrmétik] a 밀봉한, 밀폐된 = airtight = completely sealed
Most boiled fish needed to be kept in hermetic containers.
대부분의 끓인 생선은 밀폐용기에 보관할 필요가 있다.

hiatus[haiéitəs] n 중단, 틈(사이) = abeyance[əbéiəns] = cessation[seséiʃən]
= pause[pɔːz] = respite[réspit]
The power failure caused a hiatus in the production of cars.
정전 때문에 자동차 생산작업이 중단되었다.

hidebound[háidbàund] a 완고한, 편협한 =bigoted[bígətid] = intolerant[intálərənt]
= jaundiced[d͡ʒɔ́ːndist]
Marcus is at odds with his hidebound parents who want him nothing but to be a lawyer.
Marcus는 그가 변호사가 되기만을 원하는 완고한 부모와 갈등을 겪고 있다.

hideous[hídiəs] a 끔찍한, 무시무시한 = horrendous[hɔːréndəs] = ugly
The development of nuclear weapons is considered a hideous activity in the international community.
핵무기 개발은 국제사회에서 끔찍한 행위로 간주된다.

hierarchy[háiərɑ̀ːrki] n 계층제도, 계급제도, 성직자 계급 = chain of command
Monks and priests belonged to a ruling hierarchy in ancient society.
스님과 성직자는 고대 사회에서 지배계급에 속했다.

histrionic[hìstriɑ́nik] a 연극조의, 꾸민 듯한, 과장된 = theatrical[θiǽtrikəl]
His histrionic way of speaking sounded like the lack of honesty.
그의 연극조의 말투는 진실성이 결여된 것처럼 들렸다.

hoary[hɔ́ːri] a 고색창연한, 백발의, 진부한 = gray
You will encounter some hoary buildings in the traditional town.
당신들은 전통 마을에서 몇몇 고색창연한 가옥들을 만날 수 있을 것이다.

hodgepodge[hɑ́dʒpɑ̀dʒ] n 뒤죽박죽, 뒤범벅 = jumble[dʒʌmbl]
= mishmash[míʃmɑ̀ːʃ] = mixture
His lab was full of a hodgepodge of a variety of tools and machinery.
그의 연구실은 여러 가지 종류의 도구와 기계류로 완전히 뒤죽박죽이었다.

homage[hɑ́midʒ] n 경의, 존경 = admiration[ædməréiʃən] = allegiance[əlíːdʒəns]
The government is planning to build a memorial hall in homage to the former president.
정부는 전직 대통령을 기리는 기념관 건립을 계획 중이다.

homily[hɑ́məli] n 설교, 훈계 = preach[priːtʃ] = sermon[sə́ːrmən]
Minister Jae ardently talked about 'Godliness' in his homily.
Jae 목사님은 설교에서 '성결(독실함)'에 대해 열정적으로 말씀하셨다.

homogeneous[hòumədʒíːniəs] a 동종의(균질의) 것으로 이루어진 = uniform
It is not easy to find a homogeneous nation in Europe.
유럽에서 단일 민족 국가를 찾기는 쉽지 않다.

hovel[hʌvəl] n 오두막집, 광 = cottage[kɑ́tidʒ] = hut[hʌt] = shack[ʃæk] = shanty[ʃǽnti]
The rebel leaders had to hide in a hovel in the mountain.
반란군 지도자들은 산 속 오두막집에 숨어야만 했다.

hubris[hjúːbris] n 오만, 자만, 거만 = arrogance[ǽrəgəns] = audacity[ɔːdǽsəti]
= chutzpah[hútspə]
The hubris of the commander brought out many deaths of his soldiers.
사령관의 자만이 많은 병사들을 죽게 만들었다.

hue[hju:] n 색조, 색깔 = color = shade = tinge[tindʒ]
The ocean around the island took on light green hue.
섬 주위의 바다는 옅은 녹색을 띠고 있었다.

QUIZ 60

Match each word in the first column with its definition in the second column.
Check your answers in the back of the book.

1.	hue		a.	pagan
2.	hermetic		b.	pagan
3.	homage		c.	loyalty = reverence
4.	heresy		d.	preach = sermon
5.	hiatus		e.	uniform
6.	heinous		f.	chain of command
7.	hubris		g.	cottage = hut
8.	hidebound		h.	arrogance = audacity
9.	hegemony		i.	airtight = completely sealed
10.	hierarchy		j.	abeyance = cessation
11.	hideous		k.	bigoted = intolerant
12.	hoary		l.	dominion = leadership
13.	hodgepodge		m.	atrocious = flagitious
14.	heretic		n.	harbinger = messenger
15.	deference		o.	jumble = mishmash
16.	homily		p.	theatrical
17.	homogeneous		q.	horrendous = ugly
18.	hovel		r.	gray
19.	histrionic		s.	color = shade
20.	herald		t.	admiration = allegiance

husbandry[hʌzbəndri] n 검약, 절약 = economy = frugality[fru:gǽləti] = thrift[θrift]
Her old shoes and worn jacket show her good husbandry.
그녀의 오래된 신발과 낡은 재킷은 그녀의 절약성을 보여준다.

hymn[him] n 찬송가, 찬가 = paean[píːən]
The congregation in the covenant church was merrily singing hymns.
카비넌트 교회의 신자들이 즐겁게 찬송가를 부르고 있었다.

hyperbole[haipə́:rbəli] n 과장, 과장법 = exaggeration[igzædʒəréiʃən]
The sales manager explained the advantages of the new product without hyperbole.
영업 담당 매니저는 신제품의 장점에 대해 과장하지 않고 설명했다.

hypocrisy[hipákrəsi] n 위선, 가장 = deception[disépʃən] = dishonesty[disánəsti]
= duplicity[dju:plísəti] = insincerity[ìnsinsérəti] = pretense[priténsprí:tens]
The hypocrisy of the politician made many voters turn their backs on him.
그 정치인의 위선이 많은 유권자들의 등을 돌리게 만들었다.

hypothetical[haɪpəθetɪkl] a 가설의, 가상적인 = theoretical[θì:ərétikəl] = unproven
The tourists will experience the hypothetical moon walk at the Space center.
관광객들은 우주센터에서 가상적인 문 워크를 경험하게 될 것이다.

QUIZ 61

Match each word in the first column with its definition in the second column.
Check your answers in the back of the book.

1. hymn   a. paean
2. hypothetical   b. economy = frugality
3. hypocrisy   c. deception = dishonesty
4. hyperbole   d. theoretical = unproven
5. husbandry   e. exaggeration

ichthyologist[ìkθiálədʒist] n 어류학자 = one who studies fish
A famous ichthyologist was called to identify the unknown fish.
지금껏 알려지지 않은 물고기를 확인하기 위해 유명한 어류학자를 요청했다.

idiosyncrasy[ìdiəsíŋkrəsi] n 특이한 성격, 개성, 특질 = characteristic[kæriktərístik]
= peculiarity[pikjù:liærəti] = singularity[sìŋgjulærəti] = trait[treit]
His idiosyncrasies made him stand out among his friends.
특이한 성격 때문에 그는 친구들 사이에서 두드러져 보였다.

idolater[aidálətər] n 우상숭배자, 이교도 = pagan[péigən]
Some emperors themselves were idolaters in the ancient empires.
고대 제국의 일부 황제들은 스스로 우상숭배자들이었다.

idyllic[aidílik] a 전원적인, 목가적인 = bucolic[bju:kálik] = pastoral[pǽstərəl]
The businessman was fascinated by the idyllic scenery.
사업가는 목가적인 경치에 매혹되었다.

ignominious[ìgnəmíniəs] a 불명예스러운, 창피한, 면목없는 = disgraceful[disgréisfəl]
= humiliating[hju:mílièitiŋ] = shameful[ʃéimfəl]
The England soccer team experienced an ignominious defeat.
영국 축구팀은 불명예스러운 패배를 당했다.

illiterate[ilítərət] a 문맹의, 잘 모르는, 무식한 = benighted[bináitid]
= ignorant[ígnərənt] = uneducated
He is ballet illiterate, rarely going to ballet performance.
그는 발레에 대해서 잘 모르기 때문에 발레 공연장에는 거의 가지 않는다.

illuminate[ilú:mənèit] v 밝히다, 조명하다 = brighten
The streets were illuminated by the street lamps. 거리는 가로등으로 밝혀졌다.

imbue[imbjú:] v ~에게 불어넣다, 물들이다 = inculcate[inkʌ́lkeit] = infuse[infjú:z]
= ingrain[ingréin] = instill[instíl] = permeate[pə́:rmièit] = pervade[pərvéid]
= saturate[sǽtʃərèit] = steep[sti:p] = suffuse[səfjú:z]
The students were imbued with a sense of responsibility. 학생들에게 책임감을 불어넣었다.

immanent[ímənənt] a 안에 있는, 내재하는 = inborn[ínbɔ́:rn] = inherent[inhíərənt]
= intrinsic[intrínsikzik]
We have to solve the polarization of wealth immanent within our society.
우리는 우리 사회 안에 내재하는 부의 양극화 문제를 해결해야 한다.

immaterial[imətíəriəl] a 중요하지 않은, 하찮은, 관계없는 = extraneous[ikstréiniəs]
= inconsequential[inkansikwénʃəl] = irrelevant[iréləvənt] = unimportant
It is immaterial to us if he runs for the election.
그가 선거에 나가는지 여부는 우리에게 중요하지 않다.

imminent[ímənənt] a 임박한, 금방이라도 닥칠 듯한, 일촉즉발의
= forthcoming[fɔːrθkʌmiŋ] = impending[impéndiŋ]= looming = on the way
Their missile launch is imminent. 그들의 미사일 발사가 임박해 있다.

immune[imjúːn] a 면역성이 있는, 면제되는 = exempt[igzémpt]
= invulnerable[invʌ́lnərəbl] = resistant[rizístənt] = unaffected
Some bugs have become immune to insecticide.
어떤 벌레는 살충제에 면역성을 띠게 되었다.

immutable[imjúːtəbl] a 불변의, 변경되지 않는 = abiding[əbáidiŋ]
= constant[kánstənt] = invariable[invέəriəbl] = unchangeable
We regard his greed for money as immutable.
우리는 돈에 대한 그의 욕심은 변하지 않을 것이라고 생각한다.

impartial[impάːrʃəl] a 공정한, 공평한, 치우치지 않은 = disinterested[disíntərèstid]
= dispassionate[dispǽʃənət] = equitable[ékwətəbl] = fair = unbiased[ʌnbaiəst]
= unprejudiced[ʌnprédʒədist]
The newspaper is famous for impartial reports. 그 신문은 공정한 보도로 유명하다.

impassion[impǽʃən] v 크게 감동시키다, 자극하다, 흥분시키다 = impress
= inspire[inspáiər] = stir[stəːr]
The new singer impassioned the entire audience. 신인 가수는 모든 관객을 크게 감동시켰다.

impasse[ímpæs] n 교착상태, 난국, 곤경 = deadlock = dilemma[dilémə]
= gridlock[grídlὰk] = predicament[pridíkəmənt] = stalemate = standoff[stǽndɔ̀(ː)f]
The negotiations reached an impasse. 협상이 난국에 봉착했다.

impassive[impǽsiv] a 무감동의, 무표정한, 냉담한 = emotionless[imóuʃənlis]
= stolid[stálid] = unemotional = unflappable[ʌnflǽpəbl] = unruffled[ʌnrʌfld]
He looked impassive when he was arrested for keeping illicit drugs.
불법마약 소지죄로 체포당할 때 그는 무표정이었다.

impeach[impíːtʃ] v 탄핵하다, 비난하다, 고발하다 = accuse[əkjúːz] = censure[sénʃər]
= criticize[krítəsàiz] = denounce[dináuns]= impugn[impjúːn] = indict[indáit]
= reprehend[rèprihénd] = reprimand = reprobate[réprəbèit]
Some lawmakers from the opposition party impeached the president for breaking the election law.
일부 야당의원들은 대통령이 선거법 위반을 했다고 탄핵을 했다.

impeccable[impékəbl] a 결점 없는, 나무랄 데 없는 = accurate[ǽkjurət]
= flawless[flɔ́ːlis] = immaculate[imǽkjulət] = infallible[infǽləbl]
His acting in the movie was impeccable. 영화에서 그의 연기는 나무랄데가 없었다.

impecunious[ìmpikjúːniəs] a 가난한, 무일푼의= destitute[déstətjùːt]
= impoverished[impávəriʃt] = indigent[índidʒənt] = penniless[pénilis] = penurious[pənjúəriəs]
= poverty-stricken[pávərti-stríkən]
The impecunious man had to work hard for 5 years to earn the cost of the wedding ceremony.
무일푼의 남자는 결혼식 비용을 버느라 5년간 열심히 일했다.

QUIZ 62

Match each word in the first column with its definition in the second column.
Check your answers in the back of the book.

1.	impeccable	a.	brighten
2.	impeach	b.	inculcate = infuse
3.	imbue	c.	pagan
4.	idyllic	d.	inborn = inherent
5.	impassion	e.	benighted = ignorant
6.	illiterate	f.	one who studies fish
7.	impasse	g.	extraneous = inconsequential
8.	idolater	h.	forthcoming = impending
9.	immanent	i.	exempt = invulnerable
10.	immutable	j.	characteristic = peculiarity
11.	impecunious	k.	abiding = constant
12.	immune	l.	disgraceful = humiliating
13.	ichthyologist	m.	impress = inspire
14.	impartial	n.	deadlock = dilemma
15.	ignominious	o.	bucolic = pastoral
16.	immaterial	p.	disinterested = dispassionate
17.	impassive	q.	emotionless = stolid
18.	illuminate	r.	accuse = censure
19.	idiosyncrasy	s.	destitute = impoverished
20.	imminent	t.	accurate = flawless

impede[impíːd] v 지체시키다, 방해하다, 훼방놓다 = block = curb[kəːrb] = deter[ditə́ːr] = hamper[hǽmpər] = hinder[híndər] = interfere[intərfíər] = obstruct[əbstrʌ́kt] = stymie[stáimi] = thwart[θwɔːrt]
Many parked cars impeded the fire trucks rushing to the scene of the fire.
주차되어 있는 많은 자동차들 때문에 소방차의 화재현장 출동이 방해를 받았다.

impending[impéndiŋ] a 임박한, 곧 일어날 듯한 = forthcoming[|fɔːrθ|kʌmiŋ] = imminent[ímənənt] = looming[luːming]
The media are reporting about the impending volcano eruption.
미디어는 곧 일어날 화산폭발에 대해 보도하고 있다.

impenetrable[impénətrəbl] a 관통할 수 없는, 꿰뚫을 수 없는, 헤아릴 수 없는 = impassable[impǽsəbl] = impermeable[impəːrmiəbl] = impervious[impəːrviəs]
A prison-breaker encountered impenetrable forests while he was on the run.
탈옥수는 도망하는 도중에 뚫고 가기 어려운 숲을 만났다.

imperative[impérətiv] a 필수의, 긴요한, 피할 수 없는 = necessary = crucial[krúːʃəl] = essential[isénʃəl] = important = indispensible = vital
It is imperative that we should abide by the law. 우리가 법을 지키는 것은 필수이다.

imperious[impíəriəs] a 오만한, 고압적인 = arrogant[ǽrəgənt] = bossy[bɑ́si] = domineering[dɑ̀məníəriŋ] = haughty[hɔ́ːti] = overbearing[òuvərberiŋ]
The new CEO showed an imperious manner. 새로운 사장은 오만한 태도를 보였다.

impermeable[impəːrmiəbl] a 통과시키지 않는, 불침투성의 = impenetrable[impénətrəbl] = impervious[impəːrviəs]
The special forces wear leather boots and jacket impermeable to water.
특수군은 물이 스며지지 않는 가죽 부츠와 재킷을 입고 있다.

imperturbable[ìmpərtəːrbəbl] a 쉽사리 동요하지 않는, 냉정한, 침착한 = calm[kaːm] = collected = unflappable[ʌnflǽpəbl] = unruffled[ʌnrʌ́fld]
He looked imperturbable in such a crisis.
그는 그 위기 속에서도 쉽사리 동요하지 않는 모습을 보였다.

impervious[impəːrviəs] a 통과시키지 않는, 불침투성의, 영향을 받지 않는 = impassable[impǽsəbl] = impenetrable[impénətrəbl] = impermeable[impəːrmiəbl]
The soldiers were wearing gas masks impervious to toxic gases.
군인들은 유해가스를 막아주는 마스크를 착용하고 있다.

impetuous[impétʃuəs] a 충동적인, 성급한, 경솔한 = abrupt[əbrʌpt] = headlong = impulsive[impʌlsiv] = offhand
The impetuous judgment of the commander led to heavy casualties.
사령관의 충동적인 판단이 많은 사상자를 불러왔다.

implacable[implǽkəbl] a 달래기 어려운, 앙심 깊은, 완강한 = cruel[krúːəl] = inexorable[inéksərəbl] = merciless[məːrsilis] = relentless[riléntlis] = ruthless[rúːθlis] = uncompromising [ʌnkɑːmprəmaɪzɪŋ] = unforgiving[ʌnfərgívɪŋ] = unrelenting = unyielding[ʌnjiːldɪŋ]
A peaceful settlement was reached between the two implacable families.
앙심이 깊은 두 가족 사이에 평화로운 합의가 이루어졌다.

implication[ìmplikéiʃən] n 함축, 암시, 포함 = connotation[kɑ̀nətéiʃən] = indication[ìndikéiʃən] = suggestion
His long face in the meeting has an implication for his resignation.
회의를 하는 동안 보여준 그의 우울한 얼굴은 그가 사임할 것임을 암시한다.

implode[implóud] v 내파하다, 자체적으로 파괴되다 = collapse[kəlǽps] inward
The old apartment building imploded. 오래된 아파트 건물이 스스로 무너졌다.

importune[ìmpɔːrtjúːn] 성가시게 졸라대다, 치근덕거리다 = appeal[əpíːl] = badger[bǽdʒər] = beseech[bisíːtʃ] = entreat[intríːt] = implore[implɔ́ːr] = solicit[səlísit] = supplicate[sʌ́pləkèit]
The politician importuned me to lend him money.
그 정치인은 나에게 돈을 빌려달라고 성가시게 졸라댔다.

impotent[ímpətənt] a 무력한, …을 할수 없는 = effete[ifíːt] = enervated[énərvèitid] = enfeebled[infíːbld] = helpless = incapable[inkéipəbl] = incompetent[inkɑ́mpətənt]
The company became impotent due to labor dispute. 그 회사는 노사문제로 무력하게 되었다.

impoverish[impɑ́vəriʃ] v 가난하게 하다 = make poor
The long economic sanctions have impoverished the nation.
오랜 경제 제재가 그 나라를 가난하게 만들었다.

impregnable[imprégnəbl] a 난공불락의, 확고한 = insuperable[insúːpərəbl] = invincible[invínsəbl] = invulnerable[invʌ́lnərəbl] = unbeatable[ʌnbiːtəbl]
The king wanted to build an impregnable castle on the cliff. 왕은 절벽 위에 난공불락의 성을 짓고 싶었다.

impresario[ìmprisɑ́ːriòu] n (오페라, 음악) 기획자, 주최자 = opera or music producer
Edward Miller has been an impresario of music concerts.
Edward Miller는 음악회의 기획자로 일하고 있다.

impromptu[imprάmptjuː] a 즉석의, 즉흥적인, 임시변통의 = ad-lib[ǽdlíb]
= extemporaneous[ekstèmpəréiniəs] = improvised[ɪmprəvaɪz] = offhand
= unrehearsed[ʌnrihə́ːrst] = unscripted[ʌnskríptid]
The audience made a request for an impromptu performance to the musician.
관객들은 그 음악가에게 즉흥적인 연주를 해달라고 부탁했다.

improvise[ímprəvàiz] v 즉석에서(즉흥적으로) 짓다, 노래하다, 연주하다.
= extemporize[ikstémpəràiz]
Asked to pray for the families of the victims, pastor Jae improvised a sermon.
희생자 가족을 위해 기도해 달라는 부탁을 받고 Jae 목사님은 즉석에서 설교를 했다.

imprudent[imprúːdnt] a 경솔한, 무분별한, 무모한 = careless = foolhardy[fuːlhɑːrdi]
= irresponsible[ìrispʌ́nsəbl] = reckless[réklis]
It would be imprudent for him to purchase the sports car as a family car.
그가 스포츠카를 패밀리 카로 구입한 것은 경솔한 짓이었다.

QUIZ 63

*Match each word in the first column with its definition in the second column.
Check your answers in the back of the book.*

1.	imprudent	a.	impenetrable = impervious
2.	impending	b.	forthcoming = imminent
3.	implode	c.	careless = foolhardy
4.	imperative	d.	extemporize
5.	impede	e.	impassable = impermeable
6.	impermeable	f.	opera or music producer
7.	imperturbable	g.	cruel = inexorable
8.	importune	h.	connotation = indication
9.	impetuous	i.	block = curb
10.	impenetrable	j.	extemporaneous = improvised
11.	implication	k.	calm = collected
12.	imperious	l.	appeal = badger
13.	impresario	m.	necessary = crucial
14.	impotent	n.	collapse inward
15.	impoverish	o.	effete = enervated
16.	impregnable	p.	make poor
17.	improvise	q.	arrogant = bossy
18.	impromptu	r.	insuperable = invincible
19.	impervious	s.	impassable = impenetrable
20.	implacable	t.	abrupt = headlong

impugn[impjú:n] v 의문을 제기하다, 논란을 일으키다, 비난 공격하다 = assail[əséil]
= contradict[kàntrədíkt] = gainsay[géinsèi] = smear[smiər] = traduce[trədjú:s]
The detectives impugned the veracity of the statement by the witness.
형사들은 목격자 진술의 진실성에 대해서 의문을 제기했다.

impunity[impjú:nəti] n 무사, 처벌을 받지 않음 = exemption[igzémpʃən]
= immunity[imjú:nəti]
The powerful businessman left the court with impunity.
힘 있는 사업가는 처벌을 받지 않고 법정을 떠났다.

inadvertent[ìnədvə́:rtnt] a 부주의한, 고의가 아닌, 우연한 = accidental[æksədéntl]
= unintentional[ʌnɪntenʃənl] = unwitting[ʌnwítiŋ]
It was an inadvertent mistake to deliver the package to the wrong address.
소포를 잘못된 주소로 보낸 것은 고의가 아닌 실수이다.

inalienable[inéiljənəbl] a 양도할 수 없는, 빼앗을 수 없는 = inviolable[inváiələbl]
The right to vote is one of the inalienable rights. 투표권은 양도할 수 없는 권리 중 하나이다.

inane[inéin] a 어리석은, 무의미한 = foolish = stupid
He asked some inane questions. 그는 몇 가지 어리석은 질문을 했다.

incandescent[ìnkəndésnt] a 백열광을 발하는, 빛나는, 눈부시게 밝은
= beaming[bí:miŋ] = fulgent[fʌldʒənt] = glowing[glóuiŋ] = luminous[lú:mənəs]
= radiant[réidiənt] = shining
The city uses incandescent light bulbs for the street lamps.
시는 가로등에 백열전구를 사용한다.

incantation[ìnkæntéiʃən] n 주문, 마법, 마술 = abracadabra[æbrəkədǽbrə]
= conjuration[kàndʒuréiʃən] = enchantment[intʃǽntmənt] = magic = necromancy[nékrəmænsi]
= spell
The female magician utters an incantation before the magic trick.
그 여자 마술사는 마술을 보여주기 전에 주문을 외운다.

incarnation[ìnka:rnéiʃən] n 구체화, 전형, 화신, 전생, 신이 인간의 모습으로 나타남
= embodiment[imbádimənt]
The vicious loan shark is the incarnation of greed.
사악한 고리대금업자는 욕망의 화신이다.

incendiary[inséndièri] a 선동적인, 교사적인, 자극적인 = agitative[ǽdʒitèitiv]
= demagogic[dèməgádʒik] = inflammatory[inflǽmətɔ̀:ri] = provocative[prəvákətiv]
= seditious[sidíʃəs] = subversive[səbvə́:rsiv]
The politician's incendiary speech made some voters confused.
그 정치인의 선동적인 연설은 일부 유권자들을 혼란스럽게 만들었다.

incense[ínsens] v 몹시 화나게 하다, 격분시키다 = anger = enrage[inréidʒ]
= exasperate[igzǽspərèit] = infuriate[infjúərièit] = irritate[írətèit] = provoke[prəvóuk]
= rile[rail]
Some diners were incensed at the poor service of the restaurant.
몇몇 식사 손님들은 식당의 형편없는 서비스에 격분했다.

incessant[insésnt] a 끊임없는, 쉴 새 없는 = ceaseless[sí:slis] = never-ending
= perpetual[pərpétʃuəl] = persistent[pərsístənt] = unremitting[ʌnrɪmɪtɪŋ]
Incessant noise was heard from the construction site. 끊임없는 소음이 공사장에서 들렸다.

incipient[insípiənt] a 막 시작된, 초기의, 시작의 = commencing[kəméns]
= embryonic[èmbriánik] = nascent[nǽsnt]
He was on the incipient stage of lung cancer. 그는 폐암 초기다.

incisive[insáisiv] a 예리한, 날카로운, 신랄한 = acute[əkjú:t] = intelligent[intélədʒənt]
= penetrating[pénətrèitiŋ] = perspicacious[pə̀:rspəkéiʃəs] = piercing[píərsiŋ]
= trenchant[trént∫ənt]
The candidate's unrealistic election pledges came under incisive criticism.
그 후보자의 비현실적인 선거공약들은 신랄한 비판을 받았다.

incite[insáit] v 자극하다, 선동하다, 조장하다 = abet[əbét] = agitate[ǽdʒitèit]
= arouse[əráuz] = encourage[inkə́:ridʒ] = foment[foumént] = inflame = instigate[ínstəgèit]
= prompt[prampt] = provoke[prəvóuk] = trigger[trígər]
The politician incited the citizens to boycott the elections.
그 정치인은 시민들에게 선거에 참가하지 말라고 선동했다.

inclement[inklémənt] a 날씨가 혹독한(사나운) = harsh[ha:rʃ] = nasty[nǽsti]
= severe[sivíər]
Polar bears have the ability to survive the inclement weather.
북극곰은 혹독한 날씨에 살 수 있는 능력을 보유하고 있다.

inclination[ìnklənéiʃən] n 경향, 성향, 의향 = disposition[dìspəzíʃən]
= penchant[pénʧənt] = proclivity[prouklívəti] = propensity[prəpénsəti] = tendency[téndənsi]
Young couples in the cities show the inclination to live in a smaller house.
도시의 젊은 부부들은 더 작은 집에 살려고 하는 경향을 보이고 있다.

incogitant[inkάdʒitənt] a 사고력이 없는, 사려(분별) 없는 = fatuous[fǽʧuəs]
= harebrained[héərbrèind] = stupid
More and more incogitant people are betting on the horse race gambling.
점점 더 많은 분별없는 사람들이 경마도박에 돈을 걸고 있다.

incongruous[inkάŋgruəs] a 조화되지 않는, 일치하지 않는 = discordant[diskɔ́:rdənt]
= inappropriate[ìnəpróupriət] = incoherent[ìnkouhíərənt] = incompatible[ìnkəmpǽtəbl]
The ancient temple stands incongruous in the tall and modern buildings.
오래된 사찰은 높고 현대적인 빌딩 속에 조화되지 않은 모습으로 자리하고 있다.

incontrovertible[ìnkὰntrəvə́:rtəbl] a 명백한, 반박의 여지가 없는 = certain
= indisputable[ìndispjú:təbl] = undeniable[ʌndınaıəbl]
It is an incontrovertible that he has climbed the Mt. Everest.
그가 에베레스트 산을 등정한 것은 명백하다.

incorrigible[inkɔ́:ridʒəbl] a 구제할 수 없는, 교정할 수 없는 = incurable[inkjúərəbl]
= irreparable[irépərəbl]
Lilly's husband is an incorrigible gambler.
Lilly의 남편은 구제불능의 도박꾼이다.

QUIZ 64

Match each word in the first column with its definition in the second column.
Check your answers in the back of the book.

1.	incorrigible		a.	exemption = immunity
2.	impunity		b.	anger = enrage
3.	inadvertent		c.	assail = contradict
4.	inclement		d.	disposition = penchant
5.	inane		e.	ceaseless = never-ending
6.	incandescent		f.	harsh = nasty
7.	incantation		g.	inviolable
8.	incarnation		h.	fatuous = harebrained
9.	incendiary		i.	foolish = stupid
10.	incite		j.	commencing = embryonic
11.	incessant		k.	accidental = unintentional
12.	incipient		l.	discordant = inappropriate
13.	incisive		m.	acute = intelligent
14.	impugn		n.	certain = indisputable
15.	incense		o.	beaming = fulgent
16.	inclination		p.	abet = agitate
17.	inalienable		q.	abracadabra = conjuration
18.	incongruous		r.	agitative = demagogic
19.	incontrovertible		s.	embodiment
20.	incogitant		t.	incurable = irreparable

increment[ínkrəmənt] n 증가, 이익 = accretion[əkríːʃən] = accruement[əkrúːmənt] = addition = augmentation[ɔ̀ːgmentéiʃən]
The increment in productivity led to the increase of the operating profit.
생산성의 증가는 영업이익의 증가를 가져왔다.

incriminate[inkrímənèit] v 죄를 씌우다 = accuse[əkjúːz] = implicate[ímplikèit] = indict[indáit] = prosecute[prásikjùːt]
His incoherent reply during the investigation incriminated himself.
조사 중에 보여준 그의 일관성 없는 대답은 스스로에게 죄를 씌우는 결과를 가져왔다.

inculcate[inkʌ́lkeit] v 주입시키다, 가르치다 = imbue[imbjúː] = infuse[infjúːz] = inject[indʒékt] = instill[instíl]
All teachers in Jefferson High tried to inculcate students with a sense of responsibility.
제퍼슨 고등학교의 모든 선생님들은 학생들에게 책임감을 심어주도록 애쓰고 있다.

inculpate[inkʌ́lpeit] v 비난하다, 죄를 뒤집어씌우다 = charge = incriminate[inkrímənèit]
The two suspects inculpated each other in the murder case.
두 명의 살인사건 용의자들은 서로에게 죄를 뒤집어씌웠다.

incursion[inkə́ːrʒən] n 급습, 습격 = aggression[əgréʃən] = foray[fɔ́ːrei] = infiltration[ìnfiltréiʃən] = inroad = intrusion[intrúːʒən] = invasion[invéiʒən] = penetration[pènətréiʃən] = raid
Guerrillas made an incursion into our territory. 게릴라들이 우리 지역을 습격했다.

indefensible[ìndifénsəbl] a 변명의 여지가 없는, 할 말 없는, 방어할 수 없는
= inexcusable[inikskjúːzəbl] = unjustifiable[ʌndʒʌ́stəfàiəbl] = untenable[ʌnténəbl]
Our national soccer team lost a game against Thai in an indefensible game operation.
우리나라 국가대표 축구팀은 변명의 여지가 없는 경기 운영으로 태국 팀에게 졌다.

indelible[indéləbl] a 잊을 수 없는, 지울 수 없는, 없앨 수 없는
I have an indelible memory about the trip to Okinawa.
나는 오키나와 여행에 관한 잊을 수 없는 기억을 가지고 있다.

indict[indáit] v 기소하다, 비난하다 = incriminate[inkrímənèit] = prosecute[prásikjùːt]
The famous singer was indicted on charges of tax evasion.
그 유명 가수는 탈세 혐의로 기소되었다.

indigenous[indídʒənəs] a 고유의, 토착의 = aboriginal[æbərídʒənl] = endemic[endémik]
He planted some trees indigenous to Africa in the backyard of his house.
그는 집 뒤뜰에 아프리카 고유의 나무들을 심었다.

indigent[índidʒənt] a 궁핍한, 가난한 = destitute[déstətjùːt]
= impoverished[impávəriʃt] = needy = poverty-stricken
We should give tax breaks to the indigent workers.
우리는 가난한 근로자들에게 세금혜택을 주어야 한다.

indignant[indígnənt] a 분개한, 화난 = furious[fjúəriəs] = incensed[insénst]
= irate[airéit] = miffed[mift] = resentful[rizéntfəl] = wrathful[rǽθfəl]
Citizens were indignant at the news of city hall relocation.
시민들은 시청 이전 소식에 분개했다.

indolent[índələnt] a 게으른, 나태한 = lazy = lackadaisical[lækədéizikəl]
= slothful[slɔ́ːθfəl] = sluggish[slʌ́giʃ]
The sales manager was fired for his indolent attitude at work.
영업담당 매니저는 게으른 근무 태도 때문에 해고되었다.

indomitable[indάmətəbl] a 불굴의, 꿋꿋한 = impregnable[imprégnəbl]
= invincible[invínsəbl] = invulnerable[invΛlnərəbl] = pertinacious[pə̀ːrtənéiʃəs]
= unassailable[Ʌnəseɪləbl] = unbeatable
He showed indomitable challenge spirit while climbing Mt. Everest.
그는 에베레스트 산을 오르는 동안 불굴의 도전정신을 보여줬다.

indubitable[indjúːbitəbl] a 의심할 여지 없는, 분명한 = apparent[əpǽrənt]
= undoubted[Ʌndáutid]
We consider it an indubitable fact that a variety of fish will disappear in the near future.
우리는 가까운 미래에 다양한 종의 물고기가 사라질 것이 분명한 사실이라고 생각한다.

induce[indjúːs] v 설득(유도)하여 하게 하다, 유도하다, 유발하다 = encourage = lead to
= urge[əːrdʒ]
His parents induced him to major in law in college.
그의 부모들은 대학에서 법률을 전공하도록 그를 설득했다.

indulge[indΛldʒ] v 빠지다, 탐닉하다 = revel[révəl] in = wallow[wɑːloʊ] in
My son indulged in reading comic books. 나의 아들은 만화책 읽는 데 빠졌다.

indulgent[indΛldʒənt] a 관대한, 멋대로 하게 하는 = clement[klémənt]
= lenient[líːniənt] = merciful[məːrsifəl]
His indulgent father was willing to buy his son anything he wanted.
그의 아버지는 그가 원하는 것이면 뭐든 사게 해줌으로써 아들을 응석받이로 키웠다.

ineffable[inéfəbl] a 말로 표현할 수 없는, 형언할 수 없는
= indescribable[indiskráibəbl] = unspeakable
He felt an ineffable pain when he lost his son in the accident.
그는 아들을 사고로 잃었을 때 말로 표현할 수 없는 고통을 느꼈다.

ineluctable[ìnilΛktəbl] a 피할 수 없는, 불가피한, 면할 수 없는 = inescapable[ìneskéipəbl]
The Chinese smart phone companies had an ineluctable confrontation with Apple in the market.
중국의 스마트폰 회사들은 시장에서 애플과 피할 수 없는 대결을 해야 했다.

inept[inépt] a 서투른, 솜씨 없는, 부적당한 = awkward[ɔ́ːkwərd] = bumbling[bΛmbliŋ]
= clumsy[klΛmzi] = gauche[gouʃ] = incompetent[inkάmpətənt] = unskilled
The inventor was inept in growing his business.
그 발명가는 사업을 키우는 데는 서툴렀다.

ineradicable[ìnirǽdikəbl] a 근절할 수 없는, 뿌리 깊은 = deep-rooted
= ingrained[ingréind] = inured[injúərd] = inveterate[invétərət] = irradicable[irǽdikəbl]
Big cities across the globe are full of ineradicable crimes.
전세계 대도시들은 근절할 수 없는 범죄로 가득 차 있다.

QUIZ 65

Match each word in the first column with its definition in the second column.
Check your answers in the back of the book.

1.	ineradicable	a.	destitute = impoverished
2.	indefensible	b.	aggression = foray
3.	inculcate	c.	furious = incensed
4.	inculpate	d.	encourage = lead to
5.	indomitable	e.	accretion = accruement
6.	induce	f.	inexcusable = unjustifiable
7.	indolent	g.	revel in = wallow
8.	indigenous	h.	lazy = lackadaisical
9.	incriminate	i.	accuse = implicate
10.	indignant	j.	incriminate = prosecute
11.	increment	k.	imbue = infuse
12.	indict	l.	clement = lenient
13.	indubitable	m.	charge = incriminate
14.	incursion	n.	aboriginal = endemic
15.	indulge	o.	impregnable = invincible
16.	indigent	p.	indescribable = unspeakable
17.	ineffable	q.	inescapable
18.	ineluctable	r.	apparent = undoubted
19.	inept	s.	deep-rooted = ingrained
20.	indulgent	t.	awkward = bumbling

inert[inə́:rt] a 활발하지 못한, 기력이 없는, 불활성의 = dormant[dɔ́:rmənt] = inactive
= listless[lístlis] = indolent[índələnt] = languid[lǽŋgwid] = leaden[lédn] = phlegmatic[flegmǽtik]
= slack[slǽk] = slothful[slɔ́:θfəl] = sluggish[slʌ́giʃ] = torpid[tɔ́:rpid]
The shipbuilding industry has been inert for the first half year.
조선업은 상반기에 활발하지 못했다.

inevitable[inévətəbl] a 불가피한, 피할 수 없는, 필연적인 = inescapable[ìneskéipəbl]
= unavoidable[ʌ̀nəvɔ́idəbl]
The downturn of the global economy seems inevitable. 전 세계적인 경기 하락은 불가피해 보인다.

inexorable[inéksərəbl] a 변경할 수 없는, 냉혹한, 가차없는 = implacable[implǽkəbl]
= merciless[məˊːrsilis] = relentless[riléntlis] = unrelenting[ʌnriléntiŋ]
We have seen the inexorable growth of imported cars in the auto market share.
우리는 자동차 시장 점유율에서 수입차의 거침없는 성장세를 보고 있다.

infamous[ínfəməs] a 악명 높은, 지독한 = despicable[déspikəbl] = egregious[igríːdʒəs]
= heinous[héinəs] = iniquitous[iníkwətəs] = miscreant[mískriənt] = notorious[noutɔ́ːriəs]
= outrageous[autréidʒəs] = vicious[víʃəs]
An infamous serial killer was said to have escaped from the prison.
악명 높은 연쇄살인범이 탈옥했다고 전해졌다.

infatuated[infǽtʃuèitid] a 미친, 열중한, 반한 = obsessed[əbsést] = possessed[pəzést]
She was infatuated with the jazz singer. 그녀는 그 재즈 가수에게 반했다.

infinitesimal[ìnfinitésəməl] a 미소한, 극소의, 극미의 = diminutive[dimínjutiv]
= microscopic[màikrəskάpik] = minuscule[mínəskjùːl] = tiny[táini]
An infinitesimal amount of lead was detected from the river water.
강물에서 극소량의 납 성분이 검출되었다.

inflame[infléim] v 흥분시키다, 격앙시키다, 격분시키다 = agitate[ǽdʒitèit]
= arouse[əráuz] = incense[inséns] = infuriate[infjúərièit]
The FTA agreement with Chile inflamed farmers in the nation.
칠레와의 자유무역협정 체결은 농부들을 격앙시켰다.

inflammatory[inflǽmətɔ̀ːri] a 선동적인, 격정을 일으키는, 자극적인
= agitative[ǽdʒitèitiv] = demagogic[dèməgάdʒik] = incendiary[inséndièri]
= provocative[prəvάkətiv] = seditious[sidíʃəs] = subversive[səbvə́ːrsiv]
Most voters were indifferent to the inflammatory speeches by politicians.
대부분의 유권자들은 정치인들의 선동적인 연설에 무관심했다.

influx[ínflʌks] n 유입, 쇄도, 도래 = inpouring[inpɔ́ːriŋ]
The tailor shop owner was happy with the influx of the orders.
양복점 주인은 쇄도하는 주문에 행복해 했다.

infraction[infrǽkʃən] n 위반, 침해 = breach[briːtʃ] = contravention[kὰntrəvénʃən]
= infringement[infríndʒmənt] = transgression[trænsgréʃən] = violation[vàiəléiʃən]
The chairman committed an infraction of the law of inheritance.
회장님은 상속법을 위반했다.

infringe[infríndʒ] v 침해하다, 어기다, 위반하다 = breach[briːtʃ]
= contravene[kɑ̀ntrəvíːn] = disobey[dìsəbéi] = encroach[inkróutʃ] = infract[infrǽkt]
= intrude[intrúːd] = offend = trespass[tréspəs] = violate[váiəlèit]
No composer is allowed to infringe on the copyright law.
어떤 작곡가도 저작권을 위반해서는 안 된다.

infuse[infjúːz] v 주입하다, 불어넣다 = imbue[imbjúː] = impregnate[imprégneit]
= inculcate[inkʌ́lkei] = instill = permeate[pə́ːrmièit] = pervade = saturate[sǽtʃərèit]
= steep[stiːp] = suffuse[səfjúːz]
His praise infused the fighting spirit into the boxers.
그의 칭찬은 복싱 선수들에게 투지를 불어넣어 주었다.

ingenious[indʒíːnjəs] a 재간 있는, 독창적인, 기발한 = creative[kriéitiv]
= imaginative[imǽdʒənətiv] = innovative[ínəvèitiv] = intelligent[intélədʒənt] = inventive[invéntiv]
The engineers proposed ingenious designs for new washing machine.
그 엔지니어는 신제품 세탁기에 적용될 독창적인 디자인을 제안했다.

ingénue[ænʒənjúː] n 순정 소녀, 천진난만한 소녀 = innocent girl
The actress will play an ingénue role in the new movie.
그 여배우는 영화에서 순정소녀 역을 맡게 될 것이다.

ingenuous[indʒénjuəs] a 순진한, 천진한, 솔직한, 숨김없는 = artless
= candid[kǽndid] = frank = guileless[gáilis] – honest = unaffected
The young girl has an ingenuous smile. 그 어린 소녀는 천진한 미소를 가지고 있다.

ingrained[ingréind] a 깊이 배어든, 뿌리 깊은, 깊이 몸에 밴 = deep-rooted
= implanted = inbred[ínbréd] = inherent[inhíərənt] = innate[inéit] = intrinsic[intrínsik] = rooted
Jogging in the morning is his ingrained habit.
아침에 조깅하는 것은 그의 몸 깊이 배어 있는 습관이다.

ingratiate[ingréiʃièit] v 환심을 사다, 비위를 맞추다 = blandish[blǽndiʃ]
= flatter[flǽtər] = grovel[grʌ́vəl] = toady[tóudi]
He has ingratiated himself with his new boss. 그는 새로 온 사장의 비위를 맞추고 있다.

inherent[inhíərənt] a 내재된, 고유의, 타고난 = congenital[kəndʒénətl] = hereditary[hərédətèri]
= inborn = inbred[ínbréd] = inherited[inhéritid] = innate[inéit] = intrinsic[intrínsik]
All firefighters are aware of the risks inherent in their jobs.
모든 소방관들은 자신들의 직업에 위험이 내재되어 있다는 것을 의식하고 있다.

inhibit[inhíbit] v 억제하다, 금하다, 금지하다 = ban = interdict[íntərdìkt] = prevent = prohibit[prouhíbit] = proscribe[prouskráib] = stymie[stáimi]
School rules inhibit the students from going to the dance club.
학교의 교칙은 학생들이 댄스클럽에 가는 것을 금하고 있다.

inimical[inímikəl] a 해로운, 반하는, 적대하는 = adverse[ædvə́:rs] = antagonistic[æntægənístik] = hostile[hástl]
The government announced some measures inimical to the growth of our company.
정부는 우리 회사의 성장에 반하는 조치들을 발표했다.

QUIZ 66

Match each word in the first column with its definition in the second column.
Check your answers in the back of the book.

1.	inimical		a.	imbue = impregnate
2.	infatuated		b.	breach = contravene
3.	inexorable		c.	inpouring
4.	inherent		d.	creative = imaginative
5.	inevitable		e.	artless = candid
6.	infinitesimal		f.	contravention = infringement
7.	ingenuous		g.	deep-rooted = implanted
8.	inflammatory		h.	innocent girl
9.	influx		i.	agitative = demagogic
10.	inert		j.	obsessed = possessed
11.	infringe		k.	adverse = antagonistic
12.	infuse		l.	diminutive = microscopic
13.	ingrained		m.	agitate = arouse
14.	ingenue		n.	implacable = merciless
15.	inflame		o.	blandish = flatter
16.	ingenious		p.	despicable = egregious
17.	inhibit		q.	congenital = hereditary
18.	infraction		r.	dormant = inactive
19.	ingratiate		s.	inescapable = unavoidable
20.	infamous		t.	ban = interdict

inimitable[inímətəbl] a 흉내 낼 수 없는, 모방할 수 없는, 비길 데 없는 = matchless = unmatched = unparalleled[ʌnpærəleld] = unrivalled[ʌnráivəld]
She makes dresses in her own inimitable manner.
그녀는 흉내 낼 수 없는 그녀만의 방법으로 옷을 만든다.

iniquitous[iníkwətəs] a 사악한, 부정한, 부당한 = depraved[dipréivd]
= heinous[héinəs] = nefarious[niféəriəs] = vicious[víʃəs] = vile[vail] = wicked[wíkid]
We can see a lot of iniquitous practices in the society.
우리는 사회에서 많은 부당한 관행들을 봅니다.

injunction[indʒʌ́ŋkʃən] n 중지(금지) 명령, 명령 = behest[bihést] = decree[dikríː]
= edict[íːdikt] = fiat[fíːaːt] = order = ordinance[ɔ́ːrdənəns]
We got an injunction keeping our rival company from using our design.
우리는 경쟁회사들이 우리 디자인을 사용하지 못하도록 할 수 있는 명령을 받아냈다.

innate[inéit] a 타고난, 선천적인 = congenital[kəndʒénətl] = hereditary[hərédətèri]
= inborn = inbred[ínbréd] = inherent[inhíərənt] = inherited[inhéritid] = intrinsic[intrínsik]
He has an innate ability to run faster. 그는 빨리 달릴 수 있는 타고난 능력이 있다.

innocuous[inάkjuəs] a 해가 없는, 무해한 = harmless[hάːrmlis] = inoffensive[inəfénsiv]
She used eco-friendly detergent innocuous to the human body.
그녀는 인체에 무해한 친환경 세제를 사용했다.

innuendo[ìnjuéndou] n 풍자, 암시, 빈정거림 = allusion[əlúːʒən]
= insinuation[insìnjuéiʃən] = suggestion
His speech was full of innuendoes. 그의 연설은 풍자로 가득 차 있었다.

inordinate[inɔ́ːrdənət] a 과도한, 지나친, 불규칙한 = excessive[iksésiv]
= exorbitant[igzɔ́ːrbətənt] = extravagant[ikstrǽvəgənt] = preposterous[pripάstərəs]
The pilots asked inordinate demands from the air line company.
조종사들은 항공회사로부터 과도한 요구를 받았다.

inquisition[ìnkwəzíʃən] n 심문, 조사 = interrogation[intèrəgéiʃən] = investigation[invèstəgéiʃən]
The prosecution conducted an intensive inquisition against the suspect.
검찰은 피의자를 상대로 강도 높은 심문을 했다.

insatiable[inséiʃəbl] a 만족할 줄 모르는, 탐욕스러운, 채울 수 없는 = gluttonous[glʌ́tənəs] =
greedy[gríːdi] = rapacious[rəpéiʃəs] = ravenous[rǽvənəs] = voracious[vɔːréiʃəs]
The old man had an insatiable greed for money.
노인은 만족할 줄 모르는 돈 욕심을 가지고 있다.

insensible[insénsəbl] a 무감각한, 의식하지 못하는, 둔감한 = indifferent = numb[nʌm]
They were insensible of the danger of war. 그들은 전쟁의 위험을 의식하지 못했다.

insidious[insídiəs] a 잠행성의, 은밀히 퍼지는, 음흉한 = sneaky[sníːki] = stealthy[stélθi] = surreptitious[sə̀ːrəptíʃəs]
There is an insidious rumor in the market that the government will raise the interest rate.
정부가 금리를 올릴 것이라는 소문이 시장에 은밀히 퍼지고 있다.

insinuate[insínjuèit] v 넌지시 비치다, 암시하다 = allude[əlúːd] = connote[kənóut] = hint = imply[implái] = suggest
The actress insinuated that she would advance to the Chinese film industry.
그 여배우는 중국 영화계로 진출할 것을 넌지시 내비쳤다.

insipid[insípid] a 진부한, 특징 없는, 맛(풍미)없는 = banal[bənǽl] = bland = dull[dʌl] = mundane[mʌndéin] = prosaic[prouzéiik] = trite[trait] = uninteresting = vapid[vǽpid]
All the food in the restaurant tasted insipid. 그 식당의 모든 음식들은 맛이 없었다.

insolent[ínsələnt] a 오만한, 무례한, 건방진 = arrogant[ǽrəgənt] = cocky[káki] = haughty[hɔ́ːti] = imperious[impíəriəs] = overbearing = pompous[pámpəs] = presumptuous[prizʌ́mptʃuəs] = pretentious[priténʃəs] = smug[smʌg]
The young supervisor was insolent to the aged employees.
젊은 감독관은 나이 든 직원들에게 오만했다.

insouciant[insúːsiənt] a 무관심한, 무심한, 태평한 = nonchalant[nɑ̀nʃəlɑ́ːnt]
Actually he was worried about the test result, but he looked insouciant.
사실 그는 시험 결과를 걱정했지만, 겉으로는 태평한 듯 보였다.

instigate[ínstəgèit] v 부추기다, 선동하다 = abet[əbét] = foment[foumént] = goad[goud] = incite[insáit] = inflame = prompt[prampt] = provoke[prəvóuk]
Some of the greedy union leaders instigated workers to go on strike.
욕심 많은 일부 노조 지도자들이 노동자를 선동하여 파업을 하게 했다.

instill[instíl] v 서서히 불어넣다, 주입하다, 주입시키다 = imbue[imbjúː] = implant = impregnate[imprégneit] = inculcate[inkʌ́lkeit] = inject
The factory manager instilled the importance of safety to the new employees' mind.
그 공장 매니저는 새로 온 신입사원들에게 안전의 중요성을 심어주었다.

institute[ínstətjùːt] v 세우다, 제정하다, 시행하다 = establish[istǽbliʃ] = set up
The company decided to institute another research center by the end of the year.
그 회사는 연말까지 또 하나의 연구센터를 세우기로 결정했다.

instrumentalist[ìnstrəméntəlist] n 기악 연주자 = musicians = players
He has lived a happy life as an instrumentalist in the city orchestra.
그는 시향의 기악연주자로 행복한 삶을 살고 있다.

insubordinate[ìnsəbɔ́:rdənət] a 복종하지 않는, 반항하는
= contumacious[kɑ̀ntjuméiʃəs] = defiant[difáiənt] = disobedient[dìsəbí:diənt]
= intractable[intrǽktəbl] = rebellious[ribéljəs] = recalcitrant[rikǽlsitrənt]
= refractory[rifrǽktəri] = uncompliant
Nick was fired from his company because he had been insubordinate to his bosses.
Nick은 그의 상사들에게 복종하지 않았기 때문에 회사에서 해고되었다.

QUIZ 67

Match each word in the first column with its definition in the second column.
Check your answers in the back of the book.

1.	inordinate	a.	sneaky = stealthy
2.	insubordinate	b.	allusion = insinuation
3.	institute	c.	excessive = exorbitant
4.	innate	d.	congenital = hereditary
5.	innocuous	e.	harmless = inoffensive
6.	instigate	f.	establish = set up
7.	inimitable	g.	behest = decree
8.	instill	h.	allude = connote
9.	insatiable	i.	banal = bland
10.	insinuate	j.	matchless = unmatched
11.	inquisition	k.	contumacious = defiant
12.	iniquitous	l.	arrogant = cocky
13.	insipid	m.	musicians = players
14.	insensible	n.	depraved = heinous
15.	insouciant	o.	nonchalant
16.	insidious	p.	abet = foment
17.	insolent	q.	interrogation = investigation
18.	innuendo	r.	imbue = implant
19.	instrumentalist	s.	gluttonous = greedy
20.	injunction	t.	indifferent = numb

insufferable[insʌfərəbl] a 참을 수 없는, 견딜 수 없는 = intolerable[intɑ́lərəbl]
= unbearable[ʌnberəbl]
His arrogance was insufferable during the meeting. 회의 중 보여준 그의 오만함은 참기 어려웠다.

insular[ínsələr] a 고립된, 편협한, 배타적인 = bigoted[bígətid]
= circumscribed[sɜ́:rkəmskraɪb] = isolated[áisəlèitid] = narrow-minded = parochial[pəróukiəl]
We should not have insular view on celibates.
독신주의자들에 대해서 편협한 의견을 가져선 안 된다. celibate[séləbət] n 독신주의자

insuperable[insú:pərəbl] a 극복하기 어려운, 무적의 = impassible[impǽsəbl]
= insurmountable[ìnsərmáuntəbl] = invincible[invínsəbl]= unbeatable[ʌnbi:təbl]
The sudden increase of the unemployment rate looked like an insuperable problem.
급격한 실업률의 증가는 극복하기 어려운 문제처럼 보였다.

insurgent[insə́:rdʒənt] a 반란의, 폭동을 일으킨 = contumacious[kɒ̀ntjuméiʃəs]
= mutinous[mjú:tənəs] = rebellious[ribéljəs] = revolting[rivóultiŋ]
= revolutionary[rèvəlú:ʃənèri] = riotous[ráiətəs] = seditious[sidíʃəs]
The former two-star general was leading the insurgent troops.
전 육군 소장이 반란군을 이끌고 있었다.

insurrection[insərékʃən] n 폭동, 반란, 반역 = mutiny[mjú:təni] = rebellion[ribéljən]
= revolt[rivóult] = riot[ráiət] = sedition[sidíʃən] = tumult[tjú:məlt] = uprising
The police suppressed an insurrection. 경찰은 폭동을 진압했다.

intangible[intǽndʒəbl] a 무형의, 만질 수 없는 = impalpable[impǽlpəbl]
= indefinite[indéfənit] = unreal
The software company has a variety of intangible assets.
그 소프트웨어 회사는 다양한 무형 자산을 보유하고 있다.

integral[íntigrəl] a 불가결한, 필수의 = elemental[èləméntl] = essential[isénʃəl]
= indispensible = intrinsic[intrínsik] = necessary
A camera is an integral part of a smart phone.
카메라는 휴대폰에 없어서는 안 될 부품이다.

intensify[inténsəfài] v 강화하다, 증대하다 = enhance = heighten[háitn] = reinforce[rì:infɔ́:rs]
Customs Service intensified the immigration control. 세관은 출입국 관리를 강화했다.

intent[intént] a 확고한, 결의하고 있는, 작정한 = determined[ditə́:rmind]
= resolute[rézəlù:t] = resolved[rizʌ́lvd]
The judo player in the hospital was intent on participating in the tournament.
부상당한 그 유도 선수는 선수권대회에 꼭 참가하려고 한다.

intercessor[ìntərsésər] n 중재자, 조정자, 알선자 = arbitrator[ɑ́:rbətrèitər]
= mediator[mí:dièitər]
The warring parties needed an intercessor to settle the dispute.
적대하고 있는 당사자들은 논쟁을 해결하기 위해 중재자가 필요했다.

interdict[íntərdìkt] v 금지하다, 금하다 = ban = inhibit[inhíbit] = prevent[privént]
= prohibit[prouhíbit] = proscribe[prouskráib]
The government put in more troops to interdict the riot from breaking out.
정부는 폭동 발생을 방지하기 위해 더 많은 병력을 투입했다.

interim[íntərəm] a 임시의, 잠시의, 중간의 = tentative
The patriots formed an interim government before they went independent.
광복 전에 애국자들은 임시정부를 조직했다.

interloper[íntərlòupər] n 침입자, 주제넘은 사람 = intruder[intrú:dər]
= trespasser[tréspəsər]
It seems that there was an interloper in the museum overnight.
간밤에 박물관에 침입자가 있었던 것 같다.

interlude[íntərlù:d] n 막간, 사이, 간주 = break = pause[pɔ:z] = respite[réspit]
There are three interludes in the play. 그 연극에는 세 번의 막간이 있다.

interminable[intə́:rmənəbl] a 끝없는, 지루하게도 긴 = infinite[ínfənət]
= eternal[itə́:rnəl] = incessant[insésnt] = perpetual[pərpétʃuəl]
Some students felt bored with his interminable lecture.
일부 학생들은 그의 끝없는 강의에 지루해 했다.

intermittent[ìntərmítnt] a 간헐적인, 간간이 일어나는, 일시적으로 멈추는
= fitful[fítfəl] = irregular[irégjulər] = periodic[pìəriɑ́dik] = sporadic[spərǽdik]
There are a lot of intermittent springs in the mountain. 많은 간헐천들이 산 속에 있다.

interrogate[intérəgèit] v 심문하다, 따져 묻다 = grill = investigate[invéstəgèit]
FBI interrogated him about the conspiracy. FBI는 음모에 대해 그를 심문했다.

intersperse[ìntərspə́:rs] v 간격을 두고 배치하다 = scatter[skǽtər]
= sprinkle[spríŋkl] = strew[stru:]
Some tall trees were interspersed in the garden.
키 큰 나무들이 간격을 두고 정원에 배치되어 있다.

intervene[ìntərvíːn] **v** 개입하다, 끼어들다, 간섭하다 = arbitrate[ɑ́ːrbətrèit]
= intercede[ìntərsíːd] = mediate[míːdièit]
Harry had no choice but to intervene in a dispute between his best two friends.
Harry는 친한 친구 두 사람의 논쟁을 중재하지 않을 수 없었다.

intimate[íntəmət] **v** 넌지시 비치다, 암시하다 = allude[əlúːd] = hint = imply = indicate
= insinuate[insínjuèit] = suggest
My coworker intimated that he would move to our rival company.
나의 동료는 우리의 경쟁회사에 갈 것이라고 암시했다.

QUIZ 68

Match each word in the first column with its definition in the second column.
Check your answers in the back of the book.

1.	intermittent	a.	impalpable = indefinite
2.	insular	b.	break = pause
3.	interlude	c.	infinite = eternal
4.	interloper	d.	elemental = essential
5.	interdict	e.	intolerable = unbearable
6.	intangible	f.	arbitrate = intercede
7.	insufferable	g.	intruder = trespasser
8.	intensify	h.	enhance = heighten
9.	intent	i.	bigoted = circumscribed
10.	intercessor	j.	determined = resolute
11.	intimate	k.	allude = hint
12.	interim	l.	impassible = insurmountable
13.	insurgent	m.	arbitrator = mediator
14.	insurrection	n.	ban = inhibit
15.	intersperse	o.	contumacious = mutinous
16.	insuperable	p.	fitful = irregular
17.	interrogate	q.	tentative
18.	interminable	r.	mutiny = rebellion
19.	intervene	s.	grill = investigate
20.	integral	t.	scatter = sprinkle

intimidate[intímədèit] **v** 두렵게 하다, 협박하다, 겁먹게 하다 = browbeat
= bully[búli] = daunt[dɔːnt] = scare = threaten[θrétn]
The robbers intimidated the hostage into lying face down on the floor.
강도들은 인질들을 협박하여 바닥에 엎드리게 했다.

intractable[intrǽktəbl] a 고집 센, 다루기 힘든, 처리하기 어려운
= headstrong[hédstrɔ̀(:)ŋ] = intransigent[intrǽnsədʒənt] = recalcitrant[rikǽlsitrənt]
= refractory[rifrǽktəri] = stubborn[stʌ́bərn] = uncompromising
Tuberculosis is still an intractable disease. 결핵은 아직도 다루기 어려운 질병이다.

intrepid[intrépid] a 용감무쌍한, 대담한, 두려움을 모르는 = audacious[ɔ:déiʃəs]
= brave = courageous[kəréidʒəs] = dauntless[dɔ́:ntlis] = fearless[fíərlis] = gallant[gǽlənt]
= plucky[plʌ́ki] = valiant[vǽljənt] = valorous[vǽlərəs]
The intrepid soldiers were ready to go into battle.
용감무쌍한 군인들은 전투 준비가 되어 있었다.

intricate[íntrikət] a 복잡한, 미묘한, 얽힌 = complex = complicated[kámpləkèitid]
= convoluted[kánvəlù:tid] = tangled[tǽŋgld]
The company has intricate financial problems. 그 회사는 복잡한 재정문제를 가지고 있다.

intrigue[intrí:g] n 음모, 음모적 사건 = artifice[ɑ́:rtəfis] = cabal[kəbǽl] = collusion[kəlú:ʒən]
= conspiracy[kənspírəsi] = machination[mæ̀kənéiʃən] = plot = ruse[ru:z] = stratagem[strǽtədʒəm]
He said he was a scapegoat trapped in a political intrigue.
그는 정치적 음모에 걸린 희생양이라고 말했다.

intrude[intrú:d] v 침범하다, 방해하다 = encroach[inkróuʧ] = invade[invéid] = trespass[tréspəs]
We don't want anyone to intrude on our private lives.
우리는 누구나 개인생활을 침범하는 것을 원하지 않는다.

intuition[ìntju:íʃən] n 직관적 통찰, 직감 = clairvoyance[klɛərvɔ́iəns] = hunch[hʌnʧ]
= insight
The chairman relies on his intuition before making an important decision.
회장님은 중요 결정을 내리기 전에 자신의 직관에 의존한다.

invective[invéktiv] n 심한 비난, 독설, 악담 = diatribe[dáiətràib] = tirade[táireid]
= verbal abuse[vɔ́:rbəl-əbjú:z]
The two candidates exchanged invective each other during the argument.
두 후보자는 논쟁 도중에 서로 심한 비난을 퍼부었다.

inveigle[invéigl] v 꾀다, 유인하다, 구슬리다 = bamboozle[bæmbú:zl] = beguile[bigáil]
= cajole[kədʒóul] = coax[kouks] = entice[intáis] = wheedle[hwí:dl]
The dealer inveigled the young man into buying a faulty car.
자동차 중개인은 젊은 남자를 속여 결함 있는 차를 사게 했다.

investigate[invéstəgèit] v 조사하다, 수사하다, 살피다 = interrogate[intérəgèit]
= probe = scrutinize[skrú:tənàiz]
A team of experts is investigating the abduction case.
전문가 팀이 그 유괴사건을 조사하고 있다.

inveterate[invétərət] a 뿌리깊은, 상습적인, 만성의= established[istǽbliʃt] = ingrained[ingréind]
He died of the inveterate liver ailment. 그는 만성 간질환으로 죽었다.

invidious[invídiəs] a 부당한, 비위에 거슬리는, 불공평한, 남의 심기를 건드리는
= abominable[əbámənəbl] = detestable[ditéstəbl] = hateful[héitfəl] = obnoxious[əbnákʃəs]
= odious[óudiəs] = repugnant[ripʌgnənt]
It would be invidious for the police to release the powerful politician.
경찰이 유력 정치인을 풀어주는 것은 부당하다.

invigorate[invígərèit] v 고무하다, 기운을 돋우다 = enliven[inláivən]
= galvanize[gǽlvənàiz] = restore = revitalize[ri:vaɪtəlaɪz] = stimulate[stímjulèit]
The government announced some measures to invigorate the economy.
정부는 경제활성화를 위한 몇 가지 대책을 발표했다.

inviolable[inváiələbl] a 침범할 수 없는, 불가침의, 신성한 = divine[diváin]
= holy[hóuli] = sacred[séikrid] = sacrosanct[sǽkrousæŋkt]
The right to vote in the democracy is the inviolable right.
민주주의 사회에서 투표권은 불가침의 권리이다.

inviolate[inváiələt] a 침범되지 않은, 존중되어야 할, 신성한 = sacred[séikrid]
= sacrosanct[sǽkrousæŋkt]
The sovereignty of each nation should be inviolate. 모든 국가의 주권은 침범되어서는 안 된다.

invoke[invóuk] v 호소하다, 탄원하다, 들먹이다, 빌다 = adjure[ədʒúər]
= appeal to = beseech[bisí:tʃ] = conjure[kándʒər] = entreat[intrí:t] = implore[implɔ́:r]
= petition[pətíʃən] = plead[pli:d] = pray = solicit[səlísit] = supplicate[sʌpləkèit]
The management will invoke the law if the illegal protest continues.
만일 불법시위가 계속되면 회사의 경영진은 법에 호소할 것이다.

inure[injúər] v 익숙하게 하다 = acclimate[ǽkləmèit] = accustom[əkʌstəm]
= familiarize[fəmíljəràiz] = habituate[həbítʃuèit]
The farmers in the area have been inured to the severe drought.
그 지역 농부들은 심한 가뭄에 익숙해져 있다.

invulnerable[invʌ́lnərəbl] a 물리칠 수 없는, 안전한, 공격할 수 없는
= impregnable[imprégnəbl] = invincible[invínsəbl] = unbeatable[ʌnbiːtəbl]
Most buildings in Tokyo were built invulnerable to moderate earthquakes.
도쿄의 대부분 빌딩들은 보통 정도의 지진에는 안전하게 지어졌다.

irascible[irǽsəbl] a 화를 잘 내는, 성미 급한, 성마른 = cantankerous[kæntǽŋkərəs]
= choleric[kálərik] = contentious[kənténʃəs] = fractious[frǽkʃəs] = irritable[írətəbl]
= peevish[píːviʃ] = petulant[pétʃulənt] = testy[tésti]
The manager is not popular among the employees because he easily gets irascible.
매니저는 쉽게 화를 내는 성미 때문에 종업원들 사이에서 인기가 없다.

iridescent[ìrədésnt] a 무지개 빛깔의, 보는 각도에 따라 색깔이 변하는
= lustrous[lʌ́strəs] = rainbow-colored = shimmering[ʃímərɪŋ]
The expedition encountered iridescent chameleons on the island.
탐험대는 섬에서 색깔이 변하는 카멜레온과 마주쳤다.

QUIZ 69

Match each word in the first column with its definition in the second column.
Check your answers in the back of the book.

1.	inviolate		a.	headstrong = intransigent
2.	invective		b.	bamboozle = beguile
3.	invigorate		c.	audacious = brave
4.	intricate		d.	sacred = sacrosanct
5.	inveigle		e.	browbeat = bully
6.	inviolable		f.	complex = complicated
7.	intimidate		g.	impregnable = invincible
8.	intractable		h.	interrogate = probe
9.	intuition		i.	artifice = cabal
10.	investigate		j.	cantankerous = choleric
11.	iridescent		k.	established = ingrained
12.	invidious		l.	encroach = invade
13.	intrigue		m.	lustrous = rainbow-colored
14.	intrude		n.	acclimate = accustom
15.	intrepid		o.	diatribe = tirade
16.	invoke		p.	adjure = appeal to
17.	inure		q.	clairvoyance = hunch
18.	invulnerable		r.	abominable = detestable
19.	irascible		s.	enliven = galvanize
20.	inveterate		t.	divine = holy

irk[əːrk] v 짜증나게 하다, 화나게 하다, 괴롭히다 = annoy = bother = gall[gɔːl]
= irritate[írətèit] = peeve[piːv] = rile[rail] = rub the wrong way
It irked me to listen to the noisy talking from the next table.
옆자리의 소음을 듣는 것은 나를 짜증나게 했다.

irrepressible[ìriprésəbl] a 억누를 수 없는, 제지할 수 없는, 감당하기 어려운
= unrestrained[ʌnrɪstreɪnd] = unruly[ʌnrúːli] = unstoppable
His sadness was irrepressible when he heard the death of his mother.
그는 어머니의 죽음을 듣고 슬픔을 억누를 수가 없었다.

irritate[írətèit] v 짜증나게 하다, 초조하게 하다, 화나게 하다 = annoy = bother
= enrage[inréidʒ] = exasperate[igzǽspərèit] = gall[gɔːl] = incense[ínsens]
= infuriate[infjúərièit] = irk[əːrk] = peeve[piːv] = rile[rail] = rub the wrong way = vex[veks]
His repeated lies have irritated his boss. 그의 반복되는 거짓말은 그의 상사를 짜증나게 했다.

QUIZ 70

Match each word in the first column with its definition in the second column.
Check your answers in the back of the book.

1. irritate   a. unrestrained = unruly
2. irrepressible   b. annoy = bother
3. irk   c. annoy = bother

jaded[dʒéidid] a 지친, 물린, 싫증난 = exhausted[igzɔ́:stid] = tired = weary[wíəri]
Some tourists felt jaded after spending 7 days in the cruise ship.
어떤 관광객들은 크루즈여행을 하는 동안 7일간 배에서 지내는 물린 느낌을 가졌다.

jargon[dʒá:rgən] n 전문어, 은어, 특수용어 argot[á:rgou] = specialized language
He couldn't understand the legal jargon that the two lawyers were saying.
그는 두 명의 변호사가 이야기하는 법률용어를 이해하지 못했다.

jaundice[dʒɔ́:ndis] v 편견을 가지게 하다 = bias[báiəs] = prepossess[prì:pəzés]
= prejudice[prédʒudis]
We should not take a jaundiced view of immigrants.
우리는 이민자들에 대해서 편견을 가져선 안 된다.

jaunt[dʒɔ:nt] n 짧은 여행, 소풍 = excursion[ikskə́:rʒən] = journey[dʒə́:rni] = trip
The writer used to enjoy going on a jaunt around the island with his wife.
그 작가는 아내와 함께 섬 주위를 짧게 여행하는 것을 즐기곤 했다.

jejune[dʒidʒú:n] a 지루한, 재미없는, 단순한 = banal[bənǽl]= bland[blænd]
= insipid[insípid] = trite[trait] = vapid[vǽpid]
His jejune speech made some audience surf the internet on their smart phones.
그의 지루한 연설은 일부 청중들이 스마트폰으로 인터넷 검색이나 하게 만들었다.

jest[dʒest] v 농담하다 = banter[bǽntər] = joke
The three were jesting about corrupt politicians. 그 세 사람은 정치인들에 대해서 농담했다.

jingoism[dʒíŋgouìzm] n 맹목적 애국주의, 대외 강경주의 = chauvinism[ʃóuvənìzm]
= nationalism[nǽʃənəlìzm]
We should prevent the jingoism from being taught in schools.
우리는 맹목적 애국주의가 학교에서 교육되는 것을 막아야 한다.

jittery[dʒítəri] a 조마조마한, 초조해하는 = anxious = edgy[édʒi] = fidgety[fídʒiti]
= nervous = restless[réstlis]
The dancer became too jittery to move before her performance.
그 댄서는 공연 전에 너무 조마조마해서 움직일 수 없었다.

jocular[dʒákjulər] a 익살스러운, 웃기는, 익살떠는, 명랑한 = blithe[blaið] = cheerful = droll[droul] = facetious[fəsí:ʃəs] = funny = humorous = jocose[dʒoukóus] = jocund[dʒákənd] = jolly[dʒáli] = jovial[dʒóuviəl] = ludicrous[lú:dəkrəs]
His jocular way of speaking made him popular among his coworkers.
그의 익살스러운 말투는 동료들 사이에서 그를 인기 있게 만들었다.

jocund[dʒákənd] a 유쾌한, 명랑한, 즐거운 = blithe[blaið] = cheerful = droll = facetious[fəsí:ʃəs] = funny = humorous = jocose[dʒoukóus] = jocular[dʒákjulər] = jolly[dʒáli] = jovial[dʒóuviəl] = ludicrous[lú:dəkrəs]
The elementary school reunion always turns into a jocund party.
초등학교 동창모임은 언제나 명랑한 파티로 변한다.

jolt[dʒoult] v 덜컹거리게 하다, 마구 흔들리다, 충격을 주다 = convulse[kənvʌls] = shake
The spacecraft jolted the astronauts for a few minutes after the blast-off.
우주선은 발사 후에 몇 분 동안 우주인들을 마구 흔들거리게 했다.

jovial[dʒóuviəl] a 쾌활한, 명랑한, 즐거운 = affable[æfəbl] = amiable[éimiəbl] = convivial[kənvíviəl] = jolly[dʒáli]
The grandparents spent their jovial time with their grandchildren.
조부모님들은 그들의 손주들과 쾌활한 시간을 보냈다.

jubilation[dʒù:bəléiʃən] n 환희, 의기양양 = exultation[ègzʌltéiʃən] = glee[gli:] = felicity[filísəti] = mirth[mə:r]
Every city and town of the country was filled with jubilation when its national soccer team advanced to the final match.
그 나라의 모든 도시와 마을은 축구국가대표 팀이 결승전에 올라갔을 때 환희로 가득 찼다.

judicious[dʒu:díʃəs] a 현명한, 사려 분별이 있는, 판단력 있는 = rational[ræʃənl] = sober[sóubər] = sagacious[səgéiʃəs]
The real estate agent advised us to make a judicious decision before we bought a land in the rural area.
그 부동산 중개인은 우리가 지방에 땅을 사기 전에 현명한 결정을 하라고 조언했다.

juggernaut[dʒʌgərnɔ̀:t] n 불가항력, 강력하고 거대한 것 = overpowering force
Modern war between two countries will surely be a juggernaut that we can't resist.
두 나라 사이의 현대전은 틀림없이 우리가 저항하기 어려운 불가항력이 될 것이다.

junction[dʒʌ́ŋkʃən] n 교차점, 합류점 = confluence[kɑ́nfluəns]
= convergence[kənvə́ːrdʒəns] = juncture[dʒʌ́ŋktʃər]
The great dam has been built at the junction of the three rivers.
그 거대 댐은 세 개의 강이 합류하는 지점에 세워졌다.

junta[húntə] n 군사 정부 = military government
The junta carried out large-scale reforms in the every sector of the government.
그 군사정부는 정부의 모든 분야에 걸쳐서 대규모 개혁을 단행했다.

juxtapose[dʒʌ́kstəpòuz] v 나란히 놓다, 병치하다 = appose[əpóuz]
Some locally provided fish were juxtaposed with the imported fish on the counter in a fish shop.
생선가게의 판매대 위에 그 지역에서 공급되는 생선들과 수입산 생선들이 나란히 놓여 있었다.

QUIZ 71

Match each word in the first column with its definition in the second column.
Check your answers in the back of the book.

1.	juxtapose	a.	affable = amiable
2.	judicious	b.	anxious = edgy
3.	jocular	c.	bias = prepossess
4.	jovial	d.	exultation = glee
5.	jocund	e.	convulse = shake
6.	jolt	f.	rational = sober
7.	jingoism	g.	blithe = cheerful
8.	jittery	h.	overpowering force
9.	jaundice	i.	exhausted = tired
10.	junta	j.	blithe = droll
11.	jest	k.	argot = specialized
12.	jejune	l.	chauvinism = nationalism
13.	jubilation	m.	confluence = convergence
14.	jaunt	n.	appose
15.	juggernaut	o.	joke
16.	junction	p.	military government
17.	jaded	q.	banal = blend
18.	jargon	r.	excursion = journey

ken[ken] n 이해(지식)의 범위, 시야 = knowledge[nάlidʒ] = perception[pərsépʃən]
His eccentric behavior was beyond our ken. 그의 별난 행동은 우리의 이해 범위를 넘었다.

kinetic[kinétik] a 운동의 = moving
The kinetic energy is concerned with the velocity and the size of mass of an object.
운동에너지는 물체의 속도와 질량과 관계가 있다.

karma[kάːrmə] n 업보, 운명 = destiny[déstəni]
My grandparents believe in karma which will affect their future lives after death.
나의 조부모님들은 사람들이 죽은 후에 맞이하는 내세에 영향을 주는 업보를 믿으신다.

QUIZ 72

Match each word in the first column with its definition in the second column.
Check your answers in the back of the book.

1. ken   a. destiny
2. karma   b. knowledge = perception
3. kinetic   c. moving

labyrinth[lǽbərìnθ] n 미로, 미궁 = maze[meiz]
The boys from the countryside wandered in the labyrinth of streets in Shanghai.
지방에서 올라온 소년들은 미로와 같은 상하이의 거리에서 방황했다.

lacerate[lǽsərèit] v 째다, 찢다, 괴롭히다 = tear[tiər] = rend[rend]
His shoulder was lacerated in the car accident.
교통사고로 그의 어깨가 찢어졌다.

laconic[ləkάnik] a 간결한, 간명한, 말수가 적은 = brusque[brʌsk] = terse[tə:rs]
The comedian was rather laconic as a boy. 그 코미디언은 어릴 때 말수가 적었다.

lament[ləmént] v 애통하다, 비탄하다, 애도하다 = bemoan[bimóun] = deplore[diplɔ́:r]
= mourn[mɔ:rn]
Tony lamented the death of his only daughter.
Tony는 외동 딸의 죽음에 애통해 했다.

lampoon[læmpú:n] v 풍자하다, 빈정거리다, 놀리다 = burlesque[bə:rlésk]
= parody[pǽrədi] = satirize[sǽtəràiz]
His poem lampoons the corruption and conspiracy of the politicians.
그의 시는 정치인들의 비리와 음모를 풍자하고 있다.

languid[lǽŋgwid] a 힘없는, 늘어진, 활기 없는 = drooping[drú:piŋ] = dull
= languorous[lǽŋgərəs] = lethargic[ləθά:rdʒik] = listless = sluggish[slʌ́giʃ]
After a bout of boxing match, the boxer felt languid.
한바탕 복싱을 한 뒤 그 복서는 나른함을 느꼈다.

languish[lǽŋgwiʃ] v 시들다, 쇠약해지다, 활기가 없어지다 = shrink[ʃriŋk]
= shrivel[ʃrívəl] = wane[wein] = wither[wíðər]
The desktop PC industry started to languish in 2000s.
데스크용 PC 산업은 2000년대에 사양길에 접어들기 시작했다.

lapse[læps] n 실수, 잘못 = mistake
The politician was defeated in the election due to a lapse of the tongue.
그 정치인은 실언 때문에 선거에서 패배했다.

larceny[lά:rsəni] n 도둑질, 절도죄, 절도 = pilfering[pílfəriŋ] = purloining[pərlɔ́in] =
stealing = theft[θeft]
He was charged with larceny. 그는 절도죄로 기소되었다.

larder[láːrdər] n 식료품 저장실, 저장 식료품 = storage of provisions
The rich man kept the larder of his house during the long period of famine.
그 부자는 긴 기근 때에 그의 집 식료품 저장실을 열어놓았다.

largess[laːrdʒés] n 아낌없이 줌, 기부금, 많은 부조 = benefaction[bénəfækʃən]
= philanthropy[filǽnθrəpi]
The charitable organization is being run by the largess of many benefactors.
그 자선단체는 많은 후원자의 기부금으로 운영되고 있다.

lascivious[ləsíviəs] a 음란한, 선정적인, 음탕한 = debauched[dibɔ́ːtʃt]
= lecherous[létʃərəs] = lewd[luːd] = libertine[líbərtìːn] = libidinous[libídənəs]
= licentious[laisénʃəs] = lustful[lʌ́stfəl] = naughty[nɔ́ːti] = obscene[əbsíːn]
= profligate[práfligət] = promiscuous[prəmískjuəs] = prurient[prúəriənt] = salacious[səléiʃəs]
The lascivious movie was being kept from showing in the theater.
그 선정적인 영화는 영화관에서 상영이 중지되었다.

lassitude[lǽsətjùːd] n 노곤함, 나른함, 무기력 = languor[lǽŋgər] = lethargy[léθərdʒi]
= listlessness = torpor[tɔ́ːrpər]
The spicy chicken soup relieved me of the lassitude.
그 매콤한 닭고기 수프가 나의 노곤함을 풀어줬다.

latent[léitnt] a 잠재성의, 잠복성의, 숨어 있는 = dormant[dɔ́ːrmənt] = hidden
= potential[pəténʃəl] = underlying
I am sure that he must have a latent ability to be the leader of our country.
그는 우리나라의 지도자가 될 잠재적인 가능성을 가지고 있다.

latitude[lǽtətjùːd] n 자유, 위도, 허용 범위 = freedom
We should allow the students considerable latitude in the dormitory.
우리는 학생들에게 기숙사에서 상당한 자유를 허용해야 한다.

laud[lɔːd] v (찬양, 찬미, 칭찬)하다 = adore[ədɔ́ːr] = commend = eulogize[júːlədʒàiz]
= extol[ikstóul]
They lauded the dead firefighter as a hero. 그들은 죽은 소방관을 영웅으로 찬양했다.

lavish[lǽviʃ] a 아끼지 않는, 아주 후한, 낭비하는, 사치스러운 = bountiful[báuntifəl]
= extravagant[ikstrǽvəgənt] = opulent[ápjulənt] = profuse
The president was very lavish in the pay to his employees.
사장은 종업원들의 급여에 매우 후했다.

lax[læks] a 느슨한, 태만한, 해이한 = flaccid[flǽksid] = negligent[néglidʒənt] = remiss[rimís] = slack
Lax discipline can lead to a fatal accident in the military.
군대에서는 규율이 느슨하면 치명적인 사고로 연결될 수 있다.

layman[leimən] n 평신도, 문외한, 비전문가 = amateur[ǽmətʃùər] = dilettante[dìlitá:nti] = follower
Even a layman can enjoy the fishing with a roll after a few practices.
비전문가도 몇 번 연습을 하면 견지낚시를 즐길 수 있다.

leaden[lédn] a 무거운, 활기 없는, 둔한 = ponderous[pάndərəs] = weighty[wéiti]
After 8 hours of hard work, his whole body felt leaden to a rock.
8시간이나 고된 노동을 한 뒤 그는 온몸이 천근만근 무겁게 느껴졌다.

QUIZ 73

*Match each word in the first column with its definition in the second column.
Check your answers in the back of the book.*

1.	leaden	a.	ponderous = weighty
2.	layman	b.	amateur = dilettante
3.	larceny	c.	mistake
4.	lavish	d.	flaccid = negligent
5.	lampoon	e.	shrink = shrivel
6.	languid	f.	dormant = hidden
7.	largess	g.	pilfering = purloining
8.	lapse	h.	languor = lethargy
9.	laconic	i.	freedom
10.	lassitude	j.	adore = commend
11.	latitude	k.	storage of provisions
12.	lascivious	l.	bemoan = deplore
13.	lament	m.	burlesque = parody
14.	latent	n.	maze
15.	larder	o.	tear = rend
16.	laud	p.	brusque = terse
17.	languish	q.	bountiful = extravagant
18.	lax	r.	debauched = lecherous
19.	labyrinth	s.	benefaction = philanthropy
20.	lacerate	t.	drooping = dull

legacy[légəsi] n 유산, 유물, 유증 = bequest[bikwést] = heritage[héritidʒ] = inheritance[inhérətəns]
The old rich man left a large legacy to his new wife.
그 부유한 노인은 많은 유산을 새 부인에게 남겼다.

lenient[líːniənt] a 관대한, 인정이 많은 = benign[bináin] = forgiving
= indulgent[indʌ́ldʒənt] = tolerant[tálərənt]
The judge was lenient towards the young thief. 판사는 어린 절도범에게 관대했다.

lethal[líːθəl] a 치명적인, 치사의 = deadly[dédli] = fatal[féitl] = pernicious[pərníʃəs] = virulent[vírjulənt]
The volcano eruption dealt a lethal blow to the tourism industry.
화산 폭발은 관광업계에 치명타를 날렸다.

lethargy[léθərdʒi] n 무기력, 권태, 기면 = inactivity = inertia[inəːrʃə]
= lassitude[lǽsətjùːd] = listlessness = torpidity[tɔːrpídəti]
He has been in a state of lethargy after losing all his money in the stock investment.
주식투자로 모든 돈을 잃고 그는 무기력 상태에 빠졌다.

levity[lévəti] n 경솔, 경박, 경솔한 행위 = frivolity[frivάləti]
You should not approach this problem with levity. 이 문제에 경솔하게 접근해서는 안 된다.

lexicographer[lèksəkάgrəfər] n 사전 편집자, 사전 편찬자 = dictionary editor
His job was a lexicographer. 그의 직업은 사전 편집자였다.

liability[làiəbíləti] n 의무, 법적 책임, 부채 = duty = obligation[àbləgéiʃən]
= responsibility[rispὰnsəbíləti]
We hold no liability for the damages caused by intentional accident.
우리는 고의 사고로 인한 손해에 대해서는 책임을 지지 않습니다.

liaison[lìːeizɔ́ːŋ] n 연락, 밀통, 간통 = communication = contact = intermediary[intərmíːdièri]
He was a liaison officer in the 8th army. 그는 미8군에서 연락장교로 근무했다.

libel[láibəl] n 명예훼손, 모욕 = defamation[dèfəméiʃən] = aspersion[əspə́ːrʃən]
= calumny[kǽləmni] = denigration[dènigréiʃən] = vituperation[vaitjùːpəréiʃən]
The actress will sue a notorious netizen for libel.
그 여배우는 악명 높은 네티즌을 명예훼손으로 고소할 것이다.

libertine[líbərtìːn] n 방탕자, 난봉꾼 = debauched[dibɔ́ːtʃt] person = lecher[létʃər]
= profligate[prάfligət] = satyr[séitər] = voluptuary[vəlʌ́ptʃuèri]
Mark was a libertine before marriage. Mark는 결혼 전 난봉꾼이었다.

licentious[laisénʃəs] a 음란한, 음탕한, 부도덕한 = debauched[dibɔ́:tʃt] = lascivious[ləsíviəs] = lecherous[létʃərəs] = lewd[lu:d] = libertine[líbərtì:n] = libidinous[libídənəs] = lustful[lʌ́stfəl] = naughty[nɔ́:ti] = obscene[əbsí:n] = profligate[práfligət] = promiscuous[prəmískjuəs] = prurient[prúəriənt] = salacious[səléiʃəs]
The priest confessed that he used to seek licentious pleasures in his youth.
신부님은 젊은 시절 음탕한 쾌락을 추구했다고 고백했다.

lien[lí:ən] n 선취 특권, 유치권 = right to dispose of property
The bank has a lien on the property of the company.
은행이 회사 재산에 대한 유치권을 가지고 있다.

liken[láikən] v 비유하다, 비교하다 = compare
Our life is likened to a long journey. 우리 삶은 긴 항해에 비유된다.

limerick[límərik] n 5행 희시 = poem[póuəm]
The poet wrote a limerick to satirize materialism.
그 시인은 물질만능주의를 풍자하는 5행 희시를 썼다.

limpid[límpid] a 맑은, 투명한, 명쾌한 = clear = comprehensible[kàmprihénsəbl] = lucid[lú:sid] = obvious[ábviəs] = pellucid[pəlú:sid] = perspicuous[pərspíkjuəs] = transparent[trænspéərənt]
The river was so limpid that we could see small fish in it.
강물이 매우 투명해서 물속의 작은 물고기들도 볼 수 있었다.

listless[lístlis] a 열의 없는, 무기력한 = drowsy[dráuzi] = inanimate[inǽnəmət] = inert[inə́:rt] = lackadaisical[lækədéizikəl] = languid[lǽŋgwid] = leaden[lédn] = lethargic[ləθɑ́:rdʒik] = lifeless = sluggish[slʌ́giʃ] = spiritless[spíritlis]
The divorce left her feeling listless in life. 그녀의 삶은 이혼으로 인해 무기력에 빠졌다.

lithe[laið] a 나긋나긋한, 유연한, 뼈가 연한 = flexible[fléksəbl] = limber[límbər] = lissome[lísəm] = pliable[pláiəbl] = pliant[pláiənt] = supple[sʌ́pl]
She was lithe while dancing. 춤출 때 그녀는 유연했다.

litigate[lítəgèit] v 소송하다, 법정에서 다투다 = indict[indáit] = prosecute[prásikjù:t]
Both sides agreed to litigate the conflict. 양측은 분쟁을 법정에서 다투기로 합의했다.

livid[lívid] a 납빛인, 검푸른, 격노한 = discolored
The victim's face turned livid with rage. 피해자의 얼굴은 노여움으로 납빛이 되었다.

loath[louθ] a 지긋지긋하여, 싫어하는, 꺼리는 = averse[əvə́ːrs] = hesitant[hézətənt] = reluctant[rilʌ́ktənt] = unwilling[ʌnwíliŋ]
She is loath to go to a restaurant alone. 그녀는 혼자서 식당에 가기를 꺼린다.

QUIZ 74

Match each word in the first column with its definition in the second column. Check your answers in the back of the book.

1.	loath		a.	communication = contact
2.	limerick		b.	duty = obligation
3.	liaison		c.	defamation = aspersion
4.	lien		d.	indict = prosecute
5.	levity		e.	debauched = lascivious
6.	lexicographer		f.	benign = forgiving
7.	listless		g.	averse = hesitant
8.	litigate		h.	debauched person = lecher
9.	libel		i.	discolored
10.	lenient		j.	bequest = heritage
11.	licentious		k.	dictionary editor
12.	lethargy		l.	frivolity
13.	liken		m.	inactivity = inertia
14.	legacy		n.	poem
15.	limpid		o.	clear = comprehensible
16.	libertine		p.	right to dispose property
17.	lithe		q.	deadly = fatal
18.	liability		r.	drowsy = inanimate
19.	livid		s.	flexible = limber
20.	lethal		t.	compare

lofty[lɔ́ːfti] a 높은, 고귀한, 숭고한, 오만한 = elevated[éləvèitid] = towering[táuəriŋ]
He has lofty goals to make the world a better place.
그는 이 세상을 더 좋은 곳으로 만들겠다는 숭고한 목표를 가지고 있다.

longing[lɔ́ːŋiŋ] n 갈망, 동경, 열망 = craving[kréiviŋ] = yearning[jə́ːrniŋ]
She has a longing to work for UN. 그녀는 UN에서 일하고 싶다는 열망을 가지고 있다.

loquacious[loukwéiʃəs] a 말하기를 좋아하는, 수다스러운 = babbling[bǽbliŋ] = chatty[tʃǽti] = garrulous[gǽrələs] = prolix[proulíks] = verbose[vəːrbóus] = voluble[vάluəbl] = wordy[wə́ːrdi]
She is so loquacious that she is rarely left alone.
그녀는 말하기를 너무 좋아해서 혼자 있는 경우가 거의 없다.

lout[laut] n 시골뜨기, 촌놈 = boor = bumpkin[bʌmpkin]
The carpenter looks like a lout. 목수는 시골뜨기처럼 보인다.

lubricate[lúːbrəkèit] v 윤활유를 치다 = grease[griːs] = oil
Lubricate the gearbox on regular basis. 규칙적으로 차량 기어박스에 윤활유를 쳐라.

lucid[lúːsid] a 명쾌한, 명료한, 바른 정신의 = clear = unambiguous[ʌnæmbígjuəs]
= unequivocal[|ʌnɪ|kwɪvəkl]
He gave a lucid explanation about the problem. 그는 그 문제에 대해 명쾌하게 설명했다.

ludicrous[lúːdəkrəs] a 터무니없는, 익살맞은, 웃음을 자아내게 하는
= farcical[fάːrsikəl] = laughable[læfəbl] = ridiculous[ridíkjuləs]
His plan sounds ludicrous. 그의 계획은 터무니없는 것처럼 들린다.

lug[lʌg] v 힘들게 끌다, 나르다 = haul[hɔːl] = tow[tou]
The hairdresser struggled to lug her huge suitcases at the airport.
미용사는 공항에서 거대한 여행가방을 힘들게 끌고 있었다.

lugubrious[lugjúːbriəs] a 우울한, 침울한, 슬퍼하는 = doleful[dóulfəl]
= mournful[mɔ́ːrnfəl] = sorrowful[sάrəfəl]
There was a lugubrious look on the face of the widow.
그 미망인의 얼굴에는 침울한 표정이 나타나 있었다.

lull[lʌl] v 달래다, 안심시키다 = calm[kaːm] = soothe[suːð]
She sang a song to lull the baby to sleep. 그녀는 아기를 재우려고 노래를 불렀다.

lumber[lʌmbər] v 쿵쿵 걷다, 육중하게 움직이다 = plod[plad] = stump[stʌmp]
= trudge[trʌdʒ] = walk heavily
A battalion of robots were lumbering in towards the city to engage in a battle with humans.
로봇 부대가 인간과 전투를 벌이기 위해 도시로 쿵쿵 걸어오고 있었다.

luminary[lúːmənèri] n 전문가, 권위자 = dignitary[dígnitèri]
He is a leading luminary in the development of the electric cars.
그는 전기차 개발에 있어 앞서가는 전문가입니다.

lurk[ləːrk] v 숨어 있다, 잠재하다, 잠복하다 = skulk[skʌlk] = sneak[sniːk]
Many archers lurked in ambush in the forest waiting for the enemy.
궁수들이 적을 기다리며 숲 속에 매복해 있었다.

lush[lʌʃ] a 푸르게 우거진, 풀이 무성한 = green = verdant[və́:rdnt]
His house has a lush garden. 그의 집에는 풀이 무성한 정원이 있다.

lustrous[lʌ́strəs] a 윤기가 흐르는, 광택 있는 = gleaming[glí:miŋ] = glistening[glísn]
= glossy = luminous[lú:mənəs] = radiant[réidiənt] = shining
Most women living around the river have thick lustrous hair.
강 근처에 사는 대부분의 여인들이 숱 많고 윤기가 흐르는 머릿결을 가지고 있다.

luxuriant[lʌgʒúəriənt] a 무성한, 풍성한, 풍부한 = opulent[ápjulənt] = profuse
= sumptuous[sʌ́mpʧuəs]
This area was once a luxuriant forest, but now it has turned into a forest of buildings.
이 땅은 한때 풍부한 숲이었으나 이제는 빌딩 숲으로 변했다.

lyrical[lírikəl] a 서정시 같은, 아름답게 표현된, 시적으로 로맨틱한 = melodic[məládik]
= rhythmic[ríðmik]
Most songs composed by JY Park have many lyrical melodies.
JY Park이 작곡한 대부분의 노래는 매우 서정적인 선율을 가지고 있다.

QUIZ 75

Match each word in the first column with its definition in the second column.
Check your answers in the back of the book.

1. lugubrious
2. lyrical
3. loquacious
4. lout
5. lubricate
6. lurk
7. ludicrous
8. lumber
9. lofty
10. lull
11. longing
12. lucid
13. lug
14. lush
15. luminary
16. luxuriant
17. lustrous

a. Dignitary
b. clear = unambiguous
c. skulk = sneak
d. green = verdant
e. farcical = laughable
f. elevated = towering
g. gleaming = glistening
h. haul = tow
i. grease = oil
j. opulent = profuse
k. doleful = mournful
l. craving = yearning
m. melodic = rhythmic
n. babbling = chatty
o. calm = soothe
p. plod = stump
q. boor = bumpkin

machination[mækənéiʃən] n 음모, 모략, 모의하기 = artifice[ɑ́:rtəfis]
= conspiracy[kənspírəsi] = intrigue[intrí:g] = ploy[plɔi] = ruse[ru:z] = scheme[ski:m]
= stratagem[strǽtədʒəm]
The third prince ascended the throne through the numerous machinations of the rivals.
세 번째 왕자가 수많은 경쟁자들의 음모를 뚫고 왕위에 올랐다.

magnanimous[mægnǽnəməs] a 관대한, 도량이 큰, 도량이 넓은
= forgiving[fərgívin] = considerate[kənsídərət] = munificent[mju:nífəsnt]
No judges should be magnanimous toward child abuse.
아동 학대에 대해서는 어떤 판사도 관대해서는 안 된다.

magnate[mǽgneit] n 거물, 유력자 = bigwig[bɪgwɪg] = mogul[móugəl]
= tycoon[taikú:n]
The financial magnate was arrested for rigging the stock price.
금융계의 거물은 주가 조작으로 체포되었다.

maladroit[mælədrɔit] a 솜씨 없는, 재치 없는, 서투른 = all thumbs
= awkward[ɔ́:kwərd] = clumsy[klʌ́mzi]
The volunteers were maladroit at organizing the charity event.
자원봉사자들은 자선행사를 조직하는 데 솜씨가 없었다.

malaise[mæléiz] n (특정 상황·집단 내에 존재하는) 문제들[불안감] = angst[a:ŋkst]
= anxiety[æŋzáiəti] = despair = discomfort = disquiet[diskwáiət] = doldrums[dóuldrəmz]
It will take much time and many efforts to solve economic malaise in our society.
우리 사회 내의 경제적 문제들을 해결하기 위해서는 많은 시간과 노력이 필요하다.

malfeasance[mælfí:zns] n 부정행위, 위법행위, 부정 = impropriety[ìmprəpráiəti]
= misbehavior[mìsbihéivjər] = misconduct
Some police officers were tempted to be involved in malfeasance in their jobs.
어떤 경찰관들은 직무 수행 중 부정행위에 관련된 유혹을 받았다.

malign[məláin] v 비방하다, 중상하다, 헐뜯다 = defame = calumniate[kəlʌ́mnièit]
= cast aspersions on = denigrate[dénigrèit] = detract = disparage[dispǽridʒ] = libel[láibəl]
= slander[slǽndər] = vilify[víləfài]
The baseball coach has been much maligned by the many fans of the team.
감독은 그 야구팀의 팬들로부터 비난을 받았다.

malinger[məlíŋgər] v 꾀병을 부리다 = shirk[ʃəːrk]
The private first class was malingering during the ranger training.
그 일병은 유격훈련 중에 꾀병을 부리고 있었다.

malleable[mǽliəbl] a 두들겨 펼 수 있는, 두드려 펼 수 있는, 가단성의
= ductile[dʌ́ktəl] = flexible[fléksəbl] = pliant[pláiənt] = supple[sʌ́pl]
Most metals can be malleable when they are heated.
대부분의 금속은 열을 받으면 두드려서 펼 수 있게 된다.

malodor[mælóudər] n 악취, 고약한 냄새 = stench[stentʃ] = stink
Malodor is coming from a big pile of garbage.
큰 쓰레기 더미에서 악취가 난다.

mandate[mǽndeit] n 권한, 명령, 위임, 위임 통치 = behest[bihést] = decree[dikríː]
= edict[íːdikt] = injunction[indʒʌ́ŋkʃən]
The winning in the election gave the ruling party a mandate to stick to the ongoing economic reform.
선거 승리 덕분에 여당은 현재 진행 중인 경제계획을 계속할 수 있게 되었다.

mangy[méindʒi] a 초라한, 누추한, 옴이 오른 = scruffy[skrʌ́fi]
A lot of mangy dogs were barking in the abandoned cages.
옴이 오른 많은 개들이 버려진 우리 안에서 짖고 있었다.

manifest[mǽnəfèst] a 명백한, 분명한 = obvious[ábviəs] = palpable[pǽlpəbl]
The will of the players to win the game felt manifest to soccer fans.
그 경기에서 이기려는 선수들의 의지가 축구 팬들에게 분명하게 느껴졌다.

manifesto[mænəféstou] n 성명서, 선언문 = proclamation[pràkləméiʃən]
The leader of the political party is scheduled to announce its manifesto about the election policies.
정당 지도자는 선거정책에 관한 그 정당의 성명서를 발표할 예정이다.

manumit[mænjmít] v 해방시키다 = free = emancipate[imǽnsəpèit]
= extricate[ékstrəkèit] = liberate[líbərèit]
All the slaves were manumitted after their landlord surrendered to the new leader.
모든 노예는 노예주들이 새로운 지도자에게 항복하고 난 후에 모두 해방되었다.

marginal[mάːrdʒinl] a 가장자리의, 중요치 않은, 변두리의, 미미한
= insignificant[ìnsignífikənt] = minor = negligible[néglidʒəbl]
The marginal land in the suburbs of the Beijing has turned into a major business center.
베이징 근교의 변두리 땅이 중요한 비즈니스 센터로 바뀌었다.

marshal[mάːrʃəl] v 집결시키다, 정렬시키다 = assemble[əsémbl] = mobilize[móubəlàiz]
= muster[mΛstər]
After the declaration of the war, the military authorities began marshaling the soldiers along. the border.
선전포고 후에 군부는 병사들을 국경선으로 집결시켰다.

martial[mάːrʃəl] a 전쟁의, 호전적인, 무용의 = bellicose[bélikòus]
= belligerent[bəlídʒərənt] = hostile[hάstl] = pugnacious[pΛgnéiʃəs] = warlike
The military authorities decided to announce the martial law.
군부는 계엄령을 내리기로 결정했다.

martinet[mὰːrtənét] n 엄격한 사람 = disciplinarian[dìsəplinέəriən]
The new commander has been known as a martinet in military discipline.
새 사령관은 군율 면에서 엄격한 사람으로 알려졌다.

martyr[mάːrtər] n 순교자, 목숨을 바치는 사람 = sacrificing person
A lot of martyrs were executed before the religion took root in the nation.
많은 순교자들이 그 나라에 그 종교가 뿌리를 내리기 전에 처형당했다.

QUIZ 76

Match each word in the first column with its definition in the second column.
Check your answers in the back of the book.

1.	martyr		a.	impropriety = misbehavior
2.	martial		b.	all thumbs = awkward
3.	magnate		c.	forgiving = considerate
4.	marginal		d.	free = emancipate
5.	malaise		e.	behest = decree
6.	malfeasance		f.	scruffy
7.	manifesto		g.	sacrificing person
8.	malinger		h.	stench = stink
9.	manifest		i.	insignificant = minor
10.	mangy		j.	obvious = palpable
11.	mandate		k.	ductile = flexible
12.	machination		l.	assemble = mobilize
13.	malleable		m.	bellicose = belligerent
14.	malodor		n.	defame = calumniate
15.	manumit		o.	artifice = conspiracy
16.	magnanimous		p.	bigwig = mogul
17.	maladroit		q.	proclamation
18.	marshal		r.	shirk
19.	martinet		s.	disciplinarian
20.	malign		t.	angst = anxiety

materialistic[mətìəriəlístik] a 물질주의적인, 유물론적인, 실리주의의
= acquisitive[əkwízətiv] = greedy[grí:di] = profane[prəféin] = secular[sékjulər]
I am afraid that our society is becoming more and more materialistic.
우리 사회가 점점 물질주의적으로 되어 가는 것 같다.

matriculate[mətríkjulèit] v 대학생이 되다
Harry finally matriculated at the Yale university. Harry는 마침내 예일대에 입학했다.

maudlin[mɔ́:dlin] a 감상적인, 눈물이 헤픈, 눈물을 짜게 하는
= lachrymose[lǽkrəmòus] = mawkish[mɔ́:kiʃ] = sentimental[sèntəméntl] = weepy[wí:pi]
My grandma sometimes weeps while watching maudlin dramas on TV.
나의 할머니는 때때로 감상적인 TV 드라마를 보시다가 운다.

maven[méivən] n 박식한 사람, 전문가 = connoisseur[kànəsə́:r] = expert
If you have a problem with your computer, talk to a computer maven.
컴퓨터에 문제가 있으면 컴퓨터 전문가에게 얘기해봐라.

maverick[mǽvərik] n 독불장군 = bohemian[bouhí:miən] = dissenter[diséntər]
= nonconformist
The presidential candidate was known as a maverick.
그 대통령 후보자는 독불장군으로 알려졌다.

mawkish[mɔ́:kiʃ] a 별나게 감상적인 = emotional = gooey[gú:i] = maudlin[mɔ́:dlin]
= mushy[mʌ́ʃi] = sentimental[sèntəméntl]
The movie director has so far produced a few maudlin works.
그 영화감독은 지금까지 몇 편의 아주 감상적인 영화를 제작했다.

meager[mí:gər] a 부족한, 빈약한, 메마른, 결핍한 = insufficient[ìnsəfíʃənt] = scant = skimpy[skímpi]
The family has lived on his meager income for 10 years.
그 가족들은 그의 빈약한 수입에 의지해서 십년 동안 살았다.

meander[miǽndər] v 굽이쳐 흐르다, 정처 없이 거닐다, 꼬불꼬불 흐르다 = drift
= ramble[rǽmbl] = roam[roum] = stray[strei] = stroll = wander[wɑ́ndər]
The Yellow River meanders through a lot of fields to the sea.
황하는 많은 들판을 굽이쳐 흘러서 바다에 이른다.

measly[mí:zli] a 쥐꼬리만 한, 시시한, 아주 조금의 = paltry[pɔ́:ltri] = puny[pjú:ni]
His measly salary is not sufficient to support his family.
그의 쥐꼬리만 한 월급은 가족을 부양하기에 충분치 않다.

mediate[mí:dièit] v 조정하다, 중재하다, 성립시키다 = arbitrate[ɑ́:rbətrèit]
= intercede[ìntərsí:d] = intervene[ìntərví:n]
USA is asked to mediate the dispute between the two nations.
미국은 두 나라 사이를 중재해달라는 요청을 받았다.

mediocre[mì:dióukər] a 평범한, 보통의, 여느 = average[ǽvəridʒ] = commonplace
The baseball player had a mediocre batting average in 2015.
그 야구선수는 2015년에 평범한 타율을 기록했다.

meek[mi:k] a 유순한, 온순한, 미약한 = compliant[kəmpláiənt] = docile[dɑ́səl]
Marcus is a very meek gentleman. Marcus는 매우 유순한 신사이다.

melancholy[mélənkàli] a 우울한, 울적한, 감성적인 = depressed[diprést]
= dismal[dízməl] = moody = pensive[pénsiv] = somber[sámbər]
She felt melancholy after her husband died in the traffic accident.
그녀는 남편이 교통사고로 죽고 우울함을 느꼈다.

melee[méilei] n 난투, 혼전, 싸움 = brawl[brɔːl] = clash[klæʃ] = fracas[fréikəs]
= fray[frei] = ruckus[rʌkəs] = scrimmage[skrímidʒ] = scuffle[skʌfl] = skirmish[skə́ːrmiʃ]
= tussle[tʌsl]
Some teenagers had a melee each other in our neighborhood at night.
몇몇 십대들은 밤에 우리 동네에서 서로 난투극을 벌였다.

mellifluous[melífluəs] a 감미로운, 달콤한, 듣기 좋은 = dulcet[dʌlsit]
= mellow[mélou]
The winner in the song contest has a very mellifluous voice.
노래 경연대회 우승자는 매우 감미로운 목소리를 가지고 있다.

membrane[mémbrein] n 막, 박막 = covering layer
The juvenile fish were covered with membrane in the water.
치어들은 물속에서 막으로 덮여 있다.

menace[ménis] v 위협하다, 협박하다 = intimidate[intímədèit] = frighten[fráitn]
= threaten[θrétn]
The local car market is being menaced by the imported cars.
국내 자동차시장은 수입자동차에 위협당하고 있다.

menagerie[mənǽdʒəri] n 야생동물들 = wild animals
The truck is carrying a menagerie for a circus show.
그 트럭은 서커스 쇼를 위해 야생동물 무리들을 이동시키고 있다.

mendacious[mendéiʃəs] a 허위의, 거짓말을 하는, 거짓의 = deceptive[diséptiv]
= fallacious[fəléiʃəs] = fraudulent[frɔ́ːdʒulənt] = lying[láiiŋ]
He was indicted on charges of mendacious testimony.
그는 허위진술 혐의로 기소되었다.

mendicant[méndikənt] n 거지 = beggar[bégər] = panhandler = pauper[pɔ́ːpər]
The businessman spent a life of mendicant for 5 years after his company went bankrupt.
사업가는 사업이 망한 뒤 5년 동안 거지 생활을 했다.

mercurial[mərkjúəriəl] a 변덕스러운, 경박한 = capricious[kəpríʃəs] = erratic[irǽtik]
= fickle[fíkl] = unpredictable[ʌnpridíktəbl] = volatile[válətil]
Her mercurial temperament estranged her from her friends.
그녀의 변덕스러운 기질은 친구들로부터 멀어지게 했다.

QUIZ 77

Match each word in the first column with its definition in the second column.
Check your answers in the back of the book.

1.	mendicant	a.	average = commonplace
2.	menagerie	b.	deceptive = fallacious
3.	meek	c.	arbitrate = intercede
4.	membrane	d.	acquisitive = greedy
5.	mendacious	e.	wild animals
6.	meager	f.	lachrymose = mawkish
7.	melee	g.	dulcet = mellow
8.	measly	h.	connoisseur = expert
9.	maven	i.	paltry = puny
10.	mediocre	j.	bohemian = dissenter
11.	materialistic	k.	capricious = erratic
12.	melancholy	l.	compliant = docile
13.	mediate	m.	drift = ramble
14.	mellifluous	n.	beggar = panhandler
15.	meander	o.	brawl = clash
16.	mercurial	p.	intimidate = frighten
17.	maverick	q.	depressed = dismal
18.	mawkish	r.	covering layer
19.	maudlin	s.	emotional = gooey
20.	menace	t.	insufficient = scant

metamorphosis[mètəmɔ́ːrfəsis] n 변형, 변화, 변이 = vicissitude[visísətjùːd]
The criminal underwent several metamorphoses to become a pastor.
그 범죄자는 목사가 되기 위해 여러 번 변신을 했다.

metaphor[métəfɔ̀ːr] n 은유, 암유, 비유 = implied comparison
The poet is famous for his exquisite use of metaphor in his poetry.
그 시인은 시에서 절묘한 은유법을 사용하는 것으로 유명하다.

meteoric[mìːtiɔ́ːrik] a 일약 …한, 유성 같은, 급속한 = momentary[móuməntèri] = swift
Some IT companies has made a meteoric rise in the smart phone field.
몇몇 IT 회사들은 스마트폰 분야에서 급속한 성장을 보였다.

meticulous[mətíkjuləs] a 세심한, 꼼꼼한, 소심한 = fastidious[fæstídiəs]
= punctilious[pʌŋktíliəs] = scrupulous[skrúːpjuləs]
The cook is very meticulous in selecting the ingredients for his foods.
그 요리사는 요리를 할 때 재료 선택에 매우 꼼꼼하다.

miff[mif] v 발끈하게 하다 = aggrieve[əgríːv] = annoy = bother = irk[əːrk] = irritate[írətèit]
= nettle[nétl] = pester[péstər] = pique[piːk] = provoke[prəvóuk] = vex[veks]
The harsh criticism of her acting in the movie miffed the famous actress.
영화에서 보여준 그녀의 연기력을 심하게 비난한 것은 그 유명 여배우를 발끈하게 했다.

milieu[miljú] n 환경, 주위, 사회적 환경 = ambience[æmbiəns] = atmosphere[ætməsfiər]
= environment[inváiərənmənt] = surroundings
The murderer has grown up in the deprived milieu. 그 살인자는 불우한 환경에서 자랐다.

mince[mins] v 잘게 썰다, 다지다 = chop up
The chef minced some beef to make hamburger steak.
셰프는 햄버그스테이크를 만들기 위해 약간의 쇠고기를 다졌다.

minuscule[mínəskjùːl] a 아주 작은, 극소의 = diminutive[dimínjutiv] = microscopic = tiny
There are a lot of minuscule components in the smart phone.
스마트폰에는 수많은 아주 작은 부품들이 들어가 있다.

mire[maiər] n 늪, 수렁, 곤경, 궁지 = bog[bag] = marsh[maːrʃ] = morass[məræs]
= quagmire[kwægmàiər]
The M&A project was stuck in the mire. 그 인수합병 계획은 수렁에 빠졌다.

mirth[məːr] n 웃음소리, 즐거움, 환희, 명랑 = great joy = hilarity[hilǽrəti]
The music concert was full of mirth and excitement.
그 음악공연은 즐거움과 흥분으로 가득 찼다.

misanthropic[mìsənθrɑ́pik] a 염세적인, 사람을 싫어하는 = antisocial[æntisouʃl]
= cynical[sínikəl]
The hermit has a misanthropic view of the world.
그 은둔자는 염세적인 세계관을 가지고 있다.

mischievous[místʃəvəs] a 짓궂은, 유해한 = impish[ímpiʃ] = playful
The mischievous prank calls interfere with the operation of the fire stations.
짓궂은 장난전화는 소방서의 업무를 방해한다.

miscreant[mískriənt] n 악한 = villain[vílən]
I don't want to see our society controlled by miscreants.
나는 우리 사회가 악한들에 지배당하는걸 보고 싶지 않다.

misdemeanor[mìsdimí:nər] n 경범죄, 비행 = offense = transgression[trænsgréʃən]
= violation[vàiəléiʃən]
Stalking belongs to misdemeanor. 스토킹은 경범죄에 속한다.

miser[máizər] n 구두쇠, 수전노 = Scrooge[skru:dʒ]
The owner of the building has been known as a miser.
그 건물 주인은 구두쇠로 알려져 있다.

mishap[míshæp] n 사고, 재난, 불운 = accident = misfortune
The police are investigating the cause of the mishap. 경찰은 그 재난의 원인을 조사 중이다.

mitigate[mítəgèit] v 누그러뜨리다, 완화하다, 가볍게 하다 = allay[əléi]
= alleviate[əlí:vièit] = appease[əpí:z] = assuage[əswéidʒ] = lull[lʌl] = mollify[máləfài]
= pacify[pǽsəfài] = palliate[pǽlièit] = placate[pléikeit] = soothe[su:ð] = temper
The government is trying to mitigate the anger of farmers who are strongly opposed to importing rice.
정부는 쌀 수입에 강력히 반대하는 농부들의 분노를 누그러뜨리려 하고 있다.

modicum[mádəkəm] n 소량, 근소, 약간 = iota[aióutə] = small amount
A modicum of truth will make him more successful in the society.
그가 약간만 더 진실하다면 사회적으로 더욱 성공할 것이다.

modulate[mádʒulèit] v 조절(조정)하다, 억양을 붙여서 말하다 = adjust[ədʒʌst] = fine-tune
Labor leaders and management representatives have met to modulate the size of the pay raise.
노조 대표와 경영진들은 급여 인상의 규모를 조절하기 위해서 만났다.

mollify[máləfài] v 진정시키다, 달래다, 완화시키다 = allay[əléi] = alleviate[əlí:vièit]
= appease[əpí:z] = assuage[əswéidʒ] = lull[lʌl] = mitigate[mítəgèit] = pacify[pǽsəfài]
= palliate[pǽlièit] = placate[pléikeit] = soothe[su:ð] = temper
The government officials are taking some steps to mollify the angry citizens.
정부 관리들은 화난 시민들을 달래기 위한 조치를 취하고 있다.

QUIZ 78

Match each word in the first column with its definition in the second column.
Check your answers in the back of the book.

1.	mollify	a.	antisocial = cynical
2.	milieu	b.	great joy = hilarity
3.	mire	c.	allay = alleviate
4.	meticulous	d.	bog = marsh
5.	miff	e.	implied comparison
6.	metaphor	f.	ambience = atmosphere
7.	mince	g.	vicissitude
8.	misanthropic	h.	scrooge
9.	miscreant	i.	diminutive = microscopic
10.	mirth	j.	adjust = fine-tune
11.	modulate	k.	impish = playful
12.	mischievous	l.	accident = misfortune
13.	minuscule	m.	momentary = swift
14.	misdemeanor	n.	iota = small amount
15.	metamorphosis	o.	villain
16.	mishap	p.	aggrieve = annoy
17.	mitigate	q.	fastidious = punctilious
18.	modicum	r.	offense = transgression
19.	miser	s.	chop up
20.	meteoric	t.	allay = alleviate

momentous[mouméntəs] a 중요한, 중대한, 비상한 = consequential[kànsəkwénʃəl]
= crucial[krúːʃəl] = important
The business group made a momentous decision of selling off the shipbuilding division.
그 대기업은 조선 부분을 매각하기로 하는 중요한 결정을 했다.

moratorium[mɔ̀ːrətɔ́ːriəm] n 지불유예(정지), 활동정지= reprieve[ripríːv]
= suspension[səspénʃən]
The country in the South America declared a moratorium on its foreign debts.
남미의 그 국가는 외채에 대해서 지불유예를 선포했다.

morbid[mɔ́ːrbid] a 병적인, 병적으로 과민한, 우울한 = gloomy[glúːmi]
= melancholy[mélənkàli] = pessimistic[pèsəmístik]
Juno has a morbid interest in the existence of zombie.
Juno는 좀비의 존재에 대해서 병적인 관심을 가지고 있다.

mordant[mɔ́:rdənt] a 신랄한, 독설적인 = acerbic[əsə́:rbik] = caustic[kɔ́:stik]
= poignant[pɔ́injənt] = sarcastic[sa:rkǽstik] = scathing[skéiðiŋ]
The mordant TV parody show about politicians is winning popularity.
정치인들을 대상으로 하는 신랄한 TV 쇼가 인기를 얻고 있다.

mores[mɔ́:reiz] n 사회적 관례, 사회적 관습 = customs = manners
Social mores are different from country to country. 사회적 관습은 국가마다 다르다.

moribund[mɔ́:rəbʌnd] a 다 죽어가는, 빈사 상태의, 소멸해 가는 = dying
= doomed[du:md] = perishing[périʃiŋ]
MP3 player industry has become moribund after the advent of smart phones.
스마트폰 출현 이후로 MP3 플레이어 산업은 빈사 상태가 되었다.

morose[məróus] a 기분이 언짢은, 시무룩한, 뚱한 = depressed = dour[duər]
= gloomy[glú:mi] = glum[glʌm] = grouchy[gráutʃi] = melancholy[mélənkàli] = sullen[sʌ́lən]
= down in the mouth
He looked morose when he was told that he was not promoted to the manager.
그는 매니저로 진급하지 못했다는 말을 듣고 시무룩해 보였다.

mortify[mɔ́:rtəfài] v 굴욕감을 주다 = chagrin[ʃəgrín] = humiliate[hju:mílièit] = snub[snʌb]
Most prisoners of war felt mortified when they were put to sexual torture.
대부분의 전쟁포로들은 성고문을 당할 때 굴욕감을 느꼈다.

motif[moutí:f] n 주제, 동기 = theme[θi:m]
Friendship is a motif in the movie. 우정은 이 영화의 주제이다.

motley[mátli] a 잡다하게 섞인, 잡색의 = mingled[míŋgld] = mixed = varied[véərid]
= variegated[véəriəgèitid]
The cheap restaurant is using motley ingredients of meat and herbs to make a stew
저급한 식당은 스튜(찌개)를 만들 때 잡다한 고기와 약초를 재료로 사용한다

mottle[mátl] v 얼룩덜룩하게 하다 = dapple[dǽpl]
The marines are wearing their uniforms mottled with green and brown.
해병대원들은 녹색과 갈색의 얼룩무늬 군복을 입고 있다.

muffle[mʌ́fl] v 소리를 죽이다, 약하게 하다 = make quiet
All the car makers are supposed to muffle the sound of the engine.
모든 자동차 제조사들은 엔진 소리를 줄여야 한다.

mulish[mjúːliʃ] a 고집 센, 다루기 힘든, 노새의 = headstrong[hédstrɔ̀(ː)ŋ]
= intractable[intrǽktəbl] = obstinate[ɑ́bstənət] = recalcitrant[rikǽlsitrənt] = tenacious[tənéiʃəs]
The union leader was mulish in the pay raise negotiations with the management of the company.
노동조합 간부는 회사 경영진과의 임금인상 협상에서 매우 고집을 피웠다.

municipal[mjuːnísəpəl] a 시정의, 시립의 = concerning cities
The museum is being managed by the municipal government.
박물관은 시청에서 관리하고 있다.

mundane[mʌndéin] a 평범한, 현세의, 세속의, 일상적인 = banal[bənǽl]
= humdrum[hʌ́mdrʌm] = routine[ruːtíːn]
Those living in the big cities spend hectic days in their mundane lives.
대도시에 사는 사람들은 정신 없이 바쁜 일상생활을 한다.

munificent[mjuːnífəsnt] a 아낌없이 주는, 손이 큰, 후한 = considerate[kənsídərət]
= forgiving = lavish[lǽviʃ] = magnanimous[mægnǽnəməs]
The businessman turned out to be a munificent benefactor of the orphanage.
그 사업가는 고아원에 후하게 은혜를 베푸는 사람으로 판명되었다.

mural[mjúərəl] n 벽화 = paintings on wall
There are a lot of murals on the wall of a museum. 박물관 벽에는 많은 벽화들이 있다.

murmur[mə́ːrmər] v 중얼거리다, 분명치 않은 소리를 내다, 속삭이다 = babble[bǽbl]
= mumble[mʌ́mbl] = mutter[mʌ́tər] = stammer[stǽmər]
The patient murmured some words in bed. 환자는 침대에서 분명치 않은 소리를 냈다.

muse[mjuːz] v 심사숙고하다, 생각에 잠기다, 명상하다 = brood[bruːd]
= cogitate[kɑ́dʒətèit] = contemplate[kɑ́ntəmplèit] = deliberate[dilíbərət] = meditate[médətèit]
= mull over = ponder[pɑ́ndər] = ruminate[rúːmənèit] = think over
The old couple mused over moving to the countryside.
노부부는 시골로 이사가는 것을 심사숙고했다.

muster[mʌ́stər] v 소집하다, 집합시키다, 모이다 = assemble[əsémbl]
= congregate[kɑ́ŋgrigèit] = convene[kənvíːn] = convoke[kənvóuk] = mobilize[móubəlàiz]
Air squadron commander mustered all the fighter pilots before the training flight.
비행대 사령관은 연습 비행 전에 모든 전투조종사들을 소집했다.

QUIZ 79

Match each word in the first column with its definition in the second column.
Check your answers in the back of the book.

1.	momentous	a.	acerbic = caustic
2.	muster	b.	concerning cities
3.	mores	c.	considerate = forgiving
4.	murmur	d.	mingled = mixed
5.	moribund	e.	banal = humdrum
6.	moratorium	f.	gloomy = melancholy
7.	municipal	g.	consequential = crucial
8.	mortify	h.	chagrin = humiliate
9.	motif	i.	assemble = congregate
10.	mordant	j.	reprieve = suspension
11.	mottle	k.	paintings on wall
12.	morose	l.	theme
13.	mulish	m.	customs = manners
14.	motley	n.	depressed = dour
15.	mundane	o.	dying = doomed
16.	munificent	p.	headstrong = intractable
17.	mural	q.	babble = mumble
18.	muffle	r.	make quiet
19.	muse	s.	brood = cogitate
20.	morbid	t.	dapple

myopia[maióupiə] n 근시 = shortsightedness
Many students suffer from myopia.
많은 학생들이 근시로 고생한다.

myriad[míriəd] a 무수히 많음 = infinite[ínfənət] = innumerable[injú:mərəbl]
You can see a myriad of stars on the sky.
하늘에서 무수한 별들을 볼 수 있다.

mystic[místik] a 신비한, 수수께끼의, 신령스러운 = arcane[a:rkéin] = cryptic[kríptik]
= enigmatic[ènigmǽtik] = esoteric[èsətérik] = mysterious[mistíəriəs]
Watching the glacier melting in the ocean was an almost mystic experience.
바다에서 빙하가 녹는 것을 지켜보는 일은 거의 신비스러운 경험이었다.

QUIZ 80

*Match each word in the first column with its definition in the second column.
Check your answers in the back of the book.*

1. myriad
2. myopia
3. mystic

a. shortsightedness
b. arcane = cryptic
c. infinite = innumerable

natty[nǽti] a 말쑥한, 산뜻한, 멋진 = dapper[dǽpər]
He was wearing a natty suit. 그는 산뜻한 정장을 입고 있었다.

nebulous[nébjuləs] a 흐린, 막연한, 모호한 = ambiguous[æmbígjuəs] = confused[kənfjú:zd] = hazy[héizi] = imprecise[ìmprisáis] = murky[má:rki] = obscure[əbskjúər] = vague[veig]
The two parties talked about the nebulous terms in the contract.
두 당사자는 계약서의 모호한 계약조건에 대해 이야기했다.

nefarious[nifɛ́əriəs] a 극악한, 사악한 = heinous[héinəs] = malignant[məlígnənt] = vicious[víʃəs] = vile[vail] = virulent[vírjulənt] = wicked[wíkid]
Some young ambitious generals in 1960s were devising a nefarious scheme.
1960년대 일부 젊고 야망 있는 장군들이 사악한 음모를 꾸미고 있었다.

negligent[néglidʒənt] a 게을리하는, 태만한 = careless = inadvertent[inədvə́:rtnt] = inattentive[ìnəténtiv] = lax[læks] = sloppy[slápi]
Jennifer was scolded by her boss because she had been negligent in her job.
Jennifer는 그녀는 직장에서 태만한 것 때문에 상사로부터 꾸지람을 들었다.

nemesis[néməsis] n 정복할 수 없는 것, 이길 수 없는 적, 감당할 수 없는 상대
= adversary[ǽdvərsèri] = opponent[əpóunənt]
The electronic company had to compete with Apple, it nemesis, in the smart phone industry.
그 전자회사는 정복할 수 없는 상대인 Apple과 스마트폰 산업에서 경쟁해야 했다.

neophyte[ní:əfàit] n 초심자, 신출내기 = apprentice[əpréntis] = beginner = novice[návis] = tyro[táiərou]
Neophytes are not allowed to apply for the job. 초심자는 그 직업에 지원할 수 없다.

nepotism[népətìzm] n 족벌주의, 친족 등용, 정실
The founder of the company left a will to reject nepotism from his company.
회사의 창업자는 그의 회사에서 친족을 등용하지 말라는 유언을 남겼다.

nettle[nétl] v 안달나게 하다, 짜증나게 하다, 화나게 하다 = annoy = bother = exasperate[igzǽspərèit] = gall[gɔ:l] = irk[ə:rk] = irritate[írətèit] = peeve[pi:v] = pique[pi:k] = rile[rail] = vex
His severe criticism of the book nettled the author.
그가 심하게 비난한 것 때문에 그 책의 저자는 화가 났다.

nibble[níbl] v 조금씩 뜯어먹다, 갉아먹다 = gnaw[nɔ:]
The deficit of the public enterprises is nibbling away on the government's budget.
공기업의 적자가 정부 예산을 조금씩 갉아먹고 있다.

241

nicety[náisəti] n 정확, 정밀, 섬세 = precision[prisíʒən]
A group of seismologist predicted the earthquake to a nicety.
일단의 지진학자들은 지진을 정확히 예측했다.

nirvana[niərvá:nə] n 열반, 해탈 = bliss[blis] = enlightenment[inláitnmənt]
After a long period of penance, the saint reached nirvana.
오랜 기간의 고행 후에 그 성인은 열반에 다다랐다. penance[pénəns] n 참회, 고행

nitpick[nítpìk] v 하찮은 일로 트집을 잡다, 시시한 일을 꼬치꼬치 캐다 = carp[ka:rp]
= cavil[kǽvəl] = criticize[krítəsàiz]
My boss sometimes nitpicks at my accent. 나의 상사는 때때로 나의 말투를 트집 잡는다.

nocturnal[naktə́:rnl] a 야행성의, 야간의, 밤에 파는 = nightly[náitli]
Most of the owls are nocturnal. 대다수의 올빼미는 야행성이다.

noisome[nɔ́isəm] a 불쾌한, 해로운, 역겨운 = deleterious[dèlitíəriəs]
= disgusting[disgʌ́stiŋ] = fetid[fétid] = noxious[nάkʃəs] = putrid[pjú:trid]
= repulsive[ripʌ́lsiv] = stinking[stíŋkiŋ]
The chemical factory in our neighborhood gives off a noisome odor.
우리 동네의 화학공장은 역겨운 냄새를 내뿜는다.

nomadic[noumǽdik] a 유목의, 방랑의 = itinerant[aitínərənt] = wandering[wάndəriŋ]
Some Mongolians are still leading a nomadic life.
일부 몽골 사람들은 아직도 유목생활을 하고 있다.

nomenclature[nóumənklèitʃər] n 명명법, 용어, 명칭 = glossary[glάsəri]
= terminology[tə̀:rmənάlədʒi] = vocabulary[voukǽbjulèri]
Many people are confused by the legal nomenclature.
많은 사람들이 법률용어를 헷갈려 한다.

nondescript[nὰndiskrípt] a 별 특징 없는 = commonplace
= undistinguished[ʌ̀ndɪstɪŋgwɪʃt]
The world famous designer's office is full of nondescript decorations.
세계적으로 유명한 디자이너의 사무실은 별 특징 없는 장식들로 가득 차 있다.

nonentity[nɑ:nentəti] n 보잘것없는 사람(물건), 실재하지 않는 것 = nobody
Most victories were won in the war by nonentities in the history.
역사상 대부분의 전쟁의 승리는 보잘것없는 사람들에 의해서 얻어진다.

noxious[nάkʃəs] a 유해한, 유독한 = baneful[béinfəl] = deadly = deleterious[dèlitíəriəs] = detrimental[dètrəméntl] = injurious[indʒúəriəs] = pernicious[pərníʃəs] = toxic = virulent[vírjulənt]
Some students in the big cities are living exposed to the noxious environment.
대도시의 일부 학생들은 유해한 환경에 노출된 채 살고 있다.

nucleate[njú:klieit] v 응집하다 = cohere[kouhíər]
We can see a lot of working bees nucleating around the queen bee
우리는 많은 일벌들이 여왕벌 주위에 응집하는 것을 볼 수 있다.

nullify[nʌ́ləfài] v 무효로 하다, 파기하다 = abolish[əbáliʃ] = abrogate[ǽbrəgèit] = annul[ənʌ́l] = cancel = invalidate[invǽlədèit] = negate[nigéit] = repeal[ripí:l] = rescind[risínd] = revoke[rivóuk] = undo = void
Fathers wanted the government to nullify the trade treaty with its neighboring country.
농부들은 정부가 이웃나라와 맺은 무역조약을 파기하기를 원했다.

QUIZ 81

Match each word in the first column with its definition in the second column.
Check your answers in the back of the book.

1.	nullify	a.	apprentice = beginner
2.	nebulous	b.	commonplace = undistinguished
3.	noxious	c.	itinerant = wandering
4.	negligent	d.	adversary = opponent
5.	natty	e.	nobody
6.	nucleate	f.	glossary = terminology
7.	nocturnal	g.	gnaw
8.	noisome	h.	deleterious = disgusting
9.	nicety	i.	abolish = abrogate
10.	nirvana	j.	dapper
11.	nitpick	k.	cohere
12.	nettle	l.	baneful = deadly
13.	nemesis	m.	precision
14.	nomadic	n.	ambiguous = confused
15.	nibble	o.	nightly
16.	nondescript	p.	annoy = bother
17.	nonentity	q.	carp = cavil
18.	neophyte	r.	heinous = malignant
19.	nomenclature	s.	careless = inadvertent
20.	nefarious	t.	bliss = enlightenment

nuance[njúːɑːns] n 뉘앙스, 미묘한 차이 = slight difference
His no comment left a positive nuance. 그의 코멘트는 긍정적 뉘앙스를 풍겼다.

nudge[nʌdʒ] v 팔꿈치로 살짝 찌르다, 살살 밀다 = poke = prod[prad]
She nudged me when I was just to doze off during the ceremony.
그녀는 내가 축하행사 도중에 막 졸려고 하는 순간 나를 팔꿈치로 살짝 찔렀다.

numb[nʌm] a 곱은, 마비된, 감각이 없는 = insensitive[insénsətiv]
I felt all my fingers and toes go numb after walking through the snow all night long.
밤새도록 눈길을 걸은 뒤 나는 손가락과 발가락이 모두 마비됨을 느꼈다.

QUIZ 82

Match each word in the first column with its definition in the second column.
Check your answers in the back of the book.

1.	nudge	a.	insensitive
2.	nuance	b.	poke = prod
3.	numb	c.	slight difference

obdurate[ábdjurit] a 고집 센, 완고한 = intransigent[intrǽnsədʒənt]
= intractable[intrǽktəbl] = obstinate[ábstənət] = pigheaded = stubborn[stʌ́bərn]
The doctor remains obdurate on the issue of abortion. 의사는 낙태 문제에 있어서 완고하다.

obedient[oubíːdiənt] a 순종하는, 말을 잘 듣는 = compliant[kəmpláiənt]
= docile[dásəl] = submissive[səbmísiv]
He has always been obedient to his parents. 그는 항상 그의 부모님께 순종한다.

obeisance[oubéisəns] n 존경, 순종, 절 = bow[bau] = homage[hámidʒ]
= reverence[révərəns] = salutation[sæljutéiʃən]
We should pay obeisance to the war veterans.
우리는 전쟁을 겪은 퇴역군인들에게 존경을 표해야 한다.

obfuscate[ábfəskèit] v 혼란스럽게 만들다, 어리둥절하게 하다, 당황시키다
= baffle[bǽfl] = bewilder[biwíldər] = confound[kanfáund] = fuddle[fʌdl] = muddle[mʌdl]
= perplex[pərpléks] = puzzle
His perjury obfuscated the trial of a murder case.
그의 위증은 살인사건 재판을 혼란스럽게 만들었다. perjury[pə́ːrdʒəri] n 위증

oblique[əblíːk] a 기울어진, 비스듬한, 완곡한 = askew[əskjúː] = inclined[inkláind]
= slanting[slǽntiŋal]
There used to be some oblique trees around the lake.
예전에는 호수 주위에 기울어진 나무들이 있었다.

obliterate[əblítərèit] v 제거하다, 지우다, 없애다 = annihilate[ənáiəlèit] = destroy
= delete[dilíːt] = efface[iféis] = eradicate[irǽdəkèit] = erase = expunge[ikspʌndʒ]
= exterminate[ikstə́ːrmənèit] = extirpate[ékstərpèit] = wipe out
The new cosmetic surgery obliterated the wrinkling from her face.
새로운 성형수술로 그녀의 얼굴에서 주름을 제거했다.

oblivion[əblíviən] n 잊혀짐, 망각 = amnesia[æmníːʒə]
= unconsciousness[ʌnkɑːnʃəsnəs]
His name as a famous writer was buried in oblivion.
유명 작가로서의 그의 이름은 세상에서 잊혀졌다.

obscure[əbskjúər] a 애매한, 불명확한, 잘 알려지지 않은 = ambiguous[æmbígjuəs]
= arcane[aːrkéin] = cryptic[kríptik] = vague[veig]
His offer sounds obscure to me. 그의 제안은 나에게 애매하게 들린다.

obsequious[əbsí:kwiəs] a 아부하는, 굽실거리는 = groveling[grʌvəliŋ]
= fawning[fɔ́:niŋ] = ingratiating[ingréiʃièitiŋ] = servile[sə́:rvil] = submissive
= sycophantic[sìkəfǽntik] = toadying[tóuding]
He has been obsequious to the powerful people. 그는 힘있는 사람들에게 아부해오고 있다.

obsess[əbsés] v 사로잡다, 늘 붙어 다니다 = preoccupy
She is obsessed with the idea of becoming a millionaire.
그녀는 백만장자가 되려는 생각에 사로잡혀 있다.

obstinate[ɑ́bstənət] a 고집 센, 완고한, 완강한 = headstrong[hédstrɔ̀(:)ŋ]
= intractable[intrǽktəbl] = obdurate[ɑ́bdjurit] = stubborn[stʌ́bərn] = tenacious[tənéiʃəs]
No one is as obstinate as him in the town. 마을에서 그 남자만큼 고집이 센 사람은 아무도 없다.

obstreperous[əbstrépərəs] a 정신 없이 날뛰는, 시끄러운, 소란한 = noisy
= rambunctious[ræmbʌ́ŋkʃəs] = unruly[ʌnrú:li]
Some college students went obstreperous during the festival.
일부 대학생들은 페스티벌 기간 중에 정신 없이 날뛰었다.

obtrusive[əbtrú:siv] a 주제 넘게 나서는, 눈에 띄는 = interfering[intərfíəriŋ]
= intrusive[intrú:siv] = meddlesome[médlsəm] = nosy[nóuzi] = officious[əfíʃəs]
Sometimes he is too obtrusive when he should not.
때때로 그는 그러지 말아야 할 때 주제 넘게 나선다.

obtuse[əbtjú:s] a 둔한, 둔감한 = blunt[blʌnt] = insensitive[insénsətiv] = stolid[stɑ́lid]
He was too obtuse to sense the danger. 그는 너무 둔감해서 그 위험을 감지하지 못했다.

obviate[ɑ́bvièit] v 제거하다, 미연에 방지하다 = avert[əvə́:rt] = deter[ditə́:r]
= forestall = hinder = preclude[priklú:d] = prevent = ward
The online banking system obviates the inconvenience of going to the banks.
온라인 은행 시스템은 은행까지 가는 번거로움을 없애준다.

occult[əkʌ́lt] a 초자연적인, 불가사의한, 신비한 = arcane[a:rkéin] = esoteric[èsətérik]
= mysterious[mistíəriəs] = mystic[místik] = secret = supernatural
We can see some occult phenomena in the far northern areas.
우리는 최북단 지역에서 초자연적인 현상을 볼 수 있다.

ode[oud] n 시, 송가 = poem[póuəm]
He composed an ode for the late queen. 그는 타계한 여왕을 위한 송가를 작곡했다.

odious[óudiəs] a 혐오스러운, 미운, 불쾌한 = abhorrent[æbhɔ́ːrənt]
= abominable[əbámənəbl] = detestable[ditéstəbl] = disgusting[disgʌ́stiŋ]
= execrable[éksikrəbl] = hateful = loathsome[lóuðsəm] = obnoxious[əbnákʃəs]
= repugnant[ripʌ́gnənt] = repulsive[ripʌ́lsiv] = revolting[rivóultiŋ] = vile[vail]
Some fish of foreign species have become odious to our ecosystem.
어떤 외래종 물고기는 우리 생태계에 혐오스러운 존재가 되었다.

odyssey[ádəsi] n 방랑여행, 모험 = adventure = expedition[èkspədíʃən]
= exploration[èkspləréiʃən] = pilgrimage[pílgrəmidʒ] = trek[trek]
The three brothers set out on an odyssey. 세 형제는 모험 여행을 시작했다.

offbeat[ɔːfbiːt] a 색다른, 비정상적인 = bizarre[bizáːr] = eccentric[ikséntrik]
= idiosyncratic[ìdiousiŋkrǽtik] = strange = unorthodox[ʌnɔːrθədɑːks]
He enjoyed some offbeat experiences on the island. 그는 섬에서 색다른 경험을 즐겼다.

QUIZ 83

*Match each word in the first column with its definition in the second column.
Check your answers in the back of the book.*

1.	offbeat		a.	headstrong = intractable
2.	obedient		b.	groveling = fawning
3.	odious		c.	preoccupy
4.	obfuscate		d.	interfering = intrusive
5.	odyssey		e.	ambiguous = arcane
6.	obliterate		f.	amnesia = unconsciousness
7.	obtrusive		g.	blunt = insensitive
8.	obscure		h.	bizarre = eccentric
9.	obstinate		i.	annihilate = destroy
10.	obtuse		j.	adventure = expedition
11.	oblivion		k.	abhorrent = abominable
12.	obstreperous		l.	askew = inclined
13.	obsequious		m.	noisy = rambunctious
14.	obsess		n.	poem
15.	obviate		o.	baffle = bewilder
16.	obdurate		p.	arcane = esoteric
17.	ode		q.	intransigent = intractable
18.	oblique		r.	compliant = docile
19.	occult		s.	avert = deter
20.	obeisance		t.	bow = homage

officious[əfíʃəs] a 참견하기 좋아하는, 주제넘게 나서는, 거만한 = inquisitive[inkwízətiv]
= intrusive[intrúːsiv] = meddlesome[médlsəm]
The production manage was considered an officious man in the company.
그 생산 담당 매니저는 회사에서 참견하기 좋아하는 남자로 간주되었다.

offish[ɔ́fiʃ] a 쌀쌀한, 새치름한 = unfriendly
The lady at the reception desk was very offish. 안내 데스크에 있는 여성은 매우 쌀쌀맞았다.

olfactory[alfǽktəri] a 후각의 = aromatic[ærəmǽtik] = fragrant[fréigrənt]
The dogs have a very sensitive olfactory system. 개는 매우 민감한 후각계를 가졌다.

oligarchy[áləgὰːrki] n 과두정치, 소수독재정치 = autocrat[ɔ́ːtəkræt] = despot[déspət]
= tyrant[táiərənt]
The country was being ruled by the oligarchy.
그 나라는 과두정치에 의해 지배되고 있었다.

ominous[ámənəs] a 불길한, 흉조를 보이는 = apocalyptic[əpὰkəlíptik]
= augural[ɔ́ːgjərəl] = doomful[dúːmful] = foreboding[fɔːrbóudiŋ] = portentous[pɔːrténtəs]
The flight of a crow at night was considered an ominous sign.
밤에 까마귀가 날아가는 것은 불길한 징조로 받아들여졌다.

omniscient[amníʃənt] a 전지의, 모든 것을 다 아는 = all-knowing = all-seeing
= almighty[ɔːlmáiti] = preeminent[priémənənt]
He considers himself omniscient. 그는 자신이 모든 것을 다 안다고 생각한다.

onerous[ánərəs] a 부담되는, 짐이 되는 = arduous[άːrdʒuəs] = burdensome[bə́ːrdnsəm]
= grueling[grúːəliŋ] = ponderous[pάndərəs]
He was given an onerous task. 그에게 부담되는 임무가 내려졌다.

opacity[oupǽsəti] n 불투명함 = cloudiness
The opacity of the glass coating kept them from looking in the car.
불투명한 유리 코팅 때문에 차 안을 보는 것이 어려웠다.

opaque[oupéik] a 불투명한, 불명료한 = blurred[bləːrd] = muddy[mʌ́di]
= murky[mə́ːrki] = turbid[tə́ːrbid]
The water in the lake has become opaque due to the sediment.
호수 물이 침전물 때문에 불투명하게 되었다.

opine[oupáin] v 의견을 밝히다 = express an opinion
The coach opined that his team would advance to the final match.
코치는 그의 팀이 결승전에 올라갈 것이라는 의견을 밝혔다.

opportune[àpərtjúːn] a 시의적절한, 알맞은 = auspicious[ɔːspíʃəs]
= felicitous[filísətəs] = timely
The rescue team came at an opportune time. 구조 팀은 시의적절한 때에 왔다.

opprobrious[əpróubriəs] a 모욕적인, 입심 사나운, 상스러운 = abusive[əbjúːsiv]
= calumnious[kəlʌmniəs] = contemptuous[kəntémptʃuəs] = defamatory[difǽmətɔ̀ːri]
= denigrating[dénigrèit] = derogative[dirǽgətiv] = despicable[déspikəbl]
= disparaging[dispǽridʒiŋ] = humiliating[hjuːmílièitiŋ] = insulting[insʌltiŋ] = invective
= libeling[láibəliŋ] = malign[məláin] = malignant[məlígnənt] = pejorative[pidʒɔ́ːrətiv]
= reproaching[ripróutʃiŋ] = reviling[riváiliŋ] = scurrilous[skə́ːrələs] = spiteful = vile[vail]
= vitriolic[vìtriálik] = vituperative[vaitjúːpərətiv] = vulgar[vʌlgər]
You should not say opprobrious words during the debate.
토론 중에 상스러운 말을 사용해서는 안 된다.

opulent[ápjulənt] a 호화로운, 부유한, 풍부한 = affluent[ǽfluənt] = profuse[prəfjúːs]
She has lived an opulent lifestyle. 그녀는 호화로운 삶을 살고 있다.

oracle[ɔ́ːrəkl] n 신탁, 하나님의 말씀, 예언 = apocalypse[əpákəlips] = augury[ɔ́ːgjuri]
= prediction[pridíkʃən] = prophecy[práfəsi]
The pastor received an oracle. 목사님은 하느님의 말씀을 받았다.

orate[ɔːréit] v 연설하다, 연설조로 말하다 = address = speak
He was orating in front of her house to propose to her .
그는 청혼을 하기 위해 그녀의 집 앞에서 연설조로 말하고 있었다.

ordinance[ɔ́ːrdənəns] n 법령, 포고, 조례 = edict[íːdikt] = law = order
= precept[príːsept] = rule
The city government enforced an ordinance banning smoking in all the public buildings.
시 정부는 모든 공공빌딩에서 금연을 하도록 하는 법령을 시행했다.

orthodox[ɔ́ːrθədàks] a 정통의, 정설의 = accepted = traditional
The religious group insists that its school teaches the orthodox theory.
그 종교단체는 자신들의 학파는 정통 이론을 가르친다고 주장한다.

oscillate[ásəlèit] v 진동하다, 동요하다, 흔들리다 = fluctuate[flʌ́ktʃuèit] = lurch[ləːrtʃ]
= stagger[stǽgər] = sway = teeter = vacillate[vǽsəlèit] = waver[wéivər] = wobble[wábl]
He oscillated between the SUV and the sedan when buying a car.
그는 SUV와 세단 중에 어떤 차를 살지 마음이 흔들렸다.

osmosis[azmóusis] n 삼투 = absorption[æbsɔ́ːrpʃən]
A lot of osmosis phenomena happen on the leaves on rainy days.
비 오는 날 나뭇잎에서 많은 삼투현상들이 일어난다.

ossify[ásəfài] v 골화되다, 경화되다 = solidify[səlídəfài]
The civil service should not ossify into a dinosaur organization.
공무원 조직은 거대한 공룡조직으로 경화되어서는 안 된다.

QUIZ 43

Match each word in the first column with its definition in the second column.
Check your answers in the back of the book.

1.	officious	a.	auspicious = felicitous
2.	oscillate	b.	fluctuate = lurch
3.	olfactory	c.	autocrat = despot
4.	oligarchy	d.	abusive = calumnious
5.	opine	e.	apocalyptic = augural
6.	ordinance	f.	accepted = traditional
7.	ossify	g.	aromatic = fragrant
8.	opacity	h.	affluent = profuse
9.	opaque	i.	edict = law
10.	omniscient	j.	inquisitive = intrusive
11.	opportune	k.	apocalypse = augury
12.	offish	l.	blurred = muddy
13.	orthodox	m.	express an opinion
14.	oracle	n.	solidify
15.	orate	o.	unfriendly
16.	ominous	p.	absorption
17.	opulent	q.	all-knowing = all-seeing
18.	opprobrious	r.	address = speak
19.	osmosis	s.	arduous = burdensome
20.	onerous	t.	cloudiness

ostensible[əsténsəbl] a (실제는 아니어도) 표면적으로는 = superficial[sù:pərfíʃəl]
The ostensible reason of the break-up of their marriage is the difference in personality.
그들의 결혼생활의 파경 원인은 표면적으로는 성격 차이이다.

ostentatious[àstəntéiʃəs] a 과시하는, 자랑해 보이는, 허세부리는 = boastful[bóustfəl]
= flashy = showy = pompous[pámpəs]
Students were tired of their professor's ostentatious display of knowledge.
학생들은 교수가 지식을 대놓고 과시하는 것에 싫증이 났다.

ostracize[ástrəsàiz] v 외면하다, 배척하다, 추방하다 = blackball = banish[bǽniʃ] = deport
= exclude = excommunicate = exile[égzail] = expatriate[ekspéitrièit] = expel = oust[aust]
The judge was ostracized by his fellow judges for supporting the same-sex marriage.
판사는 동성결혼을 지지한다는 이유로 동료 판사들에게 배척당했다.

oust[aust] v 몰아내다, 축출하다, 내쫓다 = banish = depose[dipóuz] = deprive =
dethrone[di:θróun] = eject[idʒékt] = evict[ivíkt] = ostracize[ástrəsàiz] = topple[tápl]
He ousted his young nephew from the throne.
그는 어린 조카를 왕위에서 축출했다.

outmaneuver[àutmənjú:vər] v 책략으로 이기다, 의표를 찌르다 = outsmart = outwit[àutwít]
Robin Hood outmaneuvered his opponents at a battle in the forest.
Robin Hood는 숲속 전투에서 책략으로 적들을 압도하였다.

overbearing[oʊvərberiŋ] a 거만한, 고압적인 = arrogant[ǽrəgənt] = bossy
= domineering[dàməníəriŋ] = haughty[hɔ́:ti] = imperious[impíəriəs] = insolent
The new boss has an overbearing manner. 새로 온 사장은 고압적 태도를 가지고 있다.

overindulge[oʊvərindʌldʒ] v 지나치게 응석받다, 너무 탐닉하다 = coddle[kádl] = cosset
His parents have overindulged their only late son.
그의 부모들은 늦둥이 외동아들의 응석을 지나치게 받아줬다.

override[oʊvərraid] v 기각하다, 뒤엎다, 무효로 하다 = abrogate[ǽbrəgèit]
= annul[ənʌ́l] = nullify[nʌ́ləfài] = reverse = revoke = supersede[sù:pərsí:d] = veto[ví:tou]
Lawmakers from the opposition party decided to override the president's veto.
야당 국회의원들은 대통령의 거부권을 뒤엎기로 결정했다.

overture[óuvərtʃər] n 제의, 제안, 서곡 = proposal = proposition[pràpəzíʃən] = suggestion
The rebel forces made a peace overture. 반란군은 평화제안을 했다.

oxymoron[ùksimɔ́ːran] **n** 모순어법 = turn of expression
Good cigarette sounds like an oxymoron. 좋은 담배는 모순어법처럼 들린다.

QUIZ 85

Match each word in the first column with its definition in the second column.
Check your answers in the back of the book.

1.	ostensible		a.	superficial
2.	oxymoron		b.	boastful = flashy
3.	override		c.	proposal = proposition
4.	overindulge		d.	turn of expression
5.	outmaneuver		e.	arrogant = bossy
6.	overbearing		f.	coddle = cosset
7.	oust		g.	outsmart = outwit
8.	ostracize		h.	abrogate = annul
9.	overture		i.	banish = depose
10.	ostentatiou		j.	blackball = banish

pacify[pǽsəfài] v 진정시키다, 달래다 = alleviate[əlí:vièit] = allay[əléi]
= appease[əpí:z] = assuage[əswéidʒ] = ease = mitigate[mítəgèit] = mollify[máləfài]
= placate[pléikeit] = soothe[su:ð]
They tried to pacify the angry farmers. 그들은 화난 농민들을 진정시키려 애썼다.

painstaking[peınzteıkıŋ] a 애쓰는, 공들인 = assiduous[əsídʒuəs] = strenuous[strénjuəs]
The doctor published his painstaking research on the lung cancer on the medical journal.
그 의사는 폐암에 관한 공들인 연구를 의학잡지에 게재했다.

palatable[pǽlətəbl] a 맛있는, 맛 좋은 = delectable[diléktəbl] = delicious
= luscious[lʌ́ʃəs] = sapid[sǽpid] = savory[séivəri]
The salmon steak looked palatable. 연어 스테이크가 맛있어 보였다.

palliate[pǽlièit] v (일시적으로) 완화시키다 = alleviate[əlí:vièit] = allay[əléi]
= appease[əpí:z] = assuage[əswéidʒ] = ease = mitigate[mítəgèit] = mollify[máləfài]
= pacify[pǽsəfài] = placate[pléikeit] = soothe[su:ð]
The morphine injection palliated a pain for the patient.
모르핀 주입은 환자의 고통을 일시적으로 완화시켰다.

pallid[pǽlid] a 창백한, 파르스름한 = pale
The girl has a pallid complexion. 소녀의 안색은 창백했다. complexion[kəmplékʃən] n 안색

pallor[pǽlər] n 창백함, 안색이 나쁨 = paleness
The pallor of her face means that there are some problems with her health.
창백한 그녀의 얼굴은 건강에 어떤 문제가 있음을 의미한다.

palmy[pá:mi] a 영광스럽던, 잘 나가던, 전성기의 =flourishing[flə́:riʃiŋ]
= prosperous[prásp ərəs] = thriving[θráiviŋ]
I used to earn U$10,000 a month in my palmy days.
전성기 때 나는 한 달에 일만 달러씩 벌었다.

palpable[pǽlpəbl] a 만질 수 있는, 뚜렷한, 명백한 = clear
= noticeable[nóutisəbl] = obvious = tangible[tǽndʒəbl]
Their hatred of violence and war was palpable. 그들이 폭력과 전쟁을 싫어하는 것은 확실하다.

palter[pɔ́:ltər] v 얼버무리다, 어름어름 넘기다 = equivocate[ikwívəkèit]
= prevaricate[privǽrəkèit] = quibble[kwíbl]
The mayor paltered with his election pledges. 시장은 그의 선거 공약을 어름어름 넘어가려 했다.

paltry[pɔ́:ltri] a 얼마 안 되는, 시시한, 하찮은 = meager[mí:gər] = petty
= picayune[pìkijú:n] = trivial[tríviəl]
His wife earns a paltry salary by working as a cashier at a mart.
그의 아내는 마트에서 캐셔로 일하면서 얼마 안 되는 급여를 받고 있다.

panache[pənǽʃ] n 기백, 위풍당당 = verve[və:rv]
Triumphant troops were returning to the capital with panache.
승전한 병사들이 위풍당당하게 수도로 돌아오고 있었다.

pandemic[pændémik] a 전국적(세계적)으로 유행하는 = ecumenical[èkjuménikəl]
= prevalent[prévələnt] = universal = widespread
The pandemic disease has killed many people in Africa.
전 세계적인 역병으로 수많은 아프리카 사람들이 죽었다.

panegyric[pænidʒírik] n 찬사, 칭찬 = encomium[enkóumiəm] = eulogy[jú:lədʒi]
= exaltation[ègzɔ:ltéiʃən] = glorification[glɔ̀:rəfikéiʃən] = hymn[him] = laud[lɔ:d]
= paean[pí:ən] = praise
The president delivered a panegyric to the marathon winner.
대통령은 마라톤 우승자에게 찬사를 보냈다.

parable[pǽrəbl] n 우화, 비유 = allegory[ǽligɔ̀:ri] = fable[féibl]
We grown-ups sometimes learn lessons from parables. 우리 어른들도 우화에서 교훈을 배운다.

paradigmatic[pærədigmǽtik] a 전형적인, 모범의 = typical
We can see a lot of changes to the paradigmatic agricultural production in China.
우리는 중국에서 전형적인 농업생산에서 발생하는 많은 변화를 볼 수 있다.

paragon[pǽrəgɑ̀n] n 모범, 전형, 귀감 = apotheosis[əpɑ̀θióusis]
= archetype[ɑ́:rkitàip] = epitome[ipítəmi] = exemplar = paradigm
The 45-year-old baseball player became a paragon to the young players.
45세의 야구선수는 젊은 선수들에게 귀감이 되었다.

paramount[pǽrəmàunt] a 가장 중요한, 최고의 = outstanding
= predominant[pridɑ́mənənt] = preeminent[priémənənt] = superior
Design is paramount in the auto industry. 디자인은 자동차산업에서 가장 중요하다.

paranoia[pærənɔ́iə] n 편집증, 피해망상 = mental illness = schizophrenia[skìtsəfrí:niə] He suffered from paranoia. 그는 편집증을 겪었다.

paranormal[pærənɔ:rml] a 과학으로 설명할 수 없는, 초자연적인
= occult[əkʌlt] = preternatural[prìːtərnǽtʃərəl] = supernatural
We sometimes see paranormal events. 우리는 때때로 과학으로 설명할 수 없는 초자연적인 현상을 본다.

parity[pǽrəti] n 동가, 등위, 동등 = balance = equality
Female workers in the software company are demanding parity of treatment with male workers.
소프트웨어 회사에서 일하는 여성 근로자들은 남성 근로자들과 같은 대우를 요구하고 있다.

QUIZ 86

*Match each word in the first column with its definition in the second column.
Check your answers in the back of the book.*

1.	palmy	a.	pale
2.	paragon	b.	clear = noticeable
3.	paradigmatic	c.	allegory = fable
4.	parity	d.	ecumenical = prevalent
5.	palter	e.	delectable = delicious
6.	pallor	f.	flourishing = prosperous
7.	pacify	g.	mental illness = schizophrenia
8.	palpable	h.	alleviate = allay
9.	parable	i.	typical
10.	paltry	j.	encomium = eulogy
11.	panache	k.	outstanding = predominant
12.	pandemic	l.	apotheosis = archetype
13.	panegyric	m.	equivocate = lie
14.	palliate	n.	occult = preternatural
15.	palatable	o.	assiduous = strenuous
16.	paranoia	p.	verve
17.	paramount	q.	paleness
18.	painstaking	r.	alleviate = allay
19.	paranormal	s.	balance = equality
20.	pallid	t.	meager = petty

---

parlance[pάːrləns] n 말투, 어조 = locution[loukjúːʃən]
Lawyers were exchanging their views in legal parlance.
변호사들은 법률적인 말투로 의견을 교환했다.

paroxysm[pǽrəksìzm] n 격발, 발작적 행동 = convulsion[kənvʌ́lʃən]
= seizure[síːʒər] = spasm[spǽzm]
On seeing the criminal suspect, the victims' parents felt a paroxysm of anger.
피의자를 보자마자 피해자 부모들은 분노가 격발됨을 느꼈다.

parry[pǽri] v 비키다, 피하다 = avoid = bypass = circumvent[sə̀ːrkəmvént] = dodge[dadʒ]
= elude[ilúːd] = evade[ivéid] = shirk[ʃəːrk] = shun[ʃʌn] = sidestep = stave off = ward off
The fighting plane parried the missile attack from the enemy.
전투기는 적의 미사일 공격을 피했다.

parse[paːrs] v 문장을 구성요소로 분석하다 = analyze
The teacher parsed the sentence to explain to his students.
선생님은 학생들에게 설명하기 위해 그 문장을 구성요소로 분석했다.

parsimonious[pɑ̀ːrsəmóuniəs] a 인색한 = miserly[máizərli] = penny-pinching
= penurious[pənjúəriəs] = stingy[stíndʒi]
He is so parsimonious that nobody wants to meet him.
그는 너무 인색해서 아무도 그를 만나려 하지 않는다.

pastoral[pǽstərəl] a 전원적인, 목가적인 = Arcadian = bucolic[bjuːkɑ́lik]
= idyllic[aidílik] = rural = rustic[rʌ́stik]
He was longing for a pastoral life after retirement. 그는 은퇴 후의 전원생활을 꿈꾼다.

pathos[péiθas] n 연민, 비애감 = sadness
The new play directed by James Miller is full of pathos.
James Miller가 감독한 새로운 연극은 비애감으로 가득하다.

patina[pǽtənə] n 녹청, 고색, 그윽한 멋 = verdigris[və́ːrdəgrìːs]
The old temple has a lot of patina on its roof tile and on the wall.
그 오래된 사찰은 지붕 기와에도 벽에도 녹청이 가득하다.

patrimony[pǽtrəmòuni] n 아버지의 세습재산, 유산 = bequeathal[bikwíːð]
= heritage = inheritance[inhérətəns]
The two daughters filed a lawsuit against their older brother who wanted to inherit the patrimony alone. 두 딸은 혼자서 아버지의 유산을 물려받으려는 오빠를 상대로 소송을 냈다.

patronize[péitrənàiz] v 후원하다, 찬조하다 = sponsor = support
The company has been patronizing the world-famous pianist.
그 회사는 세계적인 피아니스트를 후원해 오고 있다.

paucity[pɔ́ːsəti] n 소량, 부족, 결핍, 부족 = dearth[dəːrθ] = lack = scarcity[skɛ́ərsəti]
Many countries will suffer from a paucity of natural resources
많은 국가들이 천연자원 부족을 겪게 될 것이다.

paunchy[pɔ́ːntʃi] a 배가 불뚝하게 나온 = corpulent[kɔ́ːrpjulənt] = fat = obese[oubíːs]
The suspect turned out to be a man who was paunchy and bald.
용의자는 배가 불뚝 나오고 머리가 벗겨진 사람으로 판명되었다.

peccadillo[pèkədílou] n 가벼운 죄, 사소한 잘못(실수) = misdemeanor
His sexual peccadilloes made him resign.
성적인 사소한 죄 때문에 그는 사임했다.

peck[pek] v 가볍게 키스하다 = kiss
She pecked the children on the cheeks. 그녀는 아이들의 볼에 가볍게 입을 맞추었다.

pedagogue[pédəgɑ̀g] n 교육자, 선생 = educator = teacher
She wanted to be a pedagogue in the field of English literature.
그녀는 영문학 분야의 교육자가 되기를 바랐다.

pedantic[pədǽntik] a 현학적인, 학자라고 뽐내는, 박식한 체하는 = erudite[érjudàit]
He used too many pedantic expressions on his report.
그는 보고서에 너무 많은 현학적인 표현을 사용했다.

pedestrian[pədéstriən] a 상상력 없는, 재미없는, 평범한 = banal[bənǽl]
= hackneyed[hǽknid] = humdrum[hʌ́mdrʌ̀m] = prosaic[prouzéiik] = trite[trait]
His proposal was too pedestrian to apply to the project in the company.
그의 제안은 회사의 프로젝트에 적용하기에는 너무 상상력이 없는 평범한 것이었다.

peeve[piːv] v 약올리다, 안달나게 하다, 화나게 하다 = annoy = bother[báðər]
= exasperate[igzǽspərèit] = gall[gɔːl] = irk[əːrk] = irritate[írətèit] = nettle[nétl] = pique[piːk]
= rile[rail] = vex
The bus driver's reckless driving peeved the passengers.
버스 운전자의 무모한 운전은 승객들을 화나게 했다.

pellucid[pəlúːsid] a 투명한, 맑은, 명료한 = clear = translucent[trænslúːsnt]
= transparent[trænspéərənt]
Travelers decided to enjoy swimming in the pellucid lake.
여행객들은 투명한 호수에서 수영을 즐기기로 했다.

penchant[péntʃənt] n 애호, 기호, 경향 = inclination[ìnklənéiʃən]
= predilection[prèdəlékʃən] = proclivity[prouklívəti] = propensity[prəpénsəti] = tendency
He has a penchant for Japanese foods. 그는 일식을 좋아한다.

QUIZ 87

Match each word in the first column with its definition in the second column.
Check your answers in the back of the book.

1.	parlance		a.	locution
2.	patronize		b.	sadness
3.	pathos		c.	convulsion = seizure
4.	paunchy		d.	educator = teacher
5.	parsimonious		e.	kiss
6.	pastoral		f.	avoid = bypass
7.	penchant		g.	erudite
8.	patina		h.	bequeathal = heritage
9.	patrimony		i.	analyze
10.	parry		j.	verdigris
11.	peeve		k.	misdemeanor
12.	pedantic		l.	miserly = penny-pinching
13.	peccadillo		m.	clear = translucent
14.	paroxysm		n.	Arcadian = bucolic
15.	pedagogue		o.	banal = hackneyed
16.	paucity		p.	inclination = predilection
17.	pedestrian		q.	corpulent = fat
18.	parse		r.	annoy = bother
19.	pellucid		s.	sponsor = support
20.	peck		t.	dearth = lack

---

penitent[pénətənt] a 뉘우치는, 참회하는 = compunctious[kəmpʌ́ŋkʃəs]
= contrite[kəntráit] = regretful[rigrétfəl] = remorseful[rimɔ́:rsfəl] = repentant[ripéntənt]
= rueful[rú:fəl]
The prisoner was penitent for the crime he committed.
그 죄수는 자신이 범한 죄에 대해 뉘우치고 있었다.

penurious[pənjúəriəs] a 매우 인색한, 몹시 가난한 = miserly[máizərli]
= parsimonious[pɑ̀:rsəmóuniəs] = penny-pinching = stingy
He was so penurious that no his neighbor went to his mother's funeral.
그는 너무 인색해서 이웃들 누구도 그의 어머니 장례식에 가지 않았다.

piquant[pí:kənt] a 톡 쏘는 듯한, 자극적인, 얼얼한 = peppery[pépəri]
= poignant[pɔ́injənt] = pungent[pʌ́ndʒənt] = tangy[tǽŋi] = zesty
The piquant taste in the spaghetti attracted many diners.
스파게티의 톡 쏘는 듯한 맛은 많은 손님들을 매혹시켰다.

porcelain[pɔ́:rsəlin] n 자기 = ceramic[sərǽmik]
She keeps a variety of crops in the porcelain jars.
그녀는 다양한 곡식을 항아리에 보관한다.

peregrination[pèrəgrinéiʃən] n 장기간 여행, 만유 = jaunt[dʒɔ:nt] = journey
The couple was preparing for the world peregrinations.
그 부부는 세계일주 여행을 준비하고 있었다.

peremptory[pərémptəri] a 독단적인, 위압적인, 단호한 = absolute
= authoritative[əθɔ́:rətèitiv] = arbitrary
The general made a peremptory command. 장군은 단호한 명령을 내렸다.

perfidious[pərfídiəs] a 불성실한, 배신하는, 믿을 수 없는 = treacherous[tréʧərəs]
I'd like to warn you not to trust Mark too much, because he can be perfidious to you.
나는 당신이 Mark를 믿지 않기를 바라네, 당신을 배신할 수가 있거든.

perforate[pə́:rfərèit] v 구멍을 내다 = puncture[pʌ́ŋkʧər]
She perforated the wall in the restroom to hang a mirror.
그녀는 거울을 걸기 위해 화장실 벽에 구멍을 냈다.

perfunctory[pərfʌ́ŋktəri] a 형식적인, 습관적인, 겉치레의, 열의가 없는
= cursory[kə́:rsəri] = superficial[sù:pərfíʃəl]
The perfunctory investigation led to the release of the real criminal.
겉치레 식의 조사 때문에 진짜 범인을 놓쳤다.

peripatetic[pèrəpətétik] a 순회하는, 돌아다니는 = itinerant[aitínərənt]
= migrant[máigrənt] = nomadic[noumǽdik] = roving[róuviŋ]
A team of peripatetic doctors and nurses receive a warm welcome from the villagers.
순회 의사와 간호사 팀은 주민들로부터 열렬한 환영을 받았다.

peripheral[pərífərəl] a 주변의, 본질적이 아닌 = tangential[tændʒénʃəl]
Home appliance business is peripheral to the biggest IT group.
가전제품 사업은 그 대형 IT 기업에게는 본질적인 사업이 아니다.

perjure[pə́:rdʒər] v (재귀용법) 위증하다 = falsify[fɔ́:lsəfài] = give false testimony
He perjured himself about the murder case.
그는 살인사건 소송에서 위증을 했다.

pernicious[pərníʃəs] a 치명적인, 해로운 = deadly = detrimental[dètrəméntl]
= harmful = lethal[líːθəl] = malicious[məlíʃəs] = nefarious[niféəriəs] = heinous[héinəs]
= malignant[məlígnənt] = vicious[víʃəs] = vile = virulent[vírjulənt] = wicked
Violent games and movies can have a pernicious influence on the youth.
폭력적인 게임과 영화는 젊은이들에게 치명적인 영향을 미친다.

perpetrator[pə́:rpitrèitər] n 가해자, 범인 = culprit[kʌ́lprit] = malefactor
= miscreant = offender = trespasser = violator[váiəlèitər] = wrongdoer
The perpetrators knelt down in front of the parents of the victims.
가해자들은 피해자 부모님들 앞에서 무릎을 꿇었다.

perpetuate[pərpétʃuèit] v 영구화하다, 영속하게 하다 = eternize[itə́:rnaiz]
= immortalize
The dictator wanted to perpetuate his political power.
독재자는 그의 정치력을 영구화하기를 원했다.

persiflage[pə́:rsəflɑ̀:ʒ] n 조롱, 희롱, 농담 = banter[bǽntər] = teasing
The persiflage from the audience made the speaker upset.
관객들의 조롱이 연사의 기분을 상하게 했다.

perspicacious[pə̀:rspəkéiʃəs] a 총명한, 통찰력 있는 = discerning[disə́:rniŋ]
= judicious[dʒu:díʃəs] = perspective = sagacious[səgéiʃəs]
He was a perspicacious king, predicting the enemy would attack his country.
총명한 왕은 적군이 그의 나라를 공격하리라 예측했다.

pertinacity[pə̀:rtənǽsəti] n 불요불굴, 끈덕짐, 집착력 = doggedness[dɔ́:gidnis]
= obstinacy[ɑ́bstənəsi] = tenacity[tənǽsəti]
He finally reached the North Pole with pertinacity. 그는 불요불굴의 집념으로 북극에 도달했다.

pertinent[pə́:rtənənt] a 적절한, 관련 있는 = germane[dʒərméin] =
opportune[ɑ̀pərtjúːn] = relevant[réləvənt]
The detective presented all the evidence pertinent to the fraudulence case.
탐정은 그 사기사건과 관련 있는 모든 증거를 제출했다.

perturb[pərtə́:rb] v 동요하게 하다, 당황하게 하다 = agitate[ǽdʒitèit] = disconcert = fluster[flʌ́stər] = muddle[mʌ́dl]

The news of the serial killer perturbed the citizens.
연쇄살인범 뉴스는 시민들을 동요하게 만들었다.

QUIZ 88

Match each word in the first column with its definition in the second column.
Check your answers in the back of the book.

1.	penitent	a.	ceramic
2.	perpetrator	b.	eternize = immortalize
3.	peremptory	c.	jaunt = journey
4.	porcelain	d.	culprit = malefactor
5.	perforate	e.	agitate = disconcert
6.	piquant	f.	treacherous
7.	persiflage	g.	banter = teasing
8.	peripatetic	h.	discerning = judicious
9.	perfunctory	i.	absolute = authoritative
10.	perfidious	j.	peppery = poignant
11.	peripheral	k.	falsify = give false testimony
12.	pertinacity	l.	puncture
13.	pernicious	m.	doggedness = obstinacy
14.	peregrination	n.	tangential
15.	perpetuate	o.	itinerant = migrant
16.	pertinent	p.	deadly = detrimental
17.	perspicacious	q.	germane = opportune
18.	perjure	r.	cursory = superficial
19.	perturb	s.	compunctious = contrite
20.	penurious	t.	miserly = parsimonious

pervade[pərvéid] v 퍼지다, 만연하다, 배어들다 = penetrate[pénətrèit] = permeate[pə́:rmièit] = suffuse[səfjú:z]

A group of priests entered a room pervaded with moldy odor.
일단의 신부님들은 곰팡이 냄새가 배어 있는 방에 들어갔다.

perverse[pərvə́:rs] a 삐딱한, 비뚤어진, 심술궂은 = cantankerous[kæntǽŋkərəs] = deviant[dí:viənt] = miscreant[mískriənt] = ornery[ɔ́:rnəri]

His perverse attitude stopped him from getting promoted to the manager title.
그는 비뚤어진 태도 때문에 매니저로 승진하지 못했다.

petrography[pitrágrəfi] n 암석분류학 = study of rocks
He spent most of his life writing books about petrography.
그는 생애 대부분을 암석분류학에 관한 책을 쓰는 데 보냈다.

petty[péti] a 사소한, 하찮은 = insignificant[insignífikənt] = trivial[tríviəl]
You are not allowed to make even petty mistakes here.
당신은 여기에서 사소한 실수조차 해서는 안 된다.

phantasm[fǽntæzm] n 환상, 환각, 유령 = apparition[æpəríʃən] = fantasy = illusion
Many children were shocked to see a strange phantasm in the abandoned house.
많은 아이들이 버려진 빈집에서 이상한 환상을 보고 놀랐다.

philanthropist[filǽnθrəpist] n 자선가, 독지가, 박애주의자 = humanitarian
The butcher turned out to be a philanthropist. 그 푸줏간 주인은 자선가로 밝혀졌다.

phlegmatic[flegmǽtik] a 냉정한, 침착한 = apathetic[æpəθétik]
= unemotional[ʌnimóuʃənl]
He remained phlegmatic in case of an emergency. 그는 비상사태 때도 침착함을 유지했다.

philistine[fíləstìːn] n 교양 없는 사람, 속물 = boor
Artists rarely hang out with philistines.
예술가들은 교양 없는 사람들과 거의 어울리지 않는다.

pigment[pígmənt] n 그림물감, 색소, 안료 = dye
The painter uses the best pigment when he draws his own painting.
그 화가는 그림을 그릴 때 최고의 그림물감을 쓴다.

pine[pain] v 애타게 그리다, 갈망하다 = crave[kreiv] = hanker[hǽŋkər] = long for = yearn
He pined for his girlfriend when she moved away.
그는 여자친구가 떠난 후 그녀를 애타게 그리워했다.

piquant[píːkənt] a 톡 쏘는 듯한, 짜릿한, 입맛을 돋우는 = peppery[pépəri]
= poignant[pɔ́injənt] = pungent[pʌ́ndʒənt] = tangy[tǽŋi] = zesty
He likes to go to the restaurant which serves piquant foods.
그는 톡 쏘는 듯한 음식을 내는 식당에 가는 것을 좋아한다.

pith[piθ] n 핵심, 요점 = core = gist[dʒist]
The pith of her lecture was not to give up. 그녀 강의의 핵심은 포기하지 말라는 것이다.

pittance[pítns] n 적은 수입, 소량 = small amount
He earns a pittance working at a small factory.
그는 작은 공장에서 일하며 적게 번다.

placate[pléikeit] v 달래다, 진정시키다 = alleviate[əlí:vièit] = allay = appease = assuage[əswéidʒ] = ease = mitigate[mítəgèit] = mollify[máləfài] = pacify[pǽsəfài] = soothe[su:ð]
Villagers tried to placate the anger of the dragon living in the mountain.
마을 사람들은 산속에 사는 용의 분노를 달래려고 노력했다.

placid[plǽsid] a 평온한, 차분한, 잔잔한 = calm = peaceful = serene[sərí:n] = tranquil[trǽŋkwil]
There were two boats in the placid lake.
평온한 호수 위에 두 대의 보트가 있었다.

plagiarism[pléidʒərìzm] n 표절 = piracy[páiərəsi]
The composer was accused of plagiarism. 그 작곡가는 표절로 고소되었다.

plangent[plǽndʒənt] a 소리가 큰, 울려 퍼지는, 구슬프게 울리는 = resonant[rézənənt]
We could hear a plangent sound of various musical instruments from the church.
우리는 교회에서 울려 퍼지는 다양한 악기 소리를 들었다.

platitude[plǽtitjù:d] n 진부한 이야기, 상투적인 문구 = banality[bənǽləti] = bromide[bróumaid]
His speech was nothing but the repeated platitude.
그의 연설은 반복적인 진부한 이야기에 불과했다.

plethora[pléθərə] n 과다, 과잉 = excess = glut[glʌt] = surfeit[sə́:rfit]
A plethora of fruits are imported from the nations in Southeast Asia.
지나치게 많은 과일들이 동남아시아 국가들에서 수입된다.

pliable[pláiəbl] a 유연한, 유순한, 고분고분한 = adaptable = bendable[béndəbl] = docile[dásəl] = flexible[fléksəbl] = limber[límbər] = malleable[mǽliəbl] = supple[sʌ́pl]
The plastic is thin but very pliable.
플라스틱은 가늘지만 유연하다.

QUIZ 89

Match each word in the first column with its definition in the second column.
Check your answers in the back of the book.

1.	petrography	a.	small amount
2.	perverse	b.	insignificant = trivial
3.	platitude	c.	alleviate = allay
4.	pith	d.	humanitarian
5.	phantasm	e.	piracy
6.	philanthropist	f.	apparition = fantasy
7.	pliable	g.	crave = hanker
8.	philistine	h.	dye
9.	plagiarism	i.	boor
10.	pine	j.	penetrate = permeate
11.	plangent	k.	cantankerous = deviant
12.	petty	l.	apathetic = unemotional
13.	pittance	m.	study of rocks
14.	phlegmatic	n.	excess = glut
15.	placid	o.	calm = peaceful
16.	piquant	p.	banality = bromide
17.	placate	q.	peppery = poignant
18.	pigment	r.	adaptable = bendable
19.	plethora	s.	resonant
20.	pervade	t.	core=gist

pliant[pláiənt] a 나긋나긋한, 유연한, 시키는 대로 하는 = adaptable = bendable
= docile[dásəl] = flexible[fléksəbl] = limber = malleable[mǽliəbl] = pliable[pláiəbl]
= supple[sʌpl]
All gymnasts have pliant bodies. 모든 체조 선수들은 유연한 몸을 가지고 있다.

plight[plait] n 곤경, 역경 = dilemma = deadlock = difficulty = imbroglio[imbróuljou]
= impasse = predicament[pridíkəmənt] = quagmire[kwǽgmàiər] = quandary[kwándəri]
The war orphans were in a hopeless plight. 전쟁 고아들은 희망 없는 곤경에 놓여 있었다.

plod[plad] v 터벅터벅 걷다 = tramp = trudge[trʌdʒ]
Hearing that he failed in the exam, he plodded home.
시험에 불합격했다는 소식을 듣고 그는 터벅터벅 집으로 걸어왔다.

pluck[plʌk] n 용기, 담력 = bravery[bréivəri] = courage = grit = guts
The hunter had enough pluck to chase a tiger alone.
그 사냥꾼은 혼자서 호랑이를 쫓을 만큼의 담력을 가지고 있었다.

plumb[plʌm] v 파헤치다, 면밀히 조사하다 = delve[delv] = fathom[fǽðəm] = probe
Scientists are trying to plumb the existence of life on other planets.
과학자들은 다른 행성의 생명체의 존재에 대해 면밀히 조사하고 있다.

plummet[plʌmit] v 곤두박질치다, 수직으로 떨어지다 = nose-dive = plunge[plʌndʒ]
After the interest rate hikes, most stocks plummeted yesterday.
금리인상 후에 대부분의 주식이 곤두박질쳤다.

plunder[plʌndər] v 약탈하다, 강탈하다 = devastate = loot = pillage[pílidʒ] = ravage[rǽvidʒ]
The pirates plundered some villages along the coast.
해적들은 해안가 마을들을 약탈했다.

pluralism[plúərəlìzm] n 다원성, 다원주의 = multiculturalism
We live in a political and social pluralism.
우리는 정치적 사회적 다원성 속에서 살고 있다.

polarize[póuləràiz] v 양극화되다, 양극화를 초래하다 = demarcate[dimá:rkeit] = divide
We have to stop our society from polarizing in annual income.
우리는 연봉의 양극화 사회가 되는 것을 막아야 한다.

polemic[pəlémik] n 논쟁, 반론 = altercation = argument = bickering = brawl[brɔ:l]
= fracas[fréikəs] = quarrel[kwɔ́:rəl] = wrangle
His writing on the euthanasia caused a lot of polemic among netizens.
그는 네티즌 사이에 많은 논란을 일으키는 안락사에 대해 썼다.

pollster[póulstər] n 여론조사원 = canvasser = polltaker
She works as a pollster. 그는 여론조사원으로 일한다.

pompous[pámpəs] a 젠체하는, 거만한 = arrogant[ǽrəgənt] = imperious
= overbearing = presumptuous[prizʌ́mptʃuəs] = pretentious[priténʃəs]
The actor answered the questions from reporters in the pompous manner.
그 배우는 거만한 태도로 리포터의 질문에 대답했다.

ponder[pándər] v 숙고하다, 곰곰이 생각하다 = brood over = contemplate = deliberate = ruminate[rú:mənèit]
She pondered on the solutions to the labor problem.
그녀는 노동문제에 대한 해결책을 곰곰이 생각했다.

pontificate[pantífəkit] v 거들먹거리며 말하다 = admonish[ædmániʃ] = dogmatize[dɔ́:gmətàiz]
The commander of the occupation forces pontificated on the new public order laws.
점령군 사령관은 새로운 공공질서법에 관해 거들먹거리는 태도로 말했다.

pore[pɔ:r] n 모공, 작은 구멍 = foramen[fɔ(:)réimən]
After running half marathon, he was sweating from every pore.
하프 마라톤을 뛰고 난 뒤 그는 몸의 모든 모공에서 땀을 흘렸다.

pore[pɔ:r] v 심사숙고하다 = brood[bru:d] = contemplate[kántəmplèit] = muse[mju:z] = ponder[pándər]
He pored over starting up his own business. 그는 회사를 창업하는 것을 심사숙고했다.

porous[pɔ́:rəs] a 작은 구멍이 많은, 다공성의 = absorbent[æbsɔ́:rbənt] = having holes = spongy[spʌ́ndʒi]
Some trees in the jungle have porous leaves.
정글의 어떤 나무들은 작은 구멍이 많은 나뭇잎을 가지고 있다.

portentous[pɔ:rténtəs] a 전조의, 징후가 되는, 불길한 = apocalyptic[əpɑ̀kəlíptik] = foreboding[fɔ:rbóudiŋ] = ominous[ámənəs]
There are some portentous signs in our economy. 우리 경제에 몇몇 불길한 징후가 보인다.

poseur[pouzə́:r] n 허식가, 젠체하는 사람 = hypocrite[hípəkrit] = pretender[priténdər]
No poseur is loved by his or her friends. 젠체하는 사람은 주위 친구들에게 사랑받지 못한다.

posterity[pastérəti] n 자손, 후세 = descendants[diséndənts] = progeny[prádʒəni]
His pottery skills should be passed down to his posterity.
그의 도예 기술은 후세에 전해져야 한다.

QUIZ 90

*Match each word in the first column with its definition in the second column.
Check your answers in the back of the book.*

1.	pliant	a.	descendants = progeny
2.	pontificate	b.	hypocrite = pretender
3.	portentous	c.	apocalyptic = foreboding
4.	plod	d.	delve = fathom
5.	plumb	e.	bravery = courage
6.	pore	f.	tramp = trudge
7.	plunder	g.	absorbent = having holes
8.	pore	h.	altercation = argument
9.	polarize	i.	canvasser = polltaker
10.	porous	j.	dilemma = deadlock
11.	pollster	k.	demarcate = divide
12.	pompous	l.	arrogant = imperious
13.	poseur	m.	brood over = contemplate
14.	plight	n.	adaptable = bendable
15.	polemic	o.	multiculturalism
16.	pluralism	p.	admonish = dogmatize
17.	posterity	q.	nose-dive = plunge
18.	plummet	r.	foramen
19.	ponder	s.	devastate = loot
20.	pluck	t.	brood = contemplate

posthumous[pástʃuməs] a 사후(死後)의, 사후에 일어나는 = postmortem
His posthumous poems are expected to be published next week.
그의 사후에 쓰여진 시들이 다음 주에 출간될 것이다.

potable[póutəbl] a 음료로 적합한, 마셔도 되는 = drinkable = edible[édəbl]
We may soon face the lack of the potable water on our planet.
우리는 곧 우리의 행성에서 마실 수 있는 물의 부족을 겪을 것이다.

potentate[póutntèit] n 통치자, 대실력자, 권세가 = leader
The potentate once ruled over two-thirds of the Europe.
그 통치자는 한때 유럽의 3분의 2를 통치했다.

potter[pátər] n 도공, 도예가 = ceramist[sérəmist]
He worked in the palace as a potter. 그는 왕궁에서 도예가로 일했다.

prate[preit] vi (on, about) 재잘거리다, 수다 떨다 = babble = chat = gabble[gǽbl]
The girls were prating about their new school uniforms.
소녀들은 새 교복에 대해 재잘거리고 있었다.

prattle[prǽtl] v 재잘재잘 지껄이다 = babble[bǽbl] = gabble[gǽbl] = gibberish[dʒíbəriʃ]
The ladies prattled on their pet animals.
여자들은 자신들의 애완동물에 대해 재잘재잘 지껄였다.

preach[priːtʃ] v 설교하다, 전도하다 = evangelize[ivǽndʒəlàiz] = sermonize[sə́ːrmənàiz]
Pastor Jae preaches the word of God at the Covenant church.
Jae 목사님은 카비넌트 교회에서 하느님의 말씀을 설교하신다.

preamble[príːæmbl] n 서문, 전문, 서두 = introduction = preface = prelude
The author mentioned his goals and intentions of the publication in the preamble.
작가는 서문에서 책의 목표와 의도를 언급했다.

precarious[prikέəriəs] a 불안정한, 위태로운 = dicey[dáisi] = hazardous[hǽzərdəs]
= insecure = perilous[pérələs] = risky = rocky = unstable
The truck mounted with a huge crane on the hill looked precarious.
거대한 크레인을 탑재한 언덕 위의 트럭이 위태로워 보였다.

precede[prisíːd] v …에 선행하다 = antecede[æntisíːd] = antedate = predate
The welcome greetings preceded the awards ceremony. 시상식에 앞서 환영인사가 있었다.

precocious[prikóuʃəs] a 조숙한, 어른스러운, 아이 같지 않은 = smart ahead of age = mature
She showed a precocious talent for cooking at the age of five.
그녀는 다섯 살 때 요리에 대한 조숙한 재능을 보였다.

precipitate[prisípitèit] v 재촉하다, 촉진하다 = accelerate[æksélərèit]
= expedite[ékspədàit] = facilitate[fəsílətèit] = hasten[héisn]
The unreasonable and hasty investment precipitated his ruin.
불합리하고 성급한 투자가 그의 파멸을 촉진했다.

precipitous[prisípətəs] a 가파른, 벼랑 같은, 절벽의
= perpendicular[pə̀ːrpəndíkjulər] = precipitate[prisípitèit] = steep[stiːp]
Some migrant birds lay eggs on the precipitous cliffs.
일부 철새들은 가파른 절벽에 알을 낳는다.

précis[preisíː] n 요약, 개요 = abridgement = abstract[ǽbstrǽkt] = epitome[ipítəmi] = synopsis[sinápsis] = summary
She is writing a précis of the project. 그녀는 그 프로젝트의 개요를 쓰고 있다.

preclude[priklúːd] v 방해하다, 가로막다 = avert[əvə́ːrt] = deter = exclude[iksklúːd] = forestall = hinder = impede[impíːd] = obviate[ábvièit] = prevent = prohibit = stave off
His poverty could not preclude him from advancing into a medical college.
가난은 그가 의대에 진학하는 것을 가로막지 못하였다.

precursor[prikə́ːrsər] n 선구자, 전조 = forerunner = harbinger[háːrbindʒər] = vanguard[vǽngàːrd]
The sudden nausea can be a precursor to the brain hemorrhage.
갑작스러운 구역질은 뇌출혈의 전조현상일 수 있다.

predecessor[prédəsèsər] n 전임자, 선배 = ancestor = antecedent[æntəsíːdnt] = forerunner = precursor[prikə́ːrsər]
The new CEO dumped the M&A plan signed by her predecessor.
새로 온 사장은 전임자가 서명한 인수합병계획을 폐기했다.

predicament[pridíkəmənt] n 곤경, 궁지 = dilemma = deadlock = difficulty = hardship[háːrdʃip] = imbroglio[imbróuljou] = impasse = plight = quagmire[kwǽgmàiər] = quandary[kwándəri]
The economic downturn put many of the businessmen in a predicament.
경기침체는 많은 사업가들을 궁지에 몰아넣었다.

predilection[prèdəlékʃən] n 경향, 애호 = disposition = inclination = penchant[péntʃənt] = predisposition = proclivity = propensity = tendency
He has a predilection for action movies. 그는 액션영화를 좋아하는 경향이 있다.

predispose[priːdɪspoʊz] v ∼하게 만들다, ∼하는 성향을 갖게 하다 = incline = inspire = prompt[prampt] = urge
Lack of exercise can predispose people to diabetes.
운동 부족은 당뇨병의 원인이 될 수 있다.

QUIZ 91

Match each word in the first column with its definition in the second column.
Check your answers in the back of the book.

1.	posthumous	a.	ceramist
2.	précis	b.	babble = gabble
3.	predicament	c.	forerunner = harbinger
4.	precocious	d.	disposition = inclination
5.	prate	e.	incline = inspire
6.	predecessor	f.	avert = deter
7.	precipitate	g.	babble = chat
8.	preamble	h.	evangelize = sermonize
9.	predispose	i.	smart ahead of age = mature
10.	precede	j.	postmortem
11.	potter	k.	ancestor = antecedent
12.	preach	l.	drinkable = edible
13.	precipitous	m.	introduction = preface
14.	potable	n.	leader
15.	precarious	o.	dicey = hazardous
16.	precursor	p.	antecede = antedate
17.	preclude	q.	abridgement = abstract
18.	prattle	r.	dilemma = deadlock
19.	predilection	s.	perpendicular = precipitate
20.	potentate	t.	accelerate = expedite

predominant[pridάmənənt] a 두드러진, 뚜렷한, 우월한 = dominant = prevailing
= prevalent[prévələnt] = leading = preponderant[pripάndərənt]
Horses played predominant roles in the ancient battles.
고대 전투에서는 말들이 두드러진 활약을 펼쳤다.

preeminent[priémənənt] a 탁월한, 발군의 = distinguished = dominant[dάmənənt]
= outstanding = predominant = superior = surpassing[sərpǽsiŋ]
The spokesperson was preeminent in defending the government policy.
대변인은 정부 정책을 옹호하는 데 탁월했다.

preempt[priémpt] v 남보다 먼저 손에 넣다, 먼저 선수를 쳐서 회피하다 = seize in advance
Some customers could preempt the newly released smart phones by waiting in the tents in front of the shops. 가게 앞에 텐트를 치고 기다렸던 일부 고객들은 새로 출시된 스마트폰을 남보다 먼저 손에 넣었다.

preen[pri:n] v 몸치장하다 = groom[gru:m] = primp[primp] = spruce[spru:s]
The panelist preened herself before going to the TV debating.
토론 패널들은 TV 토론을 하기 전에 몸치장을 했다.

pregnant[prégnənt] a 충만한, 풍부한, 가득 찬 = abundant = fecund[fíkənd]
= fertile[fə́:rtl] = fraught[frɔ:t] = productive = prolific[prəlífik] = replete[riplí:t]
= teeming[tí:miŋ]
The members of the expedition entered the cave pregnant with a variety of treasures.
탐험대원들은 여러 가지 보물이 가득 찬 동굴로 들어갔다.

prelude[prélju:d] n 전주, 서곡 = introduction = preamble[prí:æmbl] = preface[préfis]
= prologue[próulɔ:g]
The demise of the king became a prelude to the power struggles among the princes.
왕의 서거는 왕자들 간의 권력싸움의 전주가 되었다.

premeditated[pri:medɪteɪtɪd] a 미리 계획된, 계획적인, 의도된
= calculated[kǽlkjulèitid] = deliberate[dilíbərət] = intended = intentional = planned = willful
The murder case turned out to be a premeditated crime.
그 살인사건은 미리 계획된 것으로 판명되었다.

premise[prémis] n 전제 = assumption
The negotiations will be settled on the premise that the management will accept the pay raise.
경영진이 임금인상을 받아들인다는 전제 하에서 그 협상은 체결될 것이다.

preponderance[pripándərəns] n 우세, 우월 = advantage
= ascendancy[əséndənsi] = dominance = predominance = prevalence[prévələns]
= superiority[səpìərió:rəti]
The enemy has preponderance over our troops in point of firepower.
적군은 화력 면에서 아군보다 우세하다.

prepossess[prì:pəzés] v 선입견을 갖게 하다, 미리 마음 품게 하다 = incline
= prejudice = slant[slænt]
His good appearance and manners prepossessed us in favor of him.
그의 훌륭한 외모와 태도는 우리에게 좋은 선입견을 갖게 했다.

preposterous[pripástərəs] a 터무니없는, 말도 안 되는
= absurd = ludicrous[lú:dəkrəs] = ridiculous
His proposal sounded preposterous. 그의 제안은 터무니없는 것처럼 들렸다.

prerogative[prirágətiv] n 특권, 특혜 = perquisite[pə́:rkwəzit] = privilege
Until recently voting was the prerogative of men in some nations.
어떤 국가에서는 최근까지 투표가 남성들만의 특권이었다.

presage[présidʒ] v 전조가 되다, 예감하다, 예지하다 = augur[ɔ́:gər] = forebode = forecast = foresee = foretell = predict = portend[pɔ:rténd] = prognosticate[pragnástikèit] = prophesy[práfəsài]
The advent of the huge swarm of locusts presage the severe drought.
거대한 메뚜기 떼의 출현은 극심한 가뭄이 올 것이라는 전조이다.

prescience[préʃəns] n 통찰, 예지, 선견 = foresight = presage[présidʒ]
Marcus has shown remarkable prescience in the IT industry.
Marcus는 IT산업에서 주목할 만한 선견지명을 보여주었다.

presentiment[prizéntəmənt] n 예감, 육감 = anticipation[æntisəpéiʃən]
= expectation = hunch[hʌntʃ] = premonition = presage[présidʒ]
I have a presentiment that an earthquake will happen.
나는 지진이 일어날 것 같은 예감을 가지고 있다.

presuppose v 예상하다, 추정하다 = assume = suppose = surmise[sərmáiz]
We presuppose that the vaccine to the new virus will be completed next month.
우리는 새로운 바이러스에 대한 백신이 다음 달에 완성되리라고 예상한다.

prevaricate[privǽrəkèit] v 얼버무리다, 거짓말하다 = equivocate[ikwívəkèit]
= falsify[fɔ́:lsəfài] = palter[pɔ́:ltər] = quibble[kwíbl] = tergiversate[tə́:rdʒivərsèit]
Asked about the bribe scandal, he prevaricated.
뇌물 스캔들에 대해서 질문을 받고 그는 얼버무렸다.

primp[primp] v 몸치장하다, 맵시 내다 = groom[gru:m] = preen[pri:n] = spruce[spru:s]
The young girl primped herself for a date with her boy friend.
어린 소녀는 남자친구와 데이트를 하기 위해 몸치장을 했다.

pristine[prísti:n] a 손대지 않은 상태의, 순박한, 원시상태의 = immaculate[imǽkjulət]
= intact[intǽkt] = primeval[praimí:vəl] = untouched
The cave has been kept in pristine condition. 그 동굴은 원시상태로 보존되어 있었다.

privation[praivéiʃən] **n** 궁핍, 부족상태 = deprivation[dèprəvéiʃən]
= destitution[dèstətjúːʃən] = indigence[índidʒəns] = poverty
He lived a life of privation during the war. 그는 전쟁 중에 궁핍한 삶을 살았다.

QUIZ 92

Match each word in the first column with its definition in the second column.
Check your answers in the back of the book.

1. prevaricate   a. advantage = ascendancy
2. privation   b. seize in advance
3. premise   c. anticipation = expectation
4. predominant   d. augur = forebode
5. pregnant   e. foresight = presage
6. prelude   f. distinguished = dominant
7. premeditated   g. incline = prejudice
8. primp   h. groom = primp
9. preponderance   i. dominant = prevailing
10. prepossess   j. assume = suppose
11. preposterous   k. abundant = fecund
12. prerogative   l. assumption
13. presage   m. immaculate = intact
14. presentiment   n. absurd = ludicrous
15. pristine   o. deprivation = destitution
16. preempt   p. calculated = deliberate
17. presuppose   q. perquisite = privilege
18. preen   r. introduction = preamble
19. prescience   s. equivocate = falsify
20. preeminent   t. groom = preen

---

probity[próubəti] **n** 정직, 성실 = honesty = integrity[intégrəti] = rectitude[réktitjùːd]
We put the probity first when we appoint the prime mister.
우리는 총리를 지명할 때 정직성을 가장 우선시한다.

proclivity[prouklívəti] **n** 성향, 경향 = inclination[ìnklənéiʃən] = penchant[péntʃənt]
= predilection[prèdəlékʃən] = propensity[prəpénsəti] = tendency
She has shown a proclivity to lavish spending.
그녀는 낭비적인 성향을 보였다.

procrastinate[proukrǽstənèit] v 미루다, 지연하다 = dawdle[dɔ́:dl] = defer[difə́:r]
= delay = postpone = prolong[prəlɔ́:ŋ] = protract[proutrǽkt] = put off
You are not supposed to procrastinate any longer. 더 이상 지연해서는 안 된다.

procure[proukjúər] v 손에 넣다, 획득하다 = acquire[əkwáiər] = obtain
She could procure the limited edition of the luxury bag. 그녀는 한정판 명품 백을 손에 넣었다.

prod[prad] v 찌르다, 재촉하다, 촉구하다 = nudge[nʌdʒ] = poke at
Some voters prodded the war hero into the election of the lawmakers.
일부 유권자들은 그 전쟁영웅이 국회의원 선거에 출마하도록 촉구했다.

prodigal[prɑ́digəl] a 낭비하는, 방탕한 = extravagant[ikstrǽvəgənt] = lavish[lǽviʃ]
= wasteful
The legal heir was very prodigal with the inherited wealth.
그 법정 상속인은 물려받은 재산을 마구 낭비했다.

prodigious[prədídʒəs] a (보통 한정적) 거대한, 엄청난 = colossal[kəlásəl]
= enormous[inɔ́:rməs] = huge = immense[iméns] = tremendous[triméndəs] = vast
The ancient temple in the city was surrounded by a number of prodigious buildings.
도심의 오래된 사찰은 수많은 거대 빌딩들에 둘러싸여 있다.

prodigy[prɑ́dədʒi] n 천재, 신동 = genius = wunderkind[vúndərkìnd]
He has been considered a prodigy in chess. 그는 체스 신동으로 간주되고 있다.

profane[prəféin] a 신성 모독적인, 불경한, 세속적인 = blasphemous[blǽsfəməs]
= irreverent[irévərənt] = sacrilegious[sækrəlídʒəs] = unhallowed = vulgar[vʌ́lgər]
You should not show profane attitude during the rituals in the shrine.
사원에서 제사가 진행되는 동안에는 불경스러운 태도를 보여서는 안 된다.

profess[prəfés] v 공언하다, 단언하다 = assert[əsə́:rt] = declare[diklέər]
= proclaim[proukléim]
The actor professed his support for the candidate from the conservative party.
배우는 보수정당 출신의 후보자를 지지한다고 공언했다.

proffer[prɑ́fər] v 제의하다, 내놓다 = offer = propound[prəpáund]
She proffered a bowl of hot soup to the exhausted boy.
그녀는 지친 소년에게 뜨거운 수프 한 그릇을 내놓았다.

profligate[práfligət] a 방탕하는, 부도덕한, 낭비하는 = debauched[dibɔ́:ʧt]
= dissolute[dísəlù:t] = libertine[líbərtì:n] = lewd[lu:d] = promiscuous[prəmískjuəs]
= reprobate[réprəbèit]
He has been living a profligate life. 그는 방탕한 삶을 살고 있다.

profuse[prəfjú:s] a 풍부한, 마음이 후한, 너그러운, 아낌없는 = abundant[əbʌ́ndənt]
= ample = bountiful = copious[kóupiəs] = opulent[ápjulənt]
She was profuse with her money to prepare for the wedding ceremony for her daughter.
그녀는 딸의 결혼식을 준비하는 데 아낌없이 돈을 썼다.

progeny[prádʒəni] n 자손 = descendants[diséndənt] = offspring = posterity[pastérəti]
Our grandfather likes to take a walk with his progeny.
우리 할아버지는 자손과 산책하는 것을 좋아한다.

proletariat[pròulətɛ́əriət] n 노동자(무산자)계급 = working class
= plebeian[pləbí:ən] = rank and file
The conflict between the proletariat and the bourgeoisie is increasing.
노동자 계급과 자본가 계급 간의 갈등이 증가하고 있다.

proliferate[prəlífərèit] v 증식하다, 급증하다 = multiply = propagate[prápəgèit]
The number of smart phone users is proliferating. 스마트폰 사용자의 숫자가 급증하고 있다.

prolific[prəlífik] v 다산하는, 다작의, 열매를 많이 맺는 = fecund[fíkənd] = fertile[fə́:rtl]
= fruitful[frú:tfəl] = productive
He used to be a prolific writer. 그는 한때 다작 작가였다.

prolix[proulíks] a 지루하게 긴, 장황한 = lengthy[léŋkθi] = verbose[və:rbóus] = wordy
The mayor made a prolix speech. 시장은 장황한 연설을 했다.

promulgate[práməlgèit] v 공포하다, 발표하다 = declare = proclaim = make public
The government promulgated a new tax law. 정부는 새로운 세법을 공포하였다.

propagate[prápəgèit] v 증식(번식)시키다, 보급하다, 전파시키다 = breed[bri:d]
= inseminate[insémənèit] = multiply = proliferate[prəlífərèit] = reproduce
Many missionaries were sent to the region to propagate the faith.
종교를 전도하기 위해 많은 선교사들이 그 지역에 파견되었다.

QUIZ 93

Match each word in the first column with its definition in the second column.
Check your answers in the back of the book.

1.	prodigy	a.	blasphemous = irreverent
2.	propagate	b.	descendants = offspring
3.	profess	c.	assert = declare
4.	procrastinate	d.	honesty = integrity
5.	promulgate	e.	fecund = fertile
6.	prodigious	f.	lengthy = verbose
7.	prolific	g.	offer = propound
8.	proclivity	h.	inclination = penchant
9.	profane	i.	working class = plebeian
10.	profligate	j.	debauched = dissolute
11.	probity	k.	dawdle = defer
12.	proffer	l.	abundant = ample
13.	profuse	m.	acquire = obtain
14.	procure	n.	multiply = propagate
15.	prolix	o.	nudge = poke at
16.	proletariat	p.	genius = wunderkind
17.	prod	q.	declare = proclaim
18.	progeny	r.	extravagant = lavish
19.	proliferate	s.	breed = inseminate
20.	prodigal	t.	colossal = enormous

propensity[prəpénsəti] n 경향, 성향 = disposition[dìspəzíʃən]
= inclination[ìnklənéiʃən] = penchant[péntʃənt] = predilection[prèdəlékʃən] = predisposition
= proclivity[prouklívəti] = tendency[téndənsi]
He has a propensity for gambling. 그는 도박 성향을 가지고 있다.

propitiate[prəpíʃièit] v 달래다, 가라앉히다, 비위를 맞추다 = appease[əpíːz]
= assuage[əswéidʒ] = mollify[máləfài] = placate[pléikeit]
We held a memorial service to propitiate the souls of the soldiers.
우리는 병사들의 영혼을 달래주기 위해 기념식을 열었다.

propitious[prəpíʃəs] v 유리한, 상서로운 = auspicious[ɔːspíʃəs] = benign[ɔːspíʃəs]
= favorable = opportune[àpərtjúːn]
The commander was waiting for a propitious time to attack the enemy on the cliff.
사령관은 언덕에서 적을 공격하기에 유리한 시간을 기다리고 있었다.

proponent[prəpóunənt] n 지지자, 찬성자, 제안자 = advocate[ǽdvəkèit]
= exponent[ikspóunənt]
He is not the proponent of the same-sex marriage. 그는 동성결혼을 찬성하는 사람은 아니다.

propound[prəpáund] v 제기하다, 제출하다, 제안하다 = proffer[práfər]
= propose[prəpóuz]
He propounded a new plan that we could move to the Mars in 50 years.
그는 우리가 50년 후에 화성으로 이주할 수 있다는 새로운 계획을 제출했다.

propriety[prəpráiəti] n 예의범절, 적당함, 타당성 = decorum[dikɔ́:rəm]
= rectitude[réktitjù:d]
The young monks in the abbey learn how to behave with propriety.
수도원의 어린 수도승들은 어떻게 예의 바르게 행동하는지 배운다.

prosaic[prouzéiik] a 평범한, 지루한, 상상력이 없는 = banal[bənǽl] = commonplace
= drab[dræb] = hackneyed[hǽknid]= humdrum[hʌmdrʌm]= mundane[mʌndéin]
= pedestrian[pədéstriən] = trite[trait]
The novel with the prosaic storyline was not popular with the readers.
평범한 줄거리로 이루어진 소설은 독자들 사이에서 인기가 없었다.

proscribe[prouskráib] v 금하다, 금지하다, 배척하다 = forbid[fərbíd]
= interdict[íntərdìkt] = outlaw = prohibit[prouhíbit]
The religion proscribes drinking in the public places. 그 종교는 공공장소에서의 음주를 금한다.

proselytize[prásəlitàiz] v 개종시키다, 전향시키다 = convert[kənvə́:rt]
Christians rarely proselytize. 기독교인들은 좀처럼 개종하지 않는다.

prostrate[prástreit] a 엎드린, 길게 누운 = procumbent[proukʌ́mbənt]
The soldier lay prostrate with his left leg injured.
그 병사는 왼쪽 다리를 다친 채 엎드려 있었다.

protagonist[proutǽgənist] n 주인공, 주창자 = hero
The protagonist in the movie finally saved our planet.
영화에서는 주인공이 마침내 우리 행성을 구했다.

protégé[próutəʒèi] n 후배, 부하, 제자 = dependent
He was the protégé of the colonel, and they shared all the information.
그는 대령의 후배로서, 대령과 모든 정보를 공유했다.

protract[proutrǽkt] v 오래 끌다, 연장하다 = elongate[ilɔ́:ŋgeit]
= procrastinate[proukrǽstənèit] = prolong[prəlɔ́:ŋ] = put off = put on hold.
The tenant wanted to protract the rental contract. 세입자는 임대계약을 연장하길 원했다.

protocol[próutəkɔ̀:l] n 외교의례, 조약의정서, 통신규약 = code
All nations should observe the diplomatic protocol in the international community.
모든 국가들은 국제사회에서 외교의례를 준수하여야 한다.

protuberance[proutjú:bərəns] n 융기된 부분, 돌기 = protrusion[proutrú:ʒən]
We can see the protuberance of the dirt on the surface of the Mars.
우리는 화성 표면에서 흙으로 구성된 돌기를 볼 수 있다.

provident[právədənt] a 선견지명이 있는, 장래를 준비하는, 신중한 = canny[kǽni]
= discreet[diskrí:t] = judicious[dʒu:díʃəs] = circumspect[sə́:rkəmspèkt] = prudent[prú:dnt]
= sagacious[səgéiʃəs]
Sarah was a provident woman. Sarah는 선견지명이 있는 여자다.

provincial[prəvínʃəl] a 편협한, 지방의 = narrow-mined = parochial[pəróukiəl]
He showed his provincial attitude during the meeting.
그는 회의 도중에 편협한 태도를 보였다.

provisional[prəvíʒənl] a 임시의, 잠정적인 = conditional = contingent[kəntíndʒənt]
= interim[íntərəm] = tentative[téntətiv]
The two nations made a provisional treaty. 두 나라는 잠정적인 조약을 맺었다.

provocation[pràvəkéiʃən] n 자극, 도발 = harassment[hərǽsmənt]
= incitement[insáitmənt] = instigation[instəgéiʃən] = vexation[vekséiʃən]
The enemy has made a deliberate provocation. 적군은 고의적인 도발을 했다.

prowess[práuis] n 용기, 기량 = bravery[bréivəri] = courage = dauntlessness
= gallantry[gǽləntri] = grit =guts = intrepidity[intrepídəti] = mettle[métl] = valor[vǽlər]
The young general showed his prowess in the his first battle.
젊은 장군은 첫 번째 전투에서 용맹을 보여줬다.

QUIZ 94

Match each word in the first column with its definition in the second column.
Check your answers in the back of the book.

1.	propriety	a.	bravery = courage
2.	provisional	b.	harassment = incitement
3.	protocol	c.	decorum = rectitude
4.	provincial	d.	narrow-mined = parochial
5.	propensity	e.	hero
6.	provident	f.	disposition = inclination
7.	protract	g.	dependent
8.	propound	h.	conditional = contingent
9.	prowess	i.	banal = commonplace
10.	propitiate	j.	appease = assuage
11.	proscribe	k.	canny = discreet
12.	proselytize	l.	proffer = propose
13.	proponent	m.	elongate = procrastinate
14.	prosaic	n.	convert
15.	prostrate	o.	auspicious = benign
16.	protuberance	p.	forbid = interdict
17.	propitious	q.	advocate = exponent
18.	provocation	r.	protrusion
19.	protagonist	s.	code
20.	protégé	t.	procumbent

prowl[praul] v (먹이를 찾아) 배회하다, 돌아다니다 = move stealthily
Bears prowled for their prey along the river.
곰들은 강가를 따라서 먹이를 찾아 배회했다.

proximity[praksíməti] n 근접, 가까움 = closeness = adjacency[ədʒéisnsi]
They set up their tent in the proximity of the lake. 그들은 호수 근처에 텐트를 쳤다.

prune[pruːn] v 잘라내다, 쳐내다 = shear[ʃiər] = trim
He pruned the branches of the trees in the backyard.
그는 뒷마당에서 나뭇가지를 쳐냈다.

prurient[prúəriənt] a 호색적인, 외설적인 = bawdy[bɔ́ːdi] = lascivious[ləsíviəs]
= lecherous[létʃərəs] = lewd[luːd] = libertine[líbərtìːn] = libidinous[líbídənəs]
= licentious[laisénʃəs] = lustful[lʌ́stfəl] = obscene[əbsíːn] = salacious[səléiʃəs]
The book containing many prurient expressions could not be published.
많은 외설적인 표현을 포함하고 있는 그 책은 출판될 수 없었다.

pry[prai] v 캐다, 들춰내다 = poke into
Paparazzi are following the actress to pry into her private life.
파파라치들은 사생활을 캐기 위해서 그 여배우를 따라다닌다.

pseudonym[súːdənim] n 필명, 익명, 가명 = alias[éiliəs]
His book was published under a pseudonym. 그의 책은 필명으로 출판되었다.

psyche[sáiki] n 마음, 정신, 심령 = soul = spirit
Someday robots can be equipped with the human psyche.
언젠가 로봇들에게도 사람과 같은 마음이 장착될 것이다.

pucker[pʌ́kər] v 주름잡다, 오므리다 = wrinkle[ríŋkl]
She puckered her lips when she was putting up the make-up.
그녀는 화장할 때에 입술을 오므렸다.

puckish[pʌ́kiʃ] a 장난치기 좋아하는, 장난꾸러기의, 멋대로의 = mischievous[místʃəvəs]
We have finally published a series of books for puckish children.
우리는 마침내 장난꾸러기 아이들을 위한 일련의 책들을 출판했다.

pulchritude[pʌ́lkrətjùːd] n 육체미, 아름다움, 미모 = beauty
They were amazed by the pulchritude of the women in the high-mountain tribe.
그들은 고산족 여인들의 아름다움에 매료되었다.

pummel[pʌ́məl] v 세게 치다, 때리다 = bash[bæʃ] = batter = pommel[pʌ́məl]
= pound = punch = trounce[trauns]
A series of thunderstorms are expected to pummel the LA area next week.
일련의 폭풍우가 다음 주 LA지역을 강타하리라 예상된다.

punctilious[pʌŋktíliəs] a 꼼꼼한, 형식을 따르는 = careful = finicky[fíniki]
= heedful[híːdfəl] = meticulous[mətíkjuləs] = scrupulous[skrúːpjuləs]
The CFO was punctilious about the figures in the financial statements.
재무담당 임원은 재무제표 수치에 관해서 매우 꼼꼼했다.

pundit[pʌ́ndit] n 전문가, 권위자 = expert = savant[sævάːnt]
The doctor is a pundit in the field of brain surgery. 그 의사는 뇌수술 분야의 권위자이다.

pungent[pʌ́ndʒənt] a 톡 쏘는 듯한, 자극적인, 신랄한 = acid = acrid[ǽkrid] = bitter = piquant[píːkənt] = poignant[pɔ́injənt] = stinging[stíŋiŋ] = tangy[tǽŋi]
His proposal received pungent criticisms from the newspaper editorials.
그의 제안은 신문 사설에서 신랄한 비판을 받았다.

punitive[pjúːnətiv] a 징벌적인, 처벌을 위한, 벌을 가하는 = disciplinary[dísəplənèri] = penal[píːnəl] = punishing = retaliatory = vindictive[vindíktiv]
Teachers are discussing the punitive actions for those who broke the school rules.
선생님들은 교칙을 어긴 학생들에게 어떤 처벌을 할 것인가에 관해 토론 중이다.

puny[pjúːni] a 왜소한, 아주 작은, 하찮은 = paltry[pɔ́ːltri] = small = tiny
Most of the starving children have puny arms and legs.
기아를 겪고 있는 어린이들은 왜소한 팔과 다리를 가지고 있다.

purblind[pə́ːrblàind] a 반소경의, 시력이 흐린 = blind = myopic[maiάpik]
The old man was purblind, doing nothing without his glasses.
그 노인은 눈이 침침해서 안경 없이는 어떤 일도 하지 않는다.

puritanical[pjùəritǽnikəl] a 청교도적인, 금욕적인, 엄격한 = abstinent[ǽbstənənt] = austere[ɔːstíər] = rigid[rídʒid] = stern = straitlaced[stréitléist] = strict
He imposes puritanical way of living on his children.
그는 자녀들에게 청교도적인 생활방식을 강요한다.

purlieu[pə́ːrljuː] n (pl) 변두리, 교외, 가장자리 = edge = outskirts
Some start-up companies moved out to the purlieus of the city.
일부 창업 회사들은 도시 교외로 이전했다.

purloin[pərlɔ́in] v 훔치다 = filch[filtʃ] = pilfer[pílfər] = steal
Some lawmakers were actually purloining money from the state coffers.
일부 국회의원들은 국고에서 돈을 훔치고 있었다.

QUIZ 95

Match each word in the first column with its definition in the second column.
Check your answers in the back of the book.

1.	pundit	a.	soul = spirit
2.	prowl	b.	bash = batter
3.	purloin	c.	abstinent = austere
4.	pummel	d.	wrinkle
5.	pucker	e.	careful = finicky
6.	pseudonym	f.	mischievous
7.	pungent	g.	blind = myopic
8.	prurient	h.	move stealthily
9.	proximity	i.	expert = savant
10.	pulchritude	j.	beauty
11.	puny	k.	closeness = adjacency
12.	prune	l.	edge = outskirts
13.	puritanical	m.	shear = trim
14.	psyche	n.	paltry = small
15.	purblind	o.	bawdy = lascivious
16.	puckish	p.	filch = pilfer
17.	pry	q.	disciplinary = penal
18.	punitive	r.	poke into
19.	purlieu	s.	acid = acrid
20.	punctilious	t.	alias

purport[pərpɔ́:rt] v 주장하다, 칭하다 = assert[əsə́:rt] = proclaim[proukléim]
We have met a man purporting to be the survivor of the plane crash.
우리는 비행기 추락에서 살아남은 생존자라고 주장하는 남자를 만났다.

purvey[pərvéi] v 공급하다, 조달하다 = furnish = provide = supply = vend[vend]
The company won the contract to purvey milk for the school.
회사는 학교에 우유를 공급하는 계약을 따냈다.

pusillanimous[pjù:səlǽnəməs] a 겁 많은, 소심한 = fearful = timid[tímid]
= timorous[tímərəs]
He was too pusillanimous to start up his own company.
그는 너무 겁이 많아서 자신의 회사를 창업하지 못했다.

putative[pjú:tətiv]a 추정되는, 추정상 = alleged[əlédʒd] = presumed[prizjú:md]
The putative suspect of the crime was caught on CCTV.
범죄 용의자로 추정되는 사람이 CCTV에 잡혔다.

QUIZ 96

*Match each word in the first column with its definition in the second column.
Check your answers in the back of the book.*

1. pusillanimous   a. furnish = provide
2. putative   b. assert = proclaim
3. purvey   c. alleged = presumed
4. purport   d. fearful = timid

quaint[kweint] a 예스럽고 매력 있는, 진기한 = curious[kjúəriəs] = fanciful[fænsifəl] = picturesque[pìktʃərésk]
The quaint castle in the village attracts a lot of tourists.
마을에 있는 예스럽고 매력적인 그 성은 많은 관광객들을 끌어들이고 있다.

qualify[kwάləfài] v 자격을 주다 = certify[sə́:rtəfài] = entitle[intáitl] = empower[impáuər]
The golfer was qualified to teach golf as a teaching professional.
그 골퍼는 티칭 프로로서 골프를 가르칠 자격을 가지고 있다.

quandary[kwάndəri] n 진퇴양난, 곤경, 난처한 입장 = deadlock = dilemma = impasse[ímpæs] = plight[plait] = predicament[pridíkəmənt] = mire[maiər] = stalemate
The mayor of the local government was in a quandary about increasing the income tax.
시장은 소득세 인상과 관련, 진퇴양난의 입장에 있었다.

quarry[kwɔ́:ri] n 사냥감 = game
The hunters have been following the huge quarry for a few hours with their dogs.
사냥꾼들은 사냥개를 데리고 거대한 사냥감을 몇 시간째 쫓고 있었다.

quash[kwaʃ] v 진압하다, 억누르다 = crush[krʌʃ] = quell[kwel] = squelch[skweltʃ] = subdue[səbdjú:]
The president ordered the chief of staff to quash a revolt.
대통령은 합참의장에게 반란을 진압하라고 명령했다.

quasi[kwéizai] a ~과 같은, 유사의, 의사의 = almost = near = semi-[semi]
The prime minister proclaimed a quasi war situation on the whole army.
총리는 전 군에 준전시상황을 선언했다.

quay[ki:] n 부두, 선창 = dock[dak] = wharf[hwɔ:rf]
A lot of ships were moored to the quay to avoid the typhoon.
많은 배들이 태풍을 피하기 위해 부두에 정박하고 있었다.   moor[muər] v 정박하다

quell[kwel] v 진압하다, 평정하다 = crush = squelch[skweltʃ] = stifle[stáifl] = subdue[səbdjú:]
Two more companies of police were requested to quell the riot in the downtown.
도심에서 일어난 폭동을 진압하기 위해서 추가로 경찰 두개 중대가 요청되었다.

quench[kwentʃ] v 끄다, 잃게 하다 = extinguish[ikstíŋgwiʃ]
Two helicopters were being used to quench a fire in the mountain.
두 대의 헬기가 산불을 끄는 데 동원되었다.

querulous[kwérjuləs] a 불평하는, 짜증내는 = grouchy[gráuʧi]
= grumbling[grʌmbliŋ] = whining[hwaining]
He didn't want to be a querulous husband about the foods of his wife.
그는 아내의 음식에 대해 불평하는 남편이 되고 싶지는 않았다.

query[kwíəri] n 문의, 의문 = question
The mayor was ready to answer any queries by reporters.
시장은 기자들의 어떤 질문에도 대답할 준비가 되어 있었다.

queue[kju:] n 줄, 대기 행렬 = line
There is always a long queue of people to buy bread in front of the bakery.
빵집 앞에는 사람들이 줄을 길게 서 있다.

quibble[kwíbl] v 트집잡다, 언쟁을 벌이다, 옥신각신하다 = altercate[ɔ́:ltərkèit]
= bicker[bíkər] = squabble[skwábl] = wrangle[ræŋgl]
The young couple quibbled over the color of the cell phone which they would buy.
젊은 부부는 그들이 사려고 하는 휴대폰의 색깔을 가지고 옥신각신했다.

quiescent[kwaiésnt] a 조용한, 잠잠한, 활발하지 않은 = dormant[dɔ́:rmənt] = inactive
= inert[inə́:rt] = stagnant[stǽgnənt]
The severe yellow dust has become quiescent these days. 심한 황사가 요즘 잠잠해졌다.

quintessential[kwintəsénʃəl] a 본질적인, 전형적인 = typical = ultimate
They were expected to enjoy the quintessential Chinese foods in Shanghai.
그들은 상하이에서 전형적인 중국요리를 즐길 예정이다.

quizzical[kwízikəl] a 기묘한, 우스꽝스러운, 어리둥절해 하는 = eccentric[ikséntrik]
= quaint[kweint] = queer[kwiər]
He showed a quizzical look to hear that he failed in the test.
그는 시험에 낙방했다는 소식에 기묘한 표정을 보였다.

quixotic[kwiksátik] a 돈키호테 같은, 비현실적인, 공상적인 = dreamy = idealistic
= unrealistic = utopian[ju:tóupiən]
His quixotic management of the company led to its bankruptcy in the end.
그의 비현실적인 회사 운영으로 결국 부도가 났다.

quotidian[kwoutídiən] a 일상적인, 매일의, 보통의 = daily = everyday = ordinary
The doctor gave a lecture about the quotidian health care.
그 의사는 일상적인 건강관리에 대한 강의를 했다.

QUIZ 97

*Match each word in the first column with its definition in the second column.
Check your answers in the back of the book.*

1. quixotic
2. quizzical
3. querulous
4. quiescent
5. quibble
6. quell
7. quarry
8. query
9. queue
10. quench
11. quintessential
12. quandary
13. quotidian
14. quash
15. qualify
16. quay
17. quaint
18. quasi

a. altercate = bicker
b. crush = quell
c. dormant = inactive
d. extinguish
e. game
f. line
g. grouchy = grumbling
h. deadlock = dilemma
i. typical = ultimate
j. crush = squelch
k. question
l. certify = entitle
m. dreamy = idealistic
n. curious = fanciful
o. eccentric = quaint
p. almost = near
q. daily = everyday
r. dock = wharf

rabble[rǽbl] n 무질서한 군중, 오합지졸, 폭도 = crowd = mob[mab]
A rabble demanded for the resignation of the mayor. 폭도들은 시장의 사임을 요구했다.

rabid[rǽbid] a 광신적인, 과격한, 격렬한 = delirious[dilíəriəs] = fanatical[fənǽtikəl]
= renzied[frénzid]
The rabid separatists want to get independent from the federal government.
과격한 분리주의자들은 연방정부로부터의 독립을 원한다.

raffish[rǽfiʃ] a (점잖지는 않지만) 특이한 매력이 있는[흥미로운] = uncouth[ʌnkúːθ]
= vulgar[vʌlgər]
The magician was raffish on the stage.
그 마술사는 저급하게 보이기는 하지만 무대에서 특이한 매력이 있었다.

ramification[ræməfikéiʃən] n 파문, 영향, 결과 = consequence[kánsəkwèns]
= result = upshot
The court's decision will have huge ramifications in our society.
법원의 판결은 우리 사회에 커다란 파문을 가져올 것이다.

rampant[rǽmpənt] a 사나운, 만연하는, 횡행하는, 미쳐 날뛰는 = prevalent[prévələnt]
= rife[raif]
The air-borne virus is rampant in the South Americas.
공기로 전파되는 그 바이러스가 남미에 만연하고 있다.

ramshackle[rǽmʃækl] a 넘어질 듯한, 금방이라도 무너질 듯한 = decrepit[dikrépit]
= flimsy[flímzi] = rickety[ríkiti]
The tourists were moving in a ramshackle jeep.
관광객들은 금방이라도 넘어질 듯한 지프를 타고 이동 중이었다.

rancor[rǽŋkər] n 원한, 증오, 앙심 = animosity[ænəmásəti]
= antagonism[æntǽgənìzm] = antipathy[æntípəθi] = aversion[əvə́ːrʒən] = bitterness[bítərnis]
= enmity[énməti] = grudge[grʌdʒ] = hatred[héitrid] = hostility[hastíləti] = malice[mǽlis]
= malignity[məlígnəti] = resentment[rizéntmənt]
The factory workers have rancor against the manager who maltreated them.
공장 노동자들은 자신들을 학대한 관리자에게 원한을 품고 있다.

rant[rænt] v 호언장담하다, 큰소리치다, 큰소리로 불평하다 = shout = yell[jel]
The coach ranted on the victory of his team in the match.
감독은 시합에서의 승리를 호언장담했다.

rapacious[rəpéiʃəs] a 약탈하는, 강탈하는, 탐욕스러운 = avaricious[ævəríʃəs]
= greedy[grí:di] = ravenous[rǽvənəs] = voracious[vɔːréiʃəs]
The rapacious landlord forcibly evicted the tenants from his building.
탐욕스러운 집주인은 세입자들을 강제로 퇴거시켰다.

rapt[ræpt] a 골몰한, 몰두해 있는, 넋이 빠진 = absorbed[æbzɔ́:rbd] = enthralled[inθrɔ́:ld] = spellbound
Recently he has been rapt in playing golf. 최근 그는 골프에 몰두해 있다.

rapprochement[ræprouʃmá:ŋ] n 친교관계의 회복, 화해, 친선 = détente[deitá:nt]
= reconciliation[rèkənsìliéiʃən]
The summit meeting brought about a rapprochement between the two hostile countries.
정상회담은 적대적인 두 나라 사이에 화해를 가져왔다.

rapture[rǽptʃər] n 황홀감, 무아지경, 환희 = ecstasy[ékstəsi] = euphoria[ju:fɔ́:riə]
All the audience watched the water show with rapture.
모든 관객들은 무아지경에 빠진 채 수중 쇼를 봤다.

rarefied[rɛ́ərəfàid] a 보통사람들과 동떨어진, 지위 계급이 매우 높은, 수준 높은
= esoteric[èsətérik] = exalted[igzɔ́:ltid] = lofty
He was born and raised in the rarefied atmosphere of rich family.
그는 보통사람들과 다른 부잣집의 환경에서 태어나고 자랐다.

rash[ræʃ] a 경솔한, 무분별한, 성급한 = foolhardy = impetuous[impétʃuəs]
= imprudent[imprú:dnt] = impulsive[impʌ́lsiv] = reckless[réklis]
It is rash of him to announce that he has a daughter from an extra-marital affair.
그 남자가 혼외에서 얻은 딸이 있다고 발표한 것은 경솔하다.

ratify[rǽtəfài] v 비준하다, 재가하다, 승인하다 = approve = endorse[indɔ́:rs] = sanction[sǽŋkʃən]
The Free Trade Agreement with China was ratified in the congress.
자유무역협정이 국회에서 비준되었다.

ratiocination[ræʃiɑ̀sənéiʃən] n 추론, 추리 = inference[ínfərəns]
The book consists of some chapters which improve the ratiocination skills for students.
그 책은 학생들의 추론기술을 향상시켜주는 몇 개의 장으로 구성되어 있다.

rationale[ræʃənǽl] n 근본적 이유, 논리적 근거 = grounds = reason
The rationale for introducing new tax law was yet to be explained.
새로운 세법을 도입하는 근본적 이유는 아직까지 설명되지 않고 있다.

raucous[rɔ́ːkəs] a 요란하고 거친, 시끌벅쩍한, 귀에 거슬리는
= cacophonous[kækáfənəs] = discordant[diskɔ́ːrdənt] = dissonant[dísənənt] = jarring[dʒáːriŋ]
= strident[stráidnt]
The venue of the shareholder's meeting was full of raucous complaints and yelling.
주주총회 장소는 요란하고 거친 불평과 고함소리로 가득했다.

reactionary[riǽkʃənèri] a 반동의, 반동적인, 보수적인 = conservative
The reactionary party regained a lot of lost seats in the recent general elections.
보수정당은 최근 총선에서 잃어버린 의석을 많이 되찾아왔다.

rebel[rebəl] a 반항하는, 반역의 = insurgent[insəˊːrdʒənt] = rebellious[ribéljəs]
= revolutionary[rèvəlúːʃənèri]
Rebel forces are trying to overthrow the government. 반란군들이 정부를 전복하려 하고 있다.

QUIZ 98

Match each word in the first column with its definition in the second column.
Check your answers in the back of the book.

1.	ratiocination	a.	uncouth = vulgar
2.	reactionary	b.	animosity = antagonism
3.	rationale	c.	decrepit = flimsy
4.	rabble	d.	crowd = mob
5.	ratify	e.	delirious = fanatical
6.	rabid	f.	ecstasy = euphoria
7.	rebel	g.	insurgent = rebellious
8.	rash	h.	prevalent = rife
9.	raffish	i.	detente = reconciliation
10.	rapt	j.	cacophonous = discordant
11.	rapprochement	k.	consequence = result
12.	rapture	l.	conservative
13.	rapacious	m.	grounds = reason
14.	ramification	n.	absorbed = enthralled
15.	rampant	o.	esoteric = exalted
16.	raucous	p.	foolhardy = impetuous
17.	ramshackle	q.	avaricious = greedy
18.	rant	r.	inference
19.	rarefied	s.	approve = endorse
20.	rancor	t.	shout = yell

rebuff[ribʌf] v 거절하다, 퇴짜 놓다 = reject = repudiate[ripjúːdièit] = snub[snʌb]
= spurn[spəːrn] = turn down
His request for pay raise was rebuffed by his boss.
임금을 인상해달라는 그의 요구는 퇴짜를 맞았다.

rebuke[ribjúːk] v 비난하다, 질책하다, 훈계하다 = chastise[tʃæstáiz] = censure
= castigate[kǽstəgèit] = criticize severely = berate[biréit] = excoriate[ikskɔ́ːrièit]
= lambaste[læmbéist] = lash out at = reprimand = reproach[ripróutʃ] = reprove = revile[riváil]
= scold = tell off = upbraid = vilify[víləfài] = vituperate[vaitjúːpərèit]
The chairman of the bank was rebuked for illegally granting loan to the company.
은행장은 그 회사에 불법대출을 해준 것 때문에 비난을 받았다.

rebut[ribʌt] v 반박하다, 반증을 들다 = disprove = refute[rifjúːt]
The female CEO rebutted a charge that she evaded a tax.
여성 최고 경영자는 세금을 회피한다는 혐의를 반박했다.

recalcitrant[rikǽlsitrənt] a 저항(반항)하는, 다루기 힘든
= contumacious[kɑ̀ntjuméiʃəs] = disobedient[dìsəbíːdiənt] = fractious[frǽkʃəs] = intractable
= obstinate[ɑ́bstənət] = refractory[rifrǽktəri] = unruly[ʌnrúːli] = wayward
There are still a lot of recalcitrant rebel forces in the southern region.
아직 남쪽 지역에는 저항하는 반란군들이 있다.

recant[rikǽnt] v 진술 등을 철회하다, 취소하다, 부인하다 = annul[ənʌ́l] = back off
= renounce = rescind[risínd] = retract[ritrǽkt] = revoke[rivóuk]
He recanted his belief in the existence of aliens. 그는 외계인들이 존재한다는 믿음을 철회했다.

recidivism[risídəvìzm] n 상습적 범행, 재범 = backsliding = relapse[rilǽps]
We see the highest recidivism rate in drug-related crimes.
우리는 마약 관련 범죄에서 가장 높은 재범률을 보고 있다.

reciprocate[risíprəkèit] v 보답하다, 보은하다, 교환하다 = exchange = repay
The players reciprocated their dedicated coach by winning the tournament.
선수들은 우승으로 헌신적인 코치에게 보답하려 했다.

reciprocal[risíprəkəl] a 상호 간의 = bilateral[bailǽtərəl] = mutual[mjúːtʃuəl]
The reciprocal trade between the countries helped each other in economic growth.
두 나라 간의 상호교역은 서로에게 경제성장의 도움을 준다.

reckless[réklis] a 앞뒤를 가리지 않는, 무모한, 무분별한 = foolhardy
=impetuous[impétʃuəs] = imprudent[imprúːdnt] = impulsive[impʌlsiv] = rash
His reckless investment made him end up being penniless.
무분별한 투자로 인해서 결국 그는 무일푼이 되었다.

reclaim[rikléim] v 되찾다, 개간하다, 갱생시키다, 개선하다 = refurbish[riːfəːrbiʃ] = restore
She reclaimed the title of the queen of the ice. 그녀는 은반의 여왕이라는 칭호를 되찾았다.

reclusive[riklúːsiv] a 세상을 버린, 은둔한, 고독한 = cloistered[klɔ́istərd]
= isolated[áisəlèitid] = secluded[siklúːdid] = sequestered[sikwéstərd]
He has been called a reclusive leader in international community.
그는 국제사회에서 은둔의 지도자로 불린다.

recondite[rékəndàit] a 난해한, 심오한, 거의 알려지지 않은 = abstruse[æbstrúːs] = esoteric[èsətérik]
His recondite theory is too difficult for students to understand.
그의 난해한 이론은 학생들이 이해하기에 정말 힘들다.

reconnoiter[rìːkənɔ́itər] v 정찰하다, 조사하다 = scout[skaut]
His job was to reconnoiter the movements of the enemy.
그의 임무는 적의 움직임을 정찰하는 것이다.

rectify[réktəfài] v 수정하다, 정정하다, 바로잡다 = amend[əménd] = redress
We need to rectify wrong statistics in his report.
우리는 그의 보고에서 잘못된 통계수치를 수정해야 한다.

rectitude[réktitjùːd] n 정직, 청렴 = integrity[intégrəti] = probity[próubəti]
Rectitude is the first virtue when public officials are designated.
청렴은 공직자가 지명될 때 가장 처음 보는 덕목이다.

redeem[ridíːm] v 되찾다, 회복하다, 상환하다, 만회하다 = recoup[rikúːp]
= recover possession = regain
He redeemed his health thanks to his continuous diet and exercise.
그는 지속적인 식이요법과 운동으로 건강을 되찾았다.

redolent[rédələnt] a 어떤 냄새가 많이 나는, …을 생각나게 하는 = aromatic[ærəmǽtik]
= fragrant[fréigrənt] = perfumed[pərfjúːmd]
He was in a hospital room redolent with disinfectants.
그는 소독약 냄새가 많이 나는 병실에 있다.

redoubtable[ridáutəbl] a 경외할 만한, 가공할 = dreadful[drédfəl]
= formidable[fɔ́:rmidəbl]
The undefeated challenger will face a redoubtable champion next wee.
무패의 도전자는 다음 주에 가공할 위력의 챔피언과 대결한다.

redress[ridrés] v 고치다, 바로 잡다, 교정하다 = amend[əménd] = rectify[réktəfài]
The new president tried to redress the wage gap between male and female workers.
신임 사장은 남직원과 여직원 사이의 부당한 임금격차를 바로 잡으려 하고 있다.

redundant[ridʌ́ndənt] a 장황한, 불필요한, 쓸데없는, 여분의 = excessive[iksésiv]
= repetitious[rèpətíʃəs] = superfluous[supə́:rfluəs]
Bus ticket has been made redundant due to the credit card or smart phone payment system.
신용카드나 휴대폰 결제 덕분에 버스표가 불필요하게 되었다.

QUIZ 99

Match each word in the first column with its definition in the second column.
Check your answers in the back of the book.

1.	rebuff	a.	recoup = recover possession
2.	redundant	b.	contumacious = disobedient
3.	recondite	c.	integrity = probity
4.	reclaim	d.	reject = repudiate
5.	redeem	e.	amend = redress
6.	redress	f.	dreadful = formidable
7.	reconnoiter	g.	annul = back off
8.	recidivism	h.	aromatic = fragrant
9.	reclusive	i.	chastise = censure
10.	redolent	j.	foolhardy = impetuous
11.	rebuke	k.	amend = rectify
12.	redoubtable	l.	disprove = refute
13.	reciprocate	m.	refurbish = restore
14.	recant	n.	excessive = repetitious
15.	rebut	o.	backsliding = relapse
16.	recalcitrant	p.	cloistered = isolated
17.	rectitude	q.	exchange = repay
18.	reciprocal	r.	abstruse = esoteric
19.	rectify	s.	bilateral = mutual
20.	reckless	t.	scout

referendum[rèfəréndəm] n 국민투표 = plebiscite[plébəsàit]
The government wanted to hold a referendum on hosting Olympic Games.
정부는 올림픽경기 유치를 위한 국민투표를 원했다.

refined[rifáind] a 사람이 세련된, 교양 있는, 물질이 정제된 = cultured = polished = urbane[əːrbéin]
The gentleman has refined manners. 그 신사는 세련된 매너를 가지고 있다.

refractory[rifræktəri] a 사람이 다루기 어려운, 순종하지 않는, 병이 난치의
= disobedient[dìsəbíːdiənt] = headstrong = incorrigible[inkɔ́ːridʒəbl] = intractable
= unmanageable
He is such a refractory child that no one wants to look after him.
그 아이는 다루기가 어려워서 어떤 사람도 돌보려 하지 않는다.

refute[rifjúːt] v 반박하다, 논박하다, 잘못을 증명하다 = disprove = rebut[ribʌt]
The professor refuted an accusation that he sexually molested a girl college student.
그 교수는 여대생을 성추행했다는 혐의에 반박했다.

regime[rəʒíːm] n 정권, 체제 = government
Some military leaders wanted to establish a new regime.
일부 군부 지도자들은 새로운 정부를 세우길 원했다.

regimen[rédʒəmən] n 식이요법, 요양법 = systematic plan
Cancer patients should follow a strict regimen. 암 환자들은 엄격한 식이요법을 준수해야 한다.

rehabilitate[rìːhəbílətèit] v 재활치료하다, 명예회복 시키다, 복원시키다 = rebuild
= recover = renovate[rénəvèit]
The four-star general has rehabilitated his lost rank. 별 네 개를 단 대장은 계급을 되찾았다.

reign[rein] v 군림하다, 지배하다, 통치하다 = dominate = govern[gʌvərn]
No one can reign over the law. 아무도 법 위에 군림하지 못한다.

reiterate[riːítəreit] v 반복하다, 되풀이하다 = repeat = restate
The candidate reiterated his stance that he would not abandon his bid in the race.
후보자는 선거 경선에서 포기하지 않겠다는 그의 입장을 반복했다.

relapse[rilæps] v 나쁜 상태로 되돌아가다, 다시 타락하다, 퇴보하다
= degenerate[didʒénərèit] = deteriorate[ditíəriərèit]
He relapsed into gambling. 그는 도박으로 다시 되돌아갔다.

relegate[réləgèit] v 좌천시키다, 격하시키다, 강등시키다 = demote
The police chief was relegated to a trivial job in the countryside.
경찰서장은 지방의 한직으로 좌천되었다.

relentless[riléntlis] a 사정없는, 가혹한, 무자비한 = cruel[krú:əl] = ferocious[fəróuʃəs]
= implacable[implǽkəbl] = inexorable[inéksərəbl] = merciless[məˊ:rsilis] = pitiless[pítilis]
= remorseless[rimɔˊ:rslis] = ruthless[rú:θlis] = unrelenting
The Attorney General ordered a relentless crackdown on drug trafficking.
법무장관은 마약거래에 대해서 가차없이 단속을 하라고 명령했다.

relevant[réləvənt] a 관련 있는, 적절한 = germane[dʒərméin] = pertinent[pəˊ:rtənənt] = related
The actress could not answer the questions relevant to her wedding.
여배우는 결혼과 관련된 질문에는 답을 할 수 없었다.

relinquish[rilíŋkwiʃ] v 포기하다, 내주다, 양도하다 = abandon = abdicate[ǽbdəkèit]
= abnegate[ǽbnigèit] = cede[si:d] = give up = let go = quit = waive[weiv]
The founder had to relinquish the ownership of the company to the creditors.
회사 창업자는 채권단에게 회사 소유권을 넘겼다.

remiss[rimís] a 태만한, 성의 없는 = careless = delinquent[dilíŋkwənt]
The mayor has been remiss in carrying out his election pledges.
시장은 선거공약을 이행하는 데 태만했다.

remission[rimíʃən] n 용서, 사면, 경감, 완화, 진정 = absolution[æbsəlú:ʃən]
= acquittal[əkwítl] = amnesty[ǽmnəsti] = exoneration[igzɑ̀nəréiʃən] = forgiveness
= pardon[pɑˊ:rdn]
Some citizens are demanding the remission of the prisoners of conscience.
일부 시민들은 양심수의 사면을 요구하고 있다.

remonstrate[rimɑ́nstreit] v 항의하다, 불평하다 = demur[dimɔˊ:r] = disapprove
Motorists remonstrated with the police about the road block.
자동차 운전자들은 도로봉쇄에 대해 경찰들에게 항의했다.

remorseful[rimɔˊ:rsfəl] a 뉘우치고 있는, 양심의 가책을 받는
= compunctious[kəmpʌ́ŋkʃəs] = contrite = penitent[pénətənt] = regretful
= repentant[ripéntənt] = rueful[rú:fəl]
He felt remorseful for having spent all his money on Internet gambling.
그는 모든 돈을 인터넷 도박에 탕진한 것을 뉘우쳤다.

remunerate[rimjúːnərèit] v 보수를 지불하다, 보답하다 = compensate
= indemnify[indémnəfài] = reimburse[rìːimbə́ːrs] = reward
She will be remunerated for her dedication to the charity organization for 30 years.
그녀는 30년간 자선단체에 헌신한 것에 대해서 보답을 받을 것이다.

renaissance[rènəsάːns] n 부흥, 부활 = rebirth = resurgence[resə́ːrdʒəns] = revival
Horror movie is enjoying its renaissance. 공포영화가 제2의 전성기를 누리고 있다.

QUIZ 100

Match each word in the first column with its definition in the second column.
Check your answers in the back of the book.

1.	renaissance	a.	systematic plan
2.	relinquish	b.	absolution = acquittal
3.	relegate	c.	demur = disapprove
4.	reign	d.	plebiscite
5.	remiss	e.	rebuild = recover
6.	reiterate	f.	compunctious = contrite
7.	remunerate	g.	careless = delinquent
8.	remission	h.	abandon = abdicate
9.	regime	i.	cultured = polished
10.	remonstrate	j.	degenerate = deteriorate
11.	relevant	k.	cruel = ferocious
12.	remorseful	l.	germane = pertinent
13.	relapse	m.	repeat = restate
14.	referendum	n.	disobedient = headstrong
15.	rehabilitate	o.	dominate = govern
16.	refined	p.	banish = demote
17.	regimen	q.	disprove = rebut
18.	refractory	r.	compensate = indemnify
19.	relentless	s.	rebirth = resurgence
20.	refute	t.	government

rend[rend] v 찢다, 찢어발기다 = rive[raiv] = rip = tear
The missile rent the enemy tank asunder. 미사일이 적군의 탱크를 박살냈다.

render[réndər] v 어떤 상태가 되게 만들다 = make
Smart phones rendered some of the electronic gadgets useless.
스마트폰이 일부 전자기기들을 무용지물로 만들었다.

renounce[rináuns] v 포기하다, 단념하다, 버리다 = abandon = disavow[dìsəváu]
= disown[disóun] = forswear = quit = recant = waive
He renounced his title as the chairman of the veterans' association.
그는 재향군인회 회장직을 포기했다.

reparation[rèpəréiʃən] n 보상, 배상, 배상금 = amends = atonement[ətóunmənt]
= compensation[kàmpənséiʃən] = indemnity[indémnəti] = remuneration[rimjùːnəréiʃən]
= restitution[rèstətjúːʃən]
The company gave U$30,000 to each employee in reparation of their exposure to the radioactivity.
회사는 방사능에 노출된 직원들 각각에게 보상으로 삼만 달러씩 주었다.

repartee[rèpərtíː] n 재치 있는 응답, 재담 = riposte = sally[sǽli]
When asked some embarrassing questions, she always gives a repartee.
그녀는 당황스러운 질문을 받아도 항상 재치 있게 대답한다.

repatriate[riːpéitrièit] v 본국으로 송환하다 = send home
The prisoner will be repatriated for trial. 죄수들은 재판을 위해 본국으로 송환된다.

repel[ripél] v 쫓아버리다, 격퇴하다 = drive away = rebuff[ribʌ́f]
The admiral repelled the enemy's attack with a dozen ships.
그 제독은 열두척의 배로 적들을 격퇴했다.

repercussion[rìːpərkʌ́ʃn] n 반향, 영향 = consequence[kánsəkwèns] = fallout = reaction
= reverberation[rivə̀ːrbəréiʃən]
The sudden death of the designer will have repercussion for the fashion industry.
그 디자이너의 갑작스런 죽음은 패션업계에 반향을 가져올 것이다.

repertoire[répərtwὰːr] n 연주(노래, 공연) 목록, 레퍼토리 = repertory
The singer has a wide variety of repertoire. 그 가수는 다양한 레퍼토리를 가지고 있다.

replenish[riplénɪʃ] v 다시 채우다, 보충하다 = refill = refresh = restock
He replenished the gas tank of his car with gas before going on a long journey.
그는 장거리 여행을 가기 전에 차의 연료 탱크를 다시 채웠다.

replete[riplíːt] a 풍부한, 가득한 = abounding = awash[əwάʃ] = brimming[brímiŋ]
= filled = loaded[lóudid] = rife = teeming
His lab was replete with a variety of chemicals. 그의 연구실은 다양한 화학제품으로 가득했다.

replicate[répləkèit] v 복사하다, 복제하다, 모사하다 = copy = duplicate[djú:plikət]
Some cells get bigger by replicating themselves. 어떤 세포들은 자기복제를 해서 크기가 커진다.

repose[ripóuz] n 휴식, 휴게, 휴양 = respite = rest
After two hours of hard work, they took repose.
두 시간의 강도 높은 일을 한 뒤에 그들은 휴식을 취했다.

reprehensible[rèprihénsəbl] a 비난받아야 할, 괘씸한 = censurable[sénʃərəbl]
= condemnable[kəndémnəbl] = culpable[kʌlpəbl] = disgraceful[disgréisfəl] = shameful
It is reprehensible for him to commit a hit-and-run accident.
그가 뺑소니 사고를 낸 것은 비난받아야 할 짓이다.

repress[riprés] v 억누르다, 억제하다, 진압하다 = restrain[ristréin] = suppress[səprés]
The boys could not repress their impulse to eat at the sight of the foods.
소년들은 음식을 보고 먹고 싶은 충동을 억누를 수 없었다.

reprimand[réprəmænd] v 질책하다, 비난하다, 견책하다 = chastise[tʃæstáiz]
= censure[sénʃər] = castigate[kǽstəgèit] = criticize severely = berate[biréit]
= excoriate[ikskɔ́:rièit] = lambaste[læmbéist] = lash out at = rebuke[ribjú:k]
= reproach[ripróutʃ] = reprove = revile[riváil] = scold = tell off = upbraid = vilify[víləfài]
= vituperate[vaitjú:pərèit]
The company commander was reprimanded for failing to detect the penetration by enemies.
중대장은 적의 침입을 탐지하지 못해 질책을 받았다.

reprisal[ripráizəl] n 보복, 앙갚음 = counterblow = requital[rikwáitl]
= retaliation[ritæliéiʃən] = retribution[rètrəbjú:ʃən] = revenge[rivéndʒ] = vengeance[véndʒəns]
The rogue nation seized a commercial ship in reprisal for the economic sanctions against it.
그 불량국가는 경제제재에 대한 보복으로 상선을 탈취했다.

reproach[ripróutʃ] v 비난하다, 책망하다 = berate[biréit] = castigate[kǽstəgèit]
= censure = chide[tʃaid] = condemn[kəndém] = criticize[krítəsàiz] = defame
= denounce[dináuns] = disparage[dispǽridʒ] = lambaste[læmbéist] = lecture = rebuke
= reprimand = reprove = reprehend[rèprihénd] = revile[riváil] = scold = upbraid
= vilify[víləfài] = vituperate[vaitjú:pərèit]
The president of the chemical company was reproached for dumping untreated sewage into the river.
화학회사 사장은 처리하지 않은 하수를 강에 버려 비난을 받았다.

reprobate[réprəbèit] n 방탕아, 타락한 사람 = prodigal[prάdigəl]
Tom is a reprobate, because he is any man's money.
Tom은 돈이면 무슨 일이든 하는 타락한 사람이다.

reprove[riprú:v] v 나무라다, 꾸짖다, 비난하다, 책망하다 = berate[biréit]
= castigate[kǽstəgèit] = censure = chide[tʃaid] = condemn[kəndém] = criticize[krítəsàiz]
= defame = denigrate[dénigrèit] = denounce = disparage[dispǽridʒ] = lambaste[læmbéist]
= lecture = rebuke = reprimand = reprehend[rèprihénd] = reproach[ripróutʃ] = revile[riváil]
= scold = upbraid = vilify[víləfài] = vituperate[vaitjú:pərèit]
The old man reproved two college students for smoking in a non-smoking building.
노인은 금연건물에서 담배를 피우는 두 명의 대학생을 꾸짖었다.

QUIZ 101

Match each word in the first column with its definition in the second column.
Check your answers in the back of the book.

1.	reprisal	a.	riposte = sally
2.	rend	b.	amends = atonement
3.	reproach	c.	berate = castigate
4.	repertoire	d.	prodigal
5.	repress	e.	refill = refresh
6.	replenish	f.	censurable = condemnable
7.	reprobate	g.	abandon = disavow
8.	reprimand	h.	rive = rip
9.	replete	i.	repertory
10.	replicate	j.	counterblow = requital
11.	repose	k.	make
12.	reparation	l.	abounding = awash
13.	reprove	m.	consequence = fallout
14.	reprehensible	n.	chastise = censure
15.	repartee	o.	restrain = suppress
16.	renounce	p.	drive away = rebuff
17.	repatriate	q.	copy = duplicate
18.	repercussion	r.	send home
19.	repel	s.	respite = rest
20.	render	t.	berate = castigate

repudiate[ripjú:dièit] v 거부하다, 물리치다, 부인하다 = abjure[æbdʒúər]
= disavow[dìsəváu] = disown[disóun] = recant = reject = renounce[rináuns] = repeal
= rescind[risínd] = retract = revoke
The suspect repudiated the charge that he had set a fire to the building.
피의자는 건물에 방화했다는 혐의를 부인했다.

repugnant[ripʌ́gnənt] a 싫은, 불쾌한, 혐오스러운 = abhorrent[æbhɔ́:rənt]
= abominable[əbámənəbl] = disgusting = distasteful[distéistfəl] = odious[óudiəs]
The sight of the animal abuse in the circus was repugnant to most tourists.
서커스단에서 동물을 학대하는 모습은 대부분의 관광객들에게 혐오감을 주었다.

requisite[rékwəzit] a 불가결한, 필수의 = essential[isénʃəl] = necessary
The explores are supposed to acquire a variety of skills requisite for the survival in the extreme
conditions. 탐험가들은 극한상황에서 생존에 필수적인 다양한 기술을 익혀야 한다.

rescind[risínd] v 폐지(폐기)하다, 철회하다 = abolish[əbáliʃ] = abrogate[ǽbrəgèit]
= annul[ənʌ́l] = invalidate[invǽlədèit] = repeal = retract = revoke = void
The UN insisted that the country should rescind the plan to fire a long-range missile.
UN은 그 나라가 장거리 미사일을 발사하려는 계획을 폐기해야 한다고 주장했다.

reserved[rizə́:rvd] a 말을 잘 하지 않는, 내성적인 = reticent[rétəsənt]
= taciturn[tǽsətə:rn] = unsociable
The successful businessman is reserved about his running for the Congress.
성공한 사업가는 국회의원 출마에 대해 말을 하지 않고 있다.

resignation[rèzignéiʃən] n 사직, 사임 = retirement
Some engineers submitted their resignations in protest against the company's unfair treatment.
일부 기술자들은 회사의 부당대우에 항의해서 사직서를 제출했다.

resilience[rizíljəns] n 탄성, 복원력, 회복력 = elasticity[ilæstísəti]
The young boxer is showing a remarkable resilience from fatigue.
젊은 복서는 피로에서 빨리 회복하는 놀라운 복원력을 보여줬다.

resolute[rézəlù:t] a 굳게 결심하고 있는, 단호한, 확고한 = adamant[ǽdəmənt]
= determined = staunch[stɔ:ntʃ] = steadfast = uncompromising = unflinching[ʌnflíntʃɪŋ]
= unwavering[ʌnwéivəriŋ]
Some doctors are resolute in the their support of the euthanasia.
일부 의사들은 안락사를 단호히 지지하고 있다.

respite[réspit] n 일시적 중단, 한숨 돌리기, 유예 = recess[ríses] = relaxation[rìːlækséiʃən]
The slaves couldn't have a respite from their hard work in the stone quarry.
노예들은 잠깐의 휴식도 취하지 못한 채 채석장에서 혹독하게 일하고 있다.

resplendent[rispléndənt] a 눈부시게 빛나는, 화려한 = blazing[bléiziŋ] = bright = brilliant[bríljənt] = dazzling[dǽzliŋ] = effulgent[ifʌ́ldʒənt] = gleaming = glittering[glítəriŋ] = luminous[lúːmənəs] = radiant[réidiənt]
The actress was walking gracefully on the red carpet, resplendent in a black dress.
검정드레스를 입은 여배우는 눈부시게 빛나는 모습으로 우아하게 레드 카펫 위를 걷고 있었다.

restive[réstiv] a 차분하지 못한, 가만히 못 있는 = impatient[impéiʃənt] = jittery[dʒítəri] = nervous
Some students in the auditorium became restive even before the middle of the speech.
강당의 일부 학생들은 연설이 아직 절반도 지나지 않았음에도 차분하게 있지 못했다.

resurgence[resə́ːrdʒəns] n 재기, 부활 = rebirth = recovery = resurrection[rèzərékʃən] = revival
Recently we have seen the resurgence of revivalism in women's clothing.
최근에 우리는 여성복에서 복고주의 부활을 보고 있다.

resurrection[rèzərékʃən] n 부활 = rebirth = recovery = resurgence[resə́ːrdʒəns] = revival
Some villagers still believe in the resurrection of the saint.
마을의 일부 사람들은 그 성인의 부활을 여전히 믿고 있다.

retaliate[ritǽlièit] v 보복하다, 앙갚음하다 = get even with someone = revenge[rivéndʒ]
The US Navy retaliated against the attack by bombing the stronghold of the guerrilla.
미국 해군은 공격에 대한 앙갚음으로 게릴라들의 본거지를 폭격했다.

reticent[rétəsənt] a 말이 적은, 과묵한 = laconic[ləkánik] = taciturn[tǽsətəːrn]
The politician was reticent about his retirement from politics.
그 정치인은 정계 은퇴에 대해서 말을 아끼고 있다

retinue[rétənjùː] n 일행들, 수행단 = entourage[àːnturáːʒ]
The Chinese president is expected to visit America with a large retinue next month.
중국의 주석은 대규모 수행단과 함께 다음 달 미국을 방문할 예정이다.

retort[ritɔ́ːrt] v 대꾸하다, 반박하다 = rebut = riposte[ripóust]
His allegations were not worth retorting. 그의 근거없는 주장은 대꾸할 가치가 없다.

retrospect[rétrəspèkt] n 회상, 회고 = hindsight = recollection = reminiscence[rèmənísns]
In retrospect, it was the best time to invest when our country was under the IMF bailout.
회상해보면 우리 나라가 IMF 구제금융 하에 있을 때가 최고의 투자 기회였다.

revamp[ri:væmp] v 개조하다, 수리하다, 개정(수정)하다 = overhaul[oʊvər|hɔ:l]
= refurbish[ri:fə́:rbiʃ] = remodel = renovate[rénəvèit]
The political leaders from the ruling and opposition parties agreed to revamp the election system.
여당과 야당의 정치 지도자들은 선거제도를 개혁하는 것에 동의했다.

revel[révəl] v 흥청거리며 놀다, 흥청대다 = carouse[kəráuz] = indulge[indʌ́ldʒ] = roister[rɔ́istər]
The players and fans of the winning team reveled all night.
우승팀 선수들과 팬들은 밤 내내 흥청거리며 놀았다.

QUIZ 102

Match each word in the first column with its definition in the second column.
Check your answers in the back of the book.

1.	resolute	a.	abjure = disavow
2.	resurgence	b.	carouse = indulge
3.	revel	c.	impatient = jittery
4.	retort	d.	abhorrent = abominable
5.	resilience	e.	rebirth = recovery
6.	retrospect	f.	get even with someone = revenge
7.	resurrection	g.	elasticity
8.	resplendent	h.	rebirth = recovery
9.	retaliate	i.	essential = necessary
10.	repudiate	j.	rebut = riposte
11.	reticent	k.	adamant = determined
12.	rescind	l.	hindsight = recollection
13.	restive	m.	abolish = abrogate
14.	retinue	n.	overhaul = refurbish
15.	requisite	o.	recess = relaxation
16.	revamp	p.	reticent = taciturn
17.	repugnant	q.	blazing = bright
18.	reserved	r.	retirement
19.	respite	s.	laconic = taciturn
20.	resignation	t.	encourage

revere[rivíər] v 숭배하다, 공경하다, 존경하다 = adore[ədɔ́:r] = esteem[istí:m] = hallow[hǽlou] = respect = venerate[vénərèit] = worship
Most people revere the president as the save-the-nation hero.
대부분의 사람들은 대통령을 나라를 구한 영웅으로 존경하고 있다.

revile[riváil] v 욕하다, 욕설을 퍼붓다 = berate[biréit] = castigate[kǽstəgèit] = censure = chide[tʃaid] = condemn[kəndém] = criticize[krítəsàiz] = defame = denigrate[dénigrèit] = denounce[dináuns] = disparage[dispǽridʒ] = lambaste[læmbéist] = lecture = rebuke[ribjú:k] = reprimand[réprəmænd] = reprehend[rèprihénd] = reproach[ripróutʃ] = reprove[riprú:v] = scold = upbraid = vilify[víləfài] = vituperate[vaitjú:pərèit]
The man was reviled by his neighbors for making a loud noise.
그 남자는 큰 소음을 내기 때문에 이웃들로부터 욕을 먹었다.

revulsion[rivʌ́lʃən] n 혐오, 반감, 증오 = abhorrence[æbhɔ́:rəns] = abomination[əbàmənéiʃən] = aversion[əvə́:rʒən] = detestation[dì:testéiʃən] = disgust[disgʌ́st] = dislike = distaste = hatred[héitrid] = loathing[lóuðiŋ] = repugnance[ripʌ́gnəns] = repulsion[ripʌ́lʃən]
I feel revulsion against crimes involving children. 나는 아이들을 관여시킨 범죄를 혐오한다.

rhapsodize[rǽpsədàiz] v 열광적으로 이야기하다 = harangue[hərǽŋ] = perorate[pérərèit] = rave[reiv]
The company president rhapsodized over the advantage of the newly released smart phone.
사장은 새로 출시된 스마트폰의 장점에 대해서 열광적으로 이야기했다.

rhetoric[rétərik] n 미사여구, 수사법 = elocution[èləkjú:ʃən]
His empty rhetoric made the participants at the new products presentation suspect the quality of the products.
그의 공허한 미사여구는 신제품 설명회장에 참석한 사람들로 하여금 제품의 품질을 의심하게 만들었다.

ribald[ríbəld] a 야한, 야비한, 상스러운 = bawdy[bɔ́:di] = lewd[lu:d] = naughty[nɔ́:ti] = obscene[əbsí:n] = vulgar[vʌ́lgər]
His ribald way of talking damaged his image. 상스러운 화법은 그의 이미지를 손상시켰다.

rickety[ríkiti] a 곧 무너질[부서질] 듯한, 허약한 = decrepit[dikrépit] = flimsy[flímzi] = ramshackle[rǽmʃækl] = unsound = wobbly[wábli]
The only way to reach the village in the forest was to cross the rickety bridge over a river.
숲속에 있는 마을로 갈 수 있는 유일한 방법은 부서질 듯한 다리를 건너는 것이다.

rife[raif] a 만연한, 널리 퍼져 있는, 가득한 = abundant[əbʌ́ndənt] = overflowing
= prevalent[prévələnt] = rampant[rǽmpənt] = replete[riplíːt]
The abandoned house is rife with mice and harmful insects.
버려진 흉가에는 쥐와 해충이 가득했다.

rigorous[rígərəs] a 철저한, 엄격한 = exacting = punctilious[pʌŋktíliəs] = rigid[rídʒid]
= strict[strikt] = stringent[stríndʒənt]
The security system produced in Korea passed the rigorous standards of the US Air Force.
한국에서 제조된 보안제품은 미국 공군의 엄격한 기준을 통과했다.

rile[rail] v 귀찮게 하다, 짜증나게 하다, 화나게 하다 = anger = annoy = bother
= disturb[distə́ːrb] = exasperate[igzǽspərèit] = gall[gɔːl] = irk[əːrk] = irritate[írətèit]
= peeve[piːv] = provoke = upset = vex
Standing in the extremely long line to get the concert tickets riled him.
티켓을 사기 위해서 매우 길게 줄을 서서 기다리는 것이 그를 짜증나게 했다.

rivet[rívit] v (흥미나 관심을) 고정시키다, 매료시키다 = absorb[æbsɔ́ːrb] = captivate[kǽptəvèit]
= engross[ingróus] = immerse[imə́ːrs]
Their eyes were riveted to the grand and imposing scale of the pyramids.
그들은 웅장하고 인상적인 피라미드의 규모에 눈을 떼지 못했다.

robust[roubʌ́st] a 강건한, 튼튼한, 확고한 = hefty[héfti] = potent = powerful = strong
= sturdy[stə́ːrdi] = vigorous[vígərəs]
He has a robust conviction that he will win the election by a large margin.
그는 선거에서 큰 표차로 승리하리라는 확고한 신념을 가지고 있다.

rogue[roug] n 악한, 불한당, 사기꾼 = con artist = crook[kruk] = rascal[rǽskl]
= swindler[swíndlər] = villain[vílən]
The country in South America was branded as the rogue nation in UN.
남미의 그 나라는 UN에서 불량국가로 낙인이 찍혔다.

roil[rɔil] v 휘젓다, 안달하게 만들다, 발끈하게 하다 = stir[stəːr]
A sharp rise in interest rate will roil the housing market.
급격한 금리 인상이 부동산 시장을 휘저을 것이다.

roster[rɑ́stər] n 근무자 명단, 근무 당번표, 직원 명단 = list of names
The duty roster was distributed to all the employees.
근무당번표가 모든 직원들에게 배포되었다.

rout[raut] v 완패(궤멸)시키다, 패주시키다 = crush = defeat[difíːt] = repulse[ripʌ́ls]
The admiral routed the enemy in the naval battle.
그 제독은 해전에서 적들을 궤멸시켰다.

rubicund[rúːbikʌnd] a 사람의 얼굴이 불그레한, 혈색 좋은 = flushed[flʌʃt]
He was a polished and rubicund gentleman. 그는 세련되고 혈색이 좋은 신사였다.

rudimentary[rùːdəméntəri] a 기초적인, 기본적인 = basic = elementary
= fundamental[fʌndəméntl]
He is still on the rudimentary stage in learning the Chinese characters.
그는 한자를 배우고 있지만 아직 초보 수준이다.

rue[ruː] v 뉘우치다, 후회하다, = deplore[diplɔ́ːr] = feel sorry = grieve[griːv]
= lament[ləmént] = mourn[mɔːrn] = regret
He rued the day when he had been caught in a crackdown on drunken driving.
그는 음주운전 단속에 걸린 걸 후회했다.

ruminate[rúːmənèit] v 심사숙고하다, 곰곰이 생각하다 = brood[bruːd]
= cogitate[kádʒətèit] = contemplate[kántəmplèit] = deliberate[dilíbərət] = meditate[médətèit]
= muse[mjuːz] = ponder[pándər]
He ruminated over whether he should accept the offer or not.
그는 그 제안을 받아들일지 심사숙고했다.

rustic[rʌ́stik] a 시골 풍의, 소박한, 검소한 = bucolic[bjuːkálik] = pastoral[pǽstərəl]
= rural[rúərəl]
There were some rustic houses in the village.
마을에는 시골 풍의 집들이 몇 채 있었다.

QUIZ 103

Match each word in the first column with its definition in the second column.
Check your answers in the back of the book.

1. rudimentary
2. rigorous
3. revere
4. rhetoric
5. rogue
6. revile
7. ruminate
8. rife
9. ribald
10. rickety
11. rustic
12. revulsion
13. roster
14. roil
15. rhapsodize
16. rout
17. rivet
18. rile
19. robust
20. rubicund
21. rue

a. con artist = crook
b. adore = esteem
c. anger = annoy
d. stir
e. abhorrence = abomination
f. hefty = potent
g. berate = castigate
h. list of names
i. crush = defeat
j. harangue = perorate
k. absorb = captivate
l. brood = cogitate
m. bucolic = pastoral
n. elocution
o. exacting = punctilious
p. deplore = feel sorry
q. bawdy = lewd
r. abundant = overflowing
s. flushed
t. decrepit = flimsy
u. basic = elementary = fundamental

saboteur[sǽbətəːr] n 사보타주하는 사람, 파괴행위를 하는 사람 = terrorist
Some saboteurs brought out the shutdown of the factory.
사보타주를 하는 사람들 때문에 공장이 폐쇄되었다.

saccharine[sǽkərin] a 지나치게 달콤한, 감상적인 = sugary[ʃúgəri] = syrupy[sírəpi]
The actress has a saccharine voice.
그 여배우는 달콤한 목소리를 가지고 있다.

sacrilege[sǽkrəlidʒ] n 신성모독 = blasphemy[blǽsfəmi] = desecration[dèsikréiʃən]
= irreverence[irévərəns] = profanity[prəfǽnəti]
It would be a sacrilege to eat pork in public in Islamic culture.
이슬람 문화에서는 공개적으로 돼지고기를 먹는 것이 신성모독이다.

sacrosanct[sǽkrousæŋkt] a 신성불가침의, 더할 나위 없이 신성한 = consecrated[kánsəkrèitid]
= divine[diváin] = hallowed[hǽloud] = pious[páiəs] = revered[rivíərd] = sacred[séikrid]
= venerated[vénərèit]
The shrine has been designated as a sacrosanct place.
그 신전은 신성불가침한 장소로 지정되었다.

sagacious[səgéiʃəs] a 현명한, 영리한 = discerning[disəːrniŋ] = judicious[dʒuːdíʃəs]
= prudent[prúːdnt] = rational[rǽʃənl]
The pilot's sagacious decision saved all of his passengers on board.
조종사의 현명한 판단이 탑승객 전원을 살렸다.

sage[seidʒ] n 현명한 사람, 현자 = wise person
A few sages were invited to the deep philosophical debate.
몇몇 현자들이 심오한 철학 토론에 초대되었다.

salacious[səléiʃəs] a 호색적인, 외설적인 = bawdy[bɔ́ːdi] = lascivious[ləsíviəs]
= lecherous[létʃərəs] = lewd[luːd] = libertine[líbərtìːn] = libidinous[libídənəs]
=licentious[laisénʃəs] = lustful[lʌstfəl] = obscene[əbsíːn] = prurient[prúəriənt]
The court order stopped the publisher from publishing salacious books.
법원의 명령으로 그 출판사는 외설스러운 책을 출판하지 못하게 되었다.

salient[séiliənt] a 두드러진, 현저한, 핵심적인 = arresting[əréstiŋ]
= conspicuous[kənspíkjuəs] = noticeable[nóutisəbl] = prominent[prámənənt] = striking
The salient points of his speech were about innovation and creativity.
그의 연설의 핵심은 혁신과 창의력에 관한 것이었다.

sally[sǽli] n 반격, 출격, 소풍 = sortie[sɔ́ːrti]
A few combat planes made a sally against the border violation by the enemy.
적의 국경선 도발에 따라 몇 대의 전투기가 출격에 나섰다.

salubrious[səlúːbriəs] a 건강에 좋은, 몸에 좋은, 건전한 = beneficial[bènəfíʃəl]
= healthful = salutary[sǽljutèri] = wholesome[hóulsəm]
The old couple was living in salubrious environment.
노부부는 건강에 좋은 환경 속에서 살고 있었다.

salutary[sǽljutèri] a 건강에 좋은, 건전한, 유익한 = healthful = salubrious[səlúːbriəs]
= wholesome
The doctor gave the patient salutary advice.
의사 선생님은 그 환자에게 건강에 유익한 충고를 해주었다.

salutation[sæljutéiʃən] n 인사 = greeting
She smiled at me in salutation. 그녀는 나에게 미소로 인사를 건넸다.

salve[sæv] v 양심을 달래다, 진정시키다 = alleviate[əlíːvièit] = assuage[əswéidʒ]
= mollify[máləfài] = pacify[pǽsəfài] = soothe[suːð]
The founder of the weapons company donates large amount of money every year to salve his conscience. 무기회사의 창업주는 자신의 양심을 달래기 위해서 매년 거액을 기부한다.

sanctimonious[sæŋktəmóuniəs] a 독실한 체하는, 신성한 체하는
= hypocritical[hìpəkrítikəl] = insincere[ìnsinsíər]
The rich man comes to Church every week to look sanctimonious.
그 부자는 독실하게 보이기 위해서 매주 교회에 나온다.

sanction[sǽŋkʃən] n 허가, 승인 = approbation[æprəbéiʃən] = approval
= authorization[ɔːθərizéiʃən] = ratification[rætəfikéiʃən]
The port authorities gave sanction for the captain to bring his ship along the pier.
항만 당국은 그 선장의 배가 부두에 정박할 수 있도록 허가를 내 주었다.

sanguine[sǽŋgwin] a 쾌활한, 낙관적인, 자신감이 넘치는 = animated = buoyant[bɔ́iənt]
= cheerful = upbeat
The coach is sanguine about his team winning the game in the semi-final match.
감독은 그의 팀이 준결승전에서 이길 것이라고 낙관하고 있다.

sarcasm[sáːrkæzm] n 비꼼, 풍자, 야유 = cynicism[sínisìzm] = satire[sǽtaiər]
During the interpellation session the opposition lawmaker distributed a statement dripping with sarcasm about the government policies.
대정부 질문 도중에 야당 정치인은 정부 정책을 신랄하게 야유하는 성명서를 돌렸다.
interpellation[ìntərpəléiʃən] n 질의, 질문

sardonic[saːrdánik] a 냉소적인, 조소적인, 비웃는 = cynical[sínikəl]
= sarcastic[saːrkǽstik] = satirical[sətírikəl]
The champion put on a sardonic smile at the challenger.
챔피언은 도전자를 향해서 냉소적인 미소를 띠었다.

satiate[séiʃièit] v 충분히 만족시키다, 배부르게 하다, 물리게 하다 = gratify[grǽtəfài]
= sate[seit] = satisfy[sǽtisfài] = slake[sleik]
While staying on the island, I was satiated with fish dishes.
섬에 머무는 동안 나는 생선요리에 물리고 말았다.

saturate[sǽtʃərèit] v 흠뻑 적시다, 흠뻑 스며들게 하다, 포화시키다 = drench[drentʃ]
= immerse[iməːrs] = soak[souk] = steep[stiːp]
The jersey of the trainer was saturated with sweat. 트레이너의 셔츠는 땀으로 흠뻑 젖었다.

QUIZ 104

Match each word in the first column with its definition in the second column. Check your answers in the back of the book.

1.	saboteur	a.	consecrated = divine
2.	satiate	b.	blasphemy = desecration
3.	salient	c.	cynicism = satire
4.	saturate	d.	healthful = salubrious
5.	sally	e.	cynical = sarcastic
6.	saccharine	f.	sugary = syrupy
7.	salubrious	g.	greeting
8.	salve	h.	hypocritica = insincere
9.	sacrilege	i.	gratify = sate
10.	sanctimonious	j.	beneficial = healthful
11.	sacrosanct	k.	approbation = approval
12.	sanction	l.	discerning = judicious
13.	sanguine	m.	wise person
14.	sagacious	n.	animated = buoyant
15.	salacious	o.	drench = immerse
16.	sage	p.	sortie
17.	sarcasm	q.	terrorist
18.	salutation	r.	alleviate = assuage
19.	salutary	s.	arresting = conspicuous
20.	sardonic	t.	bawdy = lascivious

saturnine[sǽtərnàin] a 음침한 = gloomy[glúːmi] = glum[glʌm] = somber[sɑ́mbər] = sullen[sʌ́lən]
The saturnine look on his face means that something bad happened.
그의 얼굴에 나타난 음침한 표정은 안 좋은 일이 생겼음을 의미한다.

savant[sævɑ́ːnt] n 대학자, 학식이 높은 사람 = pundit[pʌ́ndit] = sage[seidʒ] = scholar[skɑ́lər]
He is regarded as a savant in the field of ancient religion.
그는 고대종교 분야에서 대학자로 간주된다.

savor[séivər] n 맛, 풍미, 향기 = flavor = relish[réliʃ] = taste
The cafeteria was filled with the savor of curry and rice.
그 식당은 카레라이스의 풍미로 가득 찼다.

savvy[sǽvi] a 지식이 있는, 잘 아는, 경험이 풍부한 = acute[əkjúːt]
= experienced[ikspíəriənst] = knowing = shrew[ʃruː]
She is a savvy customer, knowing when and where to buy things cheap.
그녀는 경험이 풍부한 고객이라 언제 어디서 물건을 싸게 사는지 알고 있다.

scamper[skǽmpər] v 허둥지둥 도망치다, 날쌔게 움직이다 = hurry = scurry[skə́ːri]
= scuttle[skʌ́tl]
A few minutes before the earthquake, a lot of mice and squirrels scampered away.
지진이 일어나기 몇 분 전에 많은 쥐와 다람쥐들이 허둥지둥 도망쳤다.

scant[skænt] a 빠듯한, 못미치는, 부족한 = insufficient[insəfíʃənt] = meager[míːgər]
The city provides a scant supply of tap water due to the severe drought.
심한 가뭄으로 도시의 수돗물 공급이 부족하게 되었다.

scathing[skéiðiŋ] a 냉혹한, 가차없는, 준열한 = harsh[haːrʃ] = trenchant[tréntʃənt]
We insist that the judge should be scanting about the child rapist.
우리는 판사가 그 아동성폭행범에게 가차없어야 한다고 주장합니다.

scheme[skiːm] n 음모, 모의, 계획 = conspiracy[kənspírəsi] = machination[mækənéiʃən] = plot
The culprits were talking about a scheme to smuggle drugs.
범인들은 마약을 밀수하려는 음모를 꾸미고 있었다.

schism[sízm] n 분열 = breakup = fissure[fíʃər] = rupture[rʌ́ptʃər] = separation[sèpəréiʃən]
The development of the gold mine created a schism between the tribes.
금광 개발은 부족 간의 분열을 일으켰다.

scintillate[síntəlèit] v (기지, 재치) 번뜩이다, 불꽃을 튀기다, 번쩍번쩍 빛나다 = flash
He proposed a sales plan that scintillates with creative ideas.
그는 창의적인 아이디어가 빛나는 영업계획을 제안했다.

scorn[skɔːrn] v 경멸하다, 깔보다, 무시하다 = contemn[kəntém] = deride[diráid] = despise[dispáiz]
= disdain[disdéin] = disparage[dispǽridʒ] = flout[flaut] = insult[insʌ́lt] = jeer[dʒiər] = make fun of
= mock[mak] = ridicule[rídikjùːl] = scoff[skɔːf] = slight[slait] = sneer[sniər] = taunt[tɔːnt]
We should not scorn gays. 우리는 동성애자들을 무시해서는 안 된다.

scour[skauər] v 샅샅이 뒤지다 = ferret[férit] out = ransack[rǽnsæk] = rummage[rʌ́midʒ]
The police are scouring the sea shore to find the debris of the crashed plane.
경찰은 추락한 비행기의 잔해를 찾기 위해서 해변을 샅샅이 뒤지고 있었다.

scrupulous[skrú:pjuləs] a 양심적인, 세심한, 꼼꼼한 = conscientious[kànʃiénʃəs]
=fastidious[fæstídiəs] = finicky[fíniki] = meticulous[mətíkjuləs] = picky[píki]
= punctilious[pʌŋktíliəs]
Mrs. Parker always teaches her young students with scrupulous care.
Parker 선생님은 항상 세심한 주의를 하면서 어린 학생들을 가르친다.

scrutinize[skrú:tənàiz] v 정밀히 조사하다, 세심히 살피다 = delve[delv]
= probe[proub]
The detectives were scrutinizing the scene of the crime.
탐정들은 범죄현장을 정밀 조사하고 있는 중이다.

scurrilous[skə́:rələs] a 상스러운, 천박한, 악의적인 = indecent[indí:snt]
= vulgar[vʌlgər]
The pirates insulted the captain of the vessel with a scurrilous curse.
해적들은 천박한 욕으로 선장을 모독했다.

scurry[skə́:ri] v 종종걸음을 치다, 허둥지둥 달리다, 서두르다 = hurry
= scamper[skǽmpər] = scuttle[skʌtl]
When the fire alarm rang, all shoppers scurried to the exit.
화재경보기가 울렸을 때 모든 쇼핑객들은 출구로 허둥지둥 달렸다.

seamless[sí:mlis] a 솔기가 없는, 끊임이 없는, 매끄러운 = smooth
Chinese government was sure about the seamless operations of the games during the Olympic Games. 중국 정부는 올림픽 기간 동안의 매끄러운 경기운행에 대해 자신감을 가지고 있었다.

secede[sisí:d] v 탈퇴하다, 탈당하다, 분리 독립하다 = break with
Greece decided not to secede from EU Bloc.
그리스는 EU연합에서 탈퇴하지 않기로 결정했다.

seclusion[siklú:ʒən] n 격리, 차단, 은둔 = detachment[ditǽtʃmənt]
= isolation[àisəléiʃən] = sequestration[sì:kwestréiʃən]
The dictator in South America ruled the country in seclusion.
남미의 독재자는 폐쇄정책 속에서 국가를 지배했다.

secrete[sikrí:t] v 분비하다 = excrete[ikskrí:t] = ooze[u:z]
Eating fish, anchovy, carrots and tofu helps secrete growth hormone.
생선, 멸치, 당근, 두부를 먹으면 성장호르몬 분비가 촉진된다.

QUIZ 105

*Match each word in the first column with its definition in the second column.
Check your answers in the back of the book.*

1.	scrupulous	a.	acute = experienced
2.	scrutinize	b.	delve = probe
3.	savvy	c.	hurry = scurry
4.	scurrilous	d.	detachment = isolation
5.	scamper	e.	flavor = relish
6.	scurry	f.	excrete = ooze
7.	seamless	g.	conscientious = fastidious
8.	savor	h.	gloomy = glum
9.	scorn	i.	break with
10.	scour	j.	ferret out = ransack
11.	scant	k.	smooth
12.	scathing	l.	pundit = sage
13.	secede	m.	hurry = scamper
14.	saturnine	n.	harsh = trenchant
15.	seclusion	o.	insufficient = meager
16.	savant	p.	contemn = deride
17.	secrete	q.	indecent = vulgar
18.	scheme	r.	conspiracy = machination
19.	scintillate	s.	flash
20.	schism	t.	breakup = fissure

sect[sekt] n 종파, 파벌, 당파 = denomination[dinὰmənéiʃən] = faction[fǽkʃən]
The chief monk emphasized solidarity among the sects in the religion.
주지 스님은 여러 종파의 단결을 강조했다.

secular[sékjulər] a 세속적인, 속세의 = profane[prəféin] = worldly[wə́:rldli]
The secular society is filled with betrayal and conspiracy.
세속적인 사회는 배신과 음모로 가득하다.

sedate[sidéit] a 차분한, 조용한, 침착한 = calm[ka:m] = collected = placid[plǽsid]
= serene[sərí:n] = unflappable[ʌnflǽpəbl]
The funeral was held in a sedate environment.
장례식은 차분한 분위기에서 거행되었다.

sedentary[sédntèri] a 앉은 자세의, 앉아서 하는, 고착성의 = motionless
= stationary[stéiʃənèri] = seated
Most workers in cities have sedentary jobs.
도시의 근로자들은 대부분 앉아서 하는 일을 한다.

sedition[sidíʃən] n 선동, 반란, 폭동 = agitation[ædʒitéiʃən] = insurgence[insə́ːrdʒəns]
= insurrection[insərékʃən] = mutiny[mjúːtəni] = rebellion[ribéljən] = revolt = treason[tríːzn]
= tumult[tjúːməlt] = uprising
A former general was reported to have incited sedition.
전직 장군이 선동을 유발했다고 보도되었다.

sedulous[sédʒuləs] a 근면한, 부지런한, 공들인 = assiduous[əsídʒuəs]
= industrious[indʌ́striəs] = laborious[ləbɔ́ːriəs]
All cotton growers were sedulous workers. 모든 면화 재배자들은 근면한 일꾼들이다.

seemly[síːmli] a 품위있는, 단정한, 알맞은, 적절한 = decent[díːsnt] = suitable[súːtəbl]
Most guests were wearing seemly attires at the party.
대부분의 손님들은 파티에 알맞은 복장을 하고 있었다.

seep[siːp] v 스며 나오다, 스며들다 = leak = ooze[uːz] = permeate[pə́ːrmièit] = soak[souk]
The flood made the contaminated river water seep into the nearby rice paddy.
홍수가 나서 오염된 강물이 근처 논으로 스며들었다.

seethe[siːð] v 들끓다, 끓어오르다 = simmer[símər]
When the neighbors saw the suspect reenact the crime at the scene, they seethed with anger.
이웃 사람들은 용의자가 현장에서 범죄를 재연하는 것을 보고 분노가 끓어올랐다.

sententious[senténʃəs] a 훈계조의, 설교투의, 금언적인 = pretentious[priténʃəs]
= pompous[pɑ́mpəs]
The professor delivered a sententious lecture. 그 교수는 훈계조로 강의를 했다.

sentient[sénʃənt] a 지각이 있는, 의식이 있는, 감각 있는 = cognizant[kɑ́gnəzənt] = conscious[kɑ́nʃəs]
The congressman is popular with sentient voters.
그 국회의원은 의식이 있는 유권자 사이에서 인기가 있다.

sentinel[séntənəl] n 파수, 감시인, 보초병 = guard = sentry[séntri]
Heavily armed soldiers were standing sentinel along the border.
중무장한 군인들이 국경을 따라 보초를 서고 있었다.

sequester[sikwéstər] v 격리하다, 고립시키다, 떼어놓다 = cloister[klɔ́istər] = close off
= insulate[ínsəlèit] = isolate[áisəlèit] = seclude[siklú:d] = segregate[ségrigèit]
The health authorities decided to sequester the virus-infected patients from people.
보건당국은 바이러스에 감염된 환자들을 일반인들과 분리하기로 결정했다.

sere[siər] a 시든, 말라빠진 = withered[wíðərd]
There are a lot of sere leaves around the trees. 나무들 주위에 말라빠진 나뭇잎들이 많이 있었다.

serendipity[sèrəndípəti] n 운 좋은 발견, 뜻밖의 재미 = fluke[flu:k] = windfall
It is said that the universal gravitation was found through serendipity.
만유인력은 운 좋게 발견되었다고 한다.

serene[sərí:n] a 고요한, 잔잔한, 평온한 = calm = composed = placid[plǽsid]
= poised[pɔizd] = sedate[sidéit] = tranquil[trǽŋkwil] = unflappable[ʌnflǽpəbl]
They were fishing around the serene lake. 그들은 고요한 호수 주위에서 낚시를 하고 있었다.

sermon[sə́:rmən] n 설교, 설법, 훈화 = homily[háməli] = preaching[prí:tʃiŋ]
Pastor Jae was delivering a sermon about the salvation by the lord.
Jae 목사님은 하느님의 구원에 관해 설교하는 중이었습니다.

serpentine[sə́:rpəntì:n] a 구불구불한, 뱀 모양의 = circuitous[sərkjú:ətəs]
= meandering[miǽndəriŋ] = sinuous[sínjuəs] = winding[wáindiŋ]
The expedition followed the serpentine roads in the snow-covered mountain.
탐험대는 눈 덮인 산속의 구불구불한 길을 따라갔다.

servile[sə́:rvil] a 비굴한, 맹종하는, 굽실거리는 = bootlicking[bú:tliking]
= cringing[krindʒing] = eating crow = fawning[fɔ́:niŋ] = groveling[grʌvəliŋ]
= obsequious[əbsí:kwiəs] = subservient[səbsə́:rviənt] = sycophantic[sìkəfǽntik]
= toadying[tóuding]
The boss demanded servile obedience from his employees.
사장은 그의 종업원들에게 맹목적인 복종을 요구했다.

shabby[ʃǽbi] a 초라한, 낡은, 허름한 = scruffy[skrʌfi] = threadbare
All the children gathered around the tourists in the remote village, wearing shabby clothes.
오지 마을의 모든 아이들은 초라한 옷을 입고 관광객 주위로 모였다.

QUIZ 106

Match each word in the first column with its definition in the second column.
Check your answers in the back of the book.

1.	sedentary		a.	profane = worldly
2.	sermon		b.	decent = suitable
3.	sedition		c.	calm = collected
4.	sect		d.	circuitous = meandering
5.	serendipity		e.	leak = ooze
6.	serene		f.	simmer
7.	secular		g.	agitation = insurgence
8.	seemly		h.	denomination = faction
9.	serpentine		i.	bootlicking = cringing
10.	sedate		j.	motionless = stationary
11.	sere		k.	withered
12.	seep		l.	fluke = windfall
13.	seethe		m.	pretentious = pompous
14.	sententious		n.	calm = composed
15.	shabby		o.	assiduous
16.	sedulous		p.	homily = preaching
17.	servile		q.	cognizant = conscious
18.	sentient		r.	scruffy = threadbare
19.	sentinel		s.	guard = sentry
20.	sequester		t.	cloister = close off

shackle[ʃǽkl] v 구속하다, 족쇄를 채우다 = bind[baind] = confine = handcuff = restrain
The giant removed the chains that were shackling his legs.
그 거인은 자신의 다리를 붙들어 매었던 족쇄를 풀었다.

sham[ʃæm] a 가짜의, 모조의 = bogus[bóugəs] = counterfeit[káuntərfit] = fake
= feigned[feind] = forged = fraudulent[frɔ́ːdʒulənt] = phony[fóuni]
Some merchants were selling sham jewelry. 몇몇 상인들은 가짜 보석들을 팔고 있었다.

shard[ʃaːrd] n 파편, 조각 = fragment
A lot of glass shards were scattered at the scene of the traffic accident.
교통사고 현장에는 많은 유리 파편들이 흩어져 있었다.

shibboleth[ʃíbəliθ] n 표어, 진부한 문구 = slogan
The opposition party still sticks to the shibboleth that democracy can solve everything.
야당은 아직도 민주주의가 모든 것을 해결할 수 있다는 진부한 문구에 매달리고 있다.

shirk[ʃəːrk] v 회피하다, 게을리하다 = avoid = dodge[dadʒ] = elude[ilúːd] = eschew[istʃúː]
= evade[ivéid] = parry[pǽri] = shun[ʃʌn] = sidestep
The captain of the ship shirked his duty related to the sinking of his ship.
선장은 배의 침몰과 관련, 자신의 의무를 회피했다.

shrewd[ʃruːd] a 약삭빠른, 영민한, 기민한 = astute[əstjúːt] = canny[kǽni] = slick[slik] = wily[wáili]
Jake and Josh brothers are shrewd in negotiations. Jake와 Josh 형제는 협상에서 영민했다.

shun[ʃʌn] v 피하다 = avoid[əvɔ́id] = bypass = circumvent[səːrkəmvént] = dodge[dadʒ]
= elude[ilúːd] = escape[iskéip] = evade[ivéid] = fend off = sidestep
He has shunned meeting his friends after he was fired from his company.
회사에서 해고된 뒤 그는 친구들과 만나는 것을 피하고 있다.

sidereal[saidíəriəl] a 항성의, 별의 = stellar[stélər]
Astronomers observe the sidereal explosions to understand the origin of the universe.
천문학자들은 우주의 기원을 알기 위해서 항성 폭발을 관측하고 있다.

simian[símiən] a 유인원의, 원숭이의 = anthropoid[ǽnθrəpɔ̀id]
Some people believe that we modern humans have some simian characteristics.
어떤 사람들은 우리 현생인류가 유인원의 특징을 일부 가지고 있다고 생각한다.

sinew[sínjuː] n 힘줄, 건, 체력 = tendon[téndən]
Most big cats have very strong sinews.
대부분의 큰 고양이과 동물들은 매우 강한 힘줄을 가지고 있다.

singular[síŋgjulər] a 뛰어난, 보기 드문, 기묘한 = bizarre[bizáːr] = eccentric[ikséntrik]
= exceptional[iksépʃənl] = peculiar[pikjúːljər] = queer[kwiər] = unique[juːníːk] = unparalleled
He is a man of singular ability in the s/w programming.
그는 소프트웨어 프로그래밍에서 뛰어난 능력을 가지고 있는 사람이다.

sinuous[sínjuəs] a 구불구불한, 물결 모양의 = crooked[krúkid] = curved[kəːrvd]
= meandering[miǽndəriŋ] = serpentine[sə́ːrpəntìːn] = winding[wáindiŋ]
The wind in the desert leaves sinuous movement of the sand.
사막의 바람은 물결 모양의 모래의 움직임을 남긴다.

sip[sip] v 홀짝홀짝 마시다, 조금씩 마시다 = drink slowly
He was looking out the window, sipping wine.
그는 와인을 홀짝홀짝 마시면서 창 밖을 보고 있었다.

skeptic[sképtik] n 회의론자, 의심 많은 사람 = doubter[dáutər] = pessimist
He was an inborn skeptic. 그는 타고난 회의론자이다.

skimp[skimp] v 인색하게 굴다, 절약하다, 아까워하다 = scrimp[skrimp]
He skimps on his dresses. 그는 자신의 옷을 사는 것에 인색하다.

skirmish[skə́:rmiʃ] n 작은 접전, 소규모 충돌 = battle = brawl[brɔ:l] = clash = combat = conflict[kɑnflíkt] = fracas[fréikəs] = mele[méilei] = scuffle[skʌfl] = tussle[tʌsl]
There have been a lot of skirmishes along the border between the two countries.
두 나라 사이의 국경에서 많은 소규모 충돌이 있었다.

skirt[skə:rt] v 회피하다, 피해가다, 모면하다 = avoid = bypass = circumvent[sə̀:rkəmvént] = dodge[dadʒ] = elude[ilú:d] = eschew[istʃú:] = evade[ivéid] = parry[pǽri] = shirk[ʃə:rk] = shun[ʃʌn] = sidestep
He skirted questions about his defection from the political party.
그는 탈당과 관련된 질문을 피해갔다.

skit[skit] n 촌극, 소희극 = sketch
College students did a skit on the high-handedness of big companies.
대학생들은 대기업의 고압적인 태도에 관한 촌극을 했다.

skittish[skítiʃ] a 잘 놀라는, 경박한, 변덕스러운, 급변하기 쉬운 = edgy[édʒi] =fickle[fíkl] = jumpy[dʒʌmpi] = nervous
The climate is skittish in the desert. 사막에서의 날씨는 변덕스럽다.

slacken[slǽkən] v 늦추다, 느슨해지다, 완화하다 = loosen = mitigate[mítəgèit] = soften
Many bolts and nuts in the factory have slackened over time.
공장의 많은 볼트와 너트는 시간이 지나면서 느슨해졌다.

QUIZ 107

Match each word in the first column with its definition in the second column.
Check your answers in the back of the book.

1.	shackle		a.	bizarre = eccentric
2.	sinew		b.	slogan
3.	shirk		c.	crooked = curved
4.	skittish		d.	sketch
5.	sham		e.	avoid = dodge
6.	simian		f.	anthropoid
7.	slacken		g.	tendon
8.	shard		h.	astute = canny
9.	skirmish		i.	drink slowly
10.	skirt		j.	battle = clash
11.	shibboleth		k.	bind = confine
12.	skit		l.	avoid = bypass
13.	singular		m.	doubter = pessimist
14.	sinuous		n.	scrimp
15.	shun		o.	bogus = counterfeit
16.	sip		p.	edgy = fickle
17.	shrewd		q.	loosen = mitigate
18.	skeptic		r.	fragment
19.	skimp		s.	stellar
20.	sidereal		t.	avoid = bypass

slake[sleik] v 채우다, 만족시키다, 해소하다 = abate = allay[əléi] = appease[əpíːz]
= assuage[əswéidʒ] = gratify = quench[kwentʃ] = satisfy[sǽtisfài]
A group of explorers slaked their thirst at the fountain.
한 무리의 탐험가들이 샘에서 갈증을 달랬다.

slander[slǽndər] v 중상하다, 명예를 훼손하다 = asperse[əspə́ːrs] = backbite
= calumniate[kəlʌ́mnièit] = defame[diféim] = denigrate[dénigrèit] = disparage[dispǽridʒ]
= libel[láibəl] = vituperate[vaitjúːpərèit]
The actor filed a suit against a netizen for slandering him.
그 영화배우는 명예훼손으로 한 네티즌을 고소했다.

slight[slait] v 얕보다, 냉대하다, 소홀히 하다 = contemn[kəntém] = deride
= despise[dispáiz] = disdain = disparage[dispǽridʒ] = flout[flaut] = insult = jeer[dʒiər]
= make fun of = mock = ridicule = scoff[skɔ:f] = scorn = sneer[sniər] = taunt[tɔ:nt]
The waitress at the restaurant slighted a shabbily dressed diner.
식당 종업원은 추레하게 옷을 입은 손님을 냉대했다.

slipshod[slipʃɑ:d] a 단정치 못한, 칠칠치 못한, 되는 대로의 = disheveled[diʃévəld]
= slovenly[slΛvənli] = unkempt[Λnkémpt] = untidy
Linda always does the dishes in a slipshod manner. Linda는 항상 설거지를 칠칠맞게 한다.

sloth[slɔ:θ] n 나태, 게으름 = laziness = indolence[índələns] = inertia[inə́:rʃə]
= lethargy[léθərdʒi] = listlessness[lístlisnis] = sluggishness[slΛgiʃnis]
Lack of efforts and sloth will bring out failure in your life.
노력 부족과 게으름이 너의 인생에 실패를 가져올 것이다.

slouch[slautʃ] v 구부리다, 수그리다, 앞으로 처지다 = crouch[krautʃ]
The exhausted soldiers went forward slouching under the hot sun in the desert.
피곤에 지친 병사들은 앞으로 수그린 채 뜨거운 태양 아래의 사막을 전진해 갔다.

slovenly[slΛvənli] a 단정치 못한, 추접스러운, 되는 대로의 = disheveled[diʃévəld]
= slipshod = unkempt[Λnkémpt]= untidy
She showed up slovenly in her hair and dress. 그녀는 머리와 옷이 단정치 못한 상태로 나왔다.

sluggard[slΛgərd] n 게으름뱅이, 건달, 나태한 사람 = idler[áidlər] = lazy person
The sluggard in the town does nothing but drink and lie down all day.
마을의 게으름뱅이는 술을 마시고 하루 종일 드러누워 있기만 한다.

slur[slə:r] v 헐뜯다, 중상하다, 비방하다 = defame = calumniate[kəlΛmnièit] = cast aspersions on
= denigrate[dénigrèit] = detract[ditrǽkt] = disparage[dispǽridʒ] = libel[láibəl]
= malign[məláin] = slander = vilify[víləfài]
The political candidates from ruling and opposition parties slurred each other.
여당과 야당 출신 후보들은 서로를 비방했다.

sly[slai] a 교활한, 간교한, 은밀한 = cunning = guileful[gáilfəl] = insidious[insídiəs]
You shouldn't lend your money to such a sly businessman.
그렇게 교활한 사업가에게는 돈을 빌려주지 말아라.

smirk[smə:rk] v 히죽히죽 웃다, 능글맞게 웃다 = sneer[sniər]
The players of the champion team smirked at their opponents.
챔피언 팀의 선수들은 상대 선수들을 보고 히죽히죽 웃었다.

smother[smʌðər] v 숨막히게 하다, 질식시키다 = stifle[stáifl] = strangle[strǽŋgl]
= suffocate[sʌfəkèit]
The heavy smoke in the burning house was smothering the firefighters.
화재가 난 집의 짙은 연기가 소방관들을 숨막히게 하고 있었다.

smug[smʌg] a 의기양양한, 자기 만족의, 잘난 체하는, 우쭐한 = complacent[kəmpléisnt]
= self-satisfied
The triumphant general had a smug smile on his face as he was passing by the crowd on the street.
개선장군은 군중으로 가득 찬 길거리를 지나며 얼굴에 의기양양한 미소를 지었다.

smuggle[smʌgl] v 밀수하다, 밀반입하다 = transfer illegal goods
He was caught trying to smuggle drugs into the country.
그는 국내로 마약을 밀반입하려다가 잡혔다.

snarl[sna:rl] v 혼란시키다, 얽히게 하다 = complicate[kámpləkèit] = entangle[intǽngl] = mess up
Traffic was snarled in the Washington DC area due to the heavy snow.
폭설로 워싱턴DC 지역 교통이 뒤엉키게 되었다.

sneer[sniər] v 비웃다, 조롱하다, 냉소하다 = contemn[kəntém] = deride[diráid]
= despise[dispáiz] = disdain[disdéin] = disparage[dispǽridʒ] = flout[flaut] = insult
= jeer[dʒiər] = make fun of = mock = ridicule[rídikjù:l] = scoff[skɔ:f] = scorn[skɔ:rn]
= slight[slait] = taunt[tɔ:nt]
At first some executives of the company sneered at the ideas of the young engineers.
처음에 그 회사의 임원들은 그 젊은 공학도의 아이디어를 비웃었다.

snobbish[snɑ́biʃ] a 속물의, 고상한 척하는, 우월감에 젖어 있는 = conceited[kənsí:tid]
= condescending[kàndəséndiŋ] = patronizing[péitrənàiziŋ]
No neighbors like him because of his snobbish attitude.
그의 속물적 태도 때문에 어떤 이웃도 그를 좋아하지 않는다.

snub[snʌb] v 냉대하다, 무시하다, 모욕하다 = deride[diráid] = disdain[disdéin]
= disregard[dìsrigá:rd] = neglect[niglékt] = scorn[skɔ:rn]
Some ancient emperors used to snub the kings of the neighboring countries.
일부 고대의 황제들은 이웃 왕들을 무시했다.

sobriety[səbráiəti] n 취해 있지 않음, 맨정신, 절주, 금주
= abstemiousness[æbstí:miəsnis] = abstinenc[ǽbstənəns] = continence[kántənəns]
= moderation[màdəréiʃən]
The drunken driver was caught in a sobriety test. 그 음주운전자는 음주 테스트에 걸렸다.

solace[sáləs] n 위로, 위안 = condolence[kəndóuləns] = consolation[kànsəléiʃən]
She found solace in seeing her son succeeding in the society.
그녀는 아들이 사회에서 성공하는 것을 보면서 위안을 찾았다.

QUIZ 108

*Match each word in the first column with its definition in the second column.
Check your answers in the back of the book.*

1.	snub		a.	abate = allay
2.	slouch		b.	stifle = strangle
3.	slovenly		c.	complacent = self-satisfied
4.	sloth		d.	asperse = backbite
5.	smuggle		e.	transfer illegal goods
6.	snarl		f.	crouch
7.	slipshod		g.	condolence = consolation
8.	sluggard		h.	contemn = deride
9.	sneer		i.	disheveled = slipshod
10.	slight		j.	disheveled = slovenly
11.	smother		k.	conceited = condescending
12.	smug		l.	idler = lazy person
13.	slander		m.	deride = disdain
14.	snobbish		n.	laziness = indolence
15.	slur		o.	defame = calumniate
16.	sly		p.	abstemiousness = abstinence
17.	slake		q.	cunning = guileful
18.	sobriety		r.	complicate = entangle
19.	solace		s.	contemn = deride
20.	smirk		t.	sneer

solemn[sáləm] a 근엄한, 엄숙한 = dignified[dígnəfàid] = serious
The coronation was performed in a solemn mood.
대관식은 근엄한 분위기에서 거행되었다.

solicitous[səlísətəs] a　걱정하는, 세심히 배려하는, 염려하는 = mindful = worried
She is always solicitous about the safety of her son when he goes abroad.
그녀는 아들이 해외로 나갈 때마다 그의 안전을 걱정한다.

solidarity[sàlədǽrəti] n　연대, 결속 = alliance[əláiəns] = unity
Factory workers strengthened their solidarity with college student leaders.
노동자들은 대학생 대표들과의 연대를 강화했다.

solidify[səlídəfài] v　굳히다, 단결시키다, 고착화시키다 = cement[simént] = stiffen[stífən]
The political party leader solidified his grip on the party by placing his aides on key posts.
정치 지도자는 그의 측근들을 주요 당직에 배치함으로써 당에 대한 장악력을 강화했다.

solvent[sálvənt] a　지급 능력이 있는 = financially sound
The president of the bankrupt company was not considered solvent to pay all the overdue wages of the employees.
파산한 회사의 사장은 직원들의 밀린 급여를 지불할 수 있을 것 같지 않았다.

somber[sámbər] a　어두운, 침울한, 우울한 = bleak[bli:k] = depressing = gloomy = melancholy[mélənkàli] = solemn[sáləm]
A serious of somber music was being played as the coffin was carried by soldiers.
시신이 든 관이 군인들에 의해서 옮겨지는 동안 침울한 음악이 계속 연주되었다.

somnolence[sámnələns] n　졸림, 졸음, 비몽사몽 = drowsiness = sleepiness
She had a hard time resisting the somnolence during the ceremony.
식이 거행되는 동안 그녀는 졸음을 참기 어려웠다.

soothe[su:ð] v　달래다, 진정시키다, 누그러뜨리다 = allay[əléi] = alleviate[əlí:vièit] = appease[əpí:z] = assuage[əswéidʒ] = lull[lʌl] = mitigate[mítəgèit] = mollify[máləfài] = pacify[pǽsəfài] = palliate[pǽlièit] = placate[pléikeit] = temper[témpər]
The company soothed the anger of the workers by raising the wages.
그 회사는 임금인상으로 근로자들의 분노를 진정시켰다.

sop[sap] n　뇌물, 비위를 맞추기 위해서 주는 것 = bribe
The director turned out to have received a sop from his junior staff in exchange for his promotion.
회사 임원이 부하직원을 승진시켜 주면서 뇌물을 받은 것으로 밝혀졌다.

sophisticate[səfístəkèit] v 세상물정에 밝게 하다, 불순하게 하다
= adulterate[ədʌ́ltərèit]
The realtor was a very sophisticated person.
부동산 중개인은 세상물정에 닳고 닳은 사람이었다.

sophomoric[sàfəmɔ́ːrik] a 미숙한, 아는 체하는, 건방진
= inexperienced[ìnikspíəriənst] = brash[bræʃ] = naïve[naːíːv] = reckless[réklis]
Most start-up companies are sophomoric in handling labor problems.
대부분의 창업 회사들은 노사문제를 처리하는 데 있어서 미숙하다.

soporific[sàpərífik] a 최면성의, 졸린 = drowsy = sleepy = slumberous[slʌ́mbərəs]
Some doctors are researching the soporific effect of the herb.
일부 의사들은 그 약초의 최면효과에 대해서 연구 중이다.

sordid[sɔ́ːrdid] a 더러운, 비도덕적인, 추악한, 야비한 = dirty = filthy[fílθi] = nasty = squalid[skwɑ́lid]
The fighter was ready to use sordid tricks to win the match.
그 선수는 경기에 이기기 위해 추악한 속임수를 쓸 준비가 되어 있었다.

sovereign[sɑ́vərin] n 군주, 국왕, 주권자 = czar[zaːr] = monarch[mɑ́nərk] = supreme ruler
His rude behavior incurred the wrath of his sovereign.
그의 무례한 행동이 왕의 노여움을 불렀다. incur[inkə́ːr] v 초래하다

spate[speit] n 빈발, 대량, 다수 = deluge[déljuːdʒ] = flood = myriad = outpouring = torrent
A spate of murder and fraud cases are being reported in our city.
많은 살인 및 사기 사건들이 우리 도시에서 벌어지고 있다.

spawn[spɔːn] v 낳다, 원인이 되다, 야기시키다 = generate = produce
The pyramid sales organization spawned a lot of victims.
그 다단계 회사는 많은 피해자를 낳았다.

specious[spíːʃəs] a 허울 좋은, 그럴듯한, 남의 눈을 속이는 = deceptive[diséptiv]
= misleading = ostensible[asténsəbl] = spurious[spjúəriəs]
You should not be blinded by the specious benefits of some savings banks.
우리는 일부 저축은행들이 내세우는 허울 좋은 혜택에 눈이 멀어서는 안 된다.

specter[spéktər] n 유령, 무서운 것, 불안의 원인 = apparition[æpəríʃən] = ghost
The specter of war prevented foreigners from investing in the local stock market.
전쟁이 일어날 듯한 불안감 때문에 외국인들은 현지 주식시장에 투자하지 않았다.

spectrum[spéktrəm] n 스펙트럼, 범위 = gamut[gǽmət] = scope
Internet helps us gain a broad spectrum of knowledge.
인터넷은 우리가 광범위한 지식을 갖도록 돕는다.

speculate[spékjulèit] v 추측하다(짐작하다), 억측하다 = guess = ruminate = surmise[sərmáiz]
The beekeepers speculated that bees had disappeared because of climate change.
양봉업자들은 벌들이 기후변화 때문에 사라졌다고 추측했다.

QUIZ 107

Match each word in the first column with its definition in the second column.
Check your answers in the back of the book.

1.	solemn	a.	apparition = ghost
2.	spectrum	b.	cement = stiffen
3.	sophisticate	c.	czar = monarch
4.	sophomoric	d.	guess = ruminate
5.	solicitous	e.	financially sound
6.	speculate	f.	deluge = flood
7.	sop	g.	allay = alleviate
8.	soporific	h.	dirty = filthy
9.	soothe	i.	generate = produce
10.	spate	j.	dignified = serious
11.	sordid	k.	drowsy = sleepy
12.	solidarity	l.	bribe
13.	spawn	m.	deceptive = misleading
14.	sovereign	n.	alliance = unity
15.	specious	o.	adulterate
16.	solidify	p.	inexperienced = brash
17.	specter	q.	mindful = worried
18.	solvent	r.	gamut = scope
19.	somnolence	s.	bleak = depressing
20.	somber	t.	drowsiness = sleepiness

---

spelunker[spilʌ́ŋkər] n 동굴 탐험가 = one who explores caves
The five spelunkers arrived at the entrance of the biggest cave in the world.
다섯 명의 동굴 탐험가는 세계에서 가장 큰 동굴 앞에 도착했다.

spendthrift[spendθrift] n 낭비자, 방탕아 = prodigal[prádigəl] = squanderer[skwάndərər]
He is such a spendthrift, spending all his income on drinks and entertainments.
그는 모든 재산을 술과 유흥에 써버린 방탕아이다.

spleen[spli:n] n 비장, 울화, 울분 = anger = ire[aiər] = rancor[ræŋkər] = wrath[ræθ]
The fired employees had a spleen against their employer.
해고당한 종업원들은 사장에게 울분을 느꼈다.

spontaneous[spantéiniəs] a 자발적인, 자연스러운 = impromptu[imprάmptju:]
= offhand = voluntary = willing
Most charity services in the city are performed through the spontaneous participation of volunteers.
도시에서 열리는 대부분의 자선행사는 자원봉사자들의 자발적인 참여로 이루어진다.

sporadic[spərǽdik] a 산발적인, 이따금 일어나는, 드문드문한 = fits and starts
= intermittent[intərmítnt] = irregular = occasional[əkéiʒənəl] = on and off
At night sporadic gunfire was heard from the border town.
밤에 산발적인 총소리가 국경 마을에서 들려왔다.

sprightly[spráitli] a 정정한, 활기 넘치는, 유쾌한 = cheerful = energetic
= jaunty[dʒɔ́:nti] = peppy = vivacious[vivéiʃəs]
Health experts are studying why there are so many sprightly seniors over 80 in the ginseng-producing village.
건강 전문가들은 인삼산지 마을에 80세가 넘는 활기 넘치는 노인들이 많은 이유를 연구 중이다.

spurious[spjúəriəs] a 거짓된, 가짜의, 그럴싸한 = apocryphal[əpάkrəfəl]
= bogus[bóugəs] = counterfeit[káuntərfit] = fake = false = feigned[feind] = phony
= pseudo[sú:dou] = specious[spí:ʃəs]
A group of swindlers tried to snatch money from innocent investors with a spurious business plan.
한 무리의 사기꾼들이 가짜 사업계획서로 순진한 투자자들로부터 돈을 낚아채려 했다.

spurn[spə:rn] v 퇴짜 놓다, 거절하다 = despise[dispáiz] = disdain = disregard[disrigά:rd] =
flout[flaut] = rebuff[ribʌ́f] = refuse = reject = repudiate[ripjú:dièit] = scorn = snub[snʌb] = turn down
The professor spurned the job offer from the electronics company.
그 교수는 전자회사의 입사 제안을 거절했다.

squabble[skwάbl] v 옥신각신하다, 말다툼하다 = argue[ά:rgju:] = bicker[bíkər] = brawl[brɔ:l] =
hassle[hǽsl] = quarrel[kwɔ́:rəl] = quibble[kwíbl] = wrangle[rǽŋgl]
The couple was squabbling over which movie to watch in front of the theater.
부부는 극장 앞에서 어떤 영화를 볼 것인가를 놓고 옥신각신하고 있었다.

squalid[skwɑ́lid] a 지저분한, 불결한, 누추한 = filthy[fílθi] = grimy = shabby[ʃǽbi]
= sordid[sɔ́ːrdid]
Many refugees were staying in the squalid cells in the detention center.
많은 난민들이 수용소의 지저분한 방에서 지내고 있었다.

squall[skwɔːl] n 질풍, 돌풍, 소나기 = flurry[fləˊːri] = gale[geil] = gust
A team of tourists encountered a strong squall while crossing the lake.
한 무리의 여행객들은 호수를 지나는 동안에 강한 돌풍을 만났다.

squalor[skwɑ́lər] n 불결함, 누추함 = filth[filθ] = foulness
Some children are suffering from malnutrition and squalor in the shanty town.
일부 아이들이 판자촌 마을에서 영양실조와 불결한 상황 때문에 고생하고 있다.

squander[skwɑ́ndər] v 낭비하다, 허비하다 = lavish[lǽviʃ] = prodigalize[prɑ́digəlàiz] = waste
It didn't take much time for him to squander all his huge inheritance.
그가 많은 유산을 낭비하는 데는 그리 많은 시간이 걸리지 않았다.

stagnation[stægnéiʃən] n 부진, 정체, 침체 = inactivity = quiescence[kwiésns]
= sluggishness = stasis[stéisis]
Many merchants are suffering from the sales decline due to the economic stagnation.
많은 상인들이 경제침체에 따른 매출 하락으로 고생하고 있다.

staid[steid] a 침착한, 근엄한, 안정된 = restrained = sedate[sidéit]
His mustache made him look staid. 그의 콧수염은 그를 침착하게 보이게 했다.

stalemate[stéilmeit] n 교착 상태, 궁지 = deadlock = gridlock = impasse[ímpæs]
The negotiations have been stuck in a stalemate for a month.
협상은 한 달 동안 교착상태에 빠져 있다.

stalk[stɔːk] v 몰래 추적하다, 몰래 접근하다 = chase = follow = haunt[hɔːnt]
A tiger secretly stalked a deer in the forest. 호랑이는 숲속에서 몰래 사슴에게 접근했다.

stalwart[stɔ́ːlwərt] a 건장한, 튼튼한, 충실한 = burly[bə́ːrli] = indomitable[indɑ́mətəbl]
= intrepid[intrépid] = staunch[stɔːntʃ] = strong = valiant[vǽljənt]
The knight was a man of stalwart build. 기사는 건장한 체격을 가지고 있었다.

stammer[stǽmər] v 말을 더듬거리다 = stutter[stʌtər]
The woman stammered in shock. 그녀는 충격으로 말을 더듬거렸다.

stark[stɑːrk] a 완전한, 극명한, 순전한 = absolute[ǽbsəlùːt] = utter[ʌ́tər]
The hectic city life is in stark contrast to the leisurely life in the countryside.
정신 없이 바쁜 도시 생활은 시골에서의 느긋한 삶과는 극명한 대조를 이룬다.

QUIZ 110

Match each word in the first column with its definition in the second column.
Check your answers in the back of the book.

1.	spurn		a.	apocryphal = bogus
2.	squabble		b.	stutter
3.	squalid		c.	one who explores caves
4.	stammer		d.	burly = indomitable
5.	spelunker		e.	despise = disdain
6.	squall		f.	deadlock = gridlock
7.	spurious		g.	prodigal = squanderer
8.	stark		h.	argue = bicker
9.	squalor		i.	filthy = grimy
10.	spendthrift		j.	anger = ire
11.	squander		k.	restrained = sedate
12.	spontaneous		l.	chase = follow
13.	spleen		m.	impromptu = offhand
14.	stagnation		n.	absolute = utter
15.	staid		o.	fits and starts = intermittent
16.	sporadic		p.	flurry = gale
17.	stalemate		q.	filth = foulness
18.	stalk		r.	lavish = prodigalize
19.	sprightly		s.	cheerful = energetic
20.	stalwart		t.	inactivity = quiescence

startle[stɑ́ːrtl] v 깜짝 놀라게 하다 = amaze[əméiz] = astonish[əstɑ́niʃ]
= astound[əstáund] = frighten[fráitn] = surprise
The sudden marriage of the famous actress startled many fans.
갑작스런 그 여배우의 결혼은 많은 팬들을 놀라게 했다.

stasis[stéisis] n 균형상태, 정지상태 = balance = equilibrium[ìːkwəlíbriəm]
= equipoise[íːkwəpɔ̀iz] = symmetry[símətri]
The passenger plane has reached the stasis at the altitude of 33,000 feet
그 여객기는 고도 33,000피트에서 균형상태에 도달했다.

static[stǽtik] a 정적인, 정지된, 거의 변화하지 않는 = changeless = immobile[imóubi:l] = motionless = stagnant[stǽgnənt] = stationary
The GDP per capita in the country has been static for 10 years.
그 나라의 1인당 GDP는 10년 동안 거의 변화하지 않고 있다.

staunch[stɔ:ntʃ] a 견고한, 튼튼한, 견실한 = ardent[ά:rdnt] = dependable = stalwart[stɔ́:lwərt] = stout[staut]
Weapons manufacturers are staunch supporters of the conservative party.
무기 제조업체들은 보수당의 충실한 지지자들이다.

steadfast[stedfǽst] a 변함 없는, 확고한, 부동의 = adamant[ǽdəmənt] = ardent[ά:rdnt] = loyal = unwavering[ʌnwéivəriŋ]
She remained steadfast in belief that her son was innocent.
그녀는 자신의 아들이 무죄라는 확고한 믿음을 가지고 있었다.

steep[sti:p] v 적시다, 담그다, 몰두하다, 열중하다 = drench[drentʃ] = immerse[imə́:rs] = saturate[sǽtʃərèit] = soak[souk] = submerge[səbmə́:rdʒ]
The chef has steeped some cabbages in the salty water for 10 hours.
그 셰프는 양배추를 소금물에 열시간 담가두었다.

stench[stentʃ] n 악취, 고약한 냄새 = foul odor = stink
Some neighbors had headaches from the severe stench of burning garbage
어떤 이웃들은 쓰레기가 타면서 나는 강렬한 악취로 두통을 겪고 있었다.

stentorian[stentɔ́:riən] a 우렁찬, 목소리가 큰 = blaring[blɛər] = loud
The general commanded his soldiers in a stentorian voice.
그 장군은 우렁찬 목소리로 부하들에게 명령했다.

sterile[stéril] a 살균한, 불임의, 불모의 = antiseptic[æntəséptik] = arid[ǽrid] = barren[bǽrən] = infertile[infə́:rtəl] = unproductive.
No crops could grow in such a sterile land. 그런 불모의 땅에서는 어떤 곡식도 자랄 수 없었다.

stickler[stíklər] n 완벽주의자, 깐깐한 사람 = perfectionist
The sales director is a stickler for financial reports.
영업이사는 재무보고에 관한 한 깐깐한 사람이다.

stifle[stáifl] v 억누르다, 억제하다, 진압하다 = curb = repress = smother[smʌðər]
= squelch[skweltʃ] = strangle[stræŋgl] = suffocate[sʌfəkèit] = suppress
Nothing could stifle the pro-democracy movement in the country.
어떤 것도 그 나라의 민주화 운동을 억누를 수 없었다.

stigmatize[stígmətàiz] v 오명을 씌우다, 낙인을 찍다 = label negatively = taint[teint]
The chairman of the company was stigmatized as a tax evader.
그 회사의 회장에게 세금탈루자의 오명이 씌워졌다.

stingy[stíndʒi] a 인색한, 쩨쩨한 = miserly[máizərli] = penny-pinching
The employer is not stingy with the salary for the employees.
사장은 종업원들의 급여에 인색하지 않다.

stint[stint] v 절약하다, 제한하다, 줄이다 = economize[ikánəmàiz] = scrimp[skrimp]
The chef doesn't stint on the ingredients. 셰프는 요리 재료에 인색하지 않다.

stipend[stáipend] n 급료, 봉급 = gratuity[grətjú:əti] = payment for services = salary
A monthly stipend was being paid to the new priest. 월급이 새로 온 성직자에게 주어졌다.

stipulate[stípjulèit] v 명시하다, 규정하다 = specify[spésəfài] = spell out
A lot of working terms are stipulated in the labor contract.
많은 근무조건들이 근로계약서에 명시된다.

stir[stəːr] v 선동하다, 동요시키다 = agitate[ǽdʒitèit] = arouse[əráuz] = incite[insáit]
The demagogue stirred up college students to protest.
선동정치인은 대학생들을 선동하여 시위를 하게 했다. demagogue[déməgàg] n 선동정치인

stodgy[stádʒi] a 지루한, 재미없는, 따분한 = boring = monotonous[mənátənəs] = tedious[tí:diəs]
His history lecture kept going stodgy. 그의 역사 강의는 지루하게 계속되었다.

stoic[stóuik] a 금욕의, 의연한, 절제심이 강한 = aloof = apathetic[æpəθétik] = detached
= indifferent
Most monks are considered patient and stoic.
대부분의 수도사들은 인내력 있고 금욕적인 걸로 간주된다.

stolid[stálid] a 둔감한, 무기력한, 무신경한 = apathetic[æpəθétik] = impassive[impǽsiv]
= phlegmatic[flegmǽtik]
He is stolid to his dress and hair style. 그는 옷과 헤어스타일에 신경쓰지 않는다.

QUIZ 111

Match each word in the first column with its definition in the second column.
Check your answers in the back of the book.

1.	steadfast	a.	changeless = immobile
2.	steep	b.	specify = spell out
3.	stench	c.	gratuity = payment
4.	stodgy	d.	ardent = dependable
5.	stoic	e.	economize = scrimp
6.	stentorian	f.	balance = equilibrium
7.	stickler	g.	antiseptic = arid
8.	stifle	h.	apathetic = impassive
9.	startle	i.	aloof = apathetic
10.	stipulate	j.	amaze = astonish
11.	stigmatize	k.	blaring = loud
12.	stasis	l.	boring = monotonous
13.	stir	m.	perfectionist
14.	stingy	n.	agitate = arouse
15.	static	o.	foul odor = stink
16.	stint	p.	miserly = penny-pinching
17.	staunch	q.	label negatively = taint
18.	stolid	r.	drench = immerse
19.	stipend	s.	curb = repress
20.	sterile	t.	adamant = ardent

stout[staut] a 뚱뚱한, 굵직한, 튼튼한 = overweight = portly[pɔ́ːrtli]
The stout butcher was not kind to the customers.
그 뚱뚱한 푸줏간 주인은 손님들에게 친절하지 않았다.

stratum[stréitəm] n 층, 단층, 계층 = layer = level
The politician was popular with people in a lower stratum of society.
그 정치인은 사회의 하층민들에게 인기가 있었다.

stratagem[strǽtədʒəm] n 전략, 책략, 술수 = gimmick[gímik] = ploy[plɔi]
= ruse[ruːz] = subterfuge[sʌ́btərfjùːdʒ] = trick = wile[wail]
The navy used the ingenious stratagem in the attack on the pirates.
해군은 해적들을 공격할 때 재치 있는 전략을 사용했다.

striate[stráieit] v 줄[줄무늬, 홈]을 넣다 = streak = stripe
The craftsman is striating on the surface of the wooden chairs.
그 장인은 나무 의자 표면에 줄무늬를 넣고 있다.

stricture[stríktʃər] n 심한 비난, 협착, 구속 = blame = censure[sénʃər]
= criticism[krítəsìzm] = obloquy[ábləkwi] = rebuke[ribjú:k] = reprobation[rèprəbéiʃən]
Newspapers are passing severe strictures on the lavish lives of the religious leaders.
신문은 종교지도자들의 사치스러운 생활을 비난했다.

stridence[stráidns] n 불협화음, 소음, 삐걱거림, 귀에 거슬림 = cacophony[kəkáfəni]
Some sort of stridence came from the machine in the factory.
뭔가 삐걱거리는 소리가 공장에 있는 기계에서 흘러나왔다.

strife[straif] n 갈등, 불화, 분쟁 = clash[klæʃ] = conflict = friction[fríkʃən]
The internal strife in the political party led to the defeat in the general election.
정당의 내분이 총선에서의 패배라는 결과를 낳았다.

stringent[stríndʒənt] a 엄중한, 엄격한 = demanding = draconian[dreikóuniən]
= exacting[igzæktiŋ] = rigid[rídʒid] = rigorous[rígərəs] = strict
Army cadets are supposed to follow stringent rules in military school.
사관생도들은 사관학교에서 엄격한 규칙을 따라야 한다.

strut[strʌt] v 점잔 빼며 걷다, 뽐내며 걷다 = stride[straid] = swagger[swǽgər]
= walk pompously[pámpəsli]
The police chief struts around the dark streets of the city like a king at night.
경찰서장은 마치 왕처럼 어두운 도시의 밤거리를 점잔 빼며 걸어다닌다.

stultify[stʌltəfài] v 무력화시키다, 무효로 하다, 못쓰게 만들다 = impede[impí:d]
= inhibit[inhíbit] = nullify[nʌləfài]
Lack of budget and indifference to the environment stultified the building of wind power stations.
예산 부족과 환경에 대한 무관심 때문에 풍력발전 건설이 무력화되었다.

stupendous[stju:péndəs] a 엄청나게 큰, 거대한, 대단한 = astonishing[əstániʃiŋ]
= astounding[əstáundiŋ] = breathtaking = colossal[kəlásəl] = enormous[inɔ́:rməs]
= fabulous[fǽbjuləs] = marvelous[má:rvələs] = prodigious[prədídʒəs] = stunning
The business group suffered stupendous losses in the semi-conductor sector.
그 회사는 반도체 분야에서 막대한 손실을 겪었다.

stupor[stjú:pər] n 인사불성, 혼수, 마비 = coma = lethargy[léθərdʒi] = torpor[tɔ́:rpər] = trance[træns]
The drunken man has finally fallen into a stupor. 그 술 취한 사람은 마침내 인사불성에 빠졌다.

stymie[stáimi] v 방해하다, 좌절시키다 = block = crimp[krimp] = cripple[krípl] = deter[ditə́:r] = hamper = hamstring = hinder[híndər] = impede[impí:d] = inhibit = preclude = prohibit = thwart[θwɔ:rt]
Fluctuation in the exchange rate will stymie the smooth flow of trade between the two countries.
환율의 급격한 변동이 두 나라 사이의 순조로운 무역 흐름을 방해할 것이다.

subdue[səbdjú:] v 정복하다, 진압하다, 제압하다 = conquer[káŋkər] = overcome = quell[kwel]
The passengers and crew are said to have subdued the terrorists.
승객들과 승무원들이 그 테러리스트를 제압했다고 알려졌다.

subjugate[sʌ́bdʒugèit] v 지배(통치)하에 두다, 복종시키다, 예속시키다 = conquer[káŋkər] = enslave[insléiv] = enthrall[inθrɔ́:l] = subdue[səbdjú:]
The nation has been subjugated over 30 years by the imperialist nation.
그 나라는 30년 넘게 제국주의 국가의 지배를 받았다.

sublime[səbláim] a 장엄한, 웅장한, 훌륭한 = grandiose[grǽndiòus] = imposing[impóuziŋ] = magnificent[mægnífəsnt]
As you climb the mountain high, you will encounter a sublime mountain view.
산에 높이 올라가면 장엄한 산악 풍경을 보게 될 것이다.

submerge[səbmə́:rdʒ] v 잠수하다, 담그다, 침수시키다 = douse[daus] = drench[drentʃ] = immerse[imə́:rs]
Most areas in the town have been submerged by the floodwater.
마을의 대부분은 홍수에 침수되었다.

submission[səbmíʃən] n 항복, 굴복 = compliance[kəmpláiəns]
The powerful nation coerced its neighboring country into submission for 20 years.
강한 나라는 이웃나라를 20년간 복종케 했다.

subordinate[səbɔ́:rdənət] a 부하의, 하위의, 부차적인, 종속된 = lesser[lésəR] = supplementary[sʌpləméntəri]
All other laws are subordinate to the Constitution.
모든 다른 법은 헌법에 종속되어 있다.

subside[səbsáid] v 가라앉다, 진정되다 = descend[disénd] = die down
The captain of the ship postponed the sail until the strong wind subsides.
배의 선장은 강한 바람이 진정될 때까지 항해를 연기했다.

QUIZ 112

Match each word in the first column with its definition in the second column.
Check your answers in the back of the book.

1.	stultify		a.	blame = censure
2.	subjugate		b.	demanding = draconian
3.	stout		c.	descend = die down
4.	stupendous		d.	clash = conflict
5.	subdue		e.	overweight = portly
6.	strut		f.	compliance
7.	stupor		g.	cacophony
8.	stratum		h.	lesser = supplementary
9.	stymie		i.	layer = level
10.	subside		j.	streak = stripe
11.	strife		k.	conquer = overcome
12.	stringent		l.	conquer = enslave
13.	stratagem		m.	block = crimp
14.	sublime		n.	gimmick = ploy
15.	submerge		o.	grandiose = imposing
16.	striate		p.	coma = lethargy
17.	submission		q.	douse = drench
18.	stricture		r.	astonishing = astounding
19.	subordinate		s.	stride = swagger
20.	stridence		t.	imped = inhibit

subsidiary[səbsídièri] a 부수적인, 보조의 = accessory = ancillary[ǽnsəlèri]
= auxiliary[ɔ:gzíljəri] = supplementary[sʌpləméntəri]
The electronic giant has a lot of subsidiary companies.
거대 전자회사는 많은 부속회사를 거느리고 있다.

subsidize[sʌ́bsədàiz] v 장려금(보조금)을 지원하다, 원조하다, 후원하다 = bankroll
= finance[fáinæns] = fund
The construction of the eco-friendly town is being heavily subsidized by the city government.
친환경마을 건설에 시 정부로부터 많은 보조금이 지원되고 있다.

substantial[səbstǽnʃəl] a 상당한, 실체의, 중대한 = considerable[kənsídərəbl] = sizable[sáizəbl]
The company invested a substantial amount of money to develop electric cars.
그 회사는 전기차 개발에 상당한 금액의 돈을 투자했다.

substantiate[səbstǽnʃièit] v 입증하다, 확증하다 = affirm[əfə́:rm] = confirm
= corroborate[kərábərèit] = verify[vérəfài]
His alibi substantiated his contention that he was involved in the murder case.
그의 알리바이는 살인사건과 무관하다는 그의 주장을 입증했다.

substantive[sʌ́bstəntiv] a 실질적인, 현실의 = actual[ǽktʃuəl] = real = truly existing
The substantive purpose of their visit to the island was to purchase a land for amusement park.
그 섬을 방문한 그들의 실질적인 목표는 놀이공원 건립을 위한 부지 매입이었다.

subterfuge[sʌ́btərfjù:dʒ] n 속임수, 구실, 핑계 = cheating = deception[disépʃən]
= ploy[plɔi] = ruse[ru:z] = stratagem[strǽtədʒəm] = trick = wile[wail]
He was caught using a subterfuge by securities in the casino.
그는 카지노에서 속임수를 쓰다가 보안요원들에게 걸렸다.

subversive[səbvə́:rsiv] a 체제를 전복시키는, 파괴적인 = incendiary[inséndièri]
= insurgent[insə́:rdʒənt] = rebellious[ribéljəs] = riotous[ráiətəs] = seditious[sidíʃəs]
He was arrested for being involved in subversive activities.
그는 체제 전복 활동과 관련되어 체포되었다.

subvert[səbvə́:rt] v 전복시키다, 타도하다, 뒤집다 = overthrow = rebel = topple[tápl]
They were devising a plot to subvert the government.
그들은 정부를 전복할 음모를 꾸미고 있었다.

succinct[səksíŋkt] a 간단명료한, 간결한 = brief = to the point = concise[kənsáis]
= curt[kə:rt] = laconic[ləkánik] = pithy[píθi] = terse[tə:rs]
My boss prefers a succinct report. 나의 상사는 간단명료한 보고서를 선호한다.

succor[sʌ́kər] n 구조, 원조 = assistance[əsístəns] = relief = rescue[réskju:]
Many charity organizations gave succor to poverty-stricken people in Africa.
많은 자선단체들이 아프리카의 가난에 찌든 사람들에게 원조를 해주었다.

succumb[səkʌ́m] v 굴복하다, 항복하다 = capitulate[kəpítʃulèit] = cave in to
= give in to = surrender[səréndər] = yield[ji:ld]
The aliens from the Mars succumbed to tiny viruses in our planet.
화성에서 온 외계인들은 우리 행성의 조그만 바이러스에 굴복했다.

suffice[səfáis] v 충분하다 = be enough
I think U$20 will suffice for him to have lunch and watch a movie.
나는 20달러면 그가 충분히 점심도 먹고 영화도 볼 수 있다고 생각한다.

suffrage[sʌ́fridʒ] n 투표권, 선거권, 참정권 = ballot[bǽlət] = vote
It is not long ago that the political suffrage was given to women.
선거권이 여성들에게 주어진 것은 그리 오래전이 아니다.

suffuse[səfjúːz] v 퍼지다, 뒤덮다 = permeate[pə́ːrmièit] = saturate[sǽtʃərèit] = steep[stiːp]
The mountain was suffused with colorful leaves. 산은 단풍으로 뒤덮였다.

sullen[sʌ́lən] a 뚱한, 시무룩한 = dour[duər] = morose[məróus] = somber[sámbər] = surly[sə́ːrli]
The sullen look of the team leader made all team members feel uneasy all day.
팀 주장의 시무룩한 표정은 팀원들을 하루 종일 불편하게 만들었다.

sully[sʌ́li] v 가치를 떨어뜨리다, 더럽히다, 손상시키다 = besmirch[bismə́ːrtʃ] = contaminate[kəntǽmənèit] = smear[smiər] = taint[teint] = tarnish[táːrniʃ]
The tax evasion sullied the reputation of the lawyer.
세금 탈루로 인해서 그 변호사의 명성이 더럽혀졌다.

summit[sʌ́mit] n 정상, 최고점, 정상회담 = acme[ǽkmi] = apex[éipeks] = culmination[kʌ̀lmənéiʃən] = peak = pinnacle[pínəkl] = vertex[vəːrteks] = zenith[zíːniθ]
The professional climbers reached the summit of the mountain.
프로 등반가는 산의 정상에 도달했다.

summon[sʌ́mən] v 소환하다, 호출하다 = subpoena[səbpíːnə]
The tax officials summoned the businessman to their office to investigate the tax evasion.
세무공무원들은 그 사업가의 세금 탈루를 조사하기 위해 그를 사무실로 소환했다.

sumptuous[sʌ́mptʃuəs] a 호화로운, 화려한 = deluxe[dəlʌ́ks] = extravagant[ikstrǽvəgənt] = lavish[lǽviʃ] = luxurious[lʌgʒúəriəs] = opulent[ápjulənt] = posh[paʃ]
The bankrupt business man was still living a sumptuous life.
파산한 사업가는 여전히 호화로운 삶을 영위하고 있었다.

sunder[sʌ́ndər] v 찢다, 분리하다, 절단하다 = rend = separate = sever[sévər]
The village was sundered by the pros and cons of the construction of nuclear power plant.
마을은 원자력발전소 건설 찬반 문제로 사분오열되었다.

QUIZ 113

Match each word in the first column with its definition in the second column.
Check your answers in the back of the book.

1. succinct
2. succor
3. subsidiary
4. summit
5. succumb
6. subsidize
7. suffice
8. suffrage
9. substantial
10. suffuse
11. sullen
12. substantiate
13. sully
14. summon
15. substantive
16. sumptuous
17. subterfuge
18. subvert
19. subversive
20. sunder

a. capitulate = cave in to
b. subpoena
c. besmirch = contaminate
d. be enough
e. assistance = relief
f. dour = morose
g. acme = apex
h. permeate = saturate
i. accessory = ancillary
j. actual = real
k. ballot = vote
l. bankroll = finance
m. brief = to the point
n. deluxe
o. considerable = sizable
p. overthrow = rebel
q. rend = separate
r. affirm = confirm
s. incendiary = insurgent
t. cheating = deception

supercilious[sùːpərsíliəs] a 거만한, 건방진, 남을 얕보는 = arrogant[ǽrəgənt]
= cavalier[kӕvəlíər] = cocky[káki] = contemptuous[kəntémptʃuəs] = disdainful[disdéinfəl]
= haughty[hɔ́ːti] = imperious[impíəriəs] = insolent[ínsələnt] = overbearing
The champion was looking at the challenger with a supercilious smile.
챔피언은 거만한 미소로 도전자를 보고 있었다.

superficial[sùːpərfíʃəl] a 외관상의, 피상적인, 허울뿐인 = cursory[kə́ːrsəri]
= perfunctory[pərfʌ́ŋktəri] = ostensible[asténsəbl]
He has superficial knowledge about artificial intelligence.
그는 인공지능에 대해서 피상적인 지식을 가지고 있다.

superfluous[supə́:rfluəs] a 여분의, 불필요한, 남아도는 = excessively[iksésivli]
= extra = redundant[ridʌ́ndənt] = unnecessary
The ministry of agriculture is trying to come up with an idea to handle the superfluous rice.
농림장관은 남아도는 여분의 쌀을 처리할 방도를 찾고 있다.

supersede[sù:pərsí:d] v 대신하다, 대체하다 = supplant[səplǽnt] = take the place of
Most of the desk top computers in the offices have been superseded by lap top computers.
사무실에 있는 대부분의 책상용 컴퓨터는 노트북 컴퓨터로 대체되었다.

supine[su:páin] a 반듯이 드러누운, 무기력한, 나태한 = decumbent[dikʌ́mbənt]
= flat on one's back = lying down
The injured man was in the supine position until the rescue team arrived.
다친 남자는 구조팀이 올 때까지 반듯하게 누워 있었다.

supplant[səplǽnt] v 대신하다, 대체하다, 찬탈하다 = replace[ripléis]
= supersede[sù:pərsí:d] = unseat = usurp[ju:sə́:rp]
I am sure that electric cars will supplant the cars using the fossil fuel in the near future.
나는 가까운 미래에 전기차가 화석연료를 사용하는 차를 대체하리라고 확신한다.

supple[sʌpl] a 부드러운, 나긋나긋한, 유순한 = limber[límbər] = lithe[laið]
= malleable[mǽliəbl] = pliable[pláiəbl] = pliant[pláiənt] = svelte[svelt]
Our yoga coach has a very supple body. 우리 요가 코치는 매우 유연한 몸을 가지고 있다.

supplicant[sʌ́pləkənt] n 탄원자, 애원자 = petitioner[pətíʃənər]
A lot of supplicants gathered in front of the court building. 많은 탄원자들이 법정 앞에 모였다.

supplication[sʌ̀pləkéiʃən] n 탄원, 애원, 간청 = adjuration[ædʒuəréiʃən]
= entreaty[intrí:ti] = invocation[invəkéiʃən]
The loan shark turned down the supplication of the debtor.
고리대금업자는 채무자의 간청을 거절했다.

suppress[səprés] v 진압하다, 억누르다, 금하다 = contain = curb = quash[kwaʃ]
= quell[kwel] = repress = stifle[stáifl] = subdue[səbdjú:]
The police were prepared to suppress violent protesters.
경찰은 폭력적인 시위자들을 진압할 준비를 하고 있었다.

surfeit[sə́:rfit] n 과다, 과잉 = excess = glut[glʌt] = plethora[pléθərə] = profusion
Having a surfeit of sugar weakens the immune system.
설탕을 과다 섭취하면 면역체계가 약화된다.

surmise[sərmáiz] v 추측하다, 추정하다, 짐작하다 = infer[infə́:r] = presume[prizú:m] = speculate[spékjulèit]
The authority surmises that the murderer has crossed the border.
당국은 그 살인자가 국경을 넘었을 거라고 추측한다.

surreal[sərí:əl] a 초현실적인, 비현실적인, 꿈같은 = dreamlike
His success story was too surreal to believe.
그의 성공스토리는 너무 비현실적이어서 믿을 수 없었다.

surrender[səréndər] v 넘겨주다, 양도하다, 항복하다 = cede[si:d] = hand over = relinquish[rilíŋkwiʃ] = succumb[səkʌm] = waive[weiv]
The rebels decided to surrender themselves to the government forces.
반란군들은 정부군에 항복하기로 결정했다.

surreptitious[sə̀:rəptíʃəs] a 몰래 한, 은밀한, 비밀리의 = clandestine[klændéstin] = covert = furtive[fə́:rtiv] = hole and corner = hush-hush = secret = sneaky[sní:ki] = stealthy[stélθi] = sub rosa[sʌb róuzə] = under the table
Their surreptitious plan was leaked out to the police.
그들의 은밀한 계획이 경찰에게 유출되었다.

surrogate[sə́:rəgèit] n 대행자, 대리인 = fill in = proxy[práksi] = stand in
The infertile couple wanted to have a baby through a surrogate mother.
그 불임부부는 대리모를 통해서 아이를 갖기 원했다.

susceptible[səséptəbl] a 영향을 받기 쉬운, 민감한, 예민한 = inclined = prone = vulnerable[vʌlnərəbl]
She is very susceptible to pollen allergy. 그녀는 꽃가루 알레르기에 매우 민감하다.

svelte[sveltt] a 날씬한, 호리호리한 = slender[sléndər] = slim
You should be svelte to become a shopping host.
쇼핑호스트가 되기 위해서는 날씬해야만 한다.

swagger[swǽgər] v 뽐내며(거드름 피우며) 걷다 = stride[straid] = strut[strʌt] = walk pompously[pámpəsli]
A group of war veterans were swaggering down the road.
한 무리의 퇴역군인들이 거리를 뽐내며 걷고 있었다.

sway[swei] v 흔들리다, 휘청거리다 = swing = wave = wobble[wάbl]
The trees on the both sides of the street were swaying to the wind.
길거리 양쪽의 나무들이 바람에 흔들거리고 있었다.

QUIZ 114

Match each word in the first column with its definition in the second column.
Check your answers in the back of the book.

1.	supple	a.	arrogant = cavalier
2.	supplication	b.	contain = curb
3.	supercilious	c.	adjuration = entreaty
4.	svelte	d.	cursory = perfunctory
5.	supplicant	e.	petitioner
6.	suppress	f.	limber = lithe
7.	superficial	g.	inclined = prone
8.	swagger	h.	slender = slim
9.	surfeit	i.	fill in = proxy
10.	supplant	j.	replace = supersede
11.	susceptible	k.	swing = wave
12.	surmise	l.	clandestine = covert
13.	superfluous	m.	infer = presume
14.	sway	n.	excess = glut
15.	surreal	o.	decumbent = flat on one's back
16.	supersede	p.	cede = hand over
17.	surrender	q.	dreamlike
18.	surreptitious	r.	stride = strut
19.	surrogate	s.	supplant = take the place of
20.	supine	t.	excessively = extra

sweeping[swíːpiŋ] a 전면적인, 광범위한, 대대적인 = across the board
= exhaustive[igzɔ́ːstiv] = extensive[iksténsiv] = wide-ranging
The chairman brought in an expert to make sweeping changes in the production line.
회장은 생산라인에서 대대적인 변화를 가져오기 위해 전문가를 영입했다.

sweltering[swéltəriŋ] a 무더운, 후덥지근한, 찌는 듯한 = scorching[skɔ́ːrtʃiŋ]
= sizzling[sízliŋ] = sultry[sʌ́ltri] = torrid[tɔ́ːrid]
Animal keepers help animals to overcome the sweltering heat during summer.
여름 동안 사육사들은 동물들이 숨막히는 더위를 이겨내도록 도와준다.

swill[swil] v 벌컥벌컥 마시다, 마구 들이켜다 = drink fast
After running 10KM, he started swilling water.
십킬로미터를 달리고 나서 그는 물을 벌컥벌컥 들이켜기 시작했다.

sybarite[síbəràit] n 방탕자, 쾌락주의자 = hedonist[híːdənist] = voluptuary[vəlʌptʃuèri]
He must be a sybarite because he always pursues sensual pleasures.
항상 관능적인 쾌락을 추구하는 걸 보면 그는 방탕자임에 틀림없다.

syntax[síntæks] n 통어론(단어배열 방법), 구문론 = words arrangement[əreɪndʒmənt]
Some younger teens don't follow a rule of syntax when writing sentences.
일부 어린 십대들은 글을 쓸 때 정확한 단어배열 규칙을 따르지 않는다.

sycophant[síkəfənt] n 아첨꾼, 알랑쇠 = bootlicker[búːtlìkər] = flatterer = toady[tóudi]
He has been a sycophant to the business tycoon. 그는 큰 사업가에게 아첨꾼으로 지내오고 있다.

syllogism[síləd͡ʒìzm] n 삼단논법, 연역추리 = deductive reasoning
'All animals die someday, a lion is an animal, therefore a lion dies someday' is an example of a syllogism.
'모든 동물은 언젠가 죽는다. 사자는 동물이다. 그러므로 사자는 언젠가 죽는다'는 삼단논법의 예이다.

symbiotic[sìmbaiátik] a 공생하는, 공생에 의한 = interdependent = reciprocal[risíprəkəl]
Bees and flowers have a symbiotic relationship. 벌과 꽃은 공생관계다.

sympathetic[sìmpəθétik] a 동정하는, 공감의 = caring = compassionate[kəmpǽʃənət]
We felt sympathetic to the flood victims. 우리는 홍수 피해자들에게 동정심을 느꼈다.

synopsis[sinápsis] n 개요, 요약 = digest[didʒést] = summary
The manager gave a synopsis to his team members about the project.
매니저는 팀원들에게 그 프로젝트에 관한 개요를 설명했다.

synthesis[sínθəsis] n 종합, 통합, 합성 = combination = fusion
= integration[ìntəgréiʃən] = unification[jùːnəfikéiʃən]
His dishes are the synthesis of traditional and modern foods.
그의 요리는 전통적 음식과 현대적 음식을 조합한 것이다.

systemic[sistémik] a 전체(전신)에 영향을 미치는 = affecting the entire system = integral[íntigrəl]
Doctors are trying to find a cure to the systemic lumbar disc disease.
의사들은 전신에 영향을 미치는 허리 디스크 질병에 대한 치료법을 찾으려 하고 있다.
lumbar[lʌ́mbər] a 허리의

QUIZ 115

Match each word in the first column with its definition in the second column.
Check your answers in the back of the book.

1. sycophant
2. syllogism
3. sweeping
4. sympathetic
5. symbiotic
6. sweltering
7. synthesis
8. swill
9. synopsis
10. sybarite
11. systemic
12. syntax

a. combination=fusion
b. hedonist=voluptuary
c. drink fast
d. caring=compassionate
e. digest=summary
f. interdependent=reciprocal
g. across the board=exhaustive
h. deductive reasoning
i. scorching=sizzling
j. bootlicker=flatterer
k. affecting the entire system=integral
l. words arrangement

tacit[tǽsit] a 암묵적인, 무언의 = allusive[əlúːsiv] = implicit[implísit] = implied[impláid]
We regarded his silence as a tacit approval. 우리는 그의 침묵을 암묵적인 승인으로 간주했다.

taciturn[tǽsətəːrn] a 뚱한, 말수가 적은, 무뚝뚝한 = laconic[ləkάnik] = reticent[rétəsənt]
The taciturn host led us into a room. 말수가 적은 집주인은 우리를 방으로 안내했다.

tact[tækt] n 재치, 약삭빠름, 요령 = acumen[əkjúːmən] = finesse[finés]
The bank manager exercised great tact while he and his employees being held hostage.
은행 매니저는 직원들과 함께 인질로 잡혀 있을 때 대단한 요령을 발휘했다.

tactical[tǽktikəl] a 전술상의, 작전의, 책략에 능한 = strategic[strətíːdʒik]
The troops made a tactical retreat at the battle. 군대는 전투에서 전술상의 후퇴를 했다.

taint[teint] v 오염시키다, 더럽히다, 손상시키다 = besmirch[bismə́ːrtʃ]
= contaminate[kəntǽmənèit] = smear[smiər] = sully[sʌ́li] = taint[teint] = tarnish[tάːrniʃ]
The reputation of the scientist was tainted by the false dissertation.
그 과학자의 명성은 거짓 논문으로 손상되었다.
dissertation[dìsərtéiʃən] n 논문

tangential[tændʒénʃəl] a 주제를 벗어난, 관계가 거의 없는 = digressing[daigrésing]
= extraneous[ikstréiniəs] = unrelated
His speech was tangential to the issue on the global warming.
그의 연설은 지구온난화라는 주제를 벗어났다.

tangible[tǽndʒəbl] a 명확한, 실재하는, 유형의, 만질 수 있는 = concrete
= palpable[pǽlpəbl] = touchable
The police are looking for tangible evidence to indict the suspect.
경찰은 피의자를 기소할 수 있는 명확한 증거를 찾고 있다.

tangy[tǽŋi] a 냄새가 톡 쏘는, 맛이 짜릿한 = peppery[pépəri] = piquant[píːkənt]
= pungent[pʌ́ndʒənt] = spicy = zesty
Some people on the island enjoy the tangy smell of the fermented fish.
섬에 사는 사람들 일부는 삭힌 물고기의 톡 쏘는 냄새를 좋아한다.

tantamount[tǽntəmàunt] a 동등한, 같은 = commensurate[kəménsərət]
= equivalent[ikwívələnt] = identical
The lung patient's smoking is tantamount to suicide.
폐 질환자가 담배를 피우는 것은 자살행위나 마찬가지다.

taper[téipər] v 점점 약해지다, 줄어들다 = abate[əbéit] = dwindle[dwíndl] = wane[wein]
Sales of cars in the domestic market are tapering off.
내수시장에서의 자동차 판매가 줄어들고 있다.

tarnish[tá:rniʃ] v 변색시키다, 더럽히다, 흐리게 하다 = blemish[blémiʃ] = mar = stain
= sully[sʌli] = taint[teint] = tar
Suzie did not want to tarnish her name because of money.
Suzie는 돈 때문에 자신의 명성이 더럽혀지는 걸 원치 않았다.

tatty[tǽti] a 초라한, 싸구려의, 닳아 해진 = shabby[ʃǽbi]
There were tatty curtains hanging at the window in the room.
방의 창문에는 초라한 커튼들이 걸려 있었다.

taunt[tɔːnt] v 놀리다, 비웃다, 조롱하다 = contemn[kəntém] = deride[diráid]
= despise[dispáiz] = disdain[disdéin] = disparage[dispǽridʒ] = flout[flaut] = insult = jeer
= make fun of = mock = ridicule[rídikjùːl] = scoff[skɔːf] = scorn = slight = sneer
Two bullies taunted a weak boy on the wheelchair.
두 명의 불량배가 휠체어를 타는 약한 소년을 놀렸다.

taut[tɔːt] a 팽팽한, 곤두 선, 긴장한 = rigid[rídʒid] = tense = tight
The fishermen pulled the rope from the fishing net taut.
어부들은 어망에 연결된 로프를 팽팽하게 당겼다.

tautological[tɔ̀ːtəládʒikl] a 동의어 중복의, 반복의 = redundant[ridʌ́ndənt]
= repetitious[rèpətíʃəs] = reiterating[riːítəreit]
It is tautological to say "huge tycoon" because "tycoon" itself include the meaning of "hugeness".
"거대한 거물"이라고 말하면 동의어 중복이 된다 왜냐하면 "거물"이라는 단어 자체가 "거대함"을 이미 포함하고 있기 때문이다.

tawdry[tɔ́ːdri] a 번쩍거리는, 야한, 화려하고 값싼 = flashy = garish[gɛ́əriʃ]
= gaudy[gɔ́ːdi]
The unknown singer was wearing a tawdry jacket.
그 무명가수는 화려하고 값싼 재킷을 입고 있었다.

tedious[tíːdiəs] a 지루한, 싫증나는 = banal[bənǽl] = dreary[dríəri] = dull[dʌl]
= humdrum[hʌ́mdrʌm] = monotonous[mənátənəs] = tiresome[táiərsəm]
The job of cleaning the stairs was tedious to her.
계단을 청소하는 일은 그녀에게 지루했다.

tedium[tí:diəm] n 지루함, 권태, 단조로움 = boredom = drabness[drǽbnis]
= ennui[a:nwí:] = monotony[mənátəni]
Some passengers enjoy the window shopping to relieve the tedium of their waiting at the airport.
어떤 승객들은 공항에서 기다리는 지루함을 해소하기 위해서 진열된 물건들을 보는 것을 즐긴다.

teem[ti:m] v 가득 차다, 풍부하다, 많이 있다 = abound[əbáund] = bustle[bʌsl] = overflow
= swarm[swɔ:rm]
The cold river teemed with salmon. 그 차가운 강에는 연어가 많이 있었다.

teeter[tí:tər] v 건들건들 움직이다, 불안정하게 걷다, 비틀거리다 = falter[fɔ́:ltər] = reel
= seesaw = stagger[stǽgər] = stumble[stʌmbl] = totter[tátər]
Sarah was teetering on the street after drinking a lot of beer.
Sarah는 맥주를 많이 마시고 길에서 비틀거리고 있었다.

QUIZ 116

Match each word in the first column with its definition in the second column.
Check your answers in the back of the book.

1.	tacit		a.	strategic
2.	taut		b.	acumen = finesse
3.	tautological		c.	laconic = reticent
4.	taciturn		d.	contemn = deride
5.	tedious		e.	rigid = tense
6.	tawdry		f.	allusive = implicit
7.	tact		g.	shabby
8.	taint		h.	falter = reel
9.	tactical		i.	besmirch = contaminate
10.	tatty		j.	abound = bustle
11.	taunt		k.	blemish = mar
12.	tangential		l.	boredom = drabness
13.	tedium		m.	banal = dreary
14.	tangible		n.	abate = dwindle
15.	teem		o.	digressing = extraneous
16.	tangy		p.	flashy = garish
17.	teeter		q.	commensurate = equivalent
18.	tantamount		r.	redundant = repetitious
19.	taper		s.	peppery = piquant
20.	tarnish		t.	concrete = palpable

temerity[təmérəti] n 만용, 무분별, 무모 = audacity[ɔːdǽsəti] = boldness
= daring[déəriŋ] = dauntlessness[dɔ́ːntlisnis] = gallantry[gǽləntri] = guts
= intrepidity[intrepídəti] = valor[vǽlər]
He had the temerity to sue the police chief.
그는 경찰서장을 고소할 정도로 무모했다.

temperate[témpərət] a 삼가는, 도를 넘지 않는 = abstemious[æbstíːmiəs]
= abstinent[ǽbstənənt] = controlled = sober[sóubər]
Diabetic should be temperate in eating. 당뇨 환자는 음식을 절제해야 한다.

temporal[témpərəl] a 일시적인, 한때의, 현세의, 속세적인 = ephemeral[ifémərəl]
= transitory[trǽnsətɔ̀ːri] = transient[trǽnʃənt]
His temporal stay on the island was too short to study its native animals.
그는 섬에 체류한 시간이 너무 짧아서 그 섬의 토착 동물들을 연구할 시간이 없었다.

temporize[témpəràiz] v 시간을 끌다, 우물쭈물하다 = gain time
The police tried to temporize with protesters waiting for backup forces.
경찰은 지원병력을 기다리면서 시위대 측에 시간을 끌고 있었다.

tenable[ténəbl] a 방어될 수 있는, 지지(변호)할 수 있는 = defensible
= justifiable[dʒʌstəfàiəbl] = rational
His view was not tenable in the shareholders meeting.
그의 견해는 주주총회에서 지지를 받을 수 없었다.

tenacious[tənéiʃəs] a 집요한, 완강한, 끈질긴 = dogged = headstrong
= intractable[intrǽktəbl] = intransigent[intrǽnsədʒənt] = mulish[mjúːliʃ] = obdurate[ábdjurit]
= obstinate[ábstənət] = ornery[ɔ́ːrnəri] = stubborn[stʌbərn] = unyielding
He is tenacious and goal-directed businessman. 그는 집요하고 목표지향적인 사업가이다.

tenet[ténit] n 교리, 주의, 신조 = belief = creed = doctrine[dáktrin] = dogma[dɔ́ːgmə]
= faith[feiθ] = precept[príːsept] = principle
Love is the fundamental tenet of the religious group. 사랑이 그 종교단체의 근본적인 교리이다.

tenuous[ténjuəs] a 미약한, 희박한, 가느다란 = attenuated[əténjuèitid] = feeble[fíːbl]
= flimsy[flímzi] = fragile[frǽdʒəl] = frail[freil] = rickety[ríkiti]
The rescue team was following the tenuous light from the survivors.
구조 팀은 생존자들로부터 나오는 미약한 빛을 따라가고 있었다.

tepid[tépid] a 미온의, 미적지근한, 열의 없는 = halfhearted = lukewarm[lúːkwɔ́ːrm]
= unenthusiastic[ʌninθjùːziǽstik]
Some moviegoers showed a tepid interest in the newly released black comedy movie.
일부 영화 팬들은 새로 개봉된 블랙코미디 영화에 미온적 관심을 보였다.

terse[təːrs] a 간결한, 명료한 = brusque[brʌsk] = curt[kəːrt] = laconic[ləkɑ́nik]
= pithy[píθi] = succinct[səksíŋkt]
The outgoing minister made a terse statement about his next move.
외향적인 장관은 그의 다음 행보에 대해서 간결한 성명을 냈다.

testimony[téstəmòuni] n 증언, 증거, 입증 = affidavit[æfidéivit] = evidence
= attestation[ætestéiʃən] = witness
His false testimony made the judges confused in the trial.
그의 위증은 판사들을 혼란스럽게 만들었다.

testimonial[tèstəmóuniəl] n 추천장, 증명서 = recommendation[rèkəməndéiʃən]
The new job required a testimonial from the previous employer.
새로운 일을 하기 위해서는 전 고용주로부터의 추천장이 필요했다.

testy[tésti] a 화를 잘 내는, 성미가 급한, 성깔 있는 = cantankerous[kæntǽŋkərəs]
= choleric[kɑ́lərik] = cranky = edgy[édʒi] = fretful[frétfəl] = grumpy = irascible[irǽsəbl]
= irritable[írətəbl] = peevish[píːviʃ] = petulant[pétʃulənt] = touchy[tʌ́tʃi]
The owner of the restaurant was a testy old woman.
식당 주인은 화를 잘 내는 나이 든 여인이었다.

tether[téðər] v 밧줄로 매다, 매어놓다, 속박하다 = fasten[fǽsnːsən] = shackle[ʃǽkl]
The wild horse was tethered to the stake in the backyard.
야생 말은 뒷마당 말뚝에 밧줄로 매여 있었다.

theatrical[θiǽtrikəl] a 연극에 관한, 과장된, 연극조의 = dramatic
The musical includes a lot of theatrical gestures. 그 뮤지컬은 많은 과장된 몸동작을 포함한다.

theology[θiɑ́lədʒi] n 신학, 신학 이론 = religious theory
Reverend Jae received doctorate in theology from RTS.
Jae 목사님은 RTS에서 신학박사 학위를 받았다.

thorny[θɔ́ːrni] a 곤란한, 가시투성이의, 괴롭히는 = bothersome[bɑ́ðərsəm] = difficult
= irksome[ə́ːrksəm] = prickly = troublesome[trʌ́blsəm]
The Education Minister shunned thorny questions. 교육부 장관은 곤란한 질문을 피했다.

349

threadbare[θrédbɛr] a 올이 다 드러난, 닳아빠진, 낡은, 초라한 = frayed[frei] = worn
The millionaire was wearing a threadbare jacket. 그 백만장자는 다 떨어진 재킷을 입고 있었다.

threshold[θréʃhould] n 문지방, 입구, 문턱, 시발점 = beginning = inception[insépʃən]
The terminally ill patient was on the threshold of death.
말기 환자는 죽음의 문턱을 넘고 있었다.

throttle[θrάtl] v 목 졸라 질식시키다 = choke[tʃouk] = smother[smʌðər] = stifle[stáifl]
= strangle[strǽŋgl]
The hijacker tried to throttle the hostage with wire.
그 납치범은 철사로 인질의 목을 조르려고 했다.

QUIZ 117

Match each word in the first column with its definition in the second column.
Check your answers in the back of the book.

1.	temporize	a.	cantankerous = choleric
2.	tenable	b.	fasten = shackle
3.	tenacious	c.	dramatic
4.	tenet	d.	belief = creed
5.	threadbare	e.	dogged = headstrong
6.	temerity	f.	ephemeral = transitory
7.	threshold	g.	choke = smother
8.	tenuous	h.	recommendation
9.	throttle	i.	defensible = justifiable
10.	temperate	j.	abstemious = abstinent
11.	theology	k.	gain time
12.	thorny	l.	beginning = inception
13.	temporal	m.	audacity = boldness
14.	testy	n.	frayed = worn
15.	tether	o.	attenuated = feeble
16.	tepid	p.	religious theory
17.	theatrical	q.	affidavit = evidence
18.	terse	r.	bothersome = difficult
19.	testimony	s.	brusque = curt
20.	testimonial	t.	halfhearted = lukewarm

thwart[θwɔːrt] v 좌절시키다, 방해하다, 훼방하다 = foil = frustrate[frʌstreit]
= hinder = impede[impíːd] = obstruct[əbstrʌkt] = prevent = stymie[stáimi]
Some brave citizens thwarted the plan of terrorists to hijacker the passenger plane.
일부 용감한 시민들이 여객기를 납치하려는 테러범들의 계획을 좌절시켰다.

ticklish[tíkliʃ] a 곤란한, 까다로운, 변덕스러운 = tricky
The construction company was faced with a ticklish problem. 건설회사는 곤란한 문제에 직면했다.

timorous[tímərəs] a 겁 많은, 소심한, 두려워하는 = timid[tímid] = tremulous[trémjuləs]
Young people should not be timorous of failures. 젊은 사람들은 실패를 두려워해서는 안 된다.

tinker[tíŋkər] v 어설프게 고치다, 만지작거리다 = dabble[dǽbl] = fiddle with
You should not tinker with the luxury watch. 어설프게 명품시계를 고쳐선 안 된다.

tirade[táireid] n 신랄한 비난, 장황한 열변 = denunciation[dinʌnsiéiʃən]
= diatribe[dáiətràib] = harangue[hərǽŋ] = invective[invéktiv] = screed[skriːd]
The opposition leader delivered a tirade against the government's tax policy.
야당 지도자는 정부의 세금정책에 대해 신랄한 비난을 퍼부었다.

titillate[títəlèit] v 간질이다, 자극하다, 흥분시키다 = arouse[əráuz] = excite = stimulate
The author of the book used some erotic illustrations to titillate the readers.
책의 저자는 독자들을 자극하기 위해서 일부 에로틱한 삽화들을 사용했다.

titular[títʃulər] a 명목상의, 이름뿐인 = nominal[nάmənl]
Ben is the titular head of the bank. Ben은 은행의 명목상의 대표이다.

toil[tɔil] v 힘들게 일하다, 애쓰다 = drudge[drʌdʒ] = labor = moil[mɔil] = strive[straiv]
= sweat = work hard
Many minors were forced to toil at a textile factory in the South East Asian country.
동남아시아의 직물공장에서는 많은 미성년자들이 강제 노역을 하고 있다.

tonic[tάnik] n 강장제, 원기를 돋우는 것 = restorative drink
Reading the bible is a tonic for most Christians.
성경을 읽는 것은 대부분의 기독교인들에게는 원기를 돋우는 일이다.

torpid[tɔːrpid] a 무기력한, 활기 없는, 휴면 중인 = inactive = lackadaisical[lækədéizikəl]
= languid[lǽŋgwid] = lethargic[ləθάːrdʒik] = listless = sluggish[slʌgiʃ]
He has become torpid at his job since he lost his son in the car accident.
아들을 교통사고로 잃은 이후 그는 업무에 무기력해졌다.

torpor[tɔ́ːrpər] n 무기력, 무감각, 휴면 = apathy[ǽpəθi] = dormancy[dɔ́ːrmənsi]
= drowsiness = lethargy[léθərdʒi] = sluggishness[slʌ́giʃnis] = stupor[stjúːpər]
= torpidity[tɔːrpídəti]
The hunters have recovered from their torpor since they saw a herd of deer.
사냥꾼들은 한 무리의 사슴 떼를 본 이후 무기력에서 회복하고 있다.

torrid[tɔ́ːrid] a 뜨거운, 작열하는, 바짝 말라버린 = arid[ǽrid] = parched[paːrtʃt] = scorching[skɔ́ːrtʃiŋ]
The escaped prisoners were to cross the torrid desert to survive.
탈출한 죄수들은 살아남기 위해 작열하는 사막을 건너야만 했다.

tortuous[tɔ́ːrtʃuəs] a 구불구불한, 길고 복잡한, 에두르는 = circuitous[sərkjúːətəs]
= convoluted[kɑ́nvəlùːtid] = labyrinthine[læbərínθin] = meandering[miǽndəriŋ]
= serpentine[səːrpəntiːn] = sinuous[sínjuəs] = twisting[twístiŋ] = winding[wáindiŋ]
The manager was not happy with the Peter's tortuous explanations.
매니저는 Peter의 길고 복잡한 설명을 좋아하지 않았다.

touchstone[tʌ́tʃstoʊn] n 시금석, 기준, 표준 = barometer[bərɑ́mitər]
= criterion[kraitíəriən] = gauge[geidʒ] = standard
The result of the election is the touchstone of the political capability of the party leader.
선거 결과는 정당 지도자의 정치력을 가늠할 수 있는 시금석이다.

tout[taut] v 극구 칭찬하다, 과대 선전하다 = brag about = laud[lɔːd] = praise = show off
The 'Survivor' has been touted as the best movie out of the works by Director James Miller.
영화 '생존자'는 James Miller 감독의 작품 중 최고의 영화로 극찬되었다.

toxic[tɑ́ksik] a 유독성의 = baneful[béinfəl] = harmful = lethal[líːθəl] = noxious[nɑ́kʃəs]
= pernicious[pərníʃəs] = poisonous = venomous[vénəməs] = virulent[vírjulənt]
The police carried out a raid on a factory sending out toxic waste into the river.
경찰은 유독성의 쓰레기를 강으로 내보내는 공장을 급습했다.

tractable[trǽktəbl] a 다루기 쉬운, 유순한, 온순한 = amenable[əmíːnəbl]
= complaisant[kəmpléisnt] = compliant[kəmpláiənt] = docile[dɑ́səl] = manageable
= meek[miːk] = obedient[oubíːdiənt] = pliable[pláiəbl] = submissive[səbmísiv]
The hawk is a more tractable bird you might expect. 매는 생각보다 다루기 쉬운 새이다.

transcend[trænsénd] v 초월하다, 능가하다 = excel = go beyond = outdo = outstrip
= surpass[sərpǽs]
I think marathoners transcend the limits of human power.
나는 마라토너들은 인간 체력의 한계를 초월한다고 생각한다.

transfix[trænsfiks] v 얼어붙게 만들다, 꼼짝 못하게 만들다 = hypnotize[hípnətàiz]
= mesmerize[mézməràiz] = petrify[pétrəfài] = rivet[rívit] = stun[stʌn]
The survivors of the plane crash in the jungle were transfixed by the roars of the lions.
정글에 추락한 비행기의 생존자들은 사자 울음소리에 그 자리에 얼어붙었다.

transgress[trænsgrés] v 위반하다, 어기다, 벗어나다 = contravene[kàntrəví:n]
= infringe[infríndʒ] = sin = trespass[tréspəs] = violate[váiəlèit]
Many immigrants are more likely to transgress the rules and laws of the new country.
많은 이민자들은 새로운 나라의 규칙과 법률을 더 잘 위반하는 것 같다.

QUIZ 118

*Match each word in the first column with its definition in the second column.
Check your answers in the back of the book.*

1.	torpor	a.	contravene = infringe
2.	torrid	b.	tricky
3.	tinker	c.	excel = go beyond
4.	transcend	d.	hypnotize = mesmerize
5.	tortuous	e.	timid = tremulous
6.	timorous	f.	barometer = criterion
7.	transfix	g.	amenable = complaisant
8.	touchstone	h.	dabble = fiddle with
9.	tout	i.	baneful = harmful
10.	thwart	j.	circuitous = convoluted
11.	toxic	k.	arouse = excite
12.	ticklish	l.	denunciation = diatribe
13.	tractable	m.	restorative drink
14.	toil	n.	brag about = laud
15.	transgress	o.	drudge = labor
16.	tonic	p.	foil = frustrate
17.	tirade	q.	arid = parched
18.	torpid	r.	apathy = dormancy
19.	titillate	s.	nominal
20.	titular	t.	inactive = lackadaisical

transient[trǽnʃənt] a 일시적인, 덧없는, 순간적인 = ephemeral[ifémərəl]
= fleeting[flí:tiŋ] = temporary[témpərèri] = transitory[trǽnsətɔ̀:ri,]
The Airport Hotel was full of transient guests due to a series of flight cancellations.
공항 호텔은 연속되는 비행 취소로 인해 일시적인 단기 손님들로 가득 찼다.

translucent[trænslúːsnt] a 반투명의, 비치는 = diaphanous[daiǽfənəs]
Most motorists prefer a translucent glass for the side window of a car.
대부분의 자동차 운전자들은 반투명의 유리를 차창으로 선호한다.

travesty[trǽvəsti] n 희화화, 희극 = burlesque[bəːrlésk] = farce[faːrs]
The black comedy movie is a travesty of the historic tragedy.
블랙코미디 영화는 역사적 비극을 희화화한 것이다.

treacherous[trétʃərəs] a 배신하는, 믿을 수 없는, 불안정한 = disloyal
= perfidious[pərfídiəs] = tricky = unreliable
The tanks were about to cross the treacherous bridge made of wood.
탱크들은 불안정한 나무다리를 막 건너려 했다.

trenchant[tréntʃənt] a 신랄한, 모진, 정통을 찌르는 = acerbic[əsə́ːrbik]
= caustic[kɔ́ːstik] = incisive[insáisiv] = mordant = pungent[pʌ́ndʒənt] = scathing[skéiðiŋ]
The blockbuster movie received a trenchant criticism. 그 대작 영화는 신랄한 비평을 받았다.

trepidation[trèpədéiʃən] n 두려움, 공포 = dread[dred] = fright = horror = panic = terror
I had much trepidation when I first started driving the huge truck.
나는 처음 대형 트럭을 운전할 때 많은 두려움을 가졌다.

trespass[tréspəs] v 침해하다, 무단 침입하다 = encroach[inkróutʃ] = infringe[infríndʒ]
= intrude = invade = misbehave = transgress
The college students trespassed on the orchard of the rich man.
대학생들은 부유한 남자의 과수원에 무단 침입했다.

trickle[tríkl] v 조금씩 흐르다, 똑똑 떨어지다 = dribble[dríbl] = ooze[uːz] = seep
The melted snow trickled down the roof of the traditional house.
녹은 눈은 전통가옥의 지붕을 따라 조금씩 똑똑 떨어졌다.

trite[trait] a 흔해 빠진, 진부한 = banal = bromide = cliché[kliːʃéi] = corny[kɔ́ːrni] = dull =
hackneyed[hǽknid] = pedestrian[pədéstriən] = prosaic[prouzéiik] = run-of-the-mill = vapid[vǽpid]
His presentation full of trite expressions made all the executives disappointed.
진부한 표현으로 가득한 그의 프레젠테이션은 회사의 모든 임원들을 실망시켰다.

triumvirate[traiʌ́mvərit] n 삼두정치 = troika[trɔ́ikə]
The triumvirate has led the empire more than 100 years.
삼두정치는 그 제국을 백년 넘게 이끌었다.

truant[trúːənt] a 꾀부려 쉬는, 결석의, 태만한 = absent[ǽbsənt]
He was accused by his classmates of playing truant.
그는 무단결석을 한다고 학급 친구들에게 욕을 먹었다.

truculent[trʌ́kjulənt] a 반항적인, 호전적인, 싸움을 좋아하는 = bellicose[bélikòus] = belligerent[bəlídʒərənt] = combative = contentious[kənténʃəs] = pugnacious[pʌgnéiʃəs] = warlike
The natives of the island were at first truculent to the missionaries.
섬에 사는 원주민들은 처음에 선교사들에게 호전적이었다.

trudge[trʌdʒ] v 터벅터벅 걷다 = lumber[lʌ́mbər] = plod[plad] = tramp[træmp]
The hunters trudged through the snow along the path.
사냥꾼들은 눈 속 오솔길을 따라 터벅터벅 걸었다.

truncate[trʌ́ŋkeit] v 길이를 줄이다, 짧게 하다 = curtail[kəːrtéil] = cut short = shorten
Due to the tight schedule, he had to truncate his speech.
빠듯한 일정 때문에 그는 연설시간을 줄일 수밖에 없었다.

tryst[trist] n 만날 약속, 밀회, 만남 = rendezvous[rάːndəvùː]
The windmill was used as a place for their tryst. 풍차는 그들의 밀회 장소로 사용되었다.

tumult[tjúːməlt] n 소란, 소동, 반란 = chaos[kéias] = confusion
= disturbance[distəːrbəns] = riot[ráiət] = turmoil[təːrmɔil] = unrest = upheaval[ʌphiːvl]
The tumult of angry farmers spread out of control.
화난 농부들의 소동이 통제할 수 없을 만큼 퍼져 나갔다.

turbid[təːrbid] a 흐린, 탁한 = cloudy = murky
The turbid water was running along the rivers after the flood.
홍수가 난 후에 흐린 물이 강을 따라 흘렀다.

turgid[təːrdʒid] a 부푼, 팽창한, 과장된 = distended = inflated = swollen
His report about the disaster was too turgid to believe.
재난과 관련한 그의 보고는 너무 과장되어서 믿기 어려웠다.

turmoil[təːrmɔil] n 소란, 혼란, 불안 = agitation[ædʒitéiʃən] = bedlam[bédləm]
= commotion[kəmóuʃən] = disturbance[distəːrbəns] = maelstrom[méilstrəm]
= pandemonium[pændəmóuniəm] = riot[ráiət] = ruckus[rʌ́kəs] = tumult[tjúːməlt]
= turbulence[təːrbjuləns] = upheaval[ʌphiːvl]
The slump in property prices caused social and economic turmoil.
부동산 가격 폭락은 사회적 경제적 혼란을 야기시켰다.

turncoat[tɜ:rnkoʊt] n 배신자, 배반자, 변절자 = apostate[əpǽsteit] = betrayer[bitréiər] = defector[difèktər] = renegade[rénigèid] = tergiversator[tə́:rdʒivərsèit] = traitor[tréitər]
He was branded as a turncoat of a drug-smuggling ring.
그는 마약 밀매단에서 변절자로 낙인 찍혔다.

turpitude[tə́:rpətjù:d] n 비열, 야비함, 타락 = baseness = corruption[kərʌ́pʃən] = depravity[diprǽvəti] = vileness = wickedness[wíkidnis]
He was kicked out of the company due to his turpitude. 그는 비열함 때문에 회사에서 쫓겨났다.

typo[táipou] n 오타, 오식 = mistake in typing
There are some typos in the report. 보고서에는 일부 오타가 있다.

QUIZ 119

Match each word in the first column with its definition in the second column. Check your answers in the back of the book.

1.	turbid	a.	curtail=cut short
2.	truncate	b.	burlesque=farce
3.	tryst	c.	bellicose=belligerent
4.	triumvirate	d.	diaphanous
5.	tumult	e.	lumber=plod
6.	truant	f.	banal=bromide
7.	turpitude	g.	ephemeral=fleeting
8.	trite	h.	rendezvous
9.	turmoil	i.	baseness=corruption
10.	truculent	j.	dribble=ooze
11.	trudge	k.	chaos=confusion
12.	trespass	l.	absent
13.	trickle	m.	encroach=infringe
14.	turncoat	n.	cloudy=murky
15.	transient	o.	troika
16.	trepidation	p.	dread=fright
17.	turgid	q.	apostate=betrayer
18.	translucent	r.	mistake in typing
19.	typo	s.	acerbic=caustic
20.	trenchant	t.	disloyal=perfidious
21.	travesty	u.	agitation=bedlam
22.	treacherous	v.	distended=inflated

ubiquitous[juːbíkwətəs] a 편재하는, 어디에서나 존재하는 = ever-present
= everywhere = omnipresent[ɑːmnpreznt]
Wireless technology is ubiquitous in our daily lives.
무선기술은 우리의 일상생활 어디에나 존재한다.

uncanny[ʌnkǽni] a 불가사의한, 신비로운 = mysterious[mistíəriəs] = supernatural
The advanced telescope provides an uncanny sight of the universe.
망원경의 발전은 우주의 신비로운 광경을 볼 수 있게 해준다.

unconscionable[ʌnkɑːnʃənəbl] a 비양심적인, 부도덕한 = immoral[imɔ́ːrəl]
= outrageous[autréidʒəs] = preposterous[pripástərəs] = unethical[ʌnéθikəl] = unfair
= unscrupulous[ʌnskruːpjələs] = wanton
Unconscionable reuse of syringes should be stopped right away.
비양심적인 주사기 재사용은 즉시 중단되어야 한다.

uncouth[ʌnkúːθ] a 거친, 무례한, 상스러운 = coarse[kɔːrs]
The uncouth manners of the host made many guests upset.
주인의 무례한 매너 때문에 많은 손님들이 불쾌해 했다.

unctuous[ʌ́ŋktʃuəs] a 번지르르한, 지나치게 상냥한 = groveling[grʌ́vəliŋ]
= ingratiating[ingréiʃièitiŋ] = obsequious[əbsíːkwiəs] = servile = sycophantic[sìkəfǽntik]
His unctuous way of speaking made some investors doubt his plan.
그의 지나치게 번지르르한 말씀씨 때문에 어떤 투자자가 그의 계획을 의심했다.

underlying[ʌ̀ndərlàiiŋ] a 기초를 이루는, 근원적인, 근본적인 = basic
= fundamental[fʌ̀ndəméntl]
The underlying cause of the ruling party's defeat in the election was a bad economy.
여당의 선거 패배의 근본적인 이유는 좋지 못한 경제 상황이다.

undermine[ʌ̀ndərmain] v 약화시키다, 손상시키다, 쇠퇴시키다 = attenuate[əténjuèit]
= debilitate[dibílətèit] = enfeeble[infíːbl] = impair = sap[sæp] = weaken
The slow response to the infectious disease undermined the authority of the government.
전염병에 늦게 대응한 것이 정부의 권위를 손상시켰다.

underpinning[ʌ́ndərpìniŋ] n 기초, 기반, 밑에서 떠받치는 것 = basis = ground
The high enthusiasm for education has been the underpinnings of the successful development. of the nation.
교육에 대한 높은 열정은 그 나라의 성공적인 발전의 기반이 되었다.

underwrite[ʌndərraɪt] v 서명하다, 인수하다, 승인하다 = approve = endorse[indɔ́:rs]
= sponsor
The city government decided to underwrite the contract to support the building of the new airport.
시 정부는 새로운 공항을 짓는 것을 지원한다는 계약서에 서명했다.

unflappable[ʌnflǽpəbl] a 동요되지 않는, 차분한, 침착한 = collected
= composed[kəmpóuzd]
The captain of the ship was unflappable even when his ship was going down.
선장은 배가 침몰할 때도 동요하지 않았다.

ungainly[ʌngéɪnli] a 보기 흉한, 볼품없는, 어색한 = awkward[ɔ́:kwərd]
= graceless[gréɪslɪs]
His ungainly hat made some guests frown in the wedding ceremony.
그의 보기 흉한 모자는 결혼식에 참석한 일부 하객들로 하여금 인상을 쓰게 만들었다.

unilateral[ju:nɪlǽtrəl] a 일방적인, 단독의 = one-sided
Most workers were opposed to the unilateral decision of the management.
대부분의 근로자들은 경영진의 일방적인 결정에 반대했다.

unkempt[ʌnkémpt] a 헝클어진, 흐트러진, 단정하지 못한 = disheveled[dɪʃévəld]
= scruffy[skrʌ́fi] = slipshod = sloppy[slápi] = slovenly[slʌ́vənli]
Some young girls with unkempt hair were working at the factory.
헝클어진 머리를 한 몇몇 어린 소녀들이 공장에서 일하고 있었다.

unobtrusive[ʌnəbtrú:sɪv] a 삼가는, 겸손한, 주제넘지 않은 = keeping a low profile
= unassuming
The millionaire tried to be as unobtrusive as possible during the press conference.
백만장자는 기자회견 도중에 최대한 겸손하려고 노력했다.

unremitting[ʌnrɪmítɪŋ] a 끊임없는, 끈기 있는, 약화되지 않는 = ceaseless[sí:slɪs]
= constant = continual = incessant[insésnt] = persistent[pərsístənt] = unflagging
His 20 years of unremitting study on the virus led to the development of new vaccine.
그는 이십년간의 끊임없는 바이러스 연구 끝에 새로운 백신을 개발했다.

unruly[ʌnrú:li] a 다루기 힘든, 제어하기 어려운= disobedient[dìsəbí:diənt]
= recalcitrant[rikǽlsitrənt] = wayward[wéɪwərd]
Grandma had a hard time taking care of her unruly two grandchildren.
할머니는 다루기 힘든 두 명의 손주를 돌보느라 애를 먹었다.

unsound[ʌnsaʊnd] a 건전하지 않은, 불합리한, 부적절한 = insecure = unstable
We don't respect a social leader with a unsound mind.
우리는 건전하지 않은 사고방식을 가진 사회지도자를 존경하지 않는다.

unsteady[ʌnstedi] a 불안정한, 불규칙한 = precarious[prikɛ́əriəs] = rickety[ríkiti]
= unstable = wobbly[wábli]
The toddler was unsteady on his feet. 아장아장 걷는 아이가 서 있는 것이 불안했다.

untenable[ʌnténəbl] a 지지할 수 없는, 옹호될 수 없는, 지킬 수 없는 = indefensible
The mayor stuck to his untenable argument of providing all newlywed couples with a house for free.
시장은 모든 신혼부부들에게 무상으로 집을 한 채씩 공급한다는 지킬 수 없는 공약을 고집했다.

untoward[ʌntɔ:rd] a 온당치 못한, 불리한 = improper = inappropriate[ìnəpróupriət]
The famous actor was involved in an untoward scandal.
유명 영화배우가 온당치 못한 스캔들에 관련되었다.

QUIZ 120

Match each word in the first column with its definition in the second column.
Check your answers in the back of the book.

1.	uncouth		a.	improper = inappropriate
2.	untoward		b.	coarse
3.	undermine		c.	immoral = outrageous
4.	unobtrusive		d.	indefensible
5.	unconscionable		e.	awkward = graceless
6.	unkempt		f.	precarious = rickety
7.	ungainly		g.	mysterious = supernatural
8.	unctuous		h.	collected = composed
9.	unilateral		i.	disheveled = scruffy
10.	ubiquitous		j.	ever-present = everywhere
11.	unsound		k.	approve = endorse
12.	uncanny		l.	one-sided
13.	unremitting		m.	insecure = unstable
14.	unruly		n.	basis = ground
15.	underpinning		o.	disobedient = recalcitrant
16.	unsteady		p.	ceaseless = constant
17.	underlying		q.	attenuate = debilitate
18.	underwrite		r.	keeping a low profile = unassuming
19.	untenable		s.	basic = fundamental
20.	unflappable		t.	groveling = ingratiation

unwitting[ʌnwítiŋ] a 자신도 모르는, 무의식적인 = ignorant[íɡnərənt]
= inadvertent[ìnədvə́ːrtnt] = oblivious[əblíviəs] = unconscious = unintentional
A lot of credit card holders have become unwitting victims.
많은 신용카드 소지자가 자신도 모르게 희생자가 된다.

unwonted[ʌnwɔ́ːntid] a 평소와 다른, 특이한, 드문 = atypical[eitípikəl]
= exceptional[iksépʃənl] = unusual
She showed up at the party wearing an unwonted dress.
그녀는 특이한 옷을 입고 파티에 나왔다.

upbraid[ʌpbreɪd] v 비난하다, 나무라다, 꾸짖다 = castigate[kǽstəgèit]
= criticize severely = berate[biréit] = censure[sénʃər] = chastise[tʃæstáiz]
= excoriate[ikskɔ́:rièit] = lambaste[læmbéist] = lash out at = rebuke[ribjú:k]
= reprimand[réprəmænd] = reproach[ripróutʃ] = reprove[riprú:v] = revile[riváil] = scold
= tell off = vilify[víləfài] = vituperate[vaitjú:pərèit]
She upbraided her husband for losing a fortune at the gamble.
그녀는 도박에서 큰 돈을 잃어버린 남편을 나무랐다.

urbane[ə:rbéin] a 세련된, 도시 풍의, 우아한 = civilized = cultured = elegant[éligənt]
= polished[páliʃt] = refined[rifáind] = sophisticated[səfístəkèitid]
Eric is said to be a kind and urbane gentleman.
Eric은 친절한 도시풍의 신사라고 전해진다.

usurp[ju:sə́:rp] v 빼앗다, 찬탈하다 = arrogate[ǽrəgèit] = supplant[səplǽnt]
The greedy uncle usurped the throne from his nephew.
욕심 많은 삼촌은 그의 조카로부터 왕위를 찬탈했다.

usury[jú:ʒəri] n 고리대금업, 고리 = lending money at a high interest rate
Many poor citizens depend on the usury companies.
많은 어려운 사람들이 고리대금업 회사에 의지하고 있다.

utilitarian[jú:tìlətɛ́əriən] a 실용적인, 공리주의의 = down-to-earth = practical
= pragmatic[prægmǽtik] = realistic
More and more people are buying utilitarian cars. 더 많은 사람들이 실용적인 차를 구매 중이다.

utopia[ju:tóupiə] n 이상향, 유토피아 = paradise = Shangri-la[ʃæŋgrilá:]
Some naïve people dream of living in a utopia. 어떤 사람들은 이상향에 사는 것을 꿈꾼다.

QUIZ 121

Match each word in the first column with its definition in the second column.
Check your answers in the back of the book.

1. upbraid
2. urbane
3. utopia
4. unwitting
5. usurp
6. unwonted
7. usury
8. utilitarian

a. down-to-earth = practical
b. civilized = cultured
c. ignorant = inadvertent
d. paradise = Shangri-la
e. castigate = criticize severely
f. atypical = exceptional
g. lending money at a high interest rate
h. arrogate = supplant

vaccinate[væksənèit] v 예방접종을 하다 = immunize[ímjunàiz]
= inoculate[inάkjulèit]
All the residents in the town need to be vaccinated against the new kind of virus.
마을의 모든 주민들은 새로운 바이러스에 대비해 예방접종을 해야 할 필요가 있다.

vacillate[væsəlèit] v 흔들리다, 동요하다, 망설이다 = lurch[lə:rtʃ] = oscillate[άsəlèit]
= stagger[stǽgər] = waver[wéivər] = wobble[wάbl]
The baseball player vacillated between joining the professional team and going to a university.
그 야구선수는 프로팀으로 갈지 대학으로 진학할지 흔들렸다.

vacuous[vækjuəs] a 빈, 공허한, 얼빠진 = empty = vacant[véikənt] = void[vɔid]
His emphasis on the protection of the environment became a vacuous echo.
환경보호를 위한 그의 주장은 공허한 메아리가 되었다.

vagary[vəgέəri] n 변덕, 예측불허의 변화 = caprice[kəprí:s] = quirk[kwə:rk]
= whim[hwim]
People on the southernmost island were always ready for the vagaries of the weather.
최남단 섬에 사는 사람들은 항상 예측불허의 날씨에 대비했다.

vagrant[véigrənt] n 부랑자, 방랑자 = itinerant[aitínərənt]
A lot of vagrants are likely to stay around train stations in the city.
많은 부랑자들이 도시의 기차역 부근에 거주하는 듯하다.

vague[veig] a 모호한, 애매한, 희미한 = ambiguous[æmbígjuəs] = equivocal[ikwívəkəl]
= nebulous[nébjuləs] = obscure[əbskjúər]
You should not use vague terms in the business contract.
사업계약서에 모호한 용어를 써서는 안 된다.

valiant[væljənt] a 용맹한, 단호한 = brave = gallant[gǽlənt] = guts = intrepid[intrépid]
= plucky[plʌki]
The 200 valiant warriors are said to have defended the castle.
이백명의 용맹한 전사들이 그 성을 방어했다고 한다.

vanish[væniʃ] v 사라지다, 자취를 감추다 = disappear
The UFO vanished from our sight in less than a second in the sky.
상공에 있던 UFO는 일초도 안 되는 사이에 우리 시야에서 사라졌다.

vanquish[vǽŋkwiʃ] v 정복하다, 항복시키다, 완파하다 = conquer[káŋkər] = crush = quell[kwel] = rout[raut] = subdue[səbdjúː] = subjugate[sʌ́bdʒugèit]
The ancient Japanese leader dispatched a lot of troops to vanquish the Korean peninsula.
고대 일본의 지도자는 한반도를 정복하기 위해서 많은 군대를 파병했다.

vapid[vǽpid] a 김 빠진, 지루한, 활기 없는 = bland = boring = dull = insipid[insípid] = stale = tedious[tíːdiəs] = trite[trait]
His proposal to find an alternative fuel sounded vapid.
대체 연료를 찾겠다는 그의 제안은 김이 빠진 것처럼 들렸다.

vapor[véipər] n 증기 = steam
We could see the vapor coming from each hot spring in the hot-spring town.
우리는 온천마을의 각 온천에서 증기가 나오는 걸 볼 수 있었다.

variable[vɛ́əriəbl] a 변동이 심한, 변화하는 = changeable = fickle[fíkl] = volatile[válətil]
The variable oil price has a considerable effect on the world economy.
변동이 심한 오일 가격은 전 세계 경제에 상당한 영향을 주었다.

variegate[vɛ́əriəgèit] v 변화를 주다, 다양 하게하다 = alter = change
We need to variegate some rules of sports games to attract more fans.
더 많은 팬들을 끌어오기 위해서는 일부 스포츠 경기의 규칙을 다양하게 할 필요가 있다.

vault[vɔːlt] n 금고, 귀중품 보관실 = safe
The thieves tried to open the bank vault in the basement.
도둑들은 지하의 은행금고를 열려고 했다.

vaunt[vɔːnt] v 자랑하다, 뽐내다 = boast[boust] = brag = flaunt[flɔːnt]
The ex-president vaunted his achievements during his 5-year tenure.
전직 대통령은 오년간의 임기 중에 달성한 업적을 자랑했다.

veer[viər] v 방향을 바꾸다, 바뀌다 = divert[divə́ːrt] = shift
The huge tornado is forecasted to veer away from the populous town.
거대한 토네이도는 인구가 많은 마을을 비껴갈 것으로 예상된다.

vehement[víːəmənt] a 열정적인, 맹렬한 = ardent[áːrdnt] = avid = enthusiastic[inθùːziǽstik] = fervent[fə́ːrvənt] = fervid[fə́ːrvid] = passionate[pǽʃənət] = zealous[zéləs]
Some voters are looking forward to watching a vehement debate among the candidates.
일부 유권자들은 후보자들 간의 열정적인 토론을 보기를 기대하고 있다.

venal[ví:nl] a 매수되는, 돈으로 좌우되는, 부패한 = bribable
They say that the victory of the soccer game was won by venal referees.
축구 경기의 승리는 돈으로 매수된 심판에 의해서 얻어진 것이라고 그들은 말한다.

veneer[vəníər] n 겉치레, 겉치장, 허식 = exterior[ikstíəriər]
The vicious enterpriser has acted under the veneer of charity.
사악한 기업가는 자선을 겉치레로 포장했다.

venial[ví:niəl] a 용서받을 수 있는, 죄가 가벼운, 사소한 = excusable[ikskjú:zəbl]
= forgivable[fərgívəbl] = pardonable[pá:rdənəbl]
Murder is never a venial sin.
살인은 결코 용서받을 수 있는 범죄가 아니다.

QUIZ 122

Match each word in the first column with its definition in the second column.
Check your answers in the back of the book.

1.	vanish	a.	lurch = oscillate
2.	vehement	b.	empty = vacant
3.	vanquish	c.	safe
4.	vaccinate	d.	immunize = inoculate
5.	venal	e.	steam
6.	vapid	f.	excusable = forgivable
7.	vapor	g.	alter = change
8.	vacillate	h.	exterior
9.	variable	i.	bland = boring
10.	variegate	j.	changeable = fickle
11.	vault	k.	bribable
12.	vacuous	l.	conquer = crush
13.	vaunt	m.	divert = shift
14.	veer	n.	boast = brag
15.	vagary	o.	disappear
16.	veneer	p.	ardent = avid
17.	vagrant	q.	caprice = quirk
18.	venial	r.	brave = gallant
19.	vague	s.	ambiguous = equivocal
20.	valiant	t.	itinerant

venerate[vénərèit] v 존경하다, 숭배하다, 경모하다 = adore[ədɔ́ːr] = hallow[hǽlou] = honor[ánər] = respect = revere[rivíər] = worship[wɔ́ːrʃip]
There are a lot of people in the world who venerated Steve Jobs.
전 세계에 Steve Jobs를 존경한 많은 사람들이 있다.

veracity[vərǽsəti] n 진실성, 정직, 정확성 = truth = authenticity[ɔ̀ːθentísəti] = credibility[krèdəbíləti] = probity[próubəti] = rectitude[réktitjùːd] = sincerity[sinsérəti]
A lot of people questioned the veracity of his apology.
많은 사람들이 그가 한 사죄의 진실성에 대해서 의심스러워했다.

verbose[vəːrbóus] a 말수가 많은, 수다스러운, 장황한 = babbling[bǽbliŋ] = chatty[tʃǽti] = garrulous[gǽrələs] = loquacious[loukwéiʃəs] = prolix[proulíks] = voluble[váluəbl] = wordy[wɔ́ːrdi]
The verbose politician never rejects to participate in the TV debate program.
말수가 많은 정치인은 TV 대담 프로그램 참가를 절대 거부하지 않는다.

verdant[vəːrdnt] a 신록의, 초록의, 젊은 = grassy[grǽsi] = green = lush[lʌʃ]
Above the horizon unfolded an endless verdant field before the eyes of the travelers.
지평선 위로 여행자들의 눈 앞에 끝없는 신록의 들판이 펼쳐졌다.

verge[vəːrdʒ] n 가장자리, 경계, 변두리 = brink = edge[edʒ]
The cruise ship was on the verge of sinking. 유람선은 침몰 직전에 있었다.

verify[vérəfài] v 증명하다, 입증하다, 확인하다 = confirm[kənfɔ́ːrm] = corroborate[kərábərèit]
A group of art experts wanted to verify the authenticity of the painting.
일단의 예술 전문가들이 그 그림의 진위 여부를 밝히길 원했다.

verisimilitude[vèrəsimílətjùːd] n 정말같음, 있을법함, 진실인듯함 = authenticity[ɔ̀ːθentísəti] = plausibility[plɔ̀ːzəbíləti] = semblance[sémbləns]
The verisimilitude of the battle scene in the movie attracted more moviegoers.
영화의 사실적인 전투장면이 관객들을 더 불러모았다.

verity[vérəti] n 진실, 진실성 = truth = veracity[vərǽsəti]
Some people doubt the verity of the government's announcement about UFO.
어떤 사람들은 UFO에 대한 정부 발표의 진실성을 의심한다.

vernacular[vərnǽkjulər] a 그 지역 언어의 = indigenous[indídʒənəs] = native
The people on the island use their own vernacular language.
섬에 사는 사람들은 고유의 언어를 사용한다.

vertigo[vɔ́:rtigòu] n 현기, 어지러움, 혼란 = dizziness[dízinis] = giddiness[gídinis]
She sometimes suffers from vertigo when she travels by air.
그녀는 비행기 여행을 할 때 때때로 현기증으로 고생한다.

verve[və:rv] n 열정, 힘, 활기 = pep = vigor[vígər] = zeal[zi:l] = zest[zest]
The circus members showed a performance of verve and energy.
서커스 단원들은 열정과 활력이 가득한 공연을 보여줬다.

vestige[véstidʒ] n 흔적, 자취, 유물 = relic[rélik] = remnant[rémnənt]
= residue[rézədjù:] = track[træk]
After 3 years of reconstruction, there were no vestiges of earthquake in the city.
삼년간의 재건설을 마친 도시에는 지진의 흔적이 없어졌다.

veto[ví:tou] v 거부하다, 기각시키다 = reject = turn down
The president was strongly asked by the Rifle Association to veto the bill from the Congress.
대통령은 총기연합회로부터 의회에서 올라온 법안을 기각시키라는 강력한 요청을 받았다.

vex[veks] v 성가시게 하다, 귀찮게 하다, 화나게 하다 = afflict[əflíkt] = annoy
= beleaguer[bilí:gər] = bother = distress = exasperate[igzǽspərèit] = gall[gɔ:l] = gnaw[nɔ:]
= infuriate[infjúərièit] = irk[ə:rk] = irritate[írətèit] = pester = peeve = plague[pleig] = rile[rail]
The noise music practice by a musician at night vexed his neighbors.
음악가가 내는 시끄러운 소음은 밤새도록 그의 이웃들을 성가시게 했다.

viable[váiəbl] a 실행 가능한, 생존 가능한, 생육할 수 있는 = applicable[ǽplikəbl]
= feasible[fí:zəbl] = practicable = workable
The government tries to come up with a viable solution to the unemployment problem.
정부는 실업 문제에 대해 실행 가능한 해결책을 내놓으려고 한다.

vibrant[váibrənt] a 활기찬, 생기가 넘치는, 힘찬 = dynamic = vigorous[vígərəs] = vital
Shanghai is a city vibrant with life. 상하이는 활기가 넘치는 도시이다.

vicarious[vaikɛ́əriəs] a 대리의, 자기도 같은 경험을 하는 듯이 느끼는 = by proxy
= surrogate[sə́:rəgèit]
She got a vicarious pleasure from watching her daughter growing up to be a great pianist.
그녀는 딸이 위대한 피아노 연주자가 되는 것을 보면서 대리 만족을 얻었다.

vicissitude[visísətjùːd] n 변천, 부침, 우여곡절 = cataclysm[kǽtəklìzm] = upheaval[ʌphíːvl]
The billionaire has experienced many vicissitudes in his life.
억만장자는 인생에서 많은 우여곡절을 겪었다.

vie[vai] v 우열을 다투다, 겨루다 = compete[kəmpíːt] = contend[kənténd]
The swimmer will vie with his Korean rival for the gold medal.
수영선수는 금메달을 놓고 한국의 라이벌과 우열을 다툴 것이다.

vigilant[vídʒələnt] a 방심하지 않는, 경계하고 있는, 방심 않는 = alert[əláːrt]
= attentive = careful = cautious[kɔ́ːʃəs] = circumspect[sə́ːrkəmspèkt] = observant[əbzə́ːrvənt]
= wary[wɛ́əri] = watchful
Soldiers in the conflict areas should remain vigilant at night.
분쟁지역의 군인들은 야간에 경계태세를 유지해야 한다.

QUIZ 123

Match each word in the first column with its definition in the second column.
Check your answers in the back of the book.

1.	venerate	a.	afflict = annoy
2.	viable	b.	applicable = feasible
3.	vibrant	c.	indigenous = native
4.	verify	d.	babbling = chatty
5.	verisimilitude	e.	alert = attentive
6.	verve	f.	compete = contend
7.	vestige	g.	truth = authenticity
8.	veracity	h.	cataclysm = upheaval
9.	vigilant	i.	by proxy = surrogate
10.	veto	j.	adore = hallow
11.	verdant	k.	truth = veracity
12.	verge	l.	dynamic = vigorous
13.	verbose	m.	dizziness = giddiness
14.	vex	n.	grassy = green
15.	verity	o.	reject = turn down
16.	vicarious	p.	pep = vigor
17.	vernacular	q.	brink = edge
18.	vicissitude	r.	relic = remnant
19.	vertigo	s.	confirm = corroborate
20.	vie	t.	authenticity = plausibility

vilify[víləfài] v 비방하다, 헐뜯다, 중상하다 = asperse[əspə́:rs] = berate[biréit]
= calumniate[kəlʌ́mnièit] = censure = decry[dikrái] = defame = denigrate[dénigrèit]
= denounce[dináuns] = disparage[dispǽridʒ] = libel[láibəl] = malign[məláin] = revile
= slander = slur[slə:r] = traduce[trədjú:s] = vituperate[vaitjú:pərèit]
The mayor was vilified by civic groups for developing the green belt area.
시장은 그린벨트 구역을 개발한다고 시민단체로부터 비난을 받았다.

vigor[vígər] n 활력, 활기, 박력 = energy = power
The soccer players were full of vigor in the final. 결승전에서 그 축구선수들은 활기가 넘쳤다.

vim[vim] n 정력, 활력 = enthusiasm[inθú:ziæzm]
The CEO of the company is filled with vim, which has made his company grow faster.
회사의 대표이사는 활기로 가득 찬 사람으로, 이것이 그의 회사가 빠르게 성장하는 원인이 되고 있다.

vindicate[víndəkèit] v 정당성을 입증하다, 옳음을 밝히다, 비난을 풀다 = defend
= disprove = justify[dʒʌ́stəfài] = prove one's innocence
The police arrested the real criminal, which vindicated his innocence.
경찰이 진짜 범인을 체포함으로써 그의 무죄가 입증되었다.

vindictive[vindíktiv] a 앙심을 품은, 보복하려는 = rancorous[rǽŋkərəs] = retaliatory
= revengeful[rivéndʒfəl] = spiteful[spáitfəl] = unforgiving
Armed rebels were preparing vindictive attacks on the government forces.
무장한 반란군들은 정부군에 대한 보복공격을 준비하고 있었다.

virtuoso[və̀:rtʃuóusou] n 거장, 대가 = musician
The conductor used to be a piano virtuoso. 그 지휘자는 과거에 피아노 거장이었다.

virtuous[və́:rtʃuəs] a 덕 있는, 고결한, 도덕적인 = ethical[éθikəl] = honorable[ánərəbl]
The retired professor has been living a virtuous life, teaching children from poor families for free.
은퇴한 교수는 어려운 환경의 아이들을 무상으로 가르치면서 고결한 삶을 살고 있다.

virulent[vírjulənt] a 유독한, 악성의 = baneful[béinfəl] = deadly = fatal[féitl]
= lethal[lí:θəl] = malignant[məlígnənt] = poisonous[pɔ́izənəs] = pernicious[pərníʃəs]
= venomous[vénəməs]
He has been hospitalized for a month because of a virulent infection.
그는 악성 전염병 때문에 한 달간 병원에 입원해 있다.

viscous[vískəs] a 점착성의, 끈적거리는, 점성이 있는 = gluey[glú:i] = sticky
There were a few viscous tapes hanging in the middle of the ceiling to catch mosquito.
모기를 잡기 위해서 천장 가운데에 몇 개의 점착성 테이프들이 매달려 있었다.

visionary[víʒənèri] n 비전의 소유자, 선지자, 예언가 = dreamer = idealist
The great CEO will be remembered as a visionary in the IT technology.
그 위대한 CEO는 IT산업계에서 선지자로 기억될 것이다.

vitiate[víʃièit] v 가치를 떨어뜨리다, 해치다 = besmirch[bismə́:rtʃ] = blemis[blémiʃ]
= corrupt[kərʌ́pt] = debase[dibéis] = defile[difáil] = deprave[dipréiv]
= deteriorate[ditíəriərèit] = hurt = impair[impέər] = mar = spoil = sully[sʌ́li] = taint[teint]
= tarnish[tá:rniʃ]
The SF movie was vitiated by the poor computer graphic technology.
그 SF 영화는 엉성한 CG 기술 때문에 가치가 떨어졌다.

vitriolic[vìtriálik] a 독설에 찬, 신랄한, 통렬한 = acerbic[əsə́:rbik] = bitter
= caustic[kɔ́:stik] = scathing[skéiðiŋ]
The unemployed and low-income bracket were crazy about the vitriolic speech of the politician.
실업자들과 저소득층 사람들은 그 정치인의 통렬한 연설에 열광했다.

vituperate[vaitjú:pərèit] v 헐뜯다, 비난하다, 매도하다 = accuse[əkjú:z] = blame
= castigate[kǽstəgèit] = censure[sénʃər] = condemn[kəndém] = criticize[krítəsàiz]
= decry[dikrái] = denounce[dináuns] = excoriate[ikskɔ́:rièit] = impeach[impí:tʃ]
= impugn[impjú:n] = rebuke[ribjú:k] = reprehend[rèprihénd] = reprimand[réprəmænd]
= reproach[ripróutʃ] = reprobate[réprəbèit] =reprove[riprú:v] = revile[riváil] = scold[skould]
= upbraid = vilify[víləfài]
He has been vituperated for his reckless M&A business deals.
그는 무모한 기업 인수합병 거래로 인해 비난을 당해왔다.

vivacious[vivéiʃəs] a 생기가 넘치는, 명랑한, 쾌활한 = active = animate = cheerful
= ebullient[ibʌ́ljənt] = effervescent[èfərvésnt] = exuberant[igzú:bərənt] = lively
= sparkling[spá:rkliŋ] = vibrant[váibrənt]
His vivacious daughter has grown up to be a famous singer.
그의 생기 넘치는 딸은 마침내 유명한 가수로 자랐다.

vocation[voukéiʃən] n 천직, 소명 = calling = occupation[àkjupéiʃən] = profession
He thought of firefighting as his vocation. 그는 소방직을 천직으로 생각했다.

vociferous[vousífərəs] a 큰 소리로 외치는, 소리 높은 = boisterous[bɔ́istərəs] = clamant[kléimənt] = clamorous[klǽmərəs] = loud =obstreperous[əbstrépərəs]
Most residents were vociferous in their opposition to building a casino complex in the neighborhood.
대부분의 시민들은 동네에 카지노 복합건물을 짓는 것에 대해 반대 목소리를 높였다.

vogue[voug] n 유행 = fad = trend
Fur boots are in vogue this winter. 털 부츠가 이번 겨울에 유행이다.

void[vɔid] v 무효로 하다, 취소하다 = abrogate[ǽbrəgèit] = annul[ənʌ́l] = invalidate[invǽlədèit] = nullify[nʌ́ləfài] = rescind[risínd]
The supplier and buyer agreed to void the exclusive sales contract.
공급자와 구매자는 독점 매매 계약서를 무효로 하기로 했다.

volatile[vάlətil] a 휘발성의, 불안정한, 변덕스런 = capricious[kəpríʃəs] = changeable = erratic[irǽtik] = fickle[fíkl] = variable
The price of the plane ticket can be volatile when the oil price is not stable.
오일 가격이 안정상태를 유지하지 않을 때는 비행기표의 가격이 불안정하다.

volition[voulíʃən] n 자유의지, 결단력 = determination[ditə̀ːrmənéiʃən] = resolution
The climber left for the summit of the mountain to save his college on his own volition.
등반가는 그의 자유의지에 따라 동료를 구하기 위해 산 정상으로 떠났다.

\

QUIZ 124

*Match each word in the first column with its definition in the second column.
Check your answers in the back of the book.*

1.	vitriolic	a.	accuse = blame
2.	vitiate	b.	acerbic = bitter
3.	vociferous	c.	besmirch = blemish
4.	vilify	d.	active = animate
5.	vituperate	e.	capricious = changeable
6.	vindictive	f.	asperse = berate
7.	vocation	g.	abrogate = annul
8.	virtuoso	h.	dreamer = idealist
9.	vigor	i.	energy = power
10.	vivacious	j.	determination = resolution
11.	vim	k.	fad = trend
12.	vogue	l.	gluey = sticky
13.	void	m.	baneful = deadly
14.	vindicate	n.	enthusiasm
15.	volatile	o.	boisterous = clamant
16.	volition	p.	ethical = honorable
17.	virtuous	q.	defend = disprove
18.	visionary	r.	calling = occupation
19.	virulent	s.	musician
20.	viscous	t.	rancorous = retaliatory

voluble[vǽluəbl] a 달변의, 입심 좋은, 열변을 토하는 = chatty[tʃǽti] = fluent[flúːənt]
= loquacious[loukwéiʃəs] = talkative
The voluble sport star has become popular after his appearance on the TV talk show.
입심 좋은 스포츠 스타는 TV 토크쇼에 출연한 이후 인기를 얻게 되었다.

voluminous[vəlúːmənəs] a 방대한, 권수가 많은, 다량의 = ample[ǽmpl]
= copious[kóupiəs] = extensive = vast
Voluminous evidence was submitted to the prosecution to prove his innocence.
그의 무죄를 증명하기 위해서 방대한 증거가 검찰에 제출되었다.

voluptuous[vəlʌptʃuəs] a 관능적인, 육감적인, 향락적인 = hedonistic[hì:dənístik]
= salacious[səléiʃəs] = sensuous[sénʃuəs] = sybaritic[sìbərítik]
The lady in the bar looked extremely voluptuous in her red dress.
붉은 드레스를 입은 술집의 그 여인은 매우 관능적으로 보였다.

voracious[vɔ:réiʃəs] a 게걸스러운, 탐욕적인 = avaricious[ævəríʃəs]
= gluttonous[glʌtənəs] = greedy = insatiable[inséiʃəbl] = rapacious[rəpéiʃəs]
= ravenous[rǽvənəs]
The businessman has a voracious appetite for the expansion of his business.
사업가는 사업의 확장에 게걸스러운 욕망을 가지고 있다.

votary[vóutəri] n 신봉자, 애호가 = adherent[ədhí:ərənt] = admirer[ædmáiərər]
= believer = follower = devotee
He has become a votary of the new religion. 그는 신흥종교의 신봉자가 되었다.

vulgar[vʌlgər] a 저속한, 천박한, 상스러운 = boorish[búəriʃ] = indecent[indí:snt]
= ribald[ríbəld]
He sometimes used some vulgar words during the conversation.
그는 때때로 대화 도중에 약간 저속한 언어를 사용했다.

QUIZ 123

Match each word in the first column with its definition in the second column.
Check your answers in the back of the book.

1.	vulgar	a.	ample = copious
2.	voluble	b.	chatty = fluent
3.	votary	c.	adherent = admirer
4.	voluminous	d.	boorish = indecent
5.	voluptuous	e.	avaricious = gluttonous
6.	voracious	f.	hedonistic = salacious

waft[wæft] v 떠돌게 하다, 떠돌다, 퍼지다 = carry = drift[drift] = float[flout]
The smells of bread wafted on the wind from the nearby bakery.
근처 빵 가게에서 나는 빵 냄새가 바람에 떠돌았다.

waive[weiv] v 포기하다, 삼가다, 보류하다 = abandon[əbǽndən] = give up = renounce[rináuns]
The debtor was forced to waive his property rights.
그 채무자는 그의 재산권을 포기하도록 강요받았다.

wake[weik] n 배가 지나간 자국, 항적(航跡); (물체가) 지나간 자국 = aftermath
A lot of people were carried to hospitals in the wake of the earthquake.
지진에 뒤이어 많은 사람들이 병원으로 실려갔다.

wan[wan] a 핏기 없는, 창백한 = pale[peil]
The girl, who is scheduled to have heart surgery, looked wan and weak.
심장병 수술을 예약한 그 소녀는 핏기가 없고 약해 보였다.

wane[wein] v 쇠퇴하다, 약해지다, 줄어지다, 이지러지다 = abate[əbéit] = decrease
= diminish = dwindle[dwíndl] = ebb[eb] = shrink[ʃriŋk] = weaken = wither[wíðər]
Korea's dependence on exports to China has been waning these days.
요즘 한국의 대중국 수출 의존도는 약해지고 있다.

wanton[wɑ́ntən] a 이유 없이 고의적인, 악의적인, 부당한 = unscrupulous = wayward[wéiwərd]
Wanton crimes are likely to become rampant when the economy is bad.
경제가 어려운 때 이유 없는 악의적인 범죄가 성행하는 경향이 있다.

watershed[wɔ:tərʃed] n 분수령, 중대한 분기점 = turning point
Her marriage to the ambitious general became a watershed in her life.
야망이 큰 군인과의 결혼은 그녀의 인생에서 분수령이 되었다.

wary[wɛ́əri] a 경계하고 있는, 조심하는, 신중한 = careful = cautious[kɔ́:ʃəs]
= circumspect[sə́:rkəmspèkt] = leery[líəri] = vigilant[vídʒələnt] = watchful
The actor has been wary of getting involved in any kind of scandal.
배우는 어떤 종류의 스캔들에도 연루되지 않으려고 경계하고 있다.

waver[wéivər] v 흔들리다, 약해지다, 망설이다 = oscillate[ɑ́səlèit] = quiver[kwívər]
= sway[swei] = vacillate[vǽsəlèit] = wobble[wɑ́bl]
His determination to quit drinking began to waver.
술을 끊겠다는 그의 결심은 흔들리기 시작했다.

waylay[weɪleɪ] v 잠복하여 습격하다, 숨어서 기다리다, 매복하다 = ambush[ǽmbuʃ]
The French army waylaid its enemy after waiting for 2 days.
프랑스군은 이틀을 기다린 후에 적군을 매복 공격했다.

weary[wíəri] a 지친, 피곤한, 싫증나는 = exhausted[igzɔ́:stid] = fatigued[fətí:gd] = jaded[dʒéidid]
All the travelers felt weary after walking along the entire island.
모든 여행객들은 섬 전체를 걷고 나서 피곤함을 느꼈다.

wheedle[hwí:dl] v 구슬리다, 꾀다 = cajole[kədʒóul] = coax[kouks] = inveigle[invéigl]
The swindlers wheedled innocent old people into buying the fake health foods.
사기꾼들은 순진한 노인들을 구슬려서 가짜 건강제품을 사게 했다.

whim[hwim] n 변덕, 일시적 기분, 종잡을 수 없는 생각 = caprice[kəprí:s] = quirk[kwə:rk] = vagary[vəgéəri]
She bought the designer brand bag on a whim.
그녀는 일시적 기분에 의해서 명품 브랜드 가방을 샀다.

wholesome[hóulsəm] a 건강에 좋은, 건전한, 유익한 = healthful = nutritious[nju:tríʃəs] = salubrious[səlú:briəs] = salutary[sǽljutèri]
The French restaurant uses only fresh and wholesome ingredients.
그 프랑스 식당은 신선하고 건강에 좋은 재료만 사용한다.

willful[wílfəl] a 계획적인, 의도적인, 옹고집의 = deliberate[dilíbərət] = intentional = premediated = purposeful
The player was given a yellow card for his willful foul during the game.
선수는 경기 도중 의도적인 반칙으로 경고를 받았다.

windbag[wɪndbæg] n 수다쟁이, 떠버리 = bigmouth
The great boxer was such a windbag. 위대한 복서는 대단한 떠버리였다.

wistful[wístfəl] a 탐나는 듯한, 아쉬워하는, 생각에 잠긴 = longing = wishful
A girl from the countryside looked with wistful eyes at the beautiful dress.
시골서 온 한 소녀가 예쁜 옷을 탐나는 듯이 쳐다보았다.

wither[wíðər] v 시들다, 활기를 잃다, 위축시키다 = dry = languish[lǽŋgwiʃ] = shrivel[ʃrívəl]
The long period of drought made most flowers and plants wither in the grassland.
장기간의 가뭄이 목초지에 있는 대부분의 꽃과 식물들을 시들게 했다.

wizened[wíznd] a 시든, 쭈글쭈글한, 주름투성이의 = dried = shriveled[ʃrívld] up = withered[wíðərd] = wrinkled[ríŋkld]
The wizened old man was smoking in the real estate agency.
주름살이 많은 노인이 부동산 사무실에서 담배를 피우고 있었다.

woe[wou] n 고민, 고통, 비통, 비애 = adversity[ædvə́ːrsəti] = affliction[əflíkʃən] = agony[ǽgəni] = anguish[ǽŋgwiʃ] = hardship
Most young couples in the cities are suffering from financial woes.
도시에 사는 대부분의 젊은 부부들은 경제적 고통을 겪고 있다.

wrath[ræθ] n 분노, 격노 = exasperation[igzæspəréiʃən] = indignation[ìndignéiʃən] = rage[reidʒ]
A conspiracy against the king led to the wrath of the king.
역적모의는 왕의 분노를 불러일으켰다.

wry[rai] a 뒤틀린, 찡그린, 심술궂은 = distorted[distɔ́ːrtid] = warped[wɔːrpt]
She made a wry face when she encountered her ex-husband in the hallway.
복도에서 전남편을 우연히 만났을 때 그녀는 얼굴을 찡그렸다.

QUIZ 126

Match each word in the first column with its definition in the second column.
Check your answers in the back of the book.

1.	wane		a.	careful = cautious
2.	wanton		b.	dried = shriveled
3.	watershed		c.	longing = wishful
4.	waver		d.	cajole = coax
5.	wary		e.	deliberate = intentional
6.	waft		f.	carry = drift
7.	wistful		g.	bigmouth
8.	wizened		h.	exhausted = fatigued
9.	woe		i.	adversity = affliction
10.	waive		j.	ambush
11.	wrath		k.	healthful = nutritious
12.	waylay		l.	abandon = give up
13.	wake		m.	oscillate = quiver
14.	wry		n.	distorted = warped
15.	weary		o.	exasperation = indignation
16.	wan		p.	turning point
17.	windbag		q.	aftermath
18.	wheedle		r.	caprice = quirk
19.	wither		s.	unscrupulous = wayward
20.	whim		t.	dry = languish

yield[ji:ld] v 산출하다, 생산하다, 낳다 = generate[dʒénərèit] = produce
The soil along the river yields a rich harvest of apples.
강 유역의 그 땅에서는 사과가 풍성하게 난다.

yoke[jouk] n 멍에, 속박, 지배 = bondage[bándidʒ]
The natives spent their whole lives living under the yoke of the invaders.
원주민들은 한평생 침략자들의 멍에 아래에서 살았다.

zealot[zélət] n 열광자, 광신자, 열중하는 사람 = enthusiast[inθú:ziæst]
= maniac[méiniæk]
Some zealots donated all their fortune to the leader of the new religion.
일부 광신자들은 그들의 모든 재산을 신흥 종교지도자에게 기부했다.

zealous[zéləs] a 열성적인, 열광적인, 열심인 = ardent[á:rdnt] = avid[ǽvid]
= enthusiastic[inθù:ziǽstik] = fervent[fə́:rvənt] = fervid[fə́:rvid] = passionate[pǽʃənət]
No one was more zealous than Mark in collecting ancient paintings.
고대 그림 수집에 있어서 Mark보다 열심인 사람은 없었다.

zeitgeist[tsáitgàist] n 시대 정신, 시대사조 = spirit of the time
The so called 'shared growth' has become the new zeitgeist of the current society.
소위 '동반성장'은 현 사회의 새로운 시대정신이 되었다.

zenith[zí:niθ] n 절정, 천장, 정상 = acme[ǽkmi] = apex[éipeks]
= culmination[kʌlmənéiʃən] = peak = pinnacle[pínəkl] = summit = vertex[və́:rteks]
George was at the zenith of his job career.
George는 직장생활에서 정상에 서 있었다.

QUIZ 127

*Match each word in the first column with its definition in the second column.
Check your answers in the back of the book.*

1.	yoke		a.	sprit of the time
2.	zealous		b.	bondage
3.	yield		c.	acme = apex
4.	zenith		d.	generate = produce
5.	zealot		e.	ardent = avid
6.	zeitgeist		f.	enthusiast = maniac

QUIZ Answer

Quiz 1
1–r 2–b 3–j 4–e 5–d 6–q 7–a 8–p 9–f 10–g 11–o 12–k 13–h 14–i 15–t 16–m 17–l 18–s 19–n 20–c

Quiz 2
1–b 2–a 3–s 4–j 5–h 6–g 7–m 8–o 9–d 10–c 11–q 12–r 13–f 14–e 15–n 16–t 17–i 18–l 19–p 20–k

Quiz 3
1–t 2–h 3–i 4–d 5–j 6–p 7–q 8–m 9–c 10–o 11–r 12–s 13–e 14–n 15–l 16–a 17–g 18–k 19–b 20–f

Quiz 4
1–l 2–o 3–f 4–k 5–t 6–d 7–s 8–m 9–a 10–r 11–j 12–n 13–p 14–q 15–h 16–c 17–e 18–i 19–b 20–g

Quiz 5
1–h 2–j 3–e 4–f 5–t 6–s 7–a 8–q 9–p 10–m 11–i 12–d 13–n 14–b 15–g 16–c 17–o 18–r 19–k 20–l

Quiz 6
1–q 2–j 3–r 4–l 5–k 6–f 7–o 8–g 9–i 10–p 11–c 12–b 13–s 14–h 15–a 16–n 17–m 18–t 19–d 20–e

Quiz 7
1–l 2–m 3–p 4–f 5–i 6–b 7–e 8–h 9–q 10–k 11–n 12–r 13–t 14–d 15–c 16–j 17–o 18–a 19–g 20–s

Quiz 8
1–e 2–f 3–j 4–s 5–m 6–q 7–a 8–g 9–t 10–o 11–d 12–n 13–c 14–r 15–l 16–h 17–p 18–b 19–k 20–i

Quiz 9
1–j 2–a 3–k 4–o 5–p 6–m 7–i 8–d 9–s 10–e 11–r 12–l 13–g 14–f 15–t 16–q 17–b 18–h 19–c 20–n

Quiz 10
1–e 2–t 3–a 4–h 5–g 6–n 7–c 8–r 9–f 10–j 11–p 12–m 13–o 14–s 15–l 16–b 17–d 18–i 19–k 20–q

Quiz 11
1–l 2–p 3–c 4–a 5–j 6–e 7–k 8–m 9–o 10–i 11–f 12–t 13–d 14–b 15–s 16–r 17–q 18–h 19–g 20–n

Quiz 12
1–a 2–i 3–n 4–g 5–b 6–h 7–j 8–s 9–k 10–f 11–o 12–t 13–d 14–c 15–p 16–e 17–q 18–r 19–l 20–m

Quiz 13
1–a 2–d 3–c 4–b 5–e 6–f

Quiz 14
1–j 2–d 3–l 4–i 5–a 6–c 7–t 8–b 9–f 10–s 11–n 12–m 13–o 14–h 15–r 16–e 17–g 18–q 19–p 20–k

Quiz 15
1–f 2–t 3–i 4–l 5–n 6–g 7–b 8–q 9–j 10–d 11–p 12–r 13–h 14–s 15–o 16–e 17–k 18–m 19–a 20–c

Quiz 16
1–n 2–d 3–f 4–j 5–q 6–a 7–b 8–r 9–e 10–g 11–c 12–k 13–l 14–s 15–h 16–m 17–t 18–o 19–i 20–p

Quiz 17
1–e 2–q 3–m 4–t 5–j 6–k 7–c 8–b 9–i 10–l 11–p 12–g 13–f 14–r 15–h 16–s 17–d 18–n 19–o 20–a

Quiz 18
1–k 2–e 3–s 4–r 5–l 6–c 7–d 8–g 9–h 10–t 11–o 12–q 13–i 14–b 15–p 16–f 17–j 18–n 19–a 20–m

Quiz 19
1–d 2–a 3–c 4–b

Quiz 20
1–c 2–r 3–m 4–p 5–b 6–n 7–f 8–o 9–a 10–e 11–l 12–t 13–s 14–d 15–j 16–h 17–g 18–i 19–q 20–k

Quiz 21
1–s 2–n 3–e 4–j 5–m 6–i 7–r 8–a 9–o 10–t 11–k 12–c 13–f 14–h 15–p 16–b 17–l 18–g 19–q 20–d

Quiz22
1–s 2–b 3–o 4–c 5–p 6–d 7–j 8–l 9–a 10–a 11–t 12–f 13–m 14–g 15–i 16–n 17–e 18–r 19–k 20–h

Quiz 23
1–k 2–r 3–p 4–h 5–g 6–a 7–d 8–b 9–t 10–c 11–f 12–q 13–m 14–e 15–l 16–j 17–n 18–s 19–i 20–o

Quiz 24
1–r 2–j 3–m 4–g 5–d 6–t 7–c 8–a 9–q 10–h 11–k 12–b 13–i 14–p 15–l 16–e 17–n 18–f 19–s 20–o

Quiz 25
1–s 2–b 3–m 4–r 5–p 6–d 7–j 8–c 9–a 10–q 11–k
12–o 13–g 14–f 15–h 16–l 17–e 18–i 19–n 20–t

Quiz 26
1–m 2–o 3–h 4–c 5–t 6–l 7–a 8–k 9–f 10–n 11–s
12–p 13–r 14–i 15–q 16–e 17–g 18–d 19–b 20–j

Quiz 27
1–s 2–m 3–b 4–a 5–n 6–c 7–q 8–j 9–d 10–k 11–r
12–p 13–h 14–e 15–l 16–t 17–f 18–g 19–i 20–o

Quiz 28
1–g 2–m 3–d 4–l 5–r 6–j 7–t 8–a 9–f 10–c 11–k
12–b 13–j 14–e 15–s 16–o 17–q 18–h 19–p 20–n

Quiz 29
1–e 2–c 3–m 4–o 5–r 6–q 7–p 8–t 9–i 10–j 11–a
12–b 13–l 14–d 15–g 16–h 17–f 18–k 19–n 20–s

Quiz 30
1–b 2–r 3–h 4–f 5–a 6–o 7–i 8–q 9–s 10–e 11–d
12–p 13–g 14–l 15–t 16–c 17–n 18–j 19–m 20–k

Quiz 31
1–r 2–f 3–c 4–k 5–b 6–d 7–s 8–m 9–u 10–e 11–q
12–p 13–i 14–v 15–t 16–o 17–a 18–h 19–n 20–g 21–l
22–j

Quiz 32
1–b 2–r 3–c 4–t 5–k 6–s 7–p 8–h 9–q 10–n 11–a
12–j 13–i 14–f 15–l 16–g 17–o 18–d 19–e 20–m

Quiz 33
1–s 2–m 3–f 4–g 5–i 6–p 7–t 8–e 9–h 10–q 11–a
12–l 13–n 14–c 15–d 16–j 17–r 18–o 19–k 20–b

Quiz 34
1–h 2–m 3–q 4–s 5–p 6–o 7–c 8–d 9–t 10–l 11–i
12–r 13–f 14–n 15–a 16–j 17–k 18–b 19–g 20–e

Quiz 35
1–f 2–o 3–n 4–i 5–q 6–l 7–d 8–r 9–b 10–a 11–g
12–c 13–s 14–e 15–j 16–p 17–t 18–m 19–k 20–h

Quiz 36
1–q 2–k 3–p 4–r 5–m 6–d 7–i 8–c 9–a 10–n 11–f
12–o 13–b 14–t 15–l 16–g 17–h 18–s 19–e 20–j

Quiz 37
1–s 2–t 3–p 4–b 5–e 6–f 7–h 8–r 9–j 10–q 11–a
12–g 13–o 14–i 15–d 16–k 17–m 18–n 19–c 20–l

Quiz 38
1–g 2–s 3–h 4–o 5–q 6–d 7–a 8–r 9–m 10–c 11–e
12–n 13–i 14–p 15–l 16–t 17–b 18–j 19–f 20–k

Quiz 39
1–f 2–p 3–e 4–a 5–o 6–q 7–b 8–l 9–g 10–s 11–k
12–r 13–n 14–m 15–i 16–h 17–t 18–d 19–j 20–c

Quiz 40
1–q 2–i 3–f 4–a 5–k 6–t 7–m 8–r 9–o 10–p 11–l
12–h 13–n 14–e 15–c 16–j 17–s 18–b 19–d 20–g

Quiz 41
1–p 2–f 3–d 4–o 5–n 6–m 7–i 8–k 9–t 10–a 11–b
12–h 13–q 14–s 15–l 16–r 17–j 18–g 19–c 20–e

Quiz 42
1–d 2–k 3–f 4–n 5–b 6–i 7–h 8–g 9–c 10–j 11–a
12–m 13–e 14–l

Quiz 43
1–f 2–s 3–i 4–d 5–l 6–p 7–q 8–n 9–t 10–e 11–o
12–a 13–c 14–r 15–k 16–b 17–m 18–h 19–g 20–j

Quiz 44
1–p 2–d 3–g 4–b 5–o 6–t 7–f 8–e 9–k 10–s 11–c
12–q 13–j 14–n 15–l 16–m 17–r 18–i 19–h 20–a

Quiz 45
1–n 2–j 3–k 4–l 5–p 6–q 7–g 8–n 9–f 10– r 11–c
12–t 13–b 14–t 15–s
16–l 17–a 18–o 19–i 20–h

Quiz 46
1–s 2–b 3–q 4–j 5–f 6–h 7–r 8–n 9–p 10–a 11–l
12–m 13–p 14–c 15–d 16–i 17–e 18–d 19–k 20–i

Quiz 47
1–t 2–n 3–f 4–o 5–a 6–e 7–j 8–s 9–q 10–m 11–p
12–d 13–i 14–l 15–c 16–r 17–g 18–k 19–b 20–h

Quiz 48
1–c 2–n 3–k 4–o 5–d 6–h 7–b 8–s 9–i 10–e 11–l
12–t 13–r 14–g 15–q 16–p 17–f 18–m 19–a 20–j

Quiz 49
1–p 2–k 3–d 4–r 5–n 6–t 7–m 8–h 9–l 10–c 11–b
12–e 13–f 14–a 15–j 16–i 17–s 18–o 19–h 20–g

Quiz 50
1–o 2–g 3–e 4–a 5–b 6–k 7–c 8–r 9–s 10–f 11–j
12–h 13–f 14–q 15–l 16–i 17–n 18–t 19–m 20–p

Quiz 51
1–c 2–g 3–f 4–b 5–d 6–h 7–e 8–a

Quiz 52
1–c 2–r 3–b 4–h 5–e 6–s 7–l 8–a 9–d 10–m 11–i
12–g 13–f 14–q 15–n 16–o 17–t 18–j 19–k 20–p

Quiz 53
1–f 2–r 3–o 4–b 5–c 6–p 7–k 8–m 9–d 10–i 11–e
12–h 13–n 14–a 15–t 16–s 17–q 18–j 19–l 20–g

Quiz 54
1–c 2–d 3–p 4–h 5–a 6–m 7–b 8–t 9–q 10–n 11–r
12–k 13–g 14–j 15–o 16–s 17–i 18–l 19–e 20–f

Quiz 55
1–p 2–n 3–k 4–c 5–f 6–e 7–a 8–q 9–g 10–l 11–h
12–b 13–r 14–d 15–o 16–m 17–j 18–i

Quiz 56
1–j 2–h 3–q 4–e 5–k 6–i 7–t 8–a 9–r 10–f 11–b
12–s 13–m 14–c 15–p 16–l 17–o 18–n 19–d 20–g

Quiz 57
1–m 2–6 3–b 4–c 5–e 6–i 7–g 8–d 9–r 10s 11–l
12–n 13–a 14–f 15–j 16–h 17–k 18–q 19–o 20–p

Quiz 58
1–g 2–j 3–f 4–l 5–b 6–n 7–h 8–i 9–k 10–a 11–e
12–c 13–m 14–d

Quiz 59
1–r 2–j 3–q 4–k 5–l 6–h 7–n 8–b 9–d 10–m 11–g
12–f 13–e 14–c 15–a 16–p 17–s 18–i 19–t 20–o

Quiz 60
1–s 2–i 3–t 4–a 5–j 6–m 7–h 8–k 9–l 10–f 11–q
12–r 13–o 14–b 15–c 16–d 17–e 18–g 19–p 20–n

Quiz 61
1–a 2–d 3–c 4–e 5–b

Quiz 62
1–t 2–r 3–b 4–o 5–m 6–e 7–n 8–c 9–d 10–k 11–s
12–i 13–f 14–p 15–l 16–g 17–q 18–a 19–j 20–h

Quiz 63
1–c 2–b 3–n 4–m 5–i 6–a 7–k 8–l 9–t 10–e 11–h
12–q 13–f 14–o 15–p 16–r 17–d 18–j 19–s 20–g

Quiz 64
1–t 2–a 3–k 4–f 5–i 6–o 7–q 8–s 9–r 10–p 11–e
12–j 13–m 14–c 15–b 16–d 17–g 18–l 19–n 20–h

Quiz 65
1–s 2–f 3–k 4–m 5–o 6–d 7–h 8–n 9–i 10–c 11–e
12–j 13–r 14–b 15–g 16–a 17–p 18–q 19–t 20–l

Quiz 66
1–k 2–j 3–n 4–q 5–s 6–l 7–e 8–i 9–c 10–r 11–b
12–a 13–g 14–h 15–m 16–d 17–t 18–f 19–o 20–p

Quiz 67
1–c 2–k 3–f 4–d 5–e 6–p 7–j 8–r 9–s 10–h 11–q
12–n 13–i 14–t 15–o 16–a 17–l 18–b 19–m 20–g

Quiz 68
1–p 2–i 3–b 4–g 5–n 6–a 7–e 8–h 9–j 10–m 11–k
12–q 13–o 14–r 15–t 16–l 17–s 18–c 19–f 20–d

Quiz 69
1–d 2–o 3–s 4–f 5–b 6–t 7–e 8–a 9–q 10–h 11–m
12–r 13–i 14–l 15–c 16–p 17–n 18–g 19–j 20–k

Quiz 70
1–c 2–a 3–b

Quiz 71
1–n 2–f 3–j 4–a 5–g 6–e 7–l 8–b 9–c 10–p 11–o
12–q 13–d 14–r 15–h 16–m 17–i 18–k

Quiz 72
1–b 2–a 3–c

Quiz 73
1–a 2–b 3–g 4–q 5–m 6–t 7–s 8–c 9–p 10–h 11–i
12–r 13–l 14–f 15–k 16–j 17–e 18–d 19–n 20–o

Quiz 74
1–g 2–n 3–a 4–p 5–l 6–k 7–r 8–d 9–c 10–f 11–e
12–m 13–t 14–j 15–o 16–h 17–s 18–b 19–i 20–q

Quiz 75
1–k 2–m 3–n 4–q 5–i 6–c 7–e 8–p 9–f 10–o 11–l
12–b 13–h 14–d 15–a 16–j 17–g

Quiz 76
1–g 2–m 3–p 4–i 5–t 6–a 7–q 8–r 9–j 10–f 11–e
12–o 13–k 14–h 15–d 16–c 17–b 18–l 19–s 20–n

Quiz 77
1–n 2–e 3–l 4–r 5–b 6–t 7–o 8–i 9–h 10–a 11–d 12–q 13–c 14–g 15–m 16–k 17–j 18–s 19–f 20–p

Quiz 78
1–t 2–f 3–d 4–q 5–p 6–e 7–s 8–a 9–o 10–b 11–j 12–k 13–i 14–r 15–g 16–l 17–c 18–n 19–h 20–m

Quiz 79
1–g 2–i 3–m 4–q 5–o 6–j 7–b 8–h 9–l 10–a 11–t 12–n 13–p 14–d 15–e 16–c 17–k 18–r 19–s 20–f

Quiz 80
1–c 2–a 3–b

Quiz 81
1–i 2–n 3–l 4–s 5–j 6–k 7–o 8–h 9–m 10–t 11–q 12–p 13–d 14–c 15–g 16–b 17–e 18–a 19–f 20–r

Quiz 82
1–b 2–c 3–a

Quiz 83
1–h 2–r 3–k 4–o 5–j 6–i 7–d 8–e 9–a 10–g 11–f 12–m 13–b 14–c 15–s 16–q 17–n 18–l 19–p 20–t

Quiz 84
1–j 2–b 3–g 4–c 5–m 6–i 7–n 8–t 9–l 10–q 11–a 12–o 13–f 14–k 15–r 16–e 17–h 18–d 19–p 20–s

Quiz 85
1–a 2–d 3–h 4–f 5–g 6–e 7–i 8–j 9–c 10–b

Quiz 86
1–f 2–l 3–i 4–s 5–m 6–q 7–r 8–b 9–c 10–t 11–p 12–d 13–j 14–h 15–e 16–g 17–k 18–o 19–n 20–a

Quiz 87
1–a 2–s 3–b 4–q 5–l 6–n 7–p 8–j 9–h 10–f 11–r 12–g 13–k 14–c 15–d 16–t 17–o 18–i 19–m 20–e

Quiz 88
1–s 2–d 3–l 4–a 5–l 6–j 7–g 8–o 9–r 10–f 11–n 12–m 13–p 14–c 15–b 16–q 17–h 18–k 19–e 20–t

Quiz 89
1–m 2–k 3–p 4–t 5–f 6–d 7–r 8–i 9–e 10–g 11–s 12–b 13–a 14–l 15–o 16–q 17–c 18–h 19–n 20–j

Quiz 90
1–n 2–p 3–c 4–f 5–d 6–r 7–s 8–t 9–k 10–g 11–i 12–l 13–b 14–j 15–h 16–o 17–a 18–q 19–m 20–e

Quiz 91
1–j 2–q 3–r 4–i 5–g 6–k 7–t 8–m 9–e 10–p 11–a 12–h 13–s 14–l 15–o 16–c 17–f 18–b 19–d 20–n

Quiz 92
1–s 2–o 3–l 4–i 5–k 6–r 7–p 8–t 9–a 10–g 11–n 12–q 13–d 14–c 15–m 16–b 17–j 18–h 19–e 20–f

Quiz 93
1–p 2–s 3–c 4–k 5–q 6–t 7–e 8–h 9–a 10–j 11–d 12–g 13–l 14–m 15–f 16–i 17–o 18–b 19–n 20–r

Quiz 94
1–c 2–h 3–s 4–d 5–f 6–k 7–m 8–l 9–a 10–j 11–p 12–n 13–q 14–i 15–t 16–r 17–o 18–b 19–e 20–g

Quiz 95
1–i 2–h 3–p 4–b 5–d 6–t 7–s 8–o 9–k 10–j 11–n 12–m 13–c 14–a 15–g 16–f 17–r 18–q 19–l 20–e

Quiz 96
1–d 2–c 3–a 4–b

Quiz 97
1–m 2–o 3–g 4–c 5–a 6–j 7–e 8–k 9–f 10–d 11–i 12–h 13–q 14–b 15–l 16–r 17–n 18–p

Quiz 98
1–r 2–l 3–m 4–d 5–s 6–e 7–g 8–p 9–a 10–n 11–i 12–f 13–q 14–k 15–h 16–j 17–c 18–t 19–o 20–b

Quiz 99
1–d 2–n 3–r 4–m 5–a 6–k 7–t 8–o 9–p 10–h 11–i 12–f 13–q 14–g 15–l 16–b 17–c 18–s 19–e 20–j

Quiz 100
1–s 2–h 3–p 4–o 5–g 6–m 7–r 8–b 9–t 10–c 11–l 12–f 13–j 14–d 15–e 16–i 17–a 18–n 19–k 20–q

Quiz 101
1–j 2–h 3–t 4–i 5–o 6–e 7–d 8–n 9–l 10–q 11–s 12–b 13–c 14–f 15–a 16–g 17–r 18–m 19–p 20–k

Quiz 102
1–k 2–h 3–b 4–j 5–g 6–l 7–e 8–q 9–f 10–a 11–s 12–m 13–c 14–t 15–i 16–n 17–d 18–p 19–o 20–r

Quiz 103
1–u 2–o 3–b 4–n 5–a 6–g 7–l 8–r 9–q 10–t 11–m 12–e 13–h 14–d 15–j 16–i 17–k 18–c 19–f 20–s 21–p

Quiz 104
1-q 2-i 3-s 4-o 5-p 6-f 7-j 8-r 9-b 10-h 11-a 12-k 13-n 14-l 15-t 16-m 17-c 18-g 19-d 20-e

Quiz 105
1-g 2-b 3-a 4-q 5-c 6-m 7-k 8-e 9-p 10-j 11-o 12-n 13-i 14-h 15-d 16-l 17-f 18-r 19-s 20-t

Quiz 106
1-j 2-p 3-g 4-h 5-l 6-n 7-a 8-b 9-d 10-c 11-k 12-e 13-f 14-m 15-r 16-o 17-i 18-q 19-s 20-t

Quiz 107
1-k 2-g 3-e 4-p 5-o 6-f 7-q 8-r 9-j 10-t 11-b 12-d 13-a 14-c 15-l 16-i 17-h 18-m 19-n 20-s

Quiz 108
1-m 2-f 3-i 4-n 5-e 6-r 7-j 8-l 9-s 10-h 11-b 12-c 13-d 14-k 15-o 16-q 17-a 18-p 19-g 20-t

Quiz 109
1-j 2-r 3-o 4-p 5-q 6-d 7-l 8-k 9-g 10-f 11-h 12-n 13-i 14-c 15-m 16-b 17-a 18-e 19-t 20-s

Quiz 110
1-e 2-h 3-i 4-b 5-c 6-p 7-a 8-n 9-q 10-g 11-r 12-m 13-j 14-t 15-k 16-o 17-f 18-l 19-s 20-d

Quiz 111
1-t 2-r 3-o 4-l 5-i 6-k 7-m 8-s 9-j 10-b 11-q 12-f 13-n 14-p 15-a 16-e 17-d 18-h 19-c 20-g

Quiz 112
1-t 2-l 3-e 4-r 5-k 6-s 7-p 8-i 9-m 10-c 11-d 12-b 13-n 14-o 15-q 16-j 17-f 18-a 19-h 20-g

Quiz 113
1-m 2-e 3-i 4-g 5-a 6-l 7-d 8-k 9-o 10-h 11-f 12-r 13-c 14-b 15-j 16-n 17-t 18-p 19-s 20-q

Quiz 114
1-f 2-c 3-a 4-h 5-e 6-b 7-d 8-r 9-n 10-j 11-g 12-m 13-t 14-k 15-q 16-s 17-p 18-l 19-i 20-o

Quiz 115
1-j 2-h 3-g 4-d 5-f 6-i 7-a 8-c 9-e 10-b 11-k 12-l

Quiz 116
1-f 2-e 3-r 4-c 5-m 6-p 7-b 8-i 9-a 10-g 11-d 12-o 13-l 14-t 15-j 16-s 17-h 18-q 19-n 20-k

Quiz 117
1-k 2-i 3-e 4-d 5-n 6-m 7-l 8-o 9-g 10-j 11-p 12-r 13-f 14-a 15-b 16-t 17-c 18-s 19-q 20-h

Quiz 118
1-r 2-q 3-h 4-c 5-j 6-e 7-d 8-f 9-n 10-p 11-i 12-b 13-g 14-o 15-a 16-m 17-l 18-t 19-k 20-s

Quiz 119
1-n 2-a 3-h 4-o 5-k 6-l 7-i 8-f 9-u 10-c 11-e 12-m 13-j 14-q 15-g 16-p 17-v 18-d 19-r 20-s 21-b 22-t

Quiz 120
1-b 2-a 3-q 4-r 5-c 6-i 7-e 8-t 9-l 10-j 11-m 12-g 13-p 14-o 15-n 16-f 17-s 18-k 19-d 20-h

Quiz 121
1-e 2-b 3-d 4-c 5-h 6-f 7-g 8-a

Quiz 122
1-o 2-p 3-l 4-d 5-k 6-i 7-e 8-a 9-j 10-g 11-c 12-b 13-n 14-m 15-t 16-h 17-t 18-f 19-s 20-r

Quiz 123
1-j 2-b 3-l 4-s 5-t 6-p 7-r 8-g 9-e 10-o 11-n 12-q 13-d 14-a 15-k 16-i 17-c 18-h 19-m 20-f

Quiz 124
1-b 2-c 3-o 4-f 5-a 6-t 7-r 8-s 9-i 10-d 11-n 12-k 13-g 14-q 15-e 16-j 17-p 18-h 19-m 20-l

Quiz 125
1-d 2-b 3-c 4-a 5-f 6-e

Quiz 126
1-u 2-s 3-p 4-m 5-a 6-f 7-c 8-b 9-i 10-l 11-o 12-j 13-q 14-n 15-h 16-v 17-g 18-d 19-t 20-r 21-k 22-e

Quiz 127
1-b 2-e 3-d 4-c 5-f 6-a